Social Interactions in Virtual Worlds

Within the rapidly growing arena of "virtual worlds," such as Massively Multiplayer Online Games (MMOGs), individuals behave in particular ways, influence one another, and develop complex relationships. This setting can be a useful tool for modeling complex social systems, cognitive factors, and interactions between groups and within organizations. To study these worlds effectively requires a cross-disciplinary approach that integrates social science theories with big data analytics. This broad-based book offers a comprehensive and holistic perspective on the field. It brings together research findings from an international team of experts in computer science (artificial intelligence, game design, and social computing), psychology, and the social sciences to help researchers and practitioners better understand the fundamental processes underpinning social behavior in virtual worlds such as *World of Warcraft*, *Rift*, *EVE Online*, and *Travian*.

KIRAN LAKKARAJU is a senior member of the technical staff in the Sandia National Laboratories Cognitive Science and Applications group. His primary research interests lie in computational models of behavior change in society and exploring links between social and cognitive structures in problems of information dissemination and attitude change. His current work revolves around developing online social experiments through the Controlled, Large Online Social Experimentation (CLOSE) platform.

GITA SUKTHANKAR is Associate Professor and Charles N. Millican Faculty Fellow in the Department of Computer Science at the University of Central Florida (UCF), and an affiliate faculty member at UCF's Institute for Simulation and Training. Her research focuses on multiagent systems and computational social models. She has received an Air Force Young Investigator award and a National Science Foundation CAREER award. She has served on the Defense Advanced Research Projects Agency (DARPA)'s Computer Science Study Panel and is currently a member of DARPA's Information Science and Technology study group and of the board of directors of the International Foundation for Autonomous Agents and Multiagent Systems (IFAAMAS).

ROLF T. WIGAND is Professor, Emeritus College, Arizona State University and Maulden-Entergy Chair and Distinguished Professor Emeritus of Information Science and Business Information Systems at the University of Arkansas at Little Rock. He is the past director of the Syracuse University Graduate Program in Information Management and its Center for Digital Commerce. His research focuses on software standards development and collective action in the mortgage, automotive, and radio frequency identification industries; development of trust and leadership in virtual organizations; the analysis of social networks in disaster situations; and novel methods for analysis and tracking of collective action on social media.

Social Interactions in Virtual Worlds

An Interdisciplinary Perspective

Edited by

KIRAN LAKKARAJU
Sandia National Laboratories, New Mexico

GITA SUKTHANKAR
University of Central Florida

ROLF T. WIGAND
Arizona State University and University of Arkansas

CAMBRIDGE UNIVERSITY PRESS

CAMBRIDGE
UNIVERSITY PRESS

University Printing House, Cambridge CB2 8BS, United Kingdom

One Liberty Plaza, 20th Floor, New York, NY 10006, USA

477 Williamstown Road, Port Melbourne, VIC 3207, Australia

314–321, 3rd Floor, Plot 3, Splendor Forum, Jasola District Centre,
New Delhi - 110025, India

79 Anson Road, #06-04/06, Singapore 079906

Cambridge University Press is part of the University of Cambridge.

It furthers the University's mission by disseminating knowledge in the pursuit of
education, learning, and research at the highest international levels of excellence.

www.cambridge.org
Information on this title: www.cambridge.org/9781107128828
DOI: 10.1017/9781316422823

© Cambridge University Press 2018

First published 2018

Printed in the United States of America by Sheridan Books, Inc.

A catalogue record for this publication is available from the British Library

Library of Congress Cataloging-in-Publication data
Names: Lakkaraju, Kiran, editor. | Sukthankar, Gita, editor. | Wigand, Rolf T., editor.
Title: Social interactions in virtual worlds : an interdisciplinary perspective / edited by
Kiran Lakkaraju, Sandia National Laboratories, New Mexico, Gita Sukthankar, University
of Central Florida, Rolf T. Wigand, University of Arkansas.
Description: Cambridge, United Kingdom ; New York, NY : Cambridge University Press,
2017. | Includes bibliographical references and index.
Identifiers: LCCN 2017042225 | ISBN 9781107128828 (hardback : alk. paper)
Subjects: LCSH: Internet games – Social aspects. | Virtual reality – Social aspects. |
Social interaction. | Human-computer interaction.
Classification: LCC GV1469.17.S63 S634   2017 | DDC 794.8 – dc23
LC record available at https://lccn.loc.gov/2017042225

ISBN 978-1-107-12882-8 Hardback

Contents

See Color Plates section between pages 132 and 133

Contributors

Nitin Agarwal
University of Arkansas at Little Rock, Little Rock, AR, USA

Iftekhar Ahmed
University of North Texas, Denton, TX, USA

Amanda Alencar
Erasmus University, Rotterdam, the Netherlands

Hamidreza Alvari
Arizona State University, Tempe, AZ, USA

William Sims Bainbridge
National Science Foundation, Washington, DC, USA

Christian Bauckhage
Fraunhofer IAIS, Sankt Augustin, Germany

Maude Bonenfant
Université du Québec à Montréal, Montréal, Québec, Canada

Thomas Chesney
Nottingham University Business School, Nottingham, UK

Swee Hoon Chuah
RMIT University, Melbourne, Australia

Elizabeth Craig
North Carolina State University, Raleigh, NC, USA

Lucile Crémier
Université du Québec à Montréal, Montréal, QC, Canada

Suzanne de Castell
Simon Fraser University, Burnaby, British Columbia, Canada

Teresa de la Hera Conde-Pumpido
Erasmus University, Rotterdam, the Netherlands

Anders Drachen
Aalborg University, Aalborg, Denmark and The Pagonis Network

Sarah Evans
North Carolina State University, Raleigh, NC, USA

Alireza Hajibagheri
University of Central Florida, Orlando, FL, USA

Robert Hoffmann
RMIT University, Melbourne, Australia

Wendy Hui
Curtin University, Perth, Australia

Ryan Hurley
North Carolina State University, Raleigh, NC, USA

Alexandru Iosup
Delft University of Technology, the Netherlands

Jennifer Jenson
York University, Toronto, ON, Canada

Fernando Kuipers
Delft University of Technology, Delft, the Netherlands

Kiran Lakkaraju
Sandia National Labs, Albuquerque, NM, USA

Jeremy Larner
Nottingham University Business School, Nottingham, UK

Lynnette G. Leonard
American University in Bulgaria, Blagoevgrad, Bulgaria

Marcus Märtens
Delft University of Technology, Delft, the Netherlands

John Murray
SRI International, Menlo Park, CA, USA

Andrew Pilny
University of Kentucky, Lexington, KY, USA

Marshall Scott Poole
University of Illinois at Urbana-Champaign, Urbana, IL, USA

Félix Prégent
Université du Québec à Montréal, Montréal, QC, Canada

Fanny Anne Ramirez
Rutgers University, New Brunswick, NJ, USA

John C. Sherblom
University of Maine, Orono, ME, USA

Rafet Sifa
Fraunhofer IAIS, Sankt Augustin, Germany

Jeffrey S. Smith
Central Michigan University, Mount Pleasant, MI, USA

Laura Iseut Lafrance St-Martin
Université du Québec à Montréal, Montréal, QC, Canada

Gita Sukthankar
University of Central Florida, Orlando, FL, USA

Nicholas Taylor
North Carolina State University, Raleigh, NC, USA

Ernst van der Hoeven
Delft University of Technology, Delft, the Netherlands

Rolf T. Wigand
University of Arkansas at Little Rock, Little Rock, and Arizona State
University, Tempe, AZ, USA

Lesley A. Withers
Central Michigan University, Mount Pleasant, MI, USA

Introduction

Games have always held a fascination for humans. The earliest games were dice games, based on chance and luck. Some of the earliest recorded board games, such as *Senet* or the *Game of Ur*,[1] developed in the 3000–3500 B.C. range, are still familiar to us, incorporating chance and strategic thinking on ornate boards.

A central factor in many games, sometimes the primary purpose, is to foster connection between the players. Games can provide an element of competition and cooperation that bridge the "air gap" between humans. Sporting events like the Olympic Games can bring countries together, while other games can knit players into communities.

Given this, it is no surprise that video games have followed this trend as well. Even before the rise of online gaming there were arcades, shared spaces for players, and specialized events such as local area network (LAN) parties during which gamers gather to share a LAN and participate in extended gaming sessions of popular games. Indeed, it would be a surprise if players *did not* communicate about their deeds and heroics and exhibit an eagerness to share them. We should remember that humans have one unique skill out of the rest of the animal kingdom – the ability to communicate with an expressive and rich language. Is it any surprise that humans crave to use this capability?

And thus we know we can study human behavior and social interaction in games, but does it really matter? The simple answer is "yes." As the chapters in this book show, human behavior in games is rich, complex, and varied, especially so in what we call "virtual worlds" that are created within massively multiplayer online games (MMOGs).

Is it worthwhile to study such behavior? Why should we study behavior in a virtual world that has no link to reality and in fact explicitly attempts to flee

[1] http://content.time.com/time/specials/2007/article/0,28804,1815747_1815707_1815665,00 .html

1

from a realistic and accurate portrayal of the world? There is a good answer to that: it is still humans who are making decisions and acting – humans with innate biases, unconscious tendencies, and implicit attitudes. These do not go away in a virtual world, but rather are mediated and applied to this realm. Just as these tendencies pervade our everyday life and experiences, games (even the most prosaic) provide another avenue to inspect these tendencies.

In fact, games provide a unique venue. They are rich enough to capture complex environments, but simple enough that a large number of people can play the game. They are monitored extensively so we know a good deal about the behaviors within the game.

What stops us from studying games? One of the major challenges (and opportunities) with studying human behavior in virtual worlds is the interdisciplinary nature of such research. Many fundamental computer science problems arise in analyzing large quantities of data ("big data"), but along with that are foundational questions on human behavior. It is clear that humans change behavior when playing a game, but what type of behavior changes? Do people put on different personalities online? (Recent evidence suggests that this is not always the case.) Studying behavior within virtual worlds is an inherently interdisciplinary endeavor, requiring the expertise of computer scientists, statisticians, economists, communication scholars, sociologists, and psychologists.

Our primary goal with organizing this book is to address the need for a single volume that encompasses the interdisciplinary nature of the field. Current offerings are focused on specific problems (for instance, analytics for better monetizing games) and generally keeping within one discipline. This multiauthor volume presents a unified perspective on the field, drawing from contributions from a variety of disciplines. Currently there is no single conference or journal where this research is published, so we hope this book can serve as a valuable resource and guide to the community – especially to new researchers who can have, in one volume, key insights from across the major areas of the field.

We have organized this book within three theme areas. Part I, "Individual Behaviors and Dyadic Relationships," primarily focuses on the behavior of individuals and pairs within a game. Part II, "Groups: Norms, Leadership, and Virtual Organizations," focuses on the patterns of behavior that exist within groups of players. Part III, "Understanding Culture with Games," looks at the interaction of games and cultures. Finally, to study games and the large data sets they engender, we need new techniques that can effectively, and scalably, analyze and extract patterns. In Part IV, "Techniques for Analyzing Game Data," we have contributions that address this important element.

Following are brief synopses for each chapter that will also provide an overview to this book.

Individual Behaviors and Dyadic Relationships

1. VERUS: A Multidisciplinary International Behavioral Study of Virtual World Users

At the central core of the study of virtual worlds is a hypothesis that player behavior in virtual worlds can say something about behavior in the real world. Establishing this relationship is of critical importance in framing and interpreting results from virtual world studies. In the "VERUS" chapter, the authors describe efforts from a multifaceted large research project on exactly this topic. Subjects were asked to play in online games, choosing from public ones (such as *World of Warcraft*) or two worlds created for this project. Subjects also provided demographic details. Using rule-learning techniques from the machine learning community, the authors identified relationships between in-game behavior and a variety of real-world characteristics. This chapter summarizes results around risk-related behavior, avatar characteristics, virtual world movement, and avatar language use.

2. Understanding Aggressive and Nonaggressive Individual Behaviors in Massively Multiplayer Online Games

Ahmed, Pilny, and Poole tackle important issues of aggression and their relationship to video games. While there is a sizable body of research (which at times is controversial) on the change in aggression among video game players, this study focuses on the correlation between aggressive behavior in video games and existing personality traits linked to aggression. Using player behavior data from *EverQuest II* and existing inventories to measure physical aggression, the authors develop several predictive models of aggression based on subject behavior within the game.

3. From Good Associates to True Friends: An Exploration of Friendship Practices in Massively Multiplayer Online Games

Quite noticeable in the last decade has been the advent of ubiquitous socialization – the ability of people to constantly display and monitor the actions of friends, family, and strangers. This no doubt provides the underpinnings for socialization. Games benefit from this, as technical underpinnings have been developed to allow for massively multiplayer environments. A key question then is: How do subjects socialize with others within the gaming environment? In this chapter by Fanny Anne Ramirez, this question is tackled through a qualitative study of players in *EVE Online*. She finds that much like real-world relationships, online relationships exist on a continuum and are continually changed through interaction in the game.

4. Couples Who Slay Together, Stay Together: Benefits, Challenges, and Relational Quality among Romantic Couples Who Game

This chapter tackles the important question of how gaming together affects real-world romantic relationships: What happens when real-world romantic relationships mix with virtual world team relationships? In multiplayer online battle arenas (MOBAs), two teams of players compete in a head-to-head fashion to control a territory within a short time period. Previous relationship studies have primarily analyzed MMOGs that differ in several ways from MOBAs: they span a longer duration, include greater character customization, and have more diversity in winning objectives, compared to the fast-paced, intense battle arena games. Evans, Craig, and Taylor study the benefits and challenges in romantic relationships among MOBA players. Despite the common perception that MOBAs are a nexus for hostility and toxicity between players, they find that MOBAs can also serve as an important tool in sustaining romantic relationships.

Groups: Norms, Leadership, and Virtual Organizations

5. Virtual Team Communication Norms: Modeling the Mediating Influences of Relational Trust, Presence, and Identity on Conversational Interactivity, Openness, and Satisfaction

The problem of creating productive virtual teams has risen in importance as workplaces become more distributed, increasing the probability that team members are not colocated and must rely on videoconferencing and chat tools. Online games are an excellent testbed for studying human team performance, since many MMOGs pose challenges that require sophisticated group coordination and problem solving. Effective communication is a prerequisite for good teamwork; however, communicating in virtual environments is a specialized skill that is acquired over time, which increases the challenge of working in virtual teams.

Sherblom, Withers, Leonard, and Smith study communication norms in virtual teams who were tasked with surveying residents in the *Second Life* virtual world. Their chapter reports the results of a path analytic study measuring the effects of relational indices, such as trust, on the virtual team conversational interactivity. They find that being competent with virtual communication is a necessary but not sufficient condition to guarantee that good team communication norms, such as interactiveness and openness, are followed.

6. Toxic Allies and Caring Friends: Social Systems and Behavioral Norms in *League of Legends* and *Guild Wars 2*

Video games can offer diverse gaming experiences. Moreover, far from being neutral, these technological platforms are sociotechnical apparatuses shaping social interactions through the institution of relationships of power. Thus, video games are contexts in which social systems develop through behavioral norms. Accordingly and following a soft technological determinism approach, the authors assert that online video games not only influence players' experience within the apparatus, but also inform the production of collective identities, as each game elaborates a specific form of video game community through which players recognize each other. Using a semiotic research approach, this chapter then presents results of a comparative analysis of the production of social norms within two games: *Guild Wars 2* and *League of Legends*. The authors affirm that while one may identify many parameters that encourage or discourage certain behaviors and influence the development of cultural practices, video games cannot entirely constrain gaming experiences. Relationships of power remain embedded within specific features, mechanisms, and uses of signs, as well as within worldviews, modes of intersubjectivity, actions, and values that are prescribed within the community. As semiotic objects, video games are effects of a cultural, ideological, and institutional context, but they also produce cultural, ideological, and institutional norms. Therefore, they are not neutral.

7. Management (Im)Material: Negotiating Leadership in Virtual Worlds

Academic research has begun to chart the leadership activities cultivated by players in commercial MMOGs such as *World of Warcraft* (WoW) and *EVE*

Online. Players form into groups, ranging from temporary small teams to large-scale, long-term associations numbering in the hundreds, in order to carry out goal-driven and cooperative activities. Directing these activities requires an array of communicational and interpersonal competencies, from establishing and communicating short-term and long-term priorities, recruiting new players, resolving conflicts between players, allocating resources, negotiating interactions with other player associations, and choreographing the actions of other players whose avatars have specific roles, skill sets, and weaknesses. This chapter offers an empirically driven account of the (dis)connects between players' dispositions and the embodied experiences of their play, and their propensity for and enactment of leadership in MMOGs. The study reports of game-based leadership styles and behaviors that found what the authors coined *self-interested* leadership to be least effective in terms of in-game progression; *autocratic* leadership was next, and *networked* leadership was demonstrably most successful. The authors also demonstrate that different kinds of gameplay invited and supported different forms of leadership, one being formal-managerial and the other contingent, networked, and task-driven.

8. Virtual Organization and Online Games

Virtual organizations have become popular in conjunction with the rapid growth of electronic commerce and are regarded as one of the promising new organizational forms of the future. MMOGs offer new promising opportunities to research virtual organizations. The characteristics of MMOGs allow researchers here to obtain objective data from a large and multinational population. Lasting over months or even years, MMOGs facilitate longitudinal studies and ensure a high involvement of participants reflective of their work and activities in real-life virtual organizations. Moreover, collecting data from online surveys and game servers keeps the costs of MMOG studies relatively low. In addition, the players on MMOGs operate and function within the game the same way as if they were in a virtual organization. The author illustrates how research in MMOGs can utilize these opportunities to overcome some limitations of traditional research and study the very features of virtual organization environments. He addresses a variety of essential characteristics, design principles, and enablers of virtual organizations, while recognizing that flexibility is the main goal when forming virtual organizations. Wigand discerns that virtual organizations manifest themselves across many boundaries: time and space, as well as legal definitions. Trust counts as a decisive coordination mechanism for virtual organizations. Several limitations, however, can be recognized, including the technical infrastructure, as well as human behavioral patterns imposed on institutions.

9. Virtual Economic Experiments

Behavioral economics, which studies economics with human psychology in mind, has grown in significance. However, many human studies have subject participants that are limited in diversity and in sterile settings. Virtual worlds provide an alluring alternative to in-lab experiments. In this chapter the authors survey a wide variety of experiments and discuss the benefits and drawbacks of virtual experimentation specifically for economic experiments. In terms of benefits, drawing from a diverse population is an important factor: this allows us to understand the impact of culture and other factors on decision making. Control of the virtual environment, and naturalistic settings, are also important.

Understanding Culture with Games

10. A Simulated Utopia: The Social System of a Virtual Ancient Egypt

This chapter is based on *A Tale in the Desert*, a noncombat MMOG emphasizing cooperation as the players construct a virtual version of ancient Egypt. It is designed to run in long cycles, i.e., "tellings," starting from scratch each time. This author has studied culture and social structure in *Tale* in both the fourth and sixth tellings, 2008–2010 and 2011–2015. Here he reports on the transition from the sixth to Seventh Telling. In contrast to many combat games, players in *Tale* are encouraged to join multiple guilds, resulting in the guilds specializing and creating a vast interlinked social structure marked by the division of labor. As could be observed in real ancient societies such as Egypt, social structure is supported by religious rituals, although unlike other fantasy games, *Tale* does not emphasize simulated magic. Rituals utilize ancient Egyptian culture and tend to be realistic, such as the marriage ceremony, which actually results in the establishment of community property between marriage partners. Because building structures ranging from small farms to huge pyramids requires a great diversity of skills and materials, individual players must help each other, although they also compete – peacefully. There even is a political system in which players may gain status and that decides some of the secondary rules of the game. A variety of methodologies are employed in this research, connected to standard concepts in a range of social theories. However, here a special emphasis is given to the classical research and theory on utopian movements. Arnold Toynbee used ancient Egypt as a prime example for his theory of challenge and response. The study concludes that online communities may be the most practical form of utopian experiments possible in today's world, because it is impractical to secede from the global economy, but feasible to create the experience of social harmony in an internet-delimited environment. The author provides new insights about human cooperation in a virtual environment.

11. Gaming in Multicultural Classrooms: The Potential of Collaborative Digital Games to Foster Intercultural Interaction

This chapter addresses the growing cultural diversity in European educational settings. This includes acculturation processes in schools having become increasingly complex as well as "problems" associated with cultural essentialisms in everyday classroom practices. Digital games have been embraced as an effective tool in efforts to learn and to utilize learning processes. The authors demonstrate in several studies how benefits in the use of digital games in educational settings were derived. In general, these studies focus on how digital games are being used for knowledge acquisition. In the present research, however, the authors created a new approach for the study of digital games in educational settings. Utilizing collaborative efforts, the potential of digital entertaining collaborative games to foster intercultural interaction in culturally diverse classrooms is explored. The authors anchor their research theoretically on mechanisms available through intergroup contact theory that, in turn, demonstrate the importance and explain intercultural interactions. In all, these efforts are seen to be embedded in long-term processes of integration, thus enhancing intercultural competence, mitigating conflicts stirred by cultural differences, and fostering processes of language and social integration among pupils in culturally diverse settings in the field of education. A key policy priority should therefore be to plan for the implementation of innovative teaching/learning approaches to tackle the problems deriving from cultural diversity in educational environments.

Techniques for Analyzing Game Data

12. The Power of Social Features in Online Gaming

This section explores novel techniques for analyzing social data extracted from online games and virtual worlds. It is clear that social interaction plays a nontrivial role in motivating players to participate in games, particularly MMOGs. An important question is to understand how social interaction can be measured in order to improve the gameplay experience. The use of social features and a "Quality of Experience" measure based on social features allows capturing how negative behavior, such as toxic comments, can impact game experience. In this chapter the authors focus on this and related problems. They describe different aspects of player experiences in online social games and survey methods for identifying social features.

13. Profiling in Games: Understanding Behavior from Telemetry

Sifa, Drachen, and Bauckhage provide an overview of commonly used profiling techniques for understanding player behavior in their chapter. The term "telemetry" refers to the software systems used to log player actions during gameplay; player profiling is the process of computationally constructing models of player behavior from data. It has numerous practical applications, including improving user experience, detecting fraud, and increasing monetization. This chapter presents a selection of case studies showing how machine learning, clustering, and low-rank matrix factorization can be applied to various profiling problems. The general aim of profiling is to cluster the players into different groups, based on their past behavior. In some cases, it is possible to predict future player behaviors; however, often the goal is providing interpretable models of player activities to game designers seeking to understand the effects of design choices on user experience.

14. Using Massively Multiplayer Online Game Data to Analyze the Dynamics of Social Interactions

While Sifa et al. focus on the commercial aspects of profiling users, Hajibagheri and his coauthors treat MMOGs as a laboratory both for conducting social science experiments and evaluating the performance of predictive models of social dynamics. Player transaction data is represented as a dynamic multiplex network in which the nodes represent players and the edges denote different types of social interactions, such as chatting, trading, or fighting. The network structure is dynamic and expressed as a time series of snapshots taken at periodic intervals. This chapter chronicles their research on *Travian*, a real-time strategy game, and introduces several new algorithms for predicting future network structure from past interactions. To succeed at *Travian*, players must form alliances and conquer territory to achieve the final civilization-building game objective. These dual processes of cooperation and conflict between players combine to shape the multiplex network and create cross-layer patterns that can be exploited to improve prediction accuracy. The authors describe their method for extracting, aggregating, and reweighting topological network features in order to predict future player actions.

Conclusion

History, as they say, repeats itself. In ancient times, games were used to understand, predict, and manipulate the world. It is perhaps appropriate, then, while considering the ocean of work on games and human behaviors (to which we humbly hope this volume makes a contribution), to think of games serving the same purpose as they did before – to help us understand the world we live in.

PART I

Individual Behaviors and Dyadic
Relationships

1

VERUS: A Multidisciplinary International Behavioral Study of Virtual World Users

JOHN MURRAY, THOMAS CHESNEY, AND
ROBERT HOFFMANN

Summary

This chapter discusses the design, insights, and findings of a multifaceted international research project that examined the relationships between player activities in virtual worlds (VWs) or massively multiplayer online games (MMOGs) on the one hand and their real-world (RW) characteristics on the other. The underlying premise was that certain RW qualities of individuals, in particular their demographics, would be reflected in their observable behaviors in the virtual environments.

The project was undertaken by a multinational team under the group name VERUS, which stands for Virtual Environment Real User Study (Murray & Arns, 2012). The goal was to draw on the expertise of a comprehensive group of research specialists spanning a broad variety of academic disciplines, who would introduce a variety of quantitative and qualitative techniques to the collection and analysis of data regarding online gameplay. With more than 1,300 participants, this 3-year project is among the largest multidisciplinary behavioral studies of online gamers to date.

The VERUS team focused on using both research laboratory and field settings for the data collection activities, which emphasized the recruitment of players to participate in-person, rather than relying on virtual or "remote" interaction techniques. This approach allowed the researchers to verify participants' identities so that their RW demographics could be ascertained and linked to measurable VW behavioral indicators. The combination of settings also afforded an opportunity to examine gameplay in conditions that were either more controlled (in the lab) or more naturalistic (in the field) than would have been possible via purely online observations.

From the outset, one of the central strategies for the project was to emphasize the exploration of gamer behaviors that were likely to transcend virtual environments. Of course, many in-game decisions and actions are significantly defined by the particular features – or affordances – of the environment. However, because participants retain their personal RW characteristics as they move between VWs, the core hypothesis in VERUS was that these RW attributes would also map to aspects of their activities in multiple worlds.

In pursuit of this strategy, VERUS participants were asked to play an online public virtual game of their choosing – for example, *MapleStory*, *World of Warcraft*, *Rift*, or *EVE Online*– or one of two specially instrumented environments that were developed for the project. This approach enabled researchers to observe behaviors in two quite different virtual contexts. In the first case, gameplay took place in a more "naturalistic" virtual milieu that players were already familiar with, allowing researchers to examine in-world activities in more ecologically valid settings where participants go about their routine gaming tasks in a "business-as-usual" context. These observations and play sessions, which took place in public gaming venues as well as laboratories and schools, enabled us to develop a detailed perspective for framing our specialized telemetry analysis work.

The two worlds created by the team, *Sherwood* and *Guardian Academy* (see Figure 1.1), provided far richer sources of log data and telemetry than could be obtained in the public worlds. These private VWs supported player tasks under controlled conditions and were guided by researchers using avatars within the virtual world. Two *Guardian Academy* parallel worlds – or "shards" – were used to segregate the youth and adult players into separate but essentially identical virtual environments. Thus, protected longitudinal studies of the population of minors could be carried out while adult players could log in and play whenever it suited them.

A broad suite of analytical techniques was used to examine the various aspects of players' in-game activities using these private virtual worlds. Examples include discourse analysis and identification of lexical features in players' text chat; behavioral economics features of interplayer transactions; analysis of in-game travel, exploration, and movement patterns; and examination of player in-game choices regarding avatar class, clothing, naming conventions, quest selection, etc. Where feasible, similar techniques were used to analyze accessible in-game telemetry data gathered in the public virtual worlds. In addition, we also used various other data collection techniques, including think-aloud protocols, keystroke logging, participant travelogs, video capture with activity coding, and researcher observations.

The individual outputs of these analyses were merged and integrated using the *Weka* workbench of machine learning tools (Hall et al., 2013) to develop predictive association rules that linked the observed VW behaviors and

Figure 1.1 VERUS dedicated virtual worlds: *Guardian Academy* (top) and *Sherwood* (bottom).

activities with the RW characteristics of the corresponding players. The final results were a suite of practical rules that predicted RW attributes with high precision; these include gender (98% predictive precision), age group (90%), and socioeconomic status (83%).

This feature and rules development methodology, with its emphasis on simplicity and ease of interpretation, ensures validity of rules and minimizes overfitting. Individual rules used at most two variables. The selected rules were subject to review by human domain experts to avoid the problem of poor generalizability that is associated with blindly accepting the top-scoring results returned by the rules-mining software. This methodology thus involves an interplay between machine learning and human judgment, generating rules of high quality. This hybrid approach offers the best of both worlds, i.e., enabling a machine to automate tasks such as sifting through the data to identify candidate rules but ensuring human participation in defining the features and interpreting the results.

As a comprehensive, transnational interdisciplinary endeavor, the VERUS project represents an important research milestone in the study of human behavior within online virtual worlds.

1.1 Overview

The structure of VERUS studies is shown in Figure 1.2. An initial set of hypotheses were designed to identify a suite of RW characteristics drawing on an integrated set of VW behavioral indicators (BIs). These preliminary hypotheses focused primarily on answering challenges in three broad categories: individual, group, and culture. Figure 1.2 summarizes our objective RW characteristics and shows how the hypotheses are used to establish these using the main VW BIs.

Controlled access to virtual environments was particularly important for several of our studies. We needed to capture avatar movements and interactions both with nonplayer characters (NPCs) and with other players. Also, because minors made up a significant portion of our participant pool, extra care was needed to protect that segment of the population. Thus we required dedicated virtual worlds that only authorized players and researchers would be able to access. It was particularly important to exclude involvement or access by individuals who were not part of our study. For this purpose we used two dedicated VWs: *Guardian Academy*, an adaptation of a flash-based fantasy questing world; and *Sherwood*, a social networking virtual environment that was

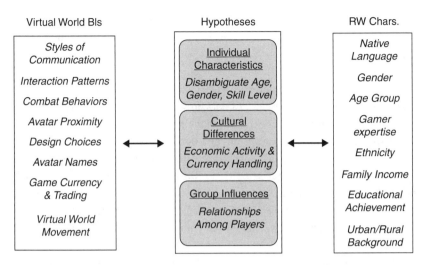

Figure 1.2 How VERUS research hypotheses link virtual world behaviors and players' real-world characteristics.

adapted primarily for our economic decision-making studies. Our strategy was to establish a pool of player accounts in these VWs, with each account used by just one participant.

The strategy for the overall project was to examine gamer activities in multiple virtual worlds, where possible. We believed that it was important to emphasize an initial exploration of broad gamer behaviors that could transcend virtual worlds, rather than prematurely focusing on activities enabled by the basic affordances of one specific environment. Thus, most of our participants were invited to play in two VWs: a popular MMOG of their choice and one of our specially instrumented worlds. This enabled us to observe gameplay in a more naturalistic context and to benefit from the richer in-world data logging that was provided by our dedicated environments.

From the outset we theorized that participants would carry their text chat characteristics into any virtual world they entered. The initial chat analysis suggested that this was probably true, since our integrated text chat models performed well in predicting several key RW characteristics. In initial work we also observed that gamers' decisions about the appearance and design of their avatars seemed to be good predictors of their RW gender. These design decisions were obviously limited – or possibly amplified – by the affordances of each game. This finding resonates with other avatar design analysis work (e.g., Kennedy et al., 2014) that also finds consistencies in such gender mapping within individual VWs. However, in our VERUS work we also noted that this relationship appears to travel across virtual worlds, a result that enhanced the basic theory.

An important topic of interest in video game studies concerns how best to characterize the levels and types of game proficiency that players may develop. For example, studying player expertise in their preferred games can pose a challenge for researchers because certain demographic factors of interest, such as age and gender, correlate with experience of particular environments. There is also the question of what actually constitutes game expertise, which may be measured along several different, game-agnostic dimensions (Taylor et al., 2011). A further issue concerns the influence of in-game affordances, such that capabilities gained in one game environment may – or may not – map or translate easily to another one.

In several parts of our work, we found it appropriate to differentiate novices for a specific virtual environment from "pure" gaming novices who play little or no digital games. Similarly, it is also useful to distinguish between players who have expertise in a particular world and those general experts who simply lack familiarity with the specific game in question.

In the VERUS project, our two dedicated VWs, *Guardian Academy* and *Sherwood*, proved to be useful research environments in this regard. As they were previously unknown to all our participants, everyone started off as a newcomer to these worlds, despite any possible previous experience with other games.

1.2 Popular Virtual Worlds and Field Studies

For the two dedicated worlds, detailed in-game behavioral activity data for all participants were completely recorded. The latter part of this chapter focuses primarily on the collection and analysis of the specialized telemetry logs that were gathered in these specific environments. However, throughout the project, VERUS researchers also undertook a comprehensive variety of laboratory and field studies that examined player activity in popular virtual environments. From the outset, these studies were carried out to provide a broader examination of the online gaming ecosystem and to set a stronger context for our specialized telemetry analysis work.

The early lab-based studies enabled researchers to examine participants' activities, primarily in small co-situated groups, in settings that incorporated multiple, multimodal forms of complementary data collection. They involved exploratory studies of gameplay across multiple MMOGs (primarily *MapleStory*, *Guild Wars*, *World of Warcraft*, *Second Life*, and *EVE Online*), which enabled researchers to gain a broad understanding of the kinds of players that different VWs attract (especially in the context of the university-based populations that we were initially working with), as well as how different online environments structure communicative action.

By their nature, the data collected in these contexts were different, in part owing to the presence of other players (i.e., non-VERUS participants) in these worlds. Rather than simply relying on the more limited in-game telemetry available in these VWs, this set of lab studies drew on various other data collection techniques, including think-aloud protocols, keystroke logging, participant travelogs, video capture with activity coding, and researcher observations (Bergstrom, Jenson, & de Castell, 2012; Jenson, Bergstrom, & de Castell, 2013).

As the project moved forward, the research procedures were refined to focus on specific recruitment priorities – including wider ethnicity and age representation, more intermediate and expert players, and co-situating multiple players in groups (two to four) to elicit more sociality and generate discursive data. To reinforce the validity of this research approach, data were collected in a coordinated fashion at two separate locations – the Multimodal Analysis of Real/Virtual Environments Laboratory (MARVEL) at Simon Fraser University in Vancouver and the Play in Computer Environments Studio (Play:CES) at York University in Toronto.

Both in scope and in methods, this type of lab study is the first of its kind: an "on the ground" exploration of the complex relationships between VWs and the localized practices of players in different cities, and in different contexts of play. The theoretical framework that the researchers deployed in these lab-based studies was Actor Network Theory (ANT), as has been developed and articulated in the field of science and technology studies (Latour, 1992, 2005; Callon, 1995). According to ANT, social interactions, institutions, and practices arise from and are reproduced through relationships between humans and nonhumans. To the extent that technologies are delegated to carry out tasks, enable or disable particular courses of action, prescribe behaviors, and generally "frame" human activity, they must be treated as full "actors" by social scientists (Latour, 1992).

For these lab studies, this meant using multiple and multimodal data collection tools, in sessions in which each participant played in at least two separate VWs, in order to reassemble the most complete range of associations between embodied players and their virtual behaviors and interactions. Failure to adopt this strategy risks confounding behavioral patterns that are more characteristic of in-game affordances, rather than of RW players, who may be playing several characters in very different – but no less predictable – ways (de Castell et al., 2014).

Using this approach, it becomes clear that connecting VW behavior to RW identities is not simply a matter of "reading back" onto a "real" person the actions or characteristics of an avatar, but of reading VW behaviors as the product and expression of a complex choreography between players in their RW environments and their (potentially multiple) game technologies.

Beyond these comprehensive cross-world studies of popular MMOGs, and to further study their usage in some typical gameplay settings, VERUS researchers developed, tested, and implemented a protocol for studying player activity in several public RW contexts. These included public gaming centers, fan culture events, and internet cafés in urban centers across a range of socioeconomically, linguistically, and culturally diverse neighborhoods and communities (Taylor et al., 2014).

As the project progressed, the research team focused fieldwork and recruitment efforts away from internet cafés and toward large-scale gaming events in several different countries. These LAN events were more amenable to fieldwork and data collection for the following reasons: MMOG players could be recruited in greater numbers (often in groups of five to fifteen at once), researchers could spend more time interacting with and observing attendees, and attendees could use their own personal computers to participate in the research. In particular, this process enabled more consistent and widespread use of the browser-based *Guardian Academy* environment among study participants, who were located in a familiar field setting rather than a laboratory.

In addition to these field studies, we undertook a preliminary feasibility study on conducting this research in broader international contexts, with exploratory visits to Bangalore, India; Guadalajara, Mexico; Seoul, South Korea; Tokyo, Japan; Dubai, UAE; and Singapore. This exploratory study was intended to characterize RW gaming centers, as well as to examine the suitability of these environments for further experimental studies, in particular, to determine the potential difficulties (travel, translation, traditions, local cultures and conditions) of conducting such ethnocentric fieldwork in international public arenas (Chee, de Castell, & Taylor, 2011).

Beyond these comprehensive cross-world studies of popular MMOGs, we also used a dedicated *Second Life* island to undertake early-stage exploratory studies of in-world social signaling and water maze search behaviors (de Castell et al., 2010; Tanenbaum et al., 2014).

The central unifying feature of all our work was the VERUS Core Survey, which was administered online to all participants. This web-based survey elicited each person's demographic details as well as his or her general experience of and engagement with digital media and video games. The demographic data were used as the source for the detailed RW characteristics that our analyses targeted. Supplementary questionnaire items were also administered to groups who participated in specific elements of our project. For example, those taking part in the economic decision-making study completed an additional questionnaire to determine their tolerance for different levels and types of risk.

1.3 Economic Decisions in Virtual Worlds

Our economic decision-making study centered primarily on our analyses of risk-related behaviors in the *Sherwood* environment. We also included data collection activities to examine behaviors in *Guardian Academy* and *EVE Online*. Both of these worlds offered our participants a more realistic, goal-oriented gaming experience, and *EVE* in particular uses a very liberal, free-form in-game economy, with few restrictions on player behavior.

We started with hypotheses from existing work that suggested economic decision-making linkages between RW and VW characteristics. A comprehensive review of the experimental economics literature identified a range of prior research relevant to this topic (Carpenter et al., 2009; Dohmen et al., 2011; Hartog, Ferreri-i-Carbonell, & Jonker, 2002; Helbok, Marinelli, & Walls, 2006; Hofstede, 2001; Inglehart, 1997). In our review, we particularly aimed to find links between the demographics of interest to our study and suitable tasks that measure behavior commonly observed in virtual worlds. Almost all of these relationships were based on four widely used laboratory tasks; from these tasks the researchers formed a number of hypotheses to be tested in the *Sherwood* environment. The tasks measured parametric risk (which has been linked with gender, age, income, education, and community type), strategic risk (income, education, social values orientation), cooperativeness (age, community type, ethnicity, social values orientation), and altruism (gender, age, social values orientation).

Sherwood was a virtual re-creation of Manhattan's Times Square. This world allowed text chat and a range of avatar gestures but no audio. Each avatar had a private apartment and could invite other avatars to be its friend. For the friendship to form the invited avatar had to agree. Friends could communicate privately with each other and could visit each other's apartments. All avatars were able to visit all the indoor and outdoor public spaces in the world. Laboratory-based play sessions were held in silence, with players positioned so that they could not see each other's screens.

Participants were first logged into a fresh account that took them to the avatar creation screen where they could customize the gender, clothing, hairstyle, hair color, and skin color of their avatars. After this, avatars appeared alone in their apartments where participants could become familiar with the interface controls (onscreen instructions were given). No RW announcements were made after participants were logged in, although two researchers were in-world and made announcements there. Avatars were asked to come to Times Square to explore the world and play an ice-breaker game designed to encourage socialization. Participants were encouraged to interact with each other inside the world using their avatars.

After 30 minutes a street fair was opened where participants could play in-world games at different booths, each of which was designed to capture a specific economic behavior implemented as a funfair activity. There were four booths: *Duck Shoot*, *Charity Booth*, *Bust*, and *Dare*. The *Duck Shoot* game was based on a classic public good game (Andreoni, 1988) and was designed to measure cooperation among groups of players. Players could use either blue or red bullets to shoot ducks on a gallery, with hits from the blue color benefitting all group members and red ones only themselves. The *Charity Booth* gave participants the chance to donate money to a popular charity and was intended to measure altruism (Eckel & Grossman, 1996). *Bust* and *Dare* were games designed to measure strategic and parametric risk-taking behavior respectively, i.e., risk in the interaction with another person or with "nature" (Chuah, Hoffmann, & Larner, 2016). In *Bust*, players' winnings were higher the later they stopped the game before it was randomly terminated, in which event they earned nothing. *Dare* was similar except two players interacted, with the one stopping later than the other earning more. If neither stopped both would lose (Chuah, Hoffmann, & Larner, 2013).

1.3.1 Guardian Academy

Guardian Academy was a multiplayer game with a "sword and sorcery" setting. Players were given quests from nonplayer characters to complete to earn points. Players could form groups with each other to complete quests or to explore the world together. The interface allowed text chat only (no audio chat). The world featured a store where health potions and other items could be bought and sold. It also featured a player versus player (PvP) arena where players could challenge each other to a duel (outside of this arena, players were unable to fight each other). The server recorded a range of telemetering information including avatar movement, avatar characteristics such as health level, battle data, chat, and trading information.

Guardian Academy provided us with an experimental environment that was different from *Sherwood* in that the decision tasks were not explicitly induced by the researchers. In this study, participants were recruited from a population of individuals with some prior experience of online game playing. As participants played, a number of metrics were logged as measures of risk-taking behavior. The health level of an avatar when entering a battle, the level of difference between an avatar and monsters fought, and the number of deaths were used as measures of parametric risk. The time spent in PvP play was used as a measure of strategic risk. The amount of buying and selling an avatar undertook was also recorded.

1.3.2 Avatar Sex, Race, and Class

Most virtual worlds provide players with a fair amount of avatar customization. In our preliminary analyses of various games, we focused our examination of feature selection on several dimensions of customization that are commonly available across virtual worlds – avatar sex, race, and class. Several prior studies have found that *avatar sex* yields a single, highly predictive, feature of the player's RW gender (Dunn & Guadagno, 2012; Hussain & Griffiths, 2008; Trepte & Reinecke, 2010).

The issue of *avatar race* is rather more subtle, and it requires some care to derive suitable features for analysis, in particular because the specific races available vary in type and range by virtual world; for example, *Rift* has six, while *World of Warcraft* has twelve. Such features must carry predictive content, but to be maximally useful they must be portable from one world to the next. Converting each race into Boolean indicators is not useful because the races are typically unique to the universe from which they originate. Similarly, races are often locked into factions, but again these factions cannot be mapped into other virtual worlds. We created groupings of races, whose characteristics were meaningful in other worlds, and that were either observed or hypothesized to correlate with RW demographic attributes. Boolean indicator variables corresponding to each of these groupings served as our avatar race features.

Players also had the ability to choose *classes* for their avatars. The choice of class (or calling), which is independent of the choice of race, defines the avatar's role and style of play: for example, fighter versus healer or ranged versus melee damage dealing. Our early analysis with *World of Warcraft* indicated that class-based features were not strong predictors; this was also observed in our subsequent work with the VERUS-dedicated world *Guardian Academy*. Moreover, we could not discern a clear correspondence in class taxonomies between virtual worlds: in some worlds players can acquire or enhance attributes; in others, the capabilities are innate, which renders class-based features less generalizable.

1.3.3 Avatar Customization in *Sherwood*

In addition to the economic decision-making activity mentioned earlier, the *Sherwood* logs also provided us with rich data on numerous other in-game activities and behaviors. For example, data on three aspects of avatar interaction were extracted as follows: avatar appearance, avatar location, and avatar communication. For avatar appearance, users could customize the gender, clothing, hairstyle, hair color, and skin color of their avatar, yielding a metric for each. Clothing options were coded as one of three classifications for an avatar's top (from the waist up) and bottom (from the waist down). The three classifications represented the amount of skin the clothing revealed and formed an ordinal scale from mostly skin (1) to medium skin (2) to fully covered (3). Amount of skin revealed was chosen as the salient measure of clothing style following previous research (Abbey et al., 1987; Grammer, Renninger, & Fischer, 2004, Rosenfeld & Plax, 1977). We chose this classification among many possible ones as universally meaningful, unlike certain fashions that mean something particular to certain groups (such as a Gothick's attitude to black clothing, or a gang member's attitude to prison issue baggy jeans).

We also coded a number of avatar appearance data including skin tone and hairstyle and color. Hairstyle was coded on the ordinal scale as short (1), medium length (2), and long (3). Hair color was coded on the following nominal scale: black, gray, red, brown, blonde, and unnatural (blue, pink, green, etc.). Participants could choose to add avatar tattoos. This was coded as 1 if at least one tattoo was chosen and 0 otherwise. Finally, users had nine choices of skin color for their avatars. These represent ordinal data and were merged into two categories, pale (1) and dark (2). These classifications of avatar options were independently generated by two observers (one of the researchers and another individual not involved in the research). In each case there was perfect agreement except for three of the male hairstyle options, indicating excellent overall interrater agreement. The three male hairstyle options were later discussed, after which agreement was reached.

From the avatar in-world location data, we extracted a proximity metric to measure the average distance that each avatar stayed to the next closest one during its interaction in the game's public space. This distance was calculated using the world's Cartesian x–y coordinate system.

We recorded friendship, coded as 1 if a participant invited another participant to become friends or accepted an offer of friendship from another participant, and 0 if a participant did not invite another participant to become friends or declined an offer of friendship from another participant. The variable captures a desire to form a friendship and could be used to identify a full friendship, an unrequited friendship, and where no desire to form a friendship exists. In addition, all text chat among avatars was recorded.

1.4 Movement in Virtual Worlds

Studies of gender and mobility in the real world suggest that the "rightful" allocation of space to women is measurably less than men's. Historically and culturally, women have been consistently less able ("free") than men to move about in general, and to explore new territory in particular; this is true across ages, over time, and across racial and cultural contexts (Ardener, 1981; Massey, 1994). In addition, in terms of objectively measured spatial abilities, females consistently prove less adept at navigation than males (Allen, 2000). Thus, we conjectured that certain behavioral characteristics related to spatial mobility and movement in VWs might provide further insights into in-game gender differences.

As noted earlier, VERUS researchers conducted a preliminary study using a virtual water maze to examine differences in spatial navigation search strategies (de Castell, 2010). They found that female participants – even "experts" – generally covered less space than males in trying to locate a hidden objective. This insight led us to design an expanded study of movement features with greater face validity using the *Guardian Academy* game (Murray, Chow, & Connolly, 2015).

The *Guardian Academy* event log files recorded the two-dimensional position of avatars as they moved around the world. For each user, the log entries detail a location identifier along with the avatar's time-stamped x, y position expressed in a location-specific coordinate frame. Metrics that distinguish the movement of different players were distilled from this position information, yielding an important class of motion-derived features that encapsulate behavior associated with the position and velocity of avatars.

Area Covered is the extent or range of a player's movement, and ***Distance Traveled*** is the length of the path traced over time. We also calculated the two-dimensional *change* of user movement at each time step, and aggregate each user's relative displacements into a *step histogram*. Figure 1.3 depicts two-step histograms; the left histogram has higher entropy, while the right one has lower entropy. The x- and y-axes represent horizontal and vertical displacement. Each histogram is colored by the frequency of visits to the corresponding positions:

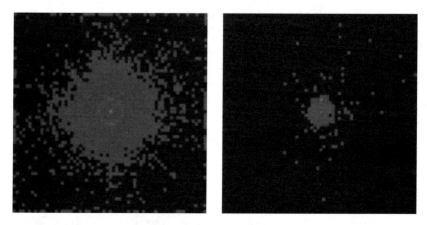

Figure 1.3 Step entropy histograms for two players: (left) higher entropy, (right) lower entropy. (This image is shown in full color in the Color Plates section.)

black is 0, blue indicates a low number of visits, and red indicates a high number. Figure 1.4 shows the effects of histogram shape on entropy. We can also compute *velocity histograms*, which are constructed from a three-point approximation to the derivative of smoothed motion.

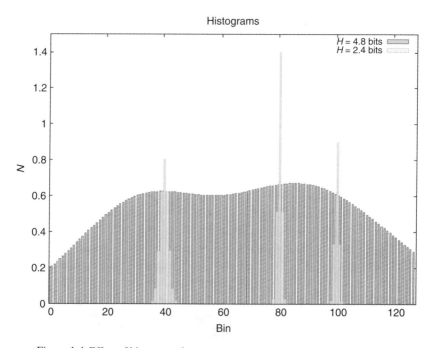

Figure 1.4 Effect of histogram shape on entropy.

Although *Area Covered* and *Distance Traveled* provide useful movement information, they do not adequately capture the frequency of a player's visits to certain locations. We therefore characterize the frequency as well as the extent of travel using *Shannon entropy* (Cover & Thomas, 1991). This gives us a measure of the "variability" or "disorder" of the travel pattern, and accounts for the frequency of visits to specific positions, as well as the variety of positions visited. The Shannon entropy $H(X)$ of random variable X is

$$H(X) = -\Sigma P(xi) \log P(xi) \qquad (1.1)$$

where $P(xi)$ is the normalized frequency for value xi. In the present context, $P(xi)$ is the fraction of the total histogram mass corresponding to bin i. The Shannon entropy can be seen as the minimum number of bits needed to encode the distribution of X. Figure 1.3 shows the qualitative effect of different entropies, where the concentrated green (lower entropy) histogram can be more easily encoded than the wider-spread red (higher entropy) one.

Entropy measures are used to assess exploratory behavior. We defined the **Propensity to Explore** as the extent to which a player travels throughout the overall environment, and quantify it as the entropy of the position histogram (the *place entropy*). This represents not just the area traveled, but also frequency of visits to specific places within the game.

We also defined the **Propensity to Wander** as the variability in the player's direction and magnitude of movement from one time point to the next, and quantify this variability by the entropy of the step histogram (the *step entropy*).

Although these entropy quantities are difficult for a human observer to calculate numerically, one can argue that they capture concepts that can be perceived rather readily: place entropy captures the tendency to *fully* explore one's surroundings, while step entropy measures the tendency to wander in undirected, irregular paths. It is nonetheless possible to familiarize the observer with place entropy and step entropy by presenting examples of player movement and the associated entropy values. Given exemplars illustrating the range of movement, one can gain a sense of the distribution of propensity, or, at minimum, what behavior exceeding the 70th percentile or 90th percentile looks like.

1.5 Analysis of Avatar Names and Language Usage

The data collection process included gathering a wide variety of in-game text chat data, as well as dedicated avatar names for several different virtual environments. In order to analyze these data, we drew on various hypotheses from the theoretical sociolinguistics literature, phonology and sound symbolism, and

Table 1.1 *Prominent chat features*

Text Chat Behavior	Class	Examples
Hedging/uncertainty	Female	Questions, "I don't know," etc.
Command forms	Male	"Heal me!"
Use of slurs	Male	"You homo!"
Direct apologies	Female	"I'm sorry"
Indirect apologies	Male	"Oops," "my bad," etc.
Empathy	Female	"I like X," "u OK?", etc.
Use of modal verbs	Female	can, could, would, should, etc.
Use of all caps	Youth	"STOP BEING DUMB," etc.
Frequent use of ellipsis	Adult	"if you bring up yr questlog...."
Commas and apostrophes	Adult	"we're done, let's turn in," etc.
Lowercase "i" for "I," "u" for "you"	Youth	"u losted to 4 pokemno," etc.
Single word utterances	Youth	"come," "yo"

semantics and discourse analysis, and made empirical observations to generate features for determining RW attributes that could be combined in a global model using statistical classifiers. Based on the literature, a selection of features were evaluated, including the following: expressions of uncertainty; swears, insults, and slurs; and expressions of empathy, and apologies. Rules for extracting each of these features were developed and the results were calculated to verify whether there were biases in the distribution across the different player classes. Table 1.1 shows examples of the prominent chat features in the text that was recorded.

It is clear that linguistic features have high predictive value for the identification of user demographics in virtual worlds. We summarize our findings in Figure 1.5, with examples of representative chat and naming phenomena and how they relate to demographics.

Analysis of the results showed that many of the existing sociolinguistic claims about gender and discourse also hold true in the VW: women were much more likely to use modal verbs, ask questions, use expressions of uncertainty, and use strong apologies than were men. Men were much more likely to use strong swears, slurs, and indirect apologies. The results also demonstrate that some of the categories suggested in the sociolinguistic studies may be too coarse. For example, women are claimed to apologize more frequently than men. However, if one analyzes the types of apologies that occur it become clear that direct apologies (e.g., "I'm sorry") are more typical of female players, while indirect apologies ("oops!" or "my bad!") are associated more with

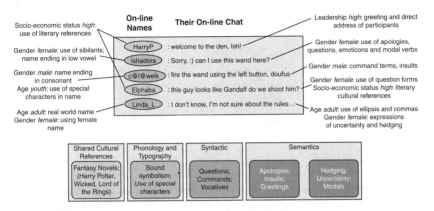

Figure 1.5 Summary of chat and avatar naming analysis (Lawson & Murray, 2014).

men. Similarly, with swears there was a breakdown between the types of words used: light swears were associated more with women and strong swears more with men. This observation is actually in keeping with the observations that men are more comfortable with profanity than women, as many of the "light swears" represent approaches to avoid offensive cursing. Slurs were the category most strongly associated with men, and most slurs were homophobic in nature (Lawson et al., 2012).

1.6 Data Analysis and Results

1.6.1 Analysis Strategy

The goal was to identify rules and patterns that identified RW characteristics from VW behavior. To start we thoroughly explored the data, using correlation analysis to retain features with predictive power and reduce them to a minimally correlated subset. The reduced feature set was then passed to the rule discovery algorithm (Flach & Lachiche, 2001) provided by the Tertius module of the Weka machine-learning workbench.

The resulting list of association rules was reviewed and validated by our subject matter experts. In some cases, our original hypotheses were confirmed, while in others, some surprising – though thoroughly plausible – insights emerged. The best combination of these rules, whose union maximizes recall while maintaining or exceeding the target precision threshold, is presented here.

We used a bootstrap approach to assess the uncertainty in the performance measures that were computed on our rules. The uncertainty is expressed as the variability in precision and recall that can be expected when the rules are applied to similar data sets. We thus introduced an innovative "assurance" technique that quantifies the degree to which the rules succeeded in meeting the target precision threshold. This feature and rules development methodology, with its emphasis on simplicity and ease of interpretation, ensures validity of rules and minimizes overfitting. We aimed for individual rules with at most two variables. We discretized continuous variables into binary indicators, each one an assertion about exceeding a quantile threshold. The advantages of this coarsening into quantiles include interpretability, seamless portability to new virtual worlds, and reduced computational effort.

We minimized overfitting by imposing a limit on the complexity of the rules. Since our rules were subject to human review, we avoided the problem of lack of generalizability associated with blindly accepting the top-scoring results returned by the rules-mining software. Because our rules generation approach is nonparametric, there are no cross-validation experiments to conduct to identify the optimal number of features to include in a discriminant function, or to select the best member from a family of competing model forms.

We believe that this methodology, a close collaboration between machine learning and human judgment, returns rules of high quality. This hybrid approach offers the best of both worlds, enabling a machine to automate tasks such as sifting through the data to identify candidate rules, but enforcing human participation in defining the features and interpreting the results.

As noted earlier, throughout the project we gathered data in various RW settings – laboratories, LAN events, summer camps, schools, etc. At the same time, we narrowed our focus to a smaller selection of virtual worlds, as the project progressed. This enabled us to pay more attention to the contexts that were proving valuable from a richness of data point of view. Our standard analysis strategy utilized an association rules methodology, which provided a consistent way to describe our hypotheses and to express our findings.

A summary of the main results for RW characteristics of interest is shown in Table 1.2. The number of our participants who played in each of the VWs studied varied and the worlds themselves offered differing selections of affordances. This resulted in a variation in the number of participants (N) who were covered by each of our analyses.

The results reporting technique reflects precision and recall (rather than overall accuracy) as the performance measure for the association rules methodology. We focused principally on precision, since our goal was primarily to find practical and useful rules about in-game features that would predict a player's RW attributes (rule precision), rather than discovering a priori the proportion of players with a given RW attribute to which a particular rule might apply (rule recall). Thus, in developing combinations of rules for our hypotheses and

Table 1.2 *Summary of VERUS predictive metrics*

N	Real-World Characteristic	Value	Precision (%)	Recall (%)	Behavioral Indicators
380	Player gender	Male	98	45	GA avatar features + movement
		Female	89	58	GA avatar features + movement
250	Approximate age group	<18	92	12	*GA* names + text chat
		18–24	80	13	*GA* text chat
		24+	83	14	*GA* text chat
91	Socioeconomic status (minors)	High	81	94	*GA* names + events
		Low	83	40	*GA* names + events
78	Ethnicity	Asian	76	41	*Rift* events
		Caucasian	83	32	*Rift* events
37	Education	HS/CC	64	50	*EVE* economic activity
		UG/GR	67	53	*EVE* economic activity
106	Income level	Low	83	28	*GA* risk aversion
		Medium	67	47	*GA* risk aversion
		High	85	30	*GA* risk aversion
540	English native speaker	Text chat features	77	22	Cross-world text chat

analyses, we aimed to maximize the recall of the combination while still meeting or exceeding our target thresholds for precision.

1.6.2 VW Movement Analysis

For our player gender analysis work with *Guardian Academy*, characterizing movement provided a convenient means to improve on the basic findings for gendered differences in behavioral gameplay. For example, combining movement features with avatar sex yields association rules that substantially improve on the default assumption that RW gender matches the VW choice; our findings on this item reflect those identified by various other games researchers (e.g., Kennedy et al., 2014; Symborski et al., 2014). The precision of our baseline avatar-gender-only rule is 93.5% (with recall 81.2%) for predicting male gender, and 60.7% (with recall 84.5%) for predicting female gender.

For the prediction of male players, augmenting this baseline rule with movement features yields rules with precision exceeding 98%, but at the cost of a significant drop in recall. The implication is that, for the relatively small proportion of players who satisfy the assertion, the prediction of male gender is near

Table 1.3 *Movement association rules to predict RW gender Male*

	In the RW, Player is Male if......			
Rule	In the VW.....	Precision (%)	Recall (%)	F
Base	Avatar is male (AM)	93.5	81.2	88.9
1	AM AND AreaCovered > 114 (i.e., 60%ile)	99.0	35.5	52.2
2	AM AND Prop.Explore > 4.46 (i.e., 60%ile)	99.0	35.5	52.2
3	AM AND Prop.Wander > 3.40 (i.e., 60%ile)	99.0	35.8	52.6
Union	RULE 1 OR 2 OR 3	98.4	44.7	61.5

perfect. For the prediction of female players, the augmentation with movement features raises the precision very close to 90%, with good recall. Tables 1.3 and 1.4 summarize these results.

1.6.3 Avatar Names

We examined the relationship between RW gender and avatar name to determine to what extent avatar names conform to predictions described in the linguistics literature. Since there is a greater degree of freedom in choosing avatar names (use of numbers, spaces, underscores, capitalization, pop-culture references, etc.), we anticipated significantly greater variability among avatar names than is the case with given or personal names. A suite of rules were proposed,

Table 1.4 *Movement association rules to predict RW gender Female*

	In the RW, Player is Female if......			
Rule	In the VW.....	Precision (%)	Recall (%)	F
Base	Avatar is female (AF)	60.7	84.5	70.7
1	AF AND Area Covered < 37 (i.e., 40%ile)	87.3	49.5	63.2
2	AF AND Prop. Explore < 3.27 (i.e., 40%ile)	87.0	48.5	62.3
3	AF AND Prop. Wander < 2.89 (i.e., 40%ile)	88.3	54.6	67.5
Union	RULE 1 OR 2 OR 3	88.9	57.7	70.0

Table 1.5 *Avatar association rules to predict RW gender*

Rule	In the VW	Precision (%)	Recall (%)	F
In the RW, Player is Male if				
1	Avatar name contains a number	99.0	4.8	9.1
2	Avatar name contains x or z	88.2	14.3	24.6
Union	RULE 1 OR 2	90.9	19.0	31.5
In the RW, Player is Female if				
1	Avatar name contains a female US census name	91.2	30.4	45.6

most were based on observations from the sound symbolism research, such as female names ending in low and front vowels; male names ending in back vowels; male names containing "z" and "x"; and female names containing "sh". Our hypothesis that names in the VW will follow similar conventions to the RW led us to the use of US Census report of 1,000 most common names for males and females as a source of data.

Each rule was evaluated against the 207 avatar names collected from *Sherwood*. Omitted from consideration were names automatically assigned to players unable to choose a name themselves. For male players, we found that avatar names containing a number, or the letters x or z were most predictive of a male player, whereas an avatar name contains a female US census name was most predictive of a female player. These summary results are shown in Table 1.5.

An examination of the patterns in the avatar names selected in *Sherwood* and *Guardian Academy* yielded very simple rules that differentiated younger from older players, and achieved a reasonable precision threshold, albeit with low recall. The hypothesis was that younger users would be more innovative and more likely to break the conventions of standard naming, while older users would create names that conformed more to traditional naming conventions. The first rule looks at whether a number is used anywhere in the name, and the second checks whether an avatar name is also a name listed in the US Census. These results are summarized in Table 1.6.

1.6.4 Text Chat

Analysis of the results (Figure 1.5) showed that many of the existing sociolinguistic claims about gender and discourse also hold true in the VW: women were much more likely to use modal verbs, ask questions, use expressions

Table 1.6 *Avatar association rules to predict RW age*

In the RW, Player is in age group......				
Age Group	If, in the VW.....	Precision (%)	Recall (%)	F
Under 18	Avatar name contains a number	85.1	33.5	48.1
18+	Avatar name is a common US census name	88.1	21.0	33.9

of uncertainty, and use strong apologies than were men. Males were much more likely to use strong swears, slurs, and indirect apologies. The results also demonstrate that some of the categories suggested in the sociolinguistic studies may be too coarse. For example, women are claimed to apologize more frequently than men. However, if one analyzes the types of apologies that occur it become clear that direct apologies (e.g., "I'm sorry") are more typical of women players, while indirect apologies ("oops!" or "my bad!") are more associated with men. Similarly, with swears there was a breakdown between the types of words used: light swears were associated more with women and strong swears more with men. This observation is actually in keeping with the observations that men are more comfortable with profanity than women, as many of the "light swears" represent approaches to avoid offensive cursing. Slurs were the category most strongly associated with men, and most slurs were homophobic in nature.

1.6.5 Economic Behavior

Rules predicting education were based on economic features observed in players of *EVE Online*. Because of the small sample size, we grouped the target into two classes: players who had completed secondary/high school or trade school/technical school/community college and players who had completed an undergraduate or graduate or professional school education. To minimize the risk of overfitting, the proposed rules are as simple as possible, consisting of only one condition. There are concerns about the generalizability of these rules due to small sample sizes, and we also found that behavior between the samples was quite different, which seems most likely explained by differing in-game conditions at the time when the sample data were collected.

Previous literature in the area of experimental economics has found that risk-seeking attitudes and behavior are often positively correlated with education. In addition, our study confirmed, to some degree, that these attitudes hold for VW

Table 1.7 *Association rules for* EVE Online *to predict education level*

In the RW, Player education is.....				
....at level	If, in the VW.....	Precision (%)	Recall (%)	*F*
High school or community college	Market trading behavior is <40%ile	63.6	50.0	56.0
University undergraduate or graduate	Market exposure is >60%ile	66.7	53.3	59.3

behavior. Previous studies have found mixed evidence with regard to age (with some studies finding a positive correlation between age and risk-taking behavior, some finding a negative one, and others finding no significant relationship). However, in many subject pools, age and education are very strongly correlated, and this is a potential confound. Our current data set is unusual in that it contains both high variance in age characteristics and a relatively weak correlation between age and education, so it offers a unique opportunity to investigate this relationship further. On this basis, we hypothesized that participants who engage in risk-taking economic behavior tend to have higher levels of educational achievement.

Our analysis confirms the hypothesis, and we find that a high level of market exposure is an indicator of high education level. We also found that participants who tend to avoid trading activity are far more likely to have lower levels of education. We confirmed that this was due to risk preferences by validating our behavioral indicators with industry-standard tasks from the experimental economics literature.

These results are summarized in Table 1.7.

1.6.6 Socioeconomic Status of Minors

While many assertions have been made about minor populations in North America, including that they are inherently "digitally native" (Prensky, 2010), based on previous VERUS researcher experience with minors, including extensive research in schools, it was found that digital "nativity" was more like naiveté for most minors.

In the first part of the project the following behaviors were observed in the population of minors, most of whom were from low socioeconomic status (SES) backgrounds:

Table 1.8 *Association rules to predict SES among minor players in* Guardian Academy

Rule	In the VW	Precision (%)	Recall (%)	F
In the RW, Player SES is Low if				
1	Quests accepted < 30%ile AND Potions purchased > 90%ile	99.0	16.0	27.6
2	PvP kills > 90%ile AND Avatar name contains an English word	83.3	20.0	32.3
3	Avatar name contains both a number and a non-word character	80.0	16.0	26.7
Union	RULE 1 OR 2 OR 3	83.3	40.0	54.1
In the RW, Player SES is High if				
1	Quests accepted is < 80%ile	99.8	31.8	48.3
2	Time spent in group is > 70%ile	96.3	39.4	55.9
3	Avatar name does not contain an English word	80.0	84.8	82.4
Union	1 OR 2 OR 3	80.5	93.9	86.7

- They were much less familiar with MMOG conventions than our adult population.
- They tended to engage in PvP when playing *Guardian Academy*, as a means of collectively learning the game's combat mechanics; as a result, they died frequently.
- They used their RW names, both when naming their avatars and when communicating with one another, despite deliberate instruction to the contrary.

Based on these observations, it was hypothesized that minors from lower SES populations would have less familiarity with MMOGs than those from higher SES populations. In addition, this lack of MMOG literacy – and in fact, the lack of broader computer-based competency in general – would lead to more PvP play, more deaths, and a greater likelihood to include their own name in their avatar name. These considerations led the team to seek out a broader range of minors from more diverse socioeconomic backgrounds, including several school populations from mid to high SES, enabling the disaggregation of SES from age.

The results shown in Table 1.8 capture each of these hypotheses, with more PvP and PvE deaths among younger and lower SES players; avatar names that make use of an English word (often simply an English name); and more overall

PvP kills. Among the higher SES participants, there were more numbers in names (indicating, we believe, that the participants anticipated not being able to select the names they wanted), more quests accepted, and more overall group play.

The rules were based on observations of minors playing *Guardian Academy*, and the data analyzed consisted of features derived from avatar names and in-game activity. The intended classifications were Low SES and High SES, which were proxy groups inferred from the school that the player attended; we regarded self-reported assertions of SES as unreliable, since most survey respondents considered themselves middle SES level.

1.6.7 Household Income Prediction

To predict household income, the categories Low, Medium, and High Income to the core survey question, "Does your family income allow you to meet your household's everyday needs?" As noted earlier, risk-seeking behavior has been found to be correlated with income (Dohmen et al., 2011; Hartog et al., 2002) those with higher income are willing to accept greater risk. Risk can be measured in *Guardian Academy* by observing battle and health behavior: which monsters a player chooses to attack, player level of health when he or she attacks, and the number of times a player purchases and uses health potions.

RW income was measured using data collected from adult players. The number and percentages falling into each category are: High income: $N = 37$ (35%), Mid income: $N = 51$ (48%), Low income: $N = 18$ (17%). As hypothesized, these data were negatively and significantly correlated with the number of health potions purchased and used as a risk measure; those with higher income used health potions less ($p = .04$).

As a validation exercise, these participants were set additional RW tasks that are known to measure risk-taking behavior including the ultimatum game. The ultimatum game is a decision task in which two players interact to decide how to divide a sum of money that is given to them. Player 1 proposes how to divide the sum between the two players, and the Player 2 can either accept or reject this proposal. If Player 2 rejects, neither player receives anything. If Player 2 accepts, the money is split according to the proposal. The offer the first player makes can be used a measure of risk – the higher the offer, the less risk-seeking the player is.

Using data collected from *GA* and from the (RW) ultimatum game task, the number of health potions used was significantly correlated with the amount offered by Player 1 ($p = .06$), giving confidence that the number of health potions used is a valid measure of risk.

1.7 Conclusions

From the outset, one of the central strategies for our project was to emphasize the exploration of gamer behaviors that we believed could transcend virtual environments and our results demonstrate that such behaviors exist. Of course, many in-game decisions and actions are significantly defined by the affordances of the environment. However, since participants retain their personal RW characteristics as they move between VWs, our core hypothesis was that these RW attributes would also map to aspects of their activities in multiple worlds. Our findings indeed suggest that individuals retain some key behavioral features across their gameplay activities – for example, attributes of their text chat and avatar naming patterns.

A core feature of the VERUS project was the researcher-driven series of qualitative gameplay observations that were mapped into the coded virtual world behaviors. This activity provided extensive subject matter expertise to support the quantitative rule development by technical analysis specialists. In addition, these structured observations formed the basis of several comprehensive examinations of player attributes along several innovative dimensions.

Both *Sherwood* and *Guardian Academy* were unfamiliar to all our participants, and therefore provided an equivalent learning curve for everyone. Hence, they enabled us to obtain data from people encountering a new game environment, all starting from the same footing. This helped us to overcome the individual differences in prior player experience that many game studies researchers encounter when merging and analyzing gameplay data in public VWs. Thus, using our *Guardian Academy* data, we were able to detect differences in ingame observable behavior between players who had played MMOGs in the past, and those who had not. To a moderate extent, we also detected such differences among the individuals who played *Rift*, which at the time of the study was a new and unfamiliar public game.

Our analysis of movement in *Guardian Academy* yielded an interesting observation that echoes findings from other studies of gender and mobility: male players tend to "occupy space" more than female players. This was evidenced by the tendency of men to cover more area during gameplay, to wander (step entropy), and to explore (place entropy).

During the project, we adjusted our analysis strategy to address several insights that were identified along the way. We eventually adopted a unified strategy of rules development that nonetheless accommodated the multimodal nature of our data streams and the multidisciplinary focus of our research team. Our laboratory and field researchers clearly had the appropriate domain experience and subject matter expertise to identify features to validate hypotheses and confirm findings from the social science literature.

From these starting points, we thoroughly explored the data, using correlation analysis to retain features with predictive power and reduce them to a minimally correlated subset. The reduced feature set was then passed to the Tertius module of the machine-learning workbench Weka. The resulting list of association rules was reviewed and validated by our subject matter experts. In some cases, the original hypotheses were confirmed, while in others, some surprising – though thoroughly plausible – insights emerged.

Our feature and rules development methodology, with its emphasis on simplicity and ease of interpretation, assures validity of rules and minimizes overfitting. We aimed for individual rules with at most two variables. We discretized continuous variables into binary indicators, each one an assertion about exceeding a quantile threshold. The advantages of this coarsening into quantiles include interpretability, seamless portability to new virtual worlds, and reduced computational effort.

We minimized overfitting by imposing a limit on the complexity of the rules. Since our rules were subject to human review, we avoided the problem of lack of generalizability associated with blindly accepting the top-scoring results returned by the rules-mining software. Because our rules generation approach is nonparametric, there are no cross-validation experiments to conduct to identify the optimal number of features to include in a discriminant function, or to select the best member from a family of competing model forms.

We believe that this methodology, a close collaboration between machine learning and human judgment, returns rules of high quality. This hybrid approach offers the best of both worlds, enabling a machine to automate tasks such as sifting through the data to identify candidate rules, but enforcing human participation in defining the features and interpreting the results.

Acknowledgments

We would like to recognize the extensive work of Suzanne de Castell, Jennifer Jenson, and Nicholas Taylor, our VERUS coinvestigators at Simon Fraser and York Universities in Canada, and their graduate students and research assistants, who were responsible for substantial amounts of the research reported here. We also acknowledge the assistance of Jeremy Larner and the research team at Nottingham University in the United Kingdom. This project was undertaken with support from the US Air Force Research Laboratory under contract FA8650–10-C-7009.

References

Abbey, A., Cozzarelli, C., McLaughlin, K., & Harnish, R. J. (1987). The effects of clothing and dyad sex composition on perceptions of sexual intent: Do women and men evaluate these cues differently? *Journal of Applied Social Psychology*, 17(2), 108–126.

Allen, G. (2000). Men and women, maps and minds: Cognitive bases of sex-related differences in reading and interpreting maps. In S. Ó. Nualláin (ed.), *Spatial cognition: Foundations and applications*. Advances in Consciousness Research. Amsterdam: John Benjamins Publishing.

Andreoni, J. (1988). Why free ride? Strategies and learning in public goods experiments. *Journal of Public Economics*, 37, 291–304.

Ardener, S. (1981). *Women and space: Ground rules and social maps*. London: Croom Helm.

Bergstrom, K., Jenson, J., & de Castell, S. (2012, May). What's 'choice' got to do with it? Avatar selection differences between novice and expert players of *World of Warcraft* and *Rift*. In *Proceedings of the International Conference on the Foundations of Digital Games* (pp. 97–104). ACM Digital Library.

Callon, M. (1995). Four models for the dynamics of science. In S. Jasanoff, G. E. Markle, J. C. Peterson, & T. J. Pinch (eds.), *Handbook of science and technology studies* (pp. 29–63). Cambridge, MA: MIT Press.

Carpenter, J. P., Bowles, S., Gintis, H., & Hwang, S-H. (2009). Strong reciprocity and team production: Theory and evidence. *Journal of Economic Behavior and Organization*, 71, 221–232.

Chee, F., de Castell, S., & Taylor, N. (2011). Public virtual world gaming in Asia: Preparatory fieldwork for site selection, protocol testing and research instrument development. Technical Report 495, Simon Fraser University, BC. Retrieved from: http://summit.sfu.ca/item/495

Chuah, S, Hoffmann, R., & Larner, J. (2013). Elicitation effects in a multi-stage bargaining experiment. *Experimental Economics*, 17, 335–345.

Chuah, S., Hoffmann, R., & Larner, J. (2016). Perceived intentionality in 2×2 experimental games. *Bulletin of Economic Research*, in press.

Cover, T., & Thomas, J. (1991). *Elements of information theory*. New York, NY: John Wiley & Sons.

de Castell, S., Bojin, N., Campbell, S. R., et al. (2010). The eyes have it: Measuring spatial orientation in virtual worlds to explain gender differences in real ones. Technical Report, Simon Fraser University Library, Vancouver, BC.

de Castell, S., Jenson, J., Taylor, N., & Thumlert, K. (2014). Re-thinking foundations: Theoretical and methodological challenges (and opportunities) in virtual worlds research. *Journal of Gaming & Virtual Worlds*, 6, 1.

de Castell, S., Larios, H., Jenson, J., & Smith, D. H. (2015). The role of video game experience in spatial learning and memory. *Journal of Gaming & Virtual Worlds*, 7(1), 21–40.

Dohmen, T., Falk, A., Huffman, D., Sunde, U., Schupp, J., & Wagner, G. G. (2011). Individual risk attitudes: Measurement, determinants and behavioral consequences. *Journal of the European Economic Association*, 9(3), 522–550.

Dunn, R. A., & Guadagno, R. E. (2012). My avatar and me: Gender and personality predictors of avatar-self discrepancy. *Computers in Human Behavior*, 28(1), 97–106.

Eckel, Catherine C., & Grossman, P. J. (1996). Altruism in anonymous dictator games. *Games and Economic Behavior*, 16, 181–191.

Flach, P., & Lachiche, N. (2001). Confirmation-guided discovery of first-order rules with Tertius. *Machine Learning*, 42(1/2), 61–95.

Grammer, K., Renninger, L., & Fischer, B. (2004). Disco clothing, female sexual motivation, and relationship status: Is she dressed to impress? *Journal of Sex Research*, 41(1), 66–74.

Hall, M., Frank, E., Holmes, G., Pfahringer, B., Reutemann, P., & Witten, I. H. (2013). Weka 3: Data mining and open source machine learning software in Java.

Hartog, J., Ferrer-i-Carbonell, A., & Jonker, N. (2002). Linking measured risk aversion to individual characteristics. *Kyklos*, 55(1), 3–26.

Helbok, C. M., Marinelli, R. P., & Walls, R. T. (2006). National survey of ethical practices across rural and urban communities. *Professional Psychology: Research and Practice*, 37(1), 36–44.

Hofstede, G. (2001). *Culture's consequences: Comparing values, behaviors, institutions, and organizations across nations*, 2nd edn. Thousand Oaks, CA: SAGE.

Hussain, Z., & Griffiths, M. D. (2008). Gender swapping and socializing in cyberspace: An exploratory study. *CyberPsychology & Behavior*, 11(1), 47–53.

Inglehart, R. (1997). *Modernization and postmodernization: Cultural, economic, and political change in 43 societies*. Princeton, NJ: Princeton University Press.

Jenson, J., Bergstrom, K., & de Castell, S. (2013). Playing 'for Real': A lab-based study of MMOGs. *Selected Papers of Internet Research*, 3.

Kennedy, T., Ratan, R. R., Kapoor, K., Pathak, N., Williams, D., & Srivastava, J. (2014). Predicting MMO player gender from in-game attributes using machine learning models. In *Predicting real world behaviors from virtual world data* (pp. 69–84). Cham, Switzerland: Springer International Publishing.

Latour, B. (1992). Where are the missing masses? The sociology of a few mundane artifacts." In W. Bilker & J. Law (eds.), *Shaping technology/building society: Studies in sociotechnical change* (pp. 225–258). Cambridge, MA: MIT Press.

Latour, B. (2005). *Reassembling the social: An introduction to actor–network theory*. New York, NY: Oxford University Press.

Lawson, A., Leveque, K., Murray, J., Wang, W., Taylor, N., Jenson, J., & de Castell, S. (2012). Socio-linguistic factors and gender mapping across real and virtual world cultures. Advances in Design for Cross-Cultural Activities, 241.

Lawson, A., & Murray, J. (2014). Identifying user demographic traits through virtual-world language use. In *Predicting real world behaviors from virtual world data* (pp. 57–67). Cham, Switzerland: Springer International Publishing.

Lejuez, C., Read, J., Kahler, C., Richards, J., Ramsey, S., Stuart, G., Strong, D., & Brown, R. (2002). Evaluation of a behavioral measure of risk taking: The balloon analogue risk task (BART), *Journal of Experimental Psychology: Applied* 8(2), 75–84.

Massey, D. (1994). *Space, place, and gender.* Minneapolis, MN: University of Minnesota Press.

Murray, J., & Arns, D. (2012). Reynard VERUS Research Project – Final Report, US Air Force Research Laboratory, Wright-Patterson AFB OH, RY-WP-TR-2012–0286.

Murray, J, Chow, E., & Connolly, C. (2015). Something in the way we move: Quantifying patterns of exploration in virtual spaces. In *Proceedings of Foundation of Digital Games Conference*, Pacific Grove, CA.

Prensky, M. (2010). *Teaching digital natives: Partnering for real learning.* Thousand Oaks, CA: Gorwin.

Rosenfeld, L. B., & Plax, T. G. (1977). Clothing as communication. *Journal of Communication* 27 (2), 24–31.

Symborski, C., Jackson, G. M., Barton, M., Cranmer, G., Raines, B., & Quinn, M. M. (2014). The use of social science methods to predict player characteristics from avatar observations. In *Predicting real world behaviors from virtual world data* (pp. 19–37). Cham, Switzerland: Springer International Publishing.

Tanenbaum, J., Seif El-Nasr, M., & Nixon, M. (2014). *Nonverbal communication in virtual worlds: Understanding and designing expressive characters.* Pittsburgh, PA: ETC Press.

Taylor, N., de Castell, S., Jenson, J., & Humphrey, M. (2011). Modeling play: Re-casting expertise in MMOGs. In *Proceedings of the 2011 ACM SIGGRAPH Symposium on Video Games*, August 10, 2011 (pp. 49–53). New York, NY: ACM.

Taylor, N., Jenson, J., de Castell, S., & Dilouya, B. (2014). Public displays of play: Studying online games in physical settings. *Journal of Computer-Mediated Communication*, 19(4), 763–779.

Trepte, S., & Reinecke, L. (2010). Avatar creation and video game enjoyment. *Journal of Media Psychology*, 22(4), 171–184.

Weka data mining toolset. Machine Learning Group, University of Waikato, NZ. Retrieved from: www.cs.waikato.ac.nz/ml/weka/

Wong, N., Tang, A., Livingston, I., Gutwin, C., & Mandryk, R. (2009). Character sharing in World of Warcraft. In Proceedings of the 11th European Conference on Computer Supported Cooperative Work, September 7–11, 2009, Vienna, Austria.

2

Understanding Aggressive and Nonaggressive Individual Behaviors in Massively Multiplayer Online Games

IFTEKHAR AHMED, ANDREW PILNY, AND
MARSHALL SCOTT POOLE

2.1 Introduction

Video games as a form of media have significantly altered the everyday experience of those who participate in them and society in general (Taylor, 2006). Despite this fact, scholarly research on games and gamers is still a growing field (Perron & Wolf, 2003) and the amount of research on video games is relatively less than that on other traditional media (Crawford, 2012). Steinkuehler and Williams (2006) argued that mediums like video games have wrongly been blamed as the root cause for the decline of traditional spaces for social interaction (e.g., cafes, bookstores, bars, etc.). Instead, they link video games as an alternative third space that corresponds to Oldenburg's (1999) space as the maintenance and restoration of civic and social life in the United States. However, a significant number of video games research continues to view video games as an erosion of traditional social avenues, consequently portraying them as a problematic interactive virtual space.

Current scholarly research on game studies is dominated by three key approaches: theoretical/aesthetical, technological/design-oriented, and sociological/ethnographic (Crawford, 2012). Within these broader categories, most scholarly approaches to video games somewhat fall short of developing a more nuanced understanding of players' relationships with video games as a kind of everyday technology (Taylor, 2006), despite the fact that the virtual world of video games is much broader and provides different spaces to observe and understand human behavior. How players interact within the virtual world of games is vital in understanding video games (Gunn, Craenen, & Hart, 2009). Distinctive patterns of interaction within the game space tell us that video games could be analyzed as communication spaces, simulation spaces, or experiential spaces ("acting" on the world) (Hew & Cheung, 2010). It is also possible to view the virtual world of video game as a "third place." Oldenburg's

(1999) idea of "third place" introduces a concept of places for socialization outside of work and home. Such a place help individuals satisfy needs for entertainment, developing groups, and spending time together.

Although there are fundamental differences in using traditional media and video games, mainly owing to the differences in interactivity and engagement, the differences are not as significant as popular perception may suggest (Crawford, 2012). We can very easily bring forward some of our lessons learned from traditional media to analyze video games. Furthermore, the unique virtual aspect of massively multiplayer online game (MMOG) space allows us to develop a nuanced understanding of how traits translate to behavior in virtual worlds. The ability of MMOGs to allow many different types of gameplay attracts different types of players (Yee, 2006). These players join gameworld with different motivations. There are three main groupings of gameplay motivations: achievement, social, and immersion (Yee, 2006). More importantly, these motivations are significantly related to players' personality dimensions (Shceck, Lee, & Pyo, 2015).

Recent studies have explored issues related to personality differences between players and nonplayers (Teng, 2008), motives to play online games (Yee, 2006; Jansz & Tanis, 2007), personality differences between groups of gamers of higher and lower video game usage (Gibb et al., 1983), reasons for online game addiction (Ng and Wiemer-Hastings, 2005; Van Rooij et al., 2011; Wan & Chiou, 2006), personality traits and online game addiction (Kim et al., 2008; Mehroof & Griffiths, 2010), anxiety (Lo, Wang, & Fang, 2005), player knowledge and selection of online games and personality traits that influence selecting games over other media forms (Hartmann & Klimmt, 2006; Quick, Atkinson, & Lin, 2012; Teng, Lo, & Wang, 2007), and the relationship among personality, values, avatar choice, and playing style (Griebel, 2006). Beyond individual level, studies have explored in-game group formation, evolution, and maintenance (Ahmed et al., 2011; Cai et al., 2013) and relationship between personality factors and in-game groups (Ahmad et al., 2014). The virtual world of games provides researchers with communication, simulation, or experiential spaces, or the "third place" that could very well be a rich ground for human behavior analysis. Despite the fact, a significant number of research related to MMOG or video games in general focuses on violence or aggression from a top-down media effects, rather than as an interactive "third space" perspective.

Aggression is a widely researched topic in relation to media and technology. Since the beginning of media effects research, scholars showed significant interest on the effect of violent media contents. Special attention had been paid to children as vulnerable section of media audience. Much of this tradition continued in analyzing new and emerging media including video games in the same manner. There are evidences of relationships between personality type and aggression response (Anderson & Bushman, 2002; Bartholow, Sestir, & Davis, 2005), preferences toward violent video games and violent behavior (Wiegman & Schie, 1998), and moderation of interactive experiences by trait aggressiveness (Tamborini et al., 2004). Although study evidences are suggesting an effect of already existing personality characteristics including aggressive tendencies and gameplay behavior, recent scholarly studies did not go beyond these discussions to develop a relationship between them. Instead, a majority of the studies related to violence or aggression and gameplay constituted a debate on whether gameplay contributes to or is even a root cause of aggressive behavior development. The goal of this study is to go beyond the current debate and understand how behavior in virtual worlds is related to already existing aggressive personalities. This study considers video games as virtual spaces of communication and experience similar to the "real world" from a behavioral perspective. We argue that the behaviors portrayed by players in the virtual world of video games are products of individuals' personality. Therefore, we can draw a relationship between personality (e.g., aggression) and gameplay behavior.

2.2 Media Effects, Video Games Research, and Aggression

Human aggression can be defined as "behavior that results in personal injury and physical destruction" (Bandura, 1978, p. 12). Moreover, "the greater the attribution of personal responsibility and injurious intent to the harm-doer, the higher the likelihood that the behavior will be judged as aggressive" (Bandura, 1978, p. 12). Previous theories of aggression explored a range of diverse perspectives including cognitive neoassociation, social learning, script, excitation transfer, and social interaction theory (for a review, see Anderson & Bushman, 2002).

A number of experimental, cross-sectional correlational and longitudinal studies have linked aggressive behavior to media violence including exposure to violent video games (Anderson & Bushman, 2002; Bushman & Huesmann, 2001). The majority of research supporting this argument is based on the General Aggression Model (GAM). The GAM posits that aggressive people tend to possess hostile attribution, hostile perception, and hostile expectation biases. Individuals with hostile attribution bias tend to perceive harmful actions by others as intentional rather than accidental. On the other hand, if an individual possesses hostile perception bias he or she is most likely to perceive social interactions as being aggressive. Similarly, having hostile expectation bias will lead individuals to expect others to react aggressively in potential conflicting situations (Bushman & Anderson, 2002). According to the GAM, an actual show of aggressive behavior will depend on exposure to cues that activate aggression-related knowledge stored in our memory system. According to this argument, any cue activation such as playing potentially aggressive video games will increase the possibility of aggressive behavior. Studies of this tradition argue that short-term exposure to violent video game can increases aggressive behaviors and long-term repeated exposure results in developing serious forms of aggression in individuals (Anderson & Bushman, 2001; Anderson & Dill, 2000; Anderson & Ford, 1986; Irwin & Gross, 1995; Silvern & Williamson, 1987). A number of researches supporting a relationship between violent video games and aggression have utilized social learning theory, general arousal model, or priming effect mechanism as their theoretical foundations (Sherry, 2001). Contrary to these lines of thoughts, a number of studies accept the hypothesis that there is no conclusive evidence to support any relationship between aggression and exposure to violent video games and also argued for video games as safe outlet for expressing aggressive behavior following the catharsis effect hypothesis (Cooper & Mackie, 1986; Scott, 1995; Sherry, 2001).

The current study views aggression not as a fragile state of mind that can be easily influenced and modified by short-term exposure to aggressive acts in various media, but more of as a *stable trait* that has developed over the course many years, including influence from various environmental and biological factors. Put this way, research questions can be more focused on investigating the behaviors that correlate to aggressive personalities, some of which may be seem obvious and some less so. Berkowitz's (1984) associative network model supports developing a framework for trait aggression. Buss and Perry's (1992) aggression questionnaire also includes items that somewhat measure trait aggression. Trait aggression or stability of aggressive behavior over time has also been supported by both social and biological scholars (Eisenberger et al., 2007; Huesmann et al., 1984; Mehroof & Griffiths, 2010; Olweus, 1979).

We argue that all individuals can be placed in a continuum ranging from nonaggressive to very high aggressive personalities. An individual's tendency and his or her place in the continuum is a product of sociopsychological processes that contribute to aggressive thoughts and feelings. Consequently, individuals' actions and behavior while playing video games could be characterized and differentiated based on their already existing aggressive personality. As a result, portrayed action and behavior in the video game outlet can help us better identify aggressive personalities that include actual behavior rather than merely responding to items on a psychological scale. The goal of this study is to understand how behavior in virtual worlds is related to already existing aggressive personalities.

2.3 *EverQuest II*

2.3.1 Context of the Study

Our data are drawn from the game *EverQuest II* (EQII). EQII, similar to other popular MMOGs, is a fantasy adventure game in which players are immersed in a virtual world. They can do a variety of things in the game such as explore the game environment, engage in challenging activities (e.g., quests), and interact with other players. Players in EQII create characters (avatars) that vary in terms of race (e.g., human, dwarf, elf), type (warrior, scout, healer), and basic moral quality (good, evil). A primary activity for players in EQII is to complete quests that involve completing a variety of different tasks (e.g., finding objects, exploring areas, and defeating nonhuman characters). Completing quests allows players to gain experience points and accumulate other resources (e.g., money, armor, weapons, etc.). Besides completing quests, players also participate in other activities such as resource building (e.g., trading, harvesting, finding rare items, etc.) and social encounters (e.g., building guilds, going on group raids, communicating with others, player versus player combat, etc.).

The groups in the game in question, EQII, are similar to the action teams described by Sundstrom et al. (1990), with clearly defined goals, clear role structure, task urgency, and clear-cut ability to ascertain how well they are doing on their task. Though an argument can be made that in-game team behavior is analogous to real-world behavior of teams (Williams et al., 2011), we do not have to go that far and would instead argue that the game represents a large experimental environment that is highly involving to subjects and that they take very seriously.

2.3.2 Theoretical Base of the Study

To examine aggression, we used two sources of data. First, we used anonymized server-side data from EQII. The servers run on EQII are set to automatically capture large volumes of data about characters and game behavior for several hundred variables at intervals of one one-hundredth of a second, yielding a very large amount of data that tracks behavior and events in the game with great precision. The variables of interest in this study were measured by creating indices from a subset of the relevant fields in the database (e.g., nonhuman characters killed per day). This in-game behavioral database is described in more detail in Williams et al. (2011) and consists of data on gameplay by 30,745 characters over the period of February 21, 2006 until August 31, 2006. These logs capture information about activities and transactions that the hosting company uses to manage the game, and hence offer data that can be used to operationalize our constructs through unobtrusive measurement.

The second source of data came from an online survey that was administered in 2008 by Sony Online Entertainment, the game producer. Players were invited to complete the survey in exchange for a special item in the game. This led players to a secure webpage and informed consent, followed by the survey. Seven thousand participants responded to the survey in the three-day period that it was available. The Survey included specific questions regarding EQII (i.e., number of characters, average playtime per day, players' virtual race and gender in EQII), demographic questionnaire (i.e., age, gender, nationality), and also several psychological measures. Both verbal and physical aggression questionnaires were part of the psychological measures. After the researchers removed any identifying information from both data sets, participants from the in-game and survey databases were matched via a universal ID number. This allowed researchers to explore how in-game behavior was related to aggression.

2.3.3 Sample

Our sample comes from an earlier study that attempted to create an algorithm to identify groups in EQII based on their interactions with other characters (Brown et al., 2012). It contains a sample of 1,972 individuals who had behavioral data with respect to group behavior in EQII and also took the survey (i.e., we wanted to have group level data available). Thus, we were able to connect both their behavioral data from EQII and demographic/psychometric data from the survey.

2.3.4 Measures

To measure aggression, we used the propensity for physical aggression by Arnold Buss and Mark Perry (Buss & Perry, 1992). The "physical" dimension of the scale was analyzed because it arguably implies one of the most severe consequences of aggression: increased likelihood for physical violence. The scale consisted of nine items along a seven-point scale (1 = strongly disagree, 7 = strongly agree).

Although the original nine items demonstrated acceptable reliability (α = 0.84), a confirmatory factor analysis showed that all nine did not result in a generally acceptable fit because of Normed Fit Index (NFI) and Comparative

Table 2.1 *Standardized factor loading for physical aggression*

	Standardized Factor Loading	A	Mean	SD
Physical aggression		0.83	3.37	1.41
I often find myself disagreeing with people.	0.78		3.37	2.05
If somebody hits me, I hit back.	0.59		4.73	1.97
If I have to resort to violence to protect my rights, I will.	0.61		4.29	1.95
There are people who pushed me so far that we came to blows.	0.73		2.57	1.89
I have threatened people I know.	0.66		2.33	1.67
I have become so mad that I have broken things.	0.65		2.91	1.97

Fit Index (CFI) values were below 0.90 (Hooper, Coughlan, & Mullen, 2008; Worthington & Whittaker, 2006). Thus, the lowest factor loading items were removed until an acceptable fit was reached. This resulted in three items being removed, which means that six remained. These six items resulted in a good fit for a single dimension confirmatory factor analysis ($\chi^2 = 35.91$, df = 9, CFI = 0.910, NFI = 0.909). More details on the items are included in Table 2.1. A binary variable was created if individuals scored above one standard deviation above the mean. We call these individuals aggressive given their high score on the scale ($N = 308$).

2.3.5 Analysis

To determine the predictors of aggressive individuals, we use machine learning classification algorithms (MLCAs). One of the advantages of MLCAs is that they use cross-validation techniques to verify patterns in the data, a more robust method than looking for patterns in the entire data set. For instance, we use a tenfold cross-validation method, which means that the algorithm will divide the sample into ten random samples, search the first nine for patterns, create probabilities or rules based on those patterns, and then test those rules on the tenth sample. It will do this ten times to determine the accuracy of the probabilities or rules (depending on which MLCA the researcher uses).

There are a wide variety of different MLCAs available. The choice of which one to use depends on the nature of the data, theoretical rationale, and desired output of the researcher. To predict aggression, we use Bayesian network classifiers (see Bouckaert, 2008 for an overview) in Weka (Hall et al., 2009).

Bayesian network MLAs use what are called *posterior probabilities* (PP) to generate classifications using Bayes' formula:

$$P(y|x) = P(x|y)P(y)/P(x)$$

whereas $P(y \mid x)$ is a posterior probability of y (dependent variable) given x (independent variable), calculated by multiplying the likelihood of an attribute (x) given y ($P(x \mid y)$) and the class prior probability of y ($P(y)$) over the raw likelihood of the dependent variable ($P(y)$). For example, consider if we wanted to predict aggression based on whether or not a character is male rather than female in a data set with five aggressive individuals and five nonaggressive individuals ($N = 10$). Of those ten, imagine that there are five males and females, but four of those males are aggressive:

$$P(y|x) = P(\text{Aggressive}|\text{Male})$$
$$= [P(x|y) = P(\text{Male}|\text{Aggressive}) = 4/5 = 0.80]$$
$$\times [P(x) = P(\text{Aggressive}) = 0.50]/P(x) = P(\text{Male})$$
$$= 0.50 = (0.80)(0.50)/0.50 = 0.80$$

Goodness of classification is determined by calculating the precision and recall for the classifier. Precision is defined as the number of "true positives" (cases correctly classified that actually belonged to the class) divided by the sum of the number true positives plus "false positives" (cases incorrectly classified that actually belonged to the class). Recall is defined as the number of true positives divided by the sum of the true positives plus the number of false negatives (cases not in the class that were put into it by the classifier). These two are often combined into a single F-measure (2 * Precision * Recall/(Precision + Recall)) [not to be confused with the statistical F-test].

When working with a data set with a large amount of cases and variables, it is important to detail why certain variables and cases were included and excluded for analysis. As such, our analysis proceeds mostly in a series of three steps.

2.3.5.1 Step 1: Variable Reduction

An advantage of MLCAs is its ability to sort through a wide variety of predictor variables. Our current data set has more than 500, making it unrealistic to develop hypotheses on each variable or even reduce them to meaningful dimensions (e.g., cluster analysis). As such, we face "an embarrassment of riches," in that we have a large number of variables and there is a need to winnow down the range of possible predictors to a manageable set. To reduce the number of variables, we used what is called "information gain." Information gain is generally defined as the mutual relationship between an attribute and a classifying variable (Quinlan, 1993, p. 22). In other words, the higher the information gain, the more accurate the algorithm can predict Y (classifying variable) from X (attribute). Variables without any information gain were removed from the sample and for each model (see later), we select a maximum of the nine best predicting variables (i.e., those with the most information gain). A maximum of nine was inspired by Miller's law, which assumes that the working mind can handle about seven plus or minus two pieces of information at a time. Indeed, an overly complex model with hundreds of variables might predict well, but will not tell us much about the big factors that have a relationship with psychical aggression. As such, the motivation here is more conceptual rather than trying to build to most accurate model possible. Instead, we are using machine learning to determine which variables are the largest discriminators with respect to physical aggression.

2.3.5.2 Step 2: Model Building

Likewise, the goal of this research, by Occam's razor, was to build to the most parsimonious models possible. Thus, variables were removed when they did not significantly improve prediction. By significantly improve, we mean a single full unit increase in the F-measure. For instance, if model 3 (three variables) had an F-measure of 65.5 and model 4 (four variables) had an F-measure of 65.9, we went with the simpler model because the difference did not yield at least a single value ($65.9 - 65.5 = 0.4$).

2.3.5.3 Step 3: Sampling

Finally, because MLCAs tend to bias the majority class in uneven distributions of the dependent variable, we randomly undersampled the nonaggressive sample ($N = 1623$) to create an equal sample size of nonaggressive and aggressive individuals ($N = 308$ for each class). The choice of undersampling was used for two reasons. First, comparing two classes with more than 300 cases is typically a sufficient sample size for cross-validation (Beleites et al., 2013). As such, there is not a problem concerning the overall sample sized used. Second, an alternative approach, such as oversampling the minority class, would produce a wealth of artificially created data. Techniques like the synthetic minority oversampling technique (SMOTE) (Chawla et al., 2002) would have meant oversampling 308 aggressive individuals into 1,623, meaning that most data would have been synthetic for that class. In the current case, we felt comfortable enough comparing two samples of 308.

2.3.6 Model Building

We built four models according to the different types of information represented by the independent variables (Table 2.2). Model 1 is what we call a behavioral model. It contains variables related to a subject's behavior in the game, ranging from play statistics (e.g., how many kills they acquired) to character information (e.g., the gender and type of character they mostly played with). Model 2 is a psychometric model. It analyzed psychological variables from the survey, including factors ranging from general personality to political ideology. Model 3 is a demographic model. It uses only demographic information such as age, gender, education, and geographic region. Finally, model 4 is a mixed model and contains variables from all three types of variables.

2.4 Results

Table 2.3 provides sample sizes and MLCAs for the four models.

Model 1: Behavioral. The overall F-measure of the behavioral model was 0.601, meaning that it was about 10% better than by chance alone. It includes variables on a character gender, their artisan class (i.e., profession for crafting items), character class (i.e., choice of twenty-six different classes), a dummy variable if they included a biography in their profile, and the amount of days their account was active during the period of data collection. Indeed, looking at the conditional probabilities gives a better sense about which variables predicted aggressive individuals more so than others. Character gender was a big factor. For instance, the PP that an aggressive individual chose to play with a female character was only 0.30 and males were 0.57, suggesting that aggressive individuals were more likely to play as male characters rather than female ones. Class was another variable seemed to discriminate well. For instance, the best predictor of aggressive individuals was a Berserker. The PP of an aggressive individual playing as a Berserker was 0.66. Berserkers are a type of *fighter* in the game, as opposed to priests, scouts, and mages. They are known for their above average strength and "unbridled aggression and fury" (http://eq2.wikia .com/wiki/Berserker). Finally, aggressive individuals were much more likely to be unskilled in crafting (PP = 0.71), meaning that they do not partake in crafting items in the game, which is often seen as a more tedious and uneventful task.

Model 2: Psychometric. The overall F-measure of the psychometric model was 0.64, slightly better than in the behavioral model. It included only two variables on general trust in people and general problematic internet use (GPIU, Caplan, 2005) because additional psychometric did not provide much

Table 2.2 *Variables and descriptive statistics*

	Aggressive	Not Aggressive
Model 1: Behavioral		
Total quests completed		
Mean	404.71*	482.92
SD	276.80	328.56
Biography text in profile		
No	134*	193
Yes	174	115
Average character level		
Mean	37.02*	34.85
SD	10.41	10.3
Average hours per day		
Mean	4.99	4.75
SD	2.99	2.38
Character gender		
Female	75*	138
Male	233	170
Character class		
Berserker	31*	14
Artisan class		
Unskilled	12*	5
Model 2: Psychometric		
Problematic internet use		
Mean	42.52*	33.59
SD	14.84	12.16
General trust in society		
Mean	2.17	2.52
SD	0.78	0.71
Model 3: Demographics		
Gender		
Female	31*	93
Male	277	215
Age		
Mean	29.39*	34.13
SD	8.33	9.75
Education		
Less than high school	25*	15
High school diploma (including GED)	64	43
Some college	118	102
Associates degree (2 years) or specialized technical training	51	57
Bachelor's degree	26	44
Some graduate training	4	15
Graduate or professional degree	20	32
Height (inches)		
Mean	70.82*	68.81
SD	4.64	4.41

Note: * indicates a t value of $p < .05$. For nominal variables, it indicates a $\chi^2 < .05$.

Table 2.3 *Sample sizes and Bayesian MLCAs*

Dependent Variable	Original Data Set			Resampled Data Set		
	High	*Not-high*	*Total*	*High*	*Not-high*	*Total*
Physical Aggression	308	1623	1931	308	308	616
	Precision	Recall	*F*-Measure	Class		
Model 1. Behavioral variables	0.604	0.584	0.594	Not-high		
	0.597	0.617	0.607	High		
	0.601	0.601	**0.601**	Weighted-average		
Model 2. Psychometric variables	0.635	0.656	0.645	Not-high		
	0.644	0.623	0.634	High		
	0.64	0.64	**0.64**	Weighted-average		
Model 3. Demographics	0.671	0.536	0.596	Not-high		
	0.614	0.737	0.67	High		
	0.642	0.636	**0.633**	Weighted-average		
Model 4: Full	0.676	0.698	0.687	Not-high		
	0.688	0.666	0.677	High		
	0.682	0.682	**0.682**	Weighted-average		

additional fit. The overall trends demonstrate that aggressive individuals were more likely to use the internet in problematic ways (if total > 45.5, then $PP = 0.75$) and less trusting of people in general (if less > 2.5 $PP = 0.61$). That is, according to the GPIU, aggressive individuals are more likely to prefer interaction via online mediums, use the internet to regulate their mood, become preoccupied by the internet, use it compulsively, and have higher odds of suffering negative consequences from its use (e.g., missing social engagements, creating difficulties in managing daily activities).

Model 3: Demographic. The overall F-measure for the demographic model was 0.633. It was the only model that had interactions when we increased the number of parent nodes. For instance, there was an interaction between gender and education. Aggressive individuals were more likely to have less education and be male; this was true if they were male and had less than a high school degree ($PP = 0.77$) as well as if they were male and had only a high school degree ($PP = 0.73$). Height also had an interaction effect. If a subject reported being male and taller than 5 feet, 5 inches, he was more likely to be aggressive ($PP = 0.65$).

Model 4: Mixed. The F-measure for the mixed model was 0.688. It contained eight variables after pruning for variables that did not significantly improve fit. Behavioral variables included character gender and if individuals had a text in their biography, psychometric variables included trust in

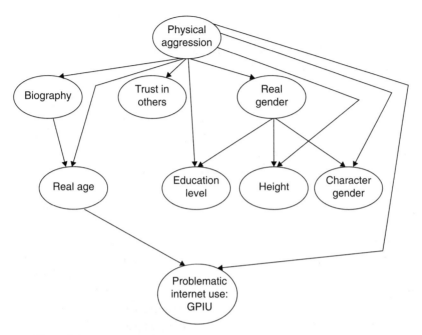

Figure 2.1 Mixed model for Bayesian network machine learning classification algorithms.

people and the GPIU, and demographic variables include gender, education, age, and height. What is interesting is the complex interactions throughout most the variables in Figure 2.1. Consider the phenomenon of gender overlap (i.e., playing a virtual gender the same as your offline gender). Subjects who identified offline as males and played as males were slightly more likely to be aggressive (PP = 0.58). And subjects under the age of 35 were more likely to be aggressive only if they also included text in their biography (PP = 0.64). Finally, age also had an interaction with higher scores on the GPIU. Those under the age of 39 who also had text in their biography were much more likely to be aggressive (PP = 0.73).

2.5 Discussion and Conclusion

The goal of this study is to go beyond the current aggression-gameplay relationship debate and demonstrate video games as a virtual space where an individual's behavior reflects his or her personality. Following this line, we sought to examine if there were differences in gameplay between aggressive and nonaggressive individuals. This research also sought to use a machine learning approach to understand the various predictors of aggression. Our results have some expected and surprising results.

First, because there is much research that demonstrates the importance of gender and aggression (i.e., Lightdale & Prentice, 1994) and because men historically have been more linked to aggressive acts like crime and war (Goldstein, 2001) and direct aggression in general (Bjorkqvist et al., 1993), we would thus expect aggressive individuals to be more likely to play as males. Moreover, we might expect individuals to play more aggressive-looking characters and like the Berserke. The fact that Berserkes even use the word "aggression" in its profile demonstrates the fact that aggressiveness, in some ways, translates quite explicitly in virtual environments. Demographically, our results support previous findings that find correlations between aggression and other factors such as education (Farrington, 1989) and age (Kay et al., 1988). Finally, the psychometric model was not surprising either. Several studies have found relationships between aggression and trust (e.g., Kinard, 1982) and other more problematic behaviors such as problematic alcohol use (Swaim et al., 2006) and general impulsivity (Ferguson et al., 2005). Although this is the first to correlate the GPIU with aggression, the result is not too surprising given that the items in the GPIU are similar to those other factors that often put individuals at risk for aggressive behavior.

There were a few surprises, however. For instance, that aggressive individuals were less likely to have an artisan class and complete quests was not something that we initially had imagined, but makes sense in hindsight. That is, neither of these activities necessarily resembles much of the stereotypical activities associated with aggression (e.g., engaging in battle). Indeed, crafting items is a mundane activity in the game and quests can often take a long time, with most of the activities sometimes designated to finding objects and secret locations. On the other hand, none of the stereotypical activities associated with aggressive individuals that we might expect them to engage in helped predict aggressive individuals at all. Our data set included a host of these variables that are considered "violent" or "aggressive" in nature such as number of kills, number of deaths, kill-death ratio, player versus player combat, and numerous attack and defense capabilities that would be higher if a character primarily engages in violent encounters. Only the choice of aggressive-looking characters and character gender (male) seemed to be good predictors of aggression. As such, our results challenge some of the prevailing research linking aggression with violent game habits (e.g., Anderson & Bushman, 2001) because we could not find any relationship between the two. That is, that real-life aggressive individuals play EQII differently than nonaggressive individuals is not surprising, but it was surprising in *how* they played it differently, by choosing stereotypical aggressive attributes such as character gender (male) and race (aggressive looking Berserke), *not* stereotypical aggressive in-game behavior.

Our study demonstrates that the game environment provides a rich ground for players' psychology and personality research. Within the virtual world of gaming, we can not only study a person as a gamer, but also explore the "real life" individual. This study looked only into one personality factor (aggression) within one game environment (EQII). More research is needed to draw relationships between other personality factors and gameplay behaviors. It is also necessary to study similar game environments to enrich our understanding and to draw general conclusions applicable across games. We consider this as a limitation of our study. Another limitation is related to group behavior. An individual's behavior as a group member could shed light on other dimensions of personality factors, which is necessary to develop a broader understanding of individuals' behavior in the game environment and their relationship with personality dimensions.

Acknowledgments

This research was supported by the National Science Foundation (NSF IIS-0729421 and NSF IIS-1247861), the Army Research Institute (ARI W91WAW-08-C-0106), and Air Force Research Lab (AFRL Contract No. FA8650-10-C-7010). This research was also supported by the National Science Foundation via the XSEDE project's Extended Collaborative Support Service under Grant NSF-OCI 1053575. We would also like to thank the Campus Cluster group at NCSA/UIUC for their help in hosting the game log database.

The data used for this research were provided by SONY Online Entertainment. The findings solely represent the opinions of the authors and not of the sponsors.

References

Ahmad, M., Shen, C., Srivastava, J., & Contractor N. (2014). *Predicting real world behaviors from virtual world data*. Springer Proceedings in Complexity. Cham, Switzerland: Springer International Publishing.

Ahmed, I., Pilny, A., Brown, C., Cai, D., Ada, Y., & Poole, M. S. (2011). Identification of groups in online environments: The twist and turns of grouping groups. In *Proceedings of the 3rd IEEE International Conference on Social Computing (SocialCom2011)*, Boston, MA.

Anderson, C. A., & Bushman, B. J. (2001). Effects of violent video games on aggressive behavior, aggressive cognition, aggressive affect, physiological arousal, and prosocial behavior: A meta-analytic review of the scientific literature. *Psychological Science*, 12(5), 353–359.

Anderson, C. A., & Bushman, B. J. (2002). Human aggression. *Psychology*, 53(1), 27.

Anderson, C. A., & Dill, K. E. (2000). Video games and aggressive thoughts, feelings, and behavior in the laboratory and in life. *Journal of Personality and Social Psychology*, 78(4), 772.

Anderson, C. A., & Ford, C. M. (1986). Affect of the game player short-term effects of highly and mildly aggressive video games. *Personality and Social Psychology Bulletin*, 12(4), 390–402.

Bandura, A. (1978). Social learning theory of aggression. *Journal of Communication*, 28(3), 12–29.

Bartholow, B. D., Sestir, M. A., & Davis, E. B. (2005). Correlates and consequences of exposure to video game violence: Hostile personality, empathy, and aggressive behavior. *Personality and Social Psychology Bulletin*, 31(11), 1573–1586.

Beleites, C., Neugebauer, U., Bocklitz, T., Krafft, C., & Popp, J. (2013). Sample size planning for classification models. *Analytica Chimica Acta*, 760, 25–33.

Berkowitz, L. (1984). Some effects of thoughts on anti-and prosocial influences of media events: A cognitive-neoassociation analysis. *Psychological Bulletin*, 95(3), 410.

Bjorkqvist, K., Lagerspetz, K. M., Osterman, K., & Kaukiainen, A. (1993). Styles of aggression and sex differences: A developmental theory. *Aggressive Behavior*, 19(1), 11–12.

Bouckaert, R. R. (2008). Bayesian network classifiers in Weka for version 3–5–7. *Artificial Intelligence Tools*, 11(3), 369–387.

Brown, C., Ahmed, I., Cai, D., Poole, M. S., Pilny, A., & Atouba, Y. (2012, July). Comparing the performance of group detection algorithm in serial and parallel processing environments. In *Proceedings of the 1st Conference of the Extreme Science and Engineering Discovery Environment: Bridging from the eXtreme to the campus and beyond* (p. 21). New York, NY: ACM Press.

Bushman, B. J., & Anderson, C. A. (2002). Violent video games and hostile expectations: A test of the general aggression model. *Personality and Social Psychology Bulletin*, 28(12), 1679–1686.

Bushman, B. J., & Huesmann, L. R. (2001). Effects of televised violence on aggression. In D. G. Singer & J. L. Singer (eds.), *Handbook of children and the media* (pp. 223–254). Thousand Oaks, CA: SAGE.

Buss, A. H., & Perry, M. (1992). The Aggression Questionnaire. *Journal of Personality and Social Psychology*, 63, 452–459.

Cai, Y. D., Ahmed, I., Pilny, A., Brown, C., Atouba, Y., & Poole, M. S. (2013). SocialMapExplorer: Visualizing social networks of massively multiplayer online games in temporal-geographic space. In *Proceedings of the Conference on Extreme Science and Engineering Discovery Environment: Gateway to Discovery* (p. 18). New York, NY: ACM Press.

Caplan, S. E. (2005). A social skill account of problematic Internet use. *Journal of Communication*, 55(4), 721–736.

Chawla, N. V., Bowyer, K. W., Hall, L. O., & Kegelmeyer, W. P. (2002). SMOTE: Synthetic minority over-sampling technique. *Journal of Artificial Intelligence Research*, 16, 321–357.

Cooper, J., & Mackie, D. (1986). Video games and aggression in children. *Journal of Applied Social Psychology*, 16(8), 726–744.

Crawford, G. (2012). *Video gamers*. New York, NY: Routledge.

Eisenberger, N. I., Way, B. M., Taylor, S. E., Welch, W. T., & Lieberman, M. D. (2007). Understanding genetic risk for aggression: Clues from the brain's response to social exclusion. *Biological Psychiatry*, 61(9), 1100–1108.

Farrington, D. P. (1989). Early predictors of adolescent aggression and adult violence. *Violence and Victims*, 4(2), 79–100.

Ferguson, C. J., Averill, P. M., Rhoades, H., Rocha, D., Gruber, N. P., & Gummattira, P. (2005). Social isolation, impulsivity and depression as predictors of aggression in a psychiatric inpatient population. *Psychiatric Quarterly*, 76(2), 123–137.

Gibb, G. D., Bailey, J. R., Lambirth, T. T., & Wilson, W. P. (1983). Personality differences between high and low electronic video game users. *Journal of Psychology*, 114(2), 159–165.

Goldstein, J. S. (2001), *War and gender: How gender shapes the war system and vice versa*. New York, NY: Cambridge University Press.

Griebel, T. (2006). Self-portrayal in a simulated life: Projecting personality and values in The Sims 2. *Game Studies*, 6(1). Retrieved from: www.gamestudies.org/0601/articles/griebel

Gunn, E. A. A., Craenen, B. G. W., & Hart, E. (April 2009). A taxonomy of video games and AI. In *AI and Games Symposium*, AISB 2009 Convention, Edinburgh, Scotland (pp. 4–14).

Hall, M., Frank, E., Holmes, G., Pfahringer, B., Reutemann, P., & Witten, I. H. (2009). The WEKA data mining software: An update. *ACM SIGKDD Explorations Newsletter*, 11(1), 10–18.

Hartmann, T., & Klimmt, C. (2006). The influence of personality factors on computer game choice. In P. Vorderer & J. Bryant (eds.), *Playing video games: Motives, responses, and consequences* (pp. 132–152). New York, NY: Routledge.

Hew, K. F., & Cheung, W. S. (2010). Use of three-dimensional (3-D) immersive virtual worlds in K-12 and higher education settings: A review of the research. *British Journal of Educational Technology*, 41(1), 33–55.

Hooper, D., Coughlan, J., & Mullen, M. (2008). Structural equation modeling: Guidelines for determining model fit. *Electronic Journal of Business Research Methods*, 6(1), 53–60.

Huesmann, L. R., Eron, L. D., Lefkowitz, M. M., & Walder, L. O. (1984). Stability of aggression over time and generations. *Developmental Psychology*, 20(6), 1120.

Irwin, A. R., & Gross, A. M. (1995). Cognitive tempo, violent video games, and aggressive behavior in young boys. *Journal of Family Violence*, 10(3), 337–350.

Jansz, J., & Tanis, M. (2007). Appeal of playing online first person shooter games. *CyberPsychology & Behavior*, 10(1), 133–136.

Kay, S. R., Wolkenfeld, F., & Murrill, L. M. (1988). Profiles of aggression among psychiatric patients: II. Covariates and predictors. *Journal of Nervous and Mental Disease*, 176(9), 547–557.

Kim, E. J., Namkoong, K., Ku, T., & Kim, S. J. (2008). The relationship between online game addiction and aggression, self-control and narcissistic personality traits. *European Psychiatry*, 23(3), 212–218.

Kinard, E. (1982). Experiencing child abuse: Effects on emotional adjustment. *American Journal of Orthopsychiatry*, 52(1), 82.

Lightdale, J. R., & Prentice, D. A. (1994). Rethinking sex differences in aggression: Aggressive behaviour in the absence of social roles. *Personality and Social Psychology Bulletin*, 20, 34–44.

Lo, S. K., Wang, C. C., & Fang, W. (2005). Physical interpersonal relationships and social anxiety among online game players. *Cyberpsychology & Behavior*, 8(1), 15–20.

Mehroof, M., & Griffiths, M. D. (2010). Online gaming addiction: The role of sensation seeking, self-control, neuroticism, aggression, state anxiety, and trait anxiety. *Cyberpsychology, Behavior, and Social Networking*, 13(3), 313–316.

Ng, B. D., & Wiemer-Hastings, P. (2005). Addiction to the internet and online gaming. *Cyberpsychology & Behavior*, 8(2), 110–113.

Oldenburg, R. (1999). *The great good place: Cafes, coffee shops, bookstores, bars, hair salons, and other hangouts at the heart of a community*. Boston, MA: Da Capo Press.

Olweus, D. (1979). Stability of aggressive reaction patterns in males: A review. *Psychological Bulletin*, 86(4), 852.

Perron, B., & Wolf, M. J. (eds.). (2003). *The video game theory reader*. New York, NY: Routledge.

Quick, J. M., Atkinson, R. K., & Lin, L. (2012). Empirical taxonomies of gameplay enjoyment: Personality and video game preference. *International Journal of Game-Based Learning (IJGBL)*, 2(3), 11–31.

Quinlan, J. R. (1993). *C4. 5: programs for machine learning*, Vol. 1. San Mateo, CA: Morgan Kaufmann.

Scott, D. (1995). The effect of video games on feelings of aggression. *The Journal of Psychology*, 129(2), 121–132.

Shceck, K., Lee, D. Y., & Pyo, K. B. (2015). The relationship between the Five Factor Personality Model and motivations for play in MMORPGs. *Indian Journal of Science and Technology*, 8(21), 1–9.

Sherry, J. L. (2001). The effects of violent video games on aggression. *Human Communication Research*, 8(4), 453–462.

Silvern, S. B., & Williamson, P. A. (1987). The effects of video game play on young children's aggression, fantasy, and prosocial behavior. *Journal of Applied Developmental Psychology*, 8(4), 453–462.

Steinkuehler, C. A., & Williams, D. (2006). Where everybody knows your (screen) name: Online games as "third places." *Journal of Computer-Mediated Communication*, 11(4), 885–909.

Sundstrom, E., De Meuse, K. P., & Futrell, D. (1990). Work teams: Applications and effectiveness. *American Psychologist*, 45(2), 120.

Swaim, R. C., Henry, K. L., & Kelly, K. (2006). Predictors of aggressive behaviors among rural middle school youth. *Journal of Primary Prevention*, 27(3), 229–243.

Tamborini, R., Eastin, M. S., Skalski, P., & Lachlan, K. (2004). Violent virtual video games and hostile thoughts. *Journal of Broadcasting & Electronic Media*, 48, 335.

Taylor, T. L. (2006). *Play between worlds: Exploring online game culture*. Cambridge, MA: MIT Press.

Teng, C. I. (2008). Personality differences between online game players and nonplayers in a student sample. *Cyber Psychology & Behavior*, 11(2), 232–234.

Teng, C. I., Lo, S. K., & Wang, P. C. (2007). How to know and choose online games: Differences between current and potential players. *Cyber Psychology & Behavior*, 10(6), 837–840.

Van Rooij, A. J., Schoenmakers, T. M., Vermulst, A. A., Van Den Eijnden, R. J., & Van DeMheen, D. (2011). Online video game addiction: Identification of addicted adolescent gamers. *Addiction*, 106(1), 205–212.

Wan, C. S., & Chiou, W. B. (2006). Psychological motives and online games addiction: A test of flow theory and humanistic needs theory for Taiwanese adolescents. *Cyber Psychology & Behavior*, 9(3), 317–324.

Wiegman, O., & Schie, E. G. (1998). Video game playing and its relations with aggressive and prosocial behaviour. *British Journal of Social Psychology*, 37(3), 367–378.

Williams, D., Contractor, N., Poole, M. S., Srivastava, J., & Cai, D. (2011). The virtual worlds exploratorium: Using large-scale data and computational techniques for communication research. *Communication Methods and Measures*, 5(2), 163–180.

Worthington, R. L., & Whittaker, T. A. (2006). Scale development research a content analysis and recommendations for best practices. *The Counseling Psychologist*, 34(6), 806–838.

Yee, N. (2006). Motivations for play in online games. *Cyber Psychology & Behavior*, 9(6), 772–775.

3

From Good Associates to True Friends: An Exploration of Friendship Practices in Massively Multiplayer Online Games

FANNY ANNE RAMIREZ

3.1 Introduction

Early text-based multiuser dungeons (MUDs) required users to read through descriptions of physical environments and type in commands in order to perform in-game actions. Player-to-player interaction was limited to text-based communication and chat room encounters. Online gaming has since come a long way. Most massively multiplayer online games (MMOs) now support a variety of communication modes, including voice chat and in-game messaging (Park et al., 2006; Williams, Xiong, & Caplan, 2007). MMOs are places of social gathering that bring players together in persistent, fictional worlds where social interaction is a key activity (Nardi, 2010; Taylor, 2009; Williams et al., 2007; Yee, 2006). Crawford, Gosling, and Light (2011) argue that such collective engagement makes MMOs appealing and encourages players to develop long-term gaming commitments: "For many players of [MMOs], the key reason they play these (and continue to do so over a long period) is not necessarily the attainment of particular goals, but rather socializing and keeping in touch with fellow players" (p. 9). The opportunity to interact with other users has also been shown to increase players' overall enjoyment of online games because playing with others makes the virtual world feel real and unpredictable (Christou et al., 2013).

While studies on social interaction in MMOs abound, there is little diversity in the games studied, with research overwhelmingly focusing on the popular massively multiplayer role-playing game (MMORPG) *World of Warcraft* (WoW). Some have expressed concern that building a generalized theory of online games from a small number of titles could be misleading since the experiences of WoW players are not necessarily representative of those who play other MMOs (Taylor, 2008). To help remediate this oversight, the MMO *EVE Online* was chosen as the research site for the study discussed in this chapter. Qualitative interviews were conducted to learn how *EVE* players socialize with each other and how they make sense of the different social connections they have formed through the game.

3.2 *EVE Online* and Backchannel Communication

EVE Online (*EVE*) is a space-themed MMO with roughly 500,000 subscribers. Over the years, it has acquired a reputation as a rather ruthless game. Antagonistic activities such as griefing[1] and scamming[2] are not only commonplace, but also tolerated by the game's developer, CCP Games. *EVE*'s dog-eat-dog ethos is accompanied by a steep learning curve that forces players who want to succeed in-game to seek outside information on third party websites, forums, and other applications (Bergstrom, 2013; Bergstrom et al., 2013; Paul, 2011). Despite its entry barriers and hostile gameworld, the game has had a strong following since its release in 2003. *EVE*'s success has been attributed to its sandbox gameplay and emphasis on player-driven initiatives (Graft, 2012). Sandbox games offer open-ended gaming experiences in that players do not follow predefined missions or goals but set up their own activities based on what is available in the game. In *EVE*, players fly spaceships, control the game's economy, explore star systems, and fight over territories, among other pursuits. Although the game has built-in communication systems, such as text-based chat channels and email accounts, most *EVE* players choose to sidestep these official communication channels and instead interact with each other through Voice over Internet Protocols (VoIPs), Instant Messaging (IM), wikis, and forums that exist outside of the game client (Bergstrom et al., 2013).

These out-of-game spaces of interaction together form what is commonly referred to as a backchannel. While intimidating to newcomers, these communication tools facilitate "play outside of the game client" and make up a central component of the gaming experience in *EVE* (Bergstrom et al., 2013, p. 5). The practice of circumventing an official channel to engage in communication is not unique to MMOs. Backchannels are commonly used to facilitate informal or clandestine negotiations in a variety of situations, ranging from personal to diplomatic and political contexts. In MMOs, backchannel communication typically spans multiple media platforms. The resulting multilayered structure of engagement "takes the social aspects of the game one step further, creating a community that not only lives in-game, but also has significant substance

---

[1] Purposely harassing and irritating other players.
[2] Fraudulent in-game market transactions.

outside of it" (Christou et al., 2013, p. 727). In MMOs backchannels are important because they have the potential to enhance players' gaming experience and increase their sense of connectedness both inside and outside of the gameworld (Williams et al., 2007).

Past studies have acknowledged the significance of in-game and out-of-game communication in facilitating social interaction and enhancing players' social lives (Williams et al., 2007; Steinkuehler & Williams, 2006). The contents of backchannel communication and the everyday experiences of multisited engagement, however, remain underexplored. This chapter examines the types of social interactions that take place on the backchannel of *EVE Online* and how players make sense of the different relationships they have developed with their fellow users. Special attention is given to what *EVE* players talk about and do while on the backchannel and how these interactions impact their lives both inside and outside of the game. This chapter highlights how MMOs function as important spaces of social interaction where a wide range of relationships are formed. Findings suggest that backchannel communication not only allows players to organize more efficiently as an organization, but also that the backchannel is an important space for casual conversations, a gathering spot during moments of downtime and a place where players engage in informational as well as emotional exchanges. Analysis of qualitative interviews with *EVE* players suggests that like offline social relations, friendships that grow out of social interaction in MMOs exist on a continuum of commitment and intimacy and are continually negotiated and reclassified as the relationship changes over time.

3.3 Literature Review

3.3.1 Social Interaction in Online Games

MMOs range widely in type and content, from role-playing games to first-person shooters, but they share one common trait: they emphasize player interaction and bring together large numbers of players from across the world. This means that a high percentage of users players encounter online are people whom they have never met face to face (Nardi & Harris, 2006). Players, however, do not remain strangers for long and social interaction in MMOs has been linked to positive outcomes such as improved personal well-being and greater social capital (Skoric & Kwan, 2011; Steinkuehler & Williams, 2006). Studies suggest that between 56% and 60% of players make friends online whom they then proceed to meet offline (Domahidi, Festl, & Quandt,

2014; Schiano et al., 2014). The opportunity to strike up new friendships that translate into offline social relations has important implications for players' personal networks and their access to social capital resources.

Social capital is often conceptualized as the social, political, and economic resources an individual can access through his or her social relations (Appel et al., 2014; Coleman, 1988; Putnam, 2000). There are two dimensions of social capital: bonding social capital and bridging social capital. The former refers to the resources accessible from intimate relations (strong ties) such as family and close friends. The latter refers to resources accessible from less intimate, but more diverse contacts (weak ties) such as coworkers, neighbors, and people from volunteer groups and other social settings (Granovetter, 1973; Putnam, 2000). Social capital is considered a valuable resource because it is associated with a wide range of social, political, informational, and emotional benefits. The interactive component of MMOs invites players to engage with each other, develop new friendships, and in the process creates opportunities for players to activate social capital resources with benefits that extend offline. A one-month panel study of online gamers found that after experiencing the sense of belonging that comes with being a member of a large online community, players reported attending in-person club meetings more frequently than before they started playing the game (Williams, 2006). This suggests that online inter-actions can have a positive impact on people's offline social lives.

Because MMOs provide a space to socialize outside of the traditional social environments of the workplace and home, researchers have argued that they function as a "third place" for informal sociability (Oldenburg, 1989; Steinkuehler & Williams, 2006). Backchannels and in-game communication systems allow players to coordinate game-related activities, but interaction is not limited to task-oriented conversation. Analyses of text-based exchanges in the online game *Jedi Knight II: Jedi Outcast*, for example, revealed that players produce three times more socioemotional communication than task-oriented communication and that a majority of these socioemotional messages are pos-itive in nature, such as jokes, declarations of solidarity, and other expressions of tension release (Peña & Hancock, 2006). In other words, MMOs can act as welcoming and comfortable spaces for casual conversations.

3.3.2 Guilds, Clans, and Other Player Organizations

Past studies on social interaction in MMOs have established that online gaming is a highly social activity in which users develop a sense of respon-sibility and commitment toward their fellow players (Nardi, 2010; Taylor, 2009; Yee, 2006). These experiences are not a byproduct of the game, but carefully planned. MMOs are intentionally designed for sociability, with built-in features that encourage or even force players to engage with each other (Christou et al., 2013; Ducheneaut, Moore, & Nickell, 2004). Common sociability designs include systems of mutual dependence between players that offer higher rewards for cooperative work. In the MMO *Star Wars Galaxies*, for example, the various character professions (medic, scout, marksman, etc.) were intentionally designed for codependence, thereby encouraging social contact between players (Ducheneaut et al., 2007). Other features likely to promote player interaction include group structures and well-defined enemies and goals that bind players through a shared in-game objective (Christou et al., 2013). Taylor (2009), in her examination of the online game *EverQuest*, found that certain in-game tasks and monster battles were more easily accomplished as a group, thus giving players an incentive to work as a team.

While MMOs offer players the possibility to interact with thousands of users, many players choose to play in smaller groups, commonly referred to as guilds or clans. These player organizations are central to the social experience of MMOs. They represent the place where one's important relationships are formed and where players spend the majority of their in-game time (Ducheneaut et al., 2006). Compared to interactions in the game at large, guilds, clans, and other player organizations represent "more permanent associations" and are often formed around "like-minded players" who share similar social and game-related interests (Williams et al., 2007, p. 429).

As distinct organizations within the broader game universe, guilds operate as online communities (Baym, 2010). They provide players with important resources for the development of interpersonal relationships, including a shared sense of space, practice, and identity, as well as mutual support and common resources. Guild members nurture each other and relate as a community by sharing gaming experiences, coordinating group efforts, offering tips for in-game success, and talking about their lives outside of the game (Ang & Zaphiris, 2010; Lee et al., 2013).

When joining a guild, players acquire a group identity and affiliation that separates them from other groups in the game. Taylor (2009) explains that *EverQuest* players who belong to the same guild are bound by a heightened sense of group identity and exhibit trust in multiple ways, including risking their characters' lives for each other, distributing loot fairly, sharing accounts, and facing difficult situations together as a group. The sense of togetherness experienced in guilds transcends the game and impacts players' personal well-being offline. Reer and Krämer (2014) argue that players who participate in the management of a guild and attend guild-related events offline are more willing to engage in self-disclosure and have higher chances of gathering social capital resources than those who are not involved in player-driven organizations.

Although guilds share many commonalities, each group is a distinct entity and player organizations vary greatly in size and type. Some guilds consist of small groups of friends who play together casually. Other guilds have upwards of a hundred members and follow a hierarchical command-and-control structure organized around various leadership roles (Ducheneaut et al., 2007). One can also find groups that were created to accommodate particular player needs such as odd work schedules and disabilities (Poisso, 2013). Lastly, it is common for guilds to be established around different in-game goals and playing preferences such as socializing, raiding, role-playing, or PvP[3] (Warmelink & Siitonen, 2013; Williams et al., 2006).

The shared responsibility that comes out of operating as a group invites users to play with the goals of the entire guild in mind and to consider the needs of the group before their own (Taylor, 2009). Trust and reputation systems are especially important at the guild level and "compared to the loose community of the MMOG as a whole, guilds provide more of the trust-building features of social institutions (interdependence, persistence of identity, and strength of reputation system)" and are therefore more likely to enable the development of meaningful relationships than the general setting of MMOs (Ratan et al., 2010, p. 96). Though research on social interaction in MMOs has found support primarily for the existence of bridging capital, some stipulate that players who stay with their guild for longer periods of time are more likely to experience bonding capital and develop close ties than those who miss out on this communal experience (Steinkuehler & Williams, 2006). Bonding capital requires frequent emotional as well as instrumental resource exchange and is more likely to be found among closely tied guild members than the general acquaintances players make when playing MMOs.

3.3.3 Social Interaction in *EVE*'s Corporations

To gain a deeper understanding of social interaction at the group level and to highlight under what circumstances players develop strong ties with fellow users, this chapter examines backchannel communication and friendship in the MMO *EVE Online*. *EVE*'s corporations can be compared to the guilds or clans commonly found in other MMOs. When players first start *EVE*, they are placed in a default nonplayer character (NPC) corporation.[4] Most players stay in this

---

[3] Player(s) versus player(s). Style of play focused on interactive conflict or combat against other players.

[4] NPC corporations are automated by the game and not organized by human players.

placeholder corporation while they complete the tutorials and familiarize themselves with the game's user interface. Once acclimated, players generally leave
the NPC corporation in favor of a player-run corporation. These groups are
long-term, formal associations of players overseen by a chief executive officer
(CEO). Although only a CEO is required to set up a corporation, for management purposes, most corporations in *EVE* have several officers who control
specific functionalities such as accounting, security, recruitment, and production management. In-game officers and regular corporation members rely on
their group's backchannel for communication.

This chapter takes a close look at player communication on *EVE*'s many
backchannels. Emphasis is placed on the types of activities that happen on the
backchannel, the processes through which players strike up new friendships,
and the maturation of online connections into off-game relations. By choosing
to focus on *EVE*, this study also examines whether findings from past studies
on social interaction in MMOs hold true for a game with a very different user
base, theme, and in-game content than the popular WoW.

Friendship is a complex concept as the term "friend" is used by different
people to mean different things. Simply saying that players have made friends
online through a game doesn't reveal much about the value individuals attach to
these relationships or how they integrate these connections into their daily lives.
By examining how *EVE Online* players make sense of the range of relationships
they have developed with their corporation members, including how they refer
to their various online connections, this chapter makes important contributions
to research on online social interaction and online friendship practices. The
following two research questions guide the study:

RQ1: How do players make sense of the various relationships they form with
their fellow corporation members?

RQ2: What types of activities are facilitated by backchannel communication
at the corporation level?

3.4 Methods

3.4.1 Data Collection

Qualitative interviews were conducted with current *EVE Online* players in
March 2014. Participants were recruited through an advertisement posted on
the popular entertainment site Reddit in a subreddit[5] dedicated to issues related

---

[5] A specific forum or subcategory of the general Reddit website.

to *EVE*. Though only registered Reddit users can post on r/Eve, the information published on the site is available to the general public. Anyone visiting r/Eve was able to see the recruitment notice. To be eligible for participation, players had to be at least 18 years of age and currently subscribed to *EVE Online*. The r/Eve recruitment post resulted in thirty-seven interested volunteers, of which fourteen individuals were purposefully selected for participation in a one-hour Skype voice interview. A purposive sample was chosen to recruit participants across a variety of criteria, including *EVE* gaming experience, preferred type of gameplay (PvP or PvE), and in-game corporation size. This approach was used to increase the diversity of players interviewed and capture a wider range of player experiences.

Interviews were semistructured to create a conversational tone and allow for follow-up questions. Interviewees were prompted to think about their relationship to their fellow corporation members, to discuss signs that a group of players has achieved a high level of trust, to talk about the kinds of activities they engage in on the backchannel, and to reflect on their experience joining a player-run corporation. Participants were compensated for their time with an *EVE* Time Code that could be redeemed for a one-month subscription to the game or in game currency and is worth the equivalent of $14.95.

3.4.2 Sample

The sample included thirteen men and one woman. Participants ranged in age from 18 to 32 years ($M = 24$). Since only about 5% of *EVE* players are female the sample is in line with the general gender distribution of the game (Bergstrom, 2013). Participants' *EVE* gaming experience ranged from 3 months to 8 years ($M = 32$ months). Efforts were made to accommodate volunteers from different time zones and the sample included participants from five different countries: United States, United Kingdom, Bulgaria, Netherlands, and Canada. The sample also included members from different size corporations. Some participants reported being part of very small corporations that counted only a handful of members; others belonged to medium-sized corporations of close to a hundred players; and a few were part of some of the game's largest corporations with upwards of 3,000 members. No exact membership numbers were recorded.

3.4.3 Data Analysis

Each interview was digitally recorded and then transcribed by the interviewer. An open coding approach was used to analyze the content of the interviews.

Part of grounded theory, open coding invites researchers to analyze data line-by-line and explore the various theoretical possibilities that emerge from the data (Charmaz, 2006). Participants' answers to the interview questions were carefully compared and contrasted in an attempt to discern common themes and develop potential activity and friendship categories. In the first step of the analysis, all the interview sections dealing with backchannel communication among corporation members and online friendship were sorted and separated for closer review. In the second step, these particular passages were again analyzed line-by-line and then reorganized and classified based on the types of activities players described and how they characterized their relationship to their fellow corporation members.

3.5 Analysis and Discussion

3.5.1 Task-Related Communication and in-Game Associates

The first type of player relationship that emerged from the open coding analysis is that of in-game associates (RQ1). Players who indicated primarily having good associates or in-game acquaintances engaged mostly in task-oriented activities focused around achieving common game goals (RQ2). They typically used the backchannel to organize as a group and discuss *EVE*-related information. Popular communication tools included the IM service Jabber, Mumble and TeamSpeak VoIPs, and corporation or alliance[6] specific internet forums. In particular, participants who were part of large corporations reported having comprehensive backchannel setups to accommodate multiple discussion groups:

> The corporation I'm in is actually quite big, upwards of 3000 members... We have an out-of-game forum, a messaging server, and a VoIP server that are used out-of-game. That's where most of the communication, coordination, and general discussion between corporation and alliance members usually goes on... There are smaller groups within the alliance or corporation, special interest groups, groups that focus on a specific type of thing, and social groups.

In large corporations where membership reaches thousands of players, it is not possible to know every player. Corporation leaders are aware of this limitation and this is why many corporations have special interest groups for players to make connections with members who share their social interests or in-game goals. Having multiple chat channels also allows corporations to synchronously

---

[6] In *EVE* corporations can ban together to form alliances against other groups.

run multiple operations (ops) such as fleet deployments, small-group roams, and wormhole explorations. This type of out-of-game communication structure is not unique to *EVE* and can be found in other games as well (Christou et al., 2013).

Off-game communication tools are very popular among player groups because they are highly versatile and allow users to tailor the application's features to the needs of the organization. IM services such as Jabber, for example, can be linked to portable devices. A participant noted that his corporation asks members to install the application on their mobile phones so that they can easily be notified of in-game activities:

> Typically I'll just receive a ping on my cell phone that's an alliance wide ping that goes out via the Jabber protocol. It details what's going on and what specific activity is happening at that time. So I can just log in and I know what's gonna happen and mostly I log on because of these pings. Mostly it's PvP oriented, so we form a group and go fight some other people, take a station, take a system, or defend a system.

Jabber is a powerful organizational tool because it allows corporations to quickly mobilize forces via a system-wide notification. Although it is efficient, this practice is not very personal. Some players like this task-oriented approach to playing *EVE*. Several interviewees stated they log on to the backchannel primarily for game-related purposes and not necessarily to socialize. When discussing their relationships with their fellow corporation members, users who played the game primarily to participate in space battles and other group ops did not refer to corporation members as friends, but said things like "they're good associates" or "I'd probably go with acquaintances." Their relationships with these other players are highly dependent on the shared practice of playing *EVE* as part of the same corporation. If they did not participate in ops together, these individuals would likely not interact. Consequently, one interviewee pointed out that he did not make any true friends in the game:

> I have not really forged any relationships within my corporation . . . I don't really have any friends or just people I really know. I know some by name and I think probably some know me, but not as a person, just my character I'd say, just what I can do, the roles that I can fulfill, but not on a personal level or anything.

Although this interviewee indicates that he enjoys playing *EVE*, his interactions with other players are limited to participating in corporation ops. He points out that others in the game know his abilities and what he can contribute to the corporation, but that they don't know his name or who he is personally. Associate-level friendships among corporation members are more task-based than emotional. Players' motivations for interacting with each other are highly dependent on the fact that they belong to the same organization and share similar in-game goals. In that respect, in-game associates can be conceived of as a type of given friend or default contact. These connections are also known as Aristotelian friendships of utility because interaction is motivated by the desire to accomplish common interests or tasks rather than mutual affinity (Aristotle, 2011; Spencer & Pahl, 2006).

3.5.2 Casual Interactions and Social Friends

The second type of player relationship is that of social friends (RQ1). Within their corporation, interviewees reported associating more closely with five to fifteen other players. They consider these players friends and socialize with them during the game and when they are on their computers throughout the day. For this smaller group, the backchannel represents an important gathering place. This is where players come not only to hear about ongoing corporation ops and the latest *EVE* activities, but to engage in small talk about videogames, popular culture, and the news, among other topics (RQ2):

> In the Jabber client we just tend to talk about anything, it doesn't necessarily have to be *EVE* related... We'll post something that may be humorous, there's a subreddit called Dirty Jokes and we'll just link to that, and then random YouTube videos of songs and things like that.
>
> It really depends on the group, but if we're just sitting around and talking on Mumble, it will usually just be about anything or everything. Sometimes I'll be doing something on my computer and I'll idle the Mumble channel and if somebody is talking about something interesting, I'll join in the conversation... We've had talks about real life politics, to fittings in the game itself, to even religion sometimes too.

While *EVE* is known for its majestic, large-scale space battles, there are many moments when not much is happening in the game. As a sandbox, *EVE* depends on players to generate game content and storylines, and sometimes days or even weeks go by before any major events happen. Individuals who play *EVE* primarily for the game don't log onto the backchannel during downtime. For those who enjoy the social aspect of MMOs, however, the backchannel becomes a highly interesting and entertaining place when in-game action subsides. These moments give players the opportunity to extend the relationships they developed in *EVE* outside of the game:

> I know a big chunk of these people. Between Jabber and the forums and fleets you get to meet a lot of different people every day... It's not a crazy intimate relationship, but we get together and we play other games not just *EVE*. I have a group where we play Dungeons and Dragons together through d20 which is a lot of

fun. There's groups where we go play League of Legends together so I mean the friendships that I've made extend outside of the game which is fun... *EVE* can get boring, it can get grindy. It's a long game, it's a long grind. You're in it for the long run so it's nice to bring those friendships outside of the game.

I've actually made quite a few friends in my player corporation and I do speak to them on the regular and I do play other games with them as well on top of that... There are about 5 or 6 people that I quite happily talk to. I'll have Skype calls with them and we'll play other games such as Dota and stuff like that... I tend to leave [Jabber] logged on pretty much every time I'm at the computer.

As players get to know each other on a more personal level, backchannel communication increases and they connect with each other not only through the off-game communication platforms provided by the corporation (IM, VoIP, and forums), but also through more personal modes of communication such as Skype and sites dedicated to virtual tabletop games.

Participants who had made social friends reported engaging in self-disclosure and knew personal details about this smaller circle of corporation members, such as birthdays, marital status, occupation, and place of living. These types of relationships are less dependent on *EVE* than task-oriented associations, but they still depend on a shared interest in videogames and popular culture more broadly. Although there is some self-disclosure in social friendships, the amount and type of information users are willing to share with their corporation members vary. One interviewee explained that he is consciously limiting what type of personal information he brings up on the backchannel:

I wouldn't talk to them about anything that was going on in the real world, or maybe I would, but it would be very broad, not very specific. So for example, at the moment me and my wife are going through the process of buying a house, they know that I'm buying a house, but they don't know where it is or how much it is or when we're moving... I want to keep [*EVE*] separate from everything else that's going on.

Although he considers several of his corporation members friends the fact that he does not want to share specific details about his personal life indicates that these relationships do not have the level of intimacy and reciprocity associated with close ties. Furthermore, his point that he likes to keep *EVE* separated from other things that are happening in his life speaks to the desire to maintain a certain distance between his online activities and his personal self. Although social friendships are more intimate than task-oriented associations, these relationships are still tied together mainly by a shared passion for videogames and some general small talk. Sharing details about one's personal life may seem outside of the scope of this type of relationship.

The social friendships described by *EVE* participants are in line with the socioemotional behaviors observed in previous studies (Peña & Hancock, 2006). *EVE*'s status as a sandbox, however, and especially its frequent moments of downtime, mean that *EVE* offers more opportunities for social interaction outside of the game than other MMOs. Indeed, interviewees indicated talking on the backchannel not only when they were actively playing the game, but also at other times throughout the day. In many ways, the backchannel of their *EVE* corporation became a hangout. They would log on to Jabber and other sites to check in on their fellow corporation members, engage in small talk, and even play other games together. In his discussion about adult friendships in the workplace, Rawlins (1992) notes that social ties are "personal ties transcending the work setting and involving some talking as well as doing things together" (p. 191). In other words, social friends engage in a few select activities and share some personal details, but lack the level of intimacy that one would find between close friends.

3.5.3 Beyond *EVE*: Forging True Friendships Online

The third category of player relationship that emerged from the interviews was that of true friends (RQ1). For corporation members who are social friends, backchannel communication binds them together during gameplay as well as during downtime. For an even smaller circle of these friends, playing *EVE* and joining a player corporation led to the development of close ties and what interviewees called "true friends." Those relationships are no longer predicated on playing *EVE* together, but on interacting across a wide range of sites, both online and offline. The relationship between true friends is different from that between social friends in that it has reached a level of camaraderie beyond casual conversation and gaming-related activities. True friends still use the corporation's backchannel as a place of social gathering, but also interact with each other on social network sites (Facebook), Skype, Steam, telephone, and email (RQ2). These other sites are not tied to the corporation's backchannel, but represent personal efforts on the part of players to connect with people they met in the game in other online venues. For true friends, social interaction on the corporation's backchannel is only one of many modes of communication. These friends engage in social activities such as watching a movie or video chatting on Skype, but personal information sharing and intimacy are much higher for true friends than for social friends:

> There's a solid maybe 10 people that have been in [the corporation] about the same amount of time that I have, those people we have each other's cell phone numbers,

we have each other's personal email addresses, Facebook, Twitter, the whole nine yards. And that's just because we want to know and be able to communicate with each other outside and inside the game. That's the camaraderie that I've grown to enjoy and take part in on a daily basis.

So there's some of them, where I have them on Skype and we have each other on Facebook. So there's a select few of them that I feel like if the game were to fall apart or the community were to fall apart, we'd still manage to be friends outside of it.

True friends exhibit greater levels of trust and emotional support than social friends. Interviewees generally had only a few friends whom they met through *EVE* and who would fall under the classification of true friends. These friendships were typically built over several years of online interaction and interviewees were confident these friendships would continue to thrive even if the gaming community where their friendship originated were to fall apart. In addition to sharing online contact information, interviewees who expressed having made true friends in the game knew each other's real names and were in touch outside of *EVE* and the backchannel. Adding someone on social media and exchanging phone numbers and email addresses are all actions that bind individuals at a more personal level than casual social interaction on the backchannel. Motivation for sharing resources and information is high among true friends. Although some interviewees had not yet met the true friends they made through *EVE* in person, they felt they could rely on these individuals for help in times of need:

A handful of them I can describe as being true friends, people I know in real life and people that could call me on my phone and ask me a favor and I'd be more than happy to help ... If I found myself through their town and needing a couch to crash on, I would feel comfortable calling them.

The people I used to play *World of Warcraft* with, I don't speak to them anymore. I don't play *EVE* a whole lot anymore and I still talk to those people from *EVE Online* every day ... In that regard the community is much better ... There's lots of different avenues for me to get in touch with people and we are all always very excited to talk to each other ... A lot of the good friends that I do have are through *EVE* so I feel they know more about me than other people might share ... I'm definitely along the lines of if something goes wrong in my life they are the first people I contact.

The availability of emotional support in addition to information exchange separates true friends from social friends. That some corporation members engage in personal socioemotional sharing is particularly interesting given that the majority of players (95%) in *EVE* are male (Bergstrom, 2013). Men are known for being less willing to engage in emotional and personal sharing and Rawlins (1992) states that "men limit their vulnerability by revealing less about themselves to their friends, avoiding the discussion of feelings or personal issues and focusing more on activities and objective issues such as sports and politics" (p. 110). While interviewees reported mostly having social friends with whom they interact casually, a handful of participants stated that they share information about their romantic relationships and other more intimate real-life details with members of their corporation to whom they feel close. This indicates that, for some men at least, MMOs are a safe place for the discussion of personal information. Further research is needed in order to explore in more depth the extent of disclosure between males in MMOs, as this study only provides initial, exploratory insights into this topic. Initial findings from this study, however, are optimistic and suggest that as long-term player organizations, *EVE*'s corporations allow players to develop a range of social relationships, including close ties.

3.6 Conclusion

This chapter examines the types of activities players engage in on the backchannel and the various degrees of friendship that exist in *EVE*. It contributes to current research on social interaction in MMOs and shows that under the right conditions, players can develop lasting friendships through online games. Findings reveal three main types of player relationships: in-game associates, social friends, and true friends. Each category of friendship is associated with different types of backchannel activities. In-game associates engage mostly in task-oriented activities that involve accomplishing shared goals. Social friends interact with each other in the game, but also make time for casual conversations and visit their corporation's backchannel even in moments of low in-game activity. In the case of true friendship, in addition to socializing, players also engage in personal and emotional exchanges. Their interaction extends outside of the corporation's backchannel to media such as email, phone, and social media.

As with most qualitative work the goal of this research is not generalizability, but to advance the current understanding on online friendships. Drawing on semistructured interviews, this chapter explores the potential of the MMO *EVE Online* to encourage the development of both bridging and bonding capital. The *EVE* players interviewed for this study developed in-game associations and social friendships with the members of their corporation and regularly engaged in casual interactions on backchannel. These findings are consistent with previous findings about the potential of guilds and player-driven groups to foster a sense of togetherness among players. Most interestingly, though, the finding that some corporation members established true friendships that are not dependent on *EVE* shows that MMOs do indeed have the ability to foster strong ties. Previous studies speculated that because MMOs commonly focus on task-based interactions and informal sociability they may lack the deeper emotional connections needed for the formation of bonding capital (Steinkuehler & Williams, 2006). *EVE*'s emphasis on sandbox interaction and its frequent moments of downtime, however, make it stand out among other MMOs in that it gives players more opportunities for backchannel socialization that extends outside of the game. This chapter highlights the crucial role played by backchannel communication and social systems in the friendship process. Although many *EVE* players are physically separated from each other, often by large geographical distances, they are not isolated socially. *EVE*'s player organizations and the various interest groups within corporations offer players a sense of shared identity and community belonging. Having friendships of different degrees of intimacy is an important aspect of one's personal well-being. By offering players the opportunity to establish task-oriented relationships, social friendships, and in some instances true friendships, MMOs help players fulfill utilitarian and hedonic needs.

References

Ang, C., & Zaphiris, P. (2010). Social roles of players in MMORPG guilds: A social network analytic perspective. *Information, Communication & Society*, 13(4), 592–614.

Appel, L., Dadlani, P., Dwyer, M., Hampton, K., Kitzie, V., Matni, Z., Moore, P., & Teodoro, R. (2014). Testing the validity of social capital measures in the study of information and communication technologies. *Information Communication & Society*, 17(4), 398–416.

Aristotle. (2011). *Aristotle's nicomachean ethics*. R. C. Bartlett & S. D. Collins, trans. Chicago, IL: The University of Chicago Press. (Original work published in 350 B.C.).

Baym, N. (2010). *Personal connections in the digital age*. Malden, MA: Polity Press.

Bergstrom, K. (2013). *EVE Online* Newbie Guides: Helpful information or gatekeeping mechanisms at work? In *Selected papers of the 2013 Association of Internet Researchers Conference*. (AOIR'14).

Bergstrom, K., Carter, M., Woodford, D., & Paul, C. (2013). Constructing the ideal *EVE Online* player. In *Proceedings of the 2013 Digital Games Research Association Conference*, August 26–29, 2013, Atlanta, GA.

Charmaz, K. (2006). *Constructing grounded theory*. Thousand Oaks, CA: SAGE.

Christou, G., Law, E., Zaphiris, P., & Ang, C. (2013). Challenges of designing for sociability to enhance player experience in massively multi-player online role-playing games. *Behavior and Information Technology*, 32(7), 724–734.

Coleman, J. (1988). Social capital in the creation of human capital. *American Journal of Sociology*, 44 (Suppl.), S95–S120.

Crawford, G., Gosling, V., & Light, B. (2011). The social and cultural significance of online gaming. In Crawford, G., Gosling, V., & Light, B. (eds.), *Online gaming in context* (pp. 3–22). New York, NY: Routledge.

Domahidi, E., Festl, R., & Quandt, T. (2014). To dwell among gamers: Investigating the relationship between social online game use and gaming-related friendships. *Computers in Human Behavior*, 35, 107–115.

Ducheneaut, N., Moore, R. J., & Nickell, E. (2004). Designing for sociability in massively multiplayer games: An examination of the "third places" of SWG. In *Proceedings of the Other Players Conference on Multiplayer Phenomena*, December 6–8, 2004, Copenhagen; Denmark. Copenhagen: IT University of Copenhagen.

Ducheneaut, N., Moore, R. J., & Nickell, E. (2007). Virtual "third places": A case study of sociability in massively multiplayer games. *Computer Supported Cooperative Work*, 16(1/2), 129–167.

Ducheneaut, N., Nickell, E., Moore, R. J., & Yee, N. (2006). "Alone together?" Exploring the social dynamics of massively multiplayer online games. In *Proceedings of Conference on Human Factors in Computing Systems* (pp. 407–416). New York, NY: ACM Press.

Ducheneaut, N., Yee, N., Nickell, E., & Moore, R. J. (2007). The life and death of online gaming communities: A look at guilds in *World of Warcraft*. In *Proceedings of CHI 2007* (pp. 839–848). New York, NY: ACM Press.

Graft, K. (2012, October 29). *EVE Online* and the meaning of sandbox. *Gamasutra*. Retrieved from: http://gamasutra.com/view/news/179811/EVE_Online_and_the_meaning_of_sandbox.php

Granovetter, M. (1973). The strength of weak ties. *American Journal of Sociology*, 78(6), 1360–1380.

Lee, H. J., Choi, J., Kim, J. W., Park, S. J., & Gloor, P. (2013). Communication, opponents, and clan performance in online games: A social network approach. *Cyberpsychology, Behavior & Social Networking*, 16(12), 878–883.

Nardi, B. (2010). *My life as a night elf priest: An anthropological account of World of Warcraft*. Ann Arbor, MI: The University of Michigan Press.

Nardi, B., & Harris, J. (2006). Strangers and friends: Collaborative play in *World of Warcraft*. In *Proceedings of the ACM Conference on Computer Supported Cooperative Work, CSCW*, November 4–8, Banff, Alberta, Canada, 2006 (pp. 149–158). New York, NY: ACM Press.

Oldenburg, R. (1989). *The great good place: Cafes, coffee shops, bookstores, bars, hair salons, and other hangouts at the heart of a community*. Cambridge, MA: Da Capo Press.

Park, J. J., Han, S. K., Won, M. K., & Na, Y. C. (2006). Communication supports for building world wide internet game communities. In *Proceedings of Entertainment Computing, ICEC 2006 – 5th International Conference*, September 20–22, Cambridge, UK (pp. 370–373).

Paul, C. (2011). Don't play me: *EVE Online*, new players and rhetoric. In *Proceedings of the 6th International Conference on Foundations of Digital Games* (FDG'11) (pp. 262–264). New York, NY: ACM Press.

Peña, J., & Hancock, J. (2006). An analysis of socioemotional and task communication in online multiplayer video games. *Communication Research*, 33(1), 92–109.

Poisso, L. (2013, February 3). Guide to choosing the right style of guild. Engadget. Retrieved from: www.engadget.com/2013/02/04/guide-to-choosing-the-right-style-of-guild/

Putnam, R. (2000). *Bowling alone*. New York, NY: Simon & Schuster.

Ratan, R. A., Chung, J., Shen, C., Williams, D., & Poole, M. (2010). Schmoozing and smiting: Trust, social institutions, and communication patterns in an MMOG. *Journal of Computer-Mediated Communication*, 16(1), 93–114.

Rawlins, W. K. (1992). *Friendship matters: Communication, dialectics, and the life course*. Hawthorne, NY: Aldine de Gruyter.

Reer, F., & Krämer, N. C. (2014). Underlying factors of social capital acquisition in the context of online-gaming: Comparing *World of Warcraft* and *Counter-Strike*. *Computers in Human Behavior*, 36, 179–189.

Schiano, D. J., Nardi, B., Debeauvais, T., Ducheneaut, N., & Yee, N. (2014). The "lonely gamer" revisited. *Entertainment Computing*, 5(1), 65–70.

Skoric, M. M., & Kwan, G. (2011). Platforms for mediated sociability and online social capital: The role of Facebook and massively multiplayer online games. *Asian Journal of Communication*, 21(5), 467–484.

Spencer, L., & Pahl, R. (2006). *Rethinking friendship: Hidden solidarities today*. Princeton, NJ: Princeton University Press.

Steinkuehler, C., & Williams, D. (2006). Where everybody knows your (screen) name: Online games as "third places." *Journal of Computer-Mediated Communication*, 11(4), 885–909.

Taylor, T. L. (2008). How a PvP server, multinational player base, and surveillance mod scene caused me pause. In H. G. Corneliussen and J. Walker-Rettberf (eds.), *Digital play and identity: A* World of Warcraft *reader* (pp. 187–202). Cambridge, MA: MIT Press.

Taylor, T. L. (2009). *Play between worlds: Exploring online game culture*. Cambridge, MA: MIT Press.

Warmelink, H., & Siitonen, M. (2013). A decade of research into player communities in online games. *Journal Of Gaming & Virtual Worlds*, 5(3), 271.

Williams, D. (2006). Groups and goblins: The social and civic impact of an online game. *Journal of Broadcasting & Electronic Media*, 50(4), 651–670.

Williams, D., Xiong, L., & Caplan, S. (2007). Can you hear me now? The impact of voice in an online gaming community. *Human Communication Research*, 33(4), 427–449.

Williams, D., Xiong, L., Zhang, Y., Ducheneaut, N., Nickell, E., & Yee, N. (2006). From tree house to barracks: The social life of guilds in *World of Warcraft*. *Games and Culture*, 1(4), 338–361.

Yee, N. (2006). The demographics, motivations, and derived experiences of users of massively multi-user online graphical environments. *Presence: Teleoperators & Virtual Environments*, 15(3), 309–329.

4

Couples Who Slay Together, Stay Together: Benefits, Challenges, and Relational Quality among Romantic Couples Who Game

SARAH EVANS, ELIZABETH CRAIG,
AND NICHOLAS TAYLOR

The old adage "couples that play together, stay together" is based on elementary understandings of how romantic relationships work. However, evidence suggests that engaging in joint activities as a romantic couple is a contributing factor to relational health (Canary & Stafford, 1992). Specifically, literature on relational maintenance demonstrates that spending time together engaging in joint activities, especially leisure activities, is positively related to relational satisfaction (Canary et al., 1993). Considering the recent exponential growth in the gaming industry (Entertainment Software Association, 2013), it should come as no surprise that a growing number of couples are spending their leisure time literally "playing together" (Carr & Oliver, 2009; Huynh, Lim & Skoric, 2013; Nardi, 2010; Williams et al., 2009).

Existing research on couples' play is largely based on a single gaming genre, namely massively multiplayer online games (MMOGs). Emerging genres such as the increasingly popular multiplayer online battle arenas (MOBAs) have been studied less often overall, especially in terms of relational behaviors and outcomes. In an effort to contribute to this significant body of literature, the current study examines couples' play through a number of theoretical frameworks from both the game studies and interpersonal communication disciplines. Specifically, the current study provides a unique look into the relational processes of players, including insights on relational maintenance behaviors and the benefits and challenges couples face when gaming together.

4.1 Literature Review

4.1.1 Massively Multiplayer Online Games

To date, there is little work on the gaming habits of romantic partners, though early game studies research explored couples' play as a way for families to connect with one another. Mitchell's (1985) study of the perceived effects of home gaming systems on family dynamics discovered families who played together reported being enthusiastic about the shared activity. These families enjoyed the new ways of communication, cooperation, and competition evoked through shared play of Atari video games like *Pac Man*, *Tennis*, and other sports games. Additionally, this enthusiasm over family gameplay was present despite mothers' self-reported lack of innate gaming skills, and their reluctance to play as often as other family members.

More recent research on couples' play is derived from studies of MMOGs. This genre historically received scholarly attention because of the games' popularity (Tassi, 2014b) and large player-driven communities. These games, such as *World of Warcraft* and *Guild Wars 2*, typically involve large, fantasy-themed environments in which players create and customize in-game characters ("avatars"), which they use to battle computer-controlled monsters and other players; craft and trade weapons, armor, and other loot; and join into formal groupings (usually "clans" or "guilds") with other players (Taylor, 2006a, 2006b; Williams et al., 2006). According to the research on couples' MMOG play, romantic partners engage in a variety of play styles, in terms of both virtual and physical intimacy. For some couples living apart, gaming provides a chance to "be" together, while other couples play side-by-side, but in different parts of the gameworld (or indeed, in different games) (Bergstrom, 2009; Carr & Oliver, 2009; Nardi, 2010; Williams et al., 2006). In a study using autoethnographic participant research and interviews, Jordan (2014) found that playing *World of Warcraft* provided a support network for couples and recommends its use for mental health professionals as a way to promote relational healing. Despite these perceived benefits, couples' gaming experiences are not without challenges, nor are they exempt from larger, sometimes damaging, trends in gaming.

In terms of in-game activities, the paradigmatic play style involves couples playing in tandem, using avatars with complementary roles – (stereo)typically with the male partner playing as a damage-dealing and damage-absorbing warrior, or "tank," and the female partner playing as a ranged magic-user or healer, supporting the tank (Carr & Oliver, 2009; Nardi, 2010). Posts and comments on MMOG forums suggest that bonding through play, and keeping in touch, for long-distance couples, were perceived benefits of gaming as a couple (Murray et al., 2012). Murray et al. also indicate that one particular source of pleasure for couples was progressing through the game at the same rate, maintaining the same player levels. Conversely, guild-related issues due to partner skill, fear of in-game interaction replacing physical-world interaction, and harassment of (typically) female players because of stereotypes were commonly reported disadvantages.

While this knowledge may be useful in documenting couples' play practices in MMOGs, these represent only one particular range of experiences in terms of couples-based gameplay. Different game genres and experiences influence player motivations and thus behavior in those spaces (Linderoth, Björk, & Olsson, 2014; Sicart, 2011; Taylor, 2009). Looking into other genres may provide a more holistic view into gaming couples' lives.

Recently, MOBAs such as *League of Legends* and *Defense of the Ancients 2* have seen a surge in popularity, eclipsing that of the more widely studied MMOGs. These games typically involve two teams of player-controlled avatars facing off for territorial supremacy on a relatively small map. Lasting on average 30 to 45 minutes, single gameplay sessions are relatively short[1] in comparison to the virtual infinitude of time one can spend logged into an MMOG. Unlike in MMOGs, there is no persistent world in MOBAs and players do not create and customize their avatars, but select from a wide range of predesigned "Champions" each with specific and highly specialized strengths, weaknesses, and attendant play strategies.

League of Legends (*League*), the MOBA context for the present study, is free-to-play and remains one of the most popular PC games in the world, supporting 27 million players daily (Tassi, 2014a). Gameplay consists of individual combat sessions where players choose from 123 different champions (with Riot Games, *League*'s developer, adding more on a regular basis), each with unique abilities and best suited to a particular role.[2] Teams of three to five players destroy turrets in two or three lanes respectively while fighting computer-controlled minions and enemy players, in hopes of ultimately destroying the opposing team's Nexus (home base), thereby winning the match. In a typical five-on-five *League* match, players on each team will sort themselves into various roles, based on preference, experience, and avatar selection.

These roles can be briefly characterized as follows: *Top* and *Mid* roles occupy the arena's top and middle lanes, respectively, and typically make use of Champions with high defensive capabilities; the *Jungler* roams the area in

---

[1] Though single matches are time constrained, players maintain account identities across matches.

[2] Roles are location based in regard to the three large routes, or "lanes" between opposing teams' bases, on the most commonly played map ("Summoner's Rift"). These include "Top" (top lane; champions that can sustain a high amount of damage); "Mid" (mid lane; balanced champions typically using ranged attacks); "Junglers" (highly mobile e champions designed to roam the areas between lanes and create outnumbered team battles); "ADC" (attack-damage-carry; heavy damage-dealers fighting in the contested bottom lane); and "Support" (champions that generally assist others, but particularly the ADC).

between lanes, in an effort to either cause or rectify outnumbered skirmishes; the *Attack Damage Carry* (ADC) role usually patrols the highly contested bottom lane, with the help of the *Support*. Teammates may communicate through *League*'s dedicated text-based chat or via an outside program such as Teamspeak. As in most MOBAs, players have the choice to play with a group of handpicked teammates or can be randomly assigned to a team on entering a *League* lobby.

While research on MOBAs and the communities they support is still in its formative stage, one clear research focus is the toxicity that players, developers, and scholars alike see in player interactions (Carlson, 2013; Kou & Nardi, 2014; McWhertor, 2012). Given the antagonism and hostility within this community, it is to be expected that players often play the game with those they already know. Meng and Williams (2012) report that 80% of the 17,995 *League* players they surveyed played with others with whom they have "preexisting social ties." Furthermore, 21% reported playing with a romantic partner. According to a mixed-methods study by Ratan and Tsai (2014) (currently the only published research focused primarily on heterosexual couples' play in *League*), 73% of female *League* players report playing with a romantic partner, often in roles that are complementary to those of their male partners. Faced with pernicious (and unfounded) stereotypes regarding sex-based differences in gaming ability (Jenson & de Castell, 2008) and an antagonistic, often misogynist player culture, the authors suggest that female players are pressured to "stand by their man," subordinating their play styles and preferences to those of their romantic partners. While the paper by Ratan and Tsai offers valuable insight into the gendered landscapes female players encounter through *League* play, it gives little attention to the relational dynamics of gaming couples. Given this understudied relational context, and the following conceptual frameworks, the current study focuses on couples' play in competitive, team-based gaming.

4.1.2 Romantic Relationships

Romantic couples experience a number of events, activities, and communicative interactions – strategic and routine – that influence the development and maintenance of relationships. In general, couples engage in a number of specific strategies such as speaking positively to one another (i.e., positivity), engaging in a number of self-disclosive behaviors to create open communicative environments (i.e., openness), declarations of commitment to ensure future togetherness (i.e., assurances), engaging in events and activities with friends (i.e., social networking), and spending time together in order to share common interests and joint activities (Canary & Stafford, 1992, 2001; Stafford, Dainton, & Hass, 2000). The use of these strategies is also linked to important relational outcomes such as satisfaction, closeness, and commitment within these relationships (Canary & Stafford, 1992). Specifically, Sidelinger et al. (2008) report relational satisfaction within couples as positively correlated with all maintenance activities (assurances, openness, positivity, advice, conflict management, shared tasks, and social networks) during computer-mediated communication such as emailing or instant messaging.

Unfortunately, there are a limited number of studies that have examined aspects of relational maintenance and video games. Chory and Banfield (2009) investigated the deleterious effects of TV and video game dependence on relational maintenance among romantic couples. Notably, these findings were based on relationships wherein only one partner engaged in game-playing activities. A similar study of Xbox Live (Ledbetter & Kuznekoff, 2012) found no clear indication of relational maintenance strategies being used when gaming was used to maintain friendships. Their research revealed that successfully using Xbox Live to maintain relational closeness in friendships was correlated to additional offline contributions to sustaining closeness. Therefore, while there exists a limited precedent for analyzing the ways video games may or may not support or erode various types of relationships, studies focusing on relational maintenance strategies within couples who game together are lacking.

By examining relational maintenance strategies in *League*, the authors seek to identify typical relational maintenance strategies romantic partners utilize in their relationships, regardless of physical location, as well as the challenges they face as they play online games together. Additionally, given the lack of focus on gameplay with one's romantic partner, we are also interested in the level of relational quality these individuals report when considering their gameplay together. Given the potential for hostile and toxic communication environments within online games, the authors are interested in examining relational maintenance and relational outcomes, specifically. Therefore, we put forth the following research questions:

RQ1: What benefits do individuals describe while playing *League of Legends* with their romantic partners?

RQ2: What challenges do individuals describe while playing *League of Legends* with their romantic partners?

RQ3: What level of relational quality do individuals report for their relationship?

4.2 Method

4.2.1 Participants and Procedures

Participants were recruited via an online survey posted to three separate sites: a geographically local *League* Facebook group, the *League* "subreddit" (specific thread) on reddit.com, and the game's official forums. Participants did not receive incentive for filling out the survey. All participation was voluntary and participants were able to stop the survey at any time. Individuals in a romantic relationship, who self-reported as gaming with their partner, were recruited for the current study. Individuals followed an internet link that provided an online informed consent page, and an online questionnaire through Qualtrics. Participants were asked to think of online gaming with their current romantic relationship when completing the survey. The online survey consisted of a number of demographic items about gameplay, as well as open-ended items regarding gameplay with their romantic partner. Researchers secured approval from North Carolina State University's Institutional Review Board.

4.2.2 Coding

For the first open-ended item regarding benefits that come from gameplay with a romantic partner, the Relational Maintenance Strategies Measure (Stafford, 2011; Stafford et al., 2000) was utilized as a template for the coding themes. Each strategy embodies certain activities that work toward both keeping the relationship in existence and, typically, fostering good feelings about relational partners and the relationship as a whole. *Positivity* encompasses actions that support cheerful, optimistic, and uncritical interactions with a partner, while self-disclosure and talk about the relationship itself define the strategy of *openness*. *Assurances* are messages that underscore one's commitment to the relationship and emphasize its continuation. *Social networks* imply shared relational affiliations including friends, family, and co-workers. Last, *joint activities* describes when partners participate engage in leisure activities together (Canary & Stafford, 1992; Johnson et al., 2008; Stafford et al., 2000). The first author utilized the dimensions from this scale as a guide to examine approximately 10% of the data. These dimensions were deemed appropriate for analyzing responses. A coauthor and the first author then coded approximately 10% of the open-ended responses and found 88% agreement (Cohen's $\kappa =$ .78) on the placement of responses into larger relational maintenance themes (e.g., positivity, assurance, social networks, etc.).

In order to code for the challenges that arise during gameplay with romantic partners, an inductive approach was developed. The first author and coauthor read through the open-ended responses several times focusing on potential themes and their characteristics (Patton, 2002). First, the primary author read through the data numerous times. Two major themes were identified: (1) whether the descriptions of the challenges were positive or negative in tone; and (2) attributions of blame for these challenges (i.e., self, partner, or both). Next, the first and second author read the data separately and created an initial category system that included labels and descriptions of possible categories under each theme. Examples from the data were used to reinforce the descriptions of each category. The first and second author then came together to discuss, modify, and agree on categories. Interrater reliability was assessed within the major themes (i.e., 100% agreement for positive vs. negative tone and whether the blame was placed on self, partner, or both). The remainder of the data were coded. Finally, the researchers revisited the data and checked them against established categories to ensure consistency (Boeije, 2002).

4.2.3 Perceived Relational Quality Components Inventory

The Perceived Relationship Quality Component (PRQC) Inventory consists of eighteen items (Fletcher, Simpson, & Thomas, 2000). Each perceived relationship quality component is assessed by three items (e.g., "I am satisfied with our relationship" and "I am committed to our relationship"), and measures outcomes related to relationships such as satisfaction, intimacy, commitment, trust, passion, and love. Each statement is answered on a five-point Likert-type scale (ranging from *1 = not at all* to *5 = extremely*). Instructions were to rate the current relationship on each item. Relational quality dimensions were found to have high reliability, satisfaction $\alpha = .88$, commitment $\alpha = .82$, intimacy $\alpha = .81$, trust $\alpha = .77$, passion $\alpha = .85$, love $\alpha = .80$.

4.3 Results

This study illuminates several aspects of how romantic partners experience relational benefits and challenges with regard to play in *League*, representing an underexplored but increasingly popular platform for networked gaming. In particular, it draws attention to the ways relational maintenance strategies and communicative practices intersect with (and are transformed by) the digitally mediated, fantasy-themed, and competition-based environment of this game.

In an effort to provide some much needed description of types of individuals who engage in MOBA play, the following highlights a number of demographic indicators. Although there were a number of responses, thirty-three individuals responded to the majority of the open-ended questions, and were included in the final data analysis. These participants included nineteen men (57.6%) and fourteen women (42.4%), with an average age of 22.15 (SD = 5.39). Twenty-four were Caucasian (72.7%), eight were Asian American (24.2%), and one was Middle Eastern-American (3.0%). Five (15.2%) reported being part of an open heterosexual relationship, twenty-five (75.8%) a monogamous heterosexual relationship, two (6.1%) a monogamous homosexual relationship, and one (3.0%) reported an asexual relationship. When asked which best describes their romantic relationships, eighteen (54.5%) indicated that they were in a dating relationship, nine (27.2%) were in a cohabiting relationship, one (3.0%) was engaged, and five (15.2%) were married. Separately, when asked if they lived with their romantic partner, fourteen (42.4%) indicated yes, and nineteen (57.6%) indicated no. Partners had been romantically involved for an average of 3.84 years (SD = 4.23). On average, players also indicated that they lived 338.15 (SD = 1,142.23) miles from their romantic partner. The median was five miles, which might be a better descriptive statistic to use when describing how far partners live from each other. Almost 68% of the sample lived closer than 20 miles from their partner, while 32% lived farther than 76 miles from their romantic partner.

The most commonly reported years for participants to begin playing *League* were 2012 ($n = 9$), and 2013 ($n = 9$). Eighteen (54.5%) reported being more knowledgeable about *League* than their partner, while nine (27.3%) indicated their partner was more knowledgeable, and six (18.2%) indicated being equally knowledgeable about *League*. Seventeen (51.5%) reported being more skilled at playing *League* than their partner, while eleven (33.3%) indicated their partner was more skilled, and five (15.2%) indicated being equally skilled. Twelve (36.4%) players indicated that Support was their most preferred in-game role, while seven (21.2%) indicated ADC and seven (21.2%) Mid, four (12.1%) responded with Top, and three (9.1%) indicated Jungler. When asked what role was most preferred when playing with their romantic partner, thirteen (39.4%) players indicated that Support was their most preferred in-game role, while nine (27.3%) indicated ADC and seven (21.2%) Mid, two (6.1%) responded with Top, and two (6.1%) indicated Jungler. Players utilized a number of communication technologies to communicate during gameplay, eighteen (54.5%) VOIP, ten (30.3%) face-to-face communication, two (6.1%) in-game chat, two (6.1%) Skype, and one (3.0%) Vsee.[3] Finally, respondents indicated that in

---

[3] Vsee is a video chat and screen-sharing program.

an average week they spend 17.79 (SD = 10.58) hours playing *League*. They also report playing *League* with their romantic partners for 10.39 (SD = 6.49) hours in a typical week.

4.3.1 "We Spend Time Together, We Understand Each Other, and We Play with Friends"

All but two individuals responded to the open-ended prompt: "In your own words, please describe any benefits playing *League* with your partner brings to your relationship." Each response involved at least one benefit that aligned with common themes from relational maintenance literature (e.g., *positivity, openness, assurances, social networks,* and *joint activities*) and many responses involved the mention of multiple strategies. The following describes some typical responses given by participants.

Positivity was identified in nearly half the responses. Individuals usually reported that when playing, "We have fun together." *Positivity* was usually paired with one or more other strategies. Participants described engaging in gameplay as a fun activity they enjoyed. More importantly, when described with other types of relational maintenance behaviors, positivity appeared to underpin productive, mutually enjoyable gaming experiences between romantic partners. Such an exemplar reads:

> We get to spend time together playing a game we both enjoy. We also usually play with friends that don't live in our area, and all talk in a group Skype call, so it's like we are all hanging out again.

In this response the participant lists their benefits as enjoying playing together, spending time together, and playing with friends. While positivity is less obviously marked, what characterizes positivity is the mention of enjoyment. Overall, despite some challenges participants reported (which we later cover in detail), answers indicate the importance of having fun, enjoyable interactions with their romantic partners, and friends. Creating these pleasurable gaming experiences were described relatively often as a benefit of playing *League* with their partner.

Twenty-four of the responses included mention of playing *League* with their partner as beneficial because of its nature as a *joint activity*. Despite the implicit assumption that participants likely play with their partner because they enjoy it together, we looked for specific language markers that directly stated some variation of "spending time together" or "something to do together" to indicate that participants understood the role of joint activities as a benefit in their relationship. One response stated very clearly: "It's a common interest we share.

We spend together and with friends without simply sitting on Skype. There's an activity we can do together while we're at home (don't live together)." This type of language regarding *League* as a "common interest" was often present, and indicates an important point of connection for these couples. As mentioned earlier, on average, individuals are spending approximately 10 of the 17 hours per week playing *League with* their romantic partners.

Openness and *assurances* were described less often as benefits, but they were included. One respondent included the following remarks:

> We understand each other more. I know what she is thinking and she knows what I'm thinking. In a game she made a good play and I followed up and in real life I know where she wants to go out and eat, etc.

The mention of "understanding each other more" and knowing what each other thinks indicate an openness based on shared communication within the game. Naturally, this openness leads to assurances among relational partners. This respondent also emphasizes how he or she might follow up an in-game action with out-of-game actions that work to bolster the relationship and perpetuate its existence.

In many instances, participants described complex relational maintenance strategies that coexist to support relational integration and health. One participant beautifully illustrates *assurances*, while concurrently describing the importance that *social networks* and engaging in *joint activities* has on this valued romantic relationship.

They note:

> We live two hours away from each other, so it is nice to have something we could still do together even while being apart physically on the weekdays. We also use *League* to hang out with other friends as well! It's nice to at least see/hear my fiancé interact with our friends, and him being so accepting of me in the 'guy' group.

Beyond the specific notation about "hang[ing] out with other friends," representing the presence of *social networks* as a benefit, the participant's mention of being accepted in the "guy group" is an indicator of *assurances* as it reinforces the importance of the participants' acceptance to their future as a couple, since serious relationships often include the blending of friend groups. Additionally, we see that playing *League* helps this couple engage in an activity that promotes communication, spending time together, fun, and access to friend groups, all while they are physically separated from one another. Thus, one can assume they are crediting playing *League* as something that helps sustain the relationship, despite geographic distance.

A variety of strategies were present in participants' answers and they manifested in various patterns. The only pair of strategies that seemed to have a strong co-presence was playing *League* as a *joint activity* and as a *social networking* opportunity. Last, although we included the potential for antisocial behavior in the coding for these reported benefits, we found no occurrences of these behaviors.

4.3.2 "It's You, It's Me, It's Us"

To understand better what players get out of playing *League* with their partners, we sought to explore the challenges they may face. To counter the benefits prompt we asked: "In your own words, please describe any challenges playing *League* with your partner brings to your relationship" and received twenty-seven responses. Overall, although individuals were asked about challenges, ten responses were coded as positive in tone. Four of these players (three female, one male) indicated they encountered no challenges while playing *League* together and answered with some variant of "None." The other six players variously listed a complaint but framed it in such a way that downplayed the challenging aspect. Three of these participants attributed the challenge to their partner and three placed responsibility on both partners equally.

An example of a positively toned, equal attribution response arises in the following response: "He's so good and I'm not that good, but we work really well which is amazing!!" The next example illustrates a positively toned, partner attribution response: "Sometimes she rages, but that gets settled down. She is working on it: P." Although these types of responses listed more negative behaviors, the overall tone remained cheerful and optimistic about the experience.

In contrast, seventeen participants' responses were coded as negatively toned, and these paired with various attributions of who was to blame for those challenges (two self, six partner, nine equally at fault). Negative responses varied linguistically in what might be described as the level of "intensity" the challenge seemed to pose for couples. For example, a fairly mild but undeniably negative response arises in the following sample response: "We rarely argue normally, but when we play *League* we are both terrible selfish people." Compare this to a more typical response found in the sample, the tone of which is much more concerning with regards to potential relational outcomes: "Sometimes, if we go on a very long loss streak, we will quietly sit there, contemplating things. Sometimes he screams or hits something, but other than that, it's just quiet. I get a little scared, but only from the random noises that comes out of nowhere, interrupting the silence."

Table 4.1 *Relational Quality Dimensions*

	Satisfaction	Commitment	Intimacy	Trust	Passion	Love	Composite Relational Quality
Mean	4.6190	4.7429	4.6476	4.6190	4.0857	4.8190	4.5889
Std. deviation	.50580	.44344	.54798	.49930	.86826	.34625	.45618

The attribution of who is at fault for the couple facing challenges also varied. First, the majority of couples, whether their responses were coded as positively or negatively toned, placed equal responsibility on both themselves and their partner for the challenges. A few responses exemplify equal placement of blame through the use of the plural pronoun "We": "We both get rather heated and will take it out on each other in the moment during games." However, some participants blamed the challenges they face on their partners ($n = 9$). One participant responded:

> Usually if I make a bad play, he gets upset, he treats every game like it's ranked[4] and that just stresses me out sometimes, and I know I don't always make perfect plays, but I do try really hard to be good at the game.

In this example the participant names her own mistakes as related to the challenge but ultimately blames her partner for overreacting, despite the participant's efforts. Last, only two participants reported that they were solely at fault for the existence of challenges. One response manifested as follows: "In our relationship, I'm the rager. As such, I'm sure it's hard for her to deal with my whining – I for one wouldn't be able to deal with it if she acted the same way I do." In this case, the participant identifies himself as "the rager" and goes as far as to commend their partner for handling the participant's aggressive frustration so well.

4.3.3 Perceived Relational Quality

We asked participants several items about different aspects of the quality of their relationship with their romantic partner. Overall, participants reported feeling high levels of satisfaction, commitment, intimacy, trust, and love in their relationship with romantic partners (Table 4.1). The composite score indicates a high relational quality score, overall.

---

[4] A ranked game is one in which the outcome counts toward players' account-wide ranking, which are seen as indicative of status and expertise; in *League* communities, ranked games are often believed to elicit the most toxic and antisocial player behavior.

4.4 Discussion

Having similar interests and spending time with romantic partners are essential parts of sustaining romantic relationships. By examining how new technologies facilitate this process, we can begin to see the ways they provide opportunities for reconceptualizing communication in these relationships. One important finding from the current study is that participants have described unique ways that they are "playing" together. Vangelisti (2011) notes that significant research on the time that couples spend with each other indicates "…that people who are happy in their relationship not only spend more time together, but they also engage in activities that make their time together particular rewarding" (p. 614). Finding time to engage in activities as a couple is not uncommon, as many couples go to the movies together, exercise together, or generally hang out with friends in their spare time. What the current study suggests is that some couples prefer to play online games as a way to date, spend time together, and solidify expectations in relationships. Specifically, these individuals spend an average of 10 hours per week together playing *League*. Further, with one-third of individuals living more than 50 miles apart, time playing *League* might be the only time they get to "be" with one another. A portion of participants also indicated that this activity was a very positive way to learn more about their partners, have fun with them, and connect in ways that distance would normally not allow. What might be useful for researchers to consider is the relationship rituals these couples are establishing within the game as ways to sustain healthy relationships long term. For example, what roles, characters, and communications are shared within gameplay that support positive communication among these couples? What types of interactions are being established that could be disrupted during shifts in relational dynamics (e.g., moving from long distance to geographically close, changes in relationship status, or birth of a child)? Additionally, how might gameplay potentially combat negative outcomes associated with some of these shifts? For example, how might promoting teamwork in games be related to coparenting skills and sharing of household responsibilities and chores? These questions should be examined in future research.

Another important finding from the current study is the emphasis that most individuals placed on the role of their social networks in their gameplay with their romantic partner. Following Parks (2006), significant work on understanding close relationships by identifying the importance of the personal networks they are embedded in, we see online gaming as a context for this examination. If couples are using this time together as a way to also spend time with friends, gameplay could be a symbolic activity used to test the strength of the romantic bond, identify the fit of a potential romantic partner into the larger social network, or provide support that romantic partners receive when working on sustaining these important relationships. We find it meaningful that online gaming can be used as a way to blend friendship groups (Shulman, 1975), regardless of whether those friendship groups developed inside or outside the game itself (Williams et al., 2006).

The current project identified some relationship-enhancing elements, as well as some typically concerning communicative behaviors couples experience with their partners during gameplay. Participants are clearly engaging in partner and self-blame during gameplay, thus creating norms for negative communication. Gottman (1994) identified the toxicity of criticism within married couples, noting that couples might develop a sequence of negative communication that can predict marital dissolution. Although complaints concerning negative behaviors is necessary for any relationship to develop and grow, when complaints are long term they can be perceived as inciting contempt toward the partner, defensiveness in conflict, and withdrawal from the partner and the relationship. Our findings suggest that although there is partner and self-blame for many of the challenges of playing online games together, these individuals describe framing these challenges as something "we" should work on together. Gottman (1994) suggests that as long as negative communication is counterbalanced with positive communication (a 5:1 ratio), then couples maintain fairly healthy perspectives of the relationship and their partner. Playing *League* has a unique benefit for couples, as they can view themselves as being part of a "team." Choosing who is on the team can provide assurances to the partner of his or her place within the partner's life, and solidify positive regard they already have established over time.

Despite the challenges some couples reported facing, these same couples report high relational quality in terms of feeling satisfaction, commitment, intimacy, trust, passion, and love. We suggest that these high relational quality scores provide insight into some of the unique ways relationships are experienced and enjoyed via gaming together. However, owing to the small sample size, questions concerning negative communication among couples (blaming partner), and relational quality remain. There is much work to be done to understand fully the communicative landscape for couples during gameplay, especially when these games are typically saturated with aggressive communication. Additionally, measuring outcomes variables in romantic relationships (e.g., satisfaction, love, and commitment) might not reflect the full range of both positive and negative communicative behaviors present within these relationships (Vangelisti, 2011). The authors suggest multimethod approaches to help understand the nuance to positive and negative communication within gameplay, as well as empirically testing predictive models to identify a number of outcome variables associated with romantic partners' online gameplay.

We believe this study also lays the foundation for meaningful contributions to the study of digital games. Placed alongside a trajectory of scholarly study that explores the instrumental roles games can play in forming and sustaining relationships – whether between "virtual" strangers (Pearce, 2009), family members (Jordan, 2014), peer groups (Domahidi et al., 2014; Taylor et al., 2014), or loved ones (Carr & Oliver, 2009; Ratan & Tsai, 2014) – this research draws from theories of relational maintenance to take a more nuanced look at the connections between MOBA play and relational health. Specifically, our work begins to document, and theorize, how joint play in the intense, often hostile communicative contexts of *League* can be both a site of nurturing, supportive interactions between romantic partners and a source of frustration and duress. Moreover, as most game studies research on romantic couples to date focuses on MMOGs (Carr & Oliver, 2009; Nardi, 2010; Williams et al., 2006), the present research offers a productive point of comparison. We can now start to address, for instance, the affordances for and challenges to conventional relational maintenance strategies posed by a game that features relatively short, action-packed, and combat-focused play sessions rather than the more "sandbox," persistent worlds of MMOGS; that leaves little time, during play, for text-based communication; and that offers no intrinsic support for the kinds of formal associations (such as "guilds" in *World of Warcraft*) typically regarded as a safe and supportive social system for couples (see, e.g., Bergstrom, 2009; Williams et al., 2006).

That said, given *League*'s reputation for its often antagonistic community (Kou & Nardi, 2014; Ratan & Tsai, 2014), it is encouraging, if not surprising, that in the majority of responses we analyzed, participants reported that shared *League* play represents a rewarding activity that is being used to sustain romantic relationships. This insight provides a degree of nuance to the commonly received perception that *League* as a site for social interactions is primarily, if not exclusively characterized by aggression and toxicity. This opens up avenues for further exploration into the broader-than-expected range of communicative dynamics that *League* supports, while also demonstrating the usefulness of interpersonal communication theories and conceptual frameworks (such as relational maintenance) to studies of networked digital play.

4.5 Limitations and Future Research

This study could benefit from a more nuanced look at the negative communicative patterns that are harmful to relationships in the long term. Additionally, a closer analysis of the role that gender and sexuality play in couples' challenges may enhance the study's importance to both game studies and interpersonal communication studies. Although not a limitation of the current study, these goals might be accomplished through strengthening the results and findings with a larger sample size and a more focused quantitative methodological approach. Recruiting participants who play MOBAs other than *League* such as *Defense of the Ancients 2* or *Heroes of the Storm* could further strengthen the generalizability of future quantitative results.

4.6 Conclusion

In exploring the specific relational processes used by couples who play *League of Legends* together, this work stands to contribute substantially to both interpersonal communication and digital game studies. With respect to the former, an understanding of how conventional relational maintenance strategies are re-mediated by the communicative affordances and constraints of games, and by MOBAs in particular, can help illuminate the novel challenges and opportunities confronting couples who play together. With respect to the latter, insights into how couples play *League of Legends* can contribute to our broader understanding of how players interact in this relatively new and increasingly popular genre, including how they navigate (and possibly, help produce) the often toxic forms these interactions take.

References

Anderson, T. L., & Emmers-Sommer, T. M. (2006). Predictors of relationship satisfaction in online romantic relationships. *Communication Studies*, 57, 153–172.

Ayres, J. (1983). Strategies to maintain relationship: Their identification and perceived usage. *Communication Quarterly*, 31, 62–67.

Bergstrom, K. (2009). *Adventuring together: Exploring how couples use MMOs as part of their shared leisure time*. MA thesis, University of Calgary.

Boeije, H. (2002). A purposeful approach to the constant comparative method in the analysis of qualitative interviews. *Quality and Quantity*, 36, 391–409.

Canary, D. J., & Stafford, L. (1992). Relational maintenance strategies and equity in marriage. *Communication Monographs*, 59, 243–266.

Canary, D. J., & Stafford, L. (2001). Equity in the preservation of personal relationships. In J. Harvey & A. Wenzel (eds.), *Close romantic relationships* (pp. 133–152). Mahwah, NJ: Lawrence Erlbaum Associates.

Canary, D. J., Stafford, L., Hause, K. S., & Wallace, L. A. (1993). An inductive analysis of relational maintenance strategies: Comparisons among lovers, relatives, friends, and other. *Communication Research Report*, 10, 5–14.

Carlson, P. (2013, Sept. 12). New *League of Legends* video uses stats to show how "rage doesn't win games". *PC Gamer*. Retrieved from: www.pcgamer.com/2013/09/12/new-league-of-legends-video-uses-stats-toshow-how-rage-doesnt-win-games/

Carr, D., & Oliver, M. (2009). Tanks, chauffeurs and backseat drivers: Competence in MMORPGs. Eludamos, 3(1), 43–53. Retrieved from: www.eludamos.org/index .php/eludamos/article/viewArticle/56/107

Chory, R. M., & Banfield, S. (2009). Media dependence and relational maintenance in interpersonal relationships. *Communication Reports*, 22, 41–53.

Dailey, R. M., Lee, C. M., & Spitzberg, B. H. (2007). Communicative aggression: Toward a more interactional view of psychological abuse. In B. H. Spitzberg & W. R. Cupach (eds.), *The dark side of interpersonal communication* (pp. 297–326). Mahwah, NJ: Lawrence Erlbaum Associates.

Dainton, M., & Aylor, B. (2002). Patterns of communication channel use in the maintenance of long-distance relationships. *Communication Research Reports*, 19, 118–129.

Dainton, M., & Gross, J. (2008). The use of negative behaviors to maintain relationships. *Communication Research Reports*, 25, 179–191.

Dainton, M., & Stafford, L. (1993). Routine maintenance behaviors: A comparison of relationship type, partner similarity and sex differences. *Journal of Social and Personal Relationships*, 10, 255–271.

Dindia, K., & Baxter, L. A. (1987). Strategies for maintaining and repairing marital relationships. *Journal of Social and Personal Relationships*, 4, 143–158.

Dindia, K., & Canary, D. J. (1993). Definitions and theoretical perspectives on maintaining relationships. *Journal of Social and Personal Relationships*, 10, 163–173.

Domahidi, E., Festl, R., & Quandt, T. (2014). To dwell among gamers: Investigating the relationship between social online game use and gaming-related friendships. *Computers in Human Behavior*, 35, 107–115.

Entertainment Software Association. (2013). Essential Facts about the computer and video game industry report. Retrieved from: http://webcache.googleusercontent .com/search?q=cache:4RKJfYQV6YQJ: www.theesa.com/facts/pdfs/ESA_EF_ 2013.pdf±&cd=1&hl=en&ct=clnk&gl=us&client=firefox-a

Fletcher, G. J. O., Simpson, J. A., & Thomas, G. (2000). The measurement of perceived relationship quality components: A confirmatory factor analytic approach. *Personality and Social Psychology Bulletin*, 26, 340–354.

Gottman, J. M. (1994). *What predicts divorce? The relationship between marital processes and marital outcomes*. Hillsdale, NJ: Lawrence Erlbaum Associates.

Houser, M., Fleuriest, C. & Estrada, D. (2012). The cyber factor: An analysis of relational maintenance through the use of computer mediated communication. *Communication Research Reports*, 29, 34–43.

Huynh, K-P., Lim, S-W. & Skoric, M. M. (2013). Stepping out of the magic circle: Regulation of play/life boundary in MMO-mediated romantic relationship. *Journal of Computer-Mediated Communication*, 18, 251–264.

Jenson, J., & de Castell, S. (2008). Theorizing gender and digital gameplay: Oversights, accidents and surprises. *Eludamos. Journal for Computer Game Culture*, 2, 15–25.

Johnson, A. J., Haigh, M. M., Becker, J. A. H., Craig, E. A., & Wigley, S. (2008). College students' use of relational management strategies in Email in longdistance and geographically close relationships. *Journal of Computer-Mediated Communication*, 13, 381–404.

Jordan, N. (2014). World of warcraft: A family therapist's journey into scapegoated culture. *The Qualitative Report*, 19(31), 1–19. Retrieved from: http://proxying.lib.ncsu.edu/index.php?url=/docview/1552716842?accountid=12725

Kou, Y., & Nardi, B (2014). Governance in *League of Legends*: A hybrid system. In *Proceedings from Foundation of Digital Games Conference*, Fort Lauderdale, FL. Retrieved from: www.ics.uci.edu/~yubok/Kou_FDG2014_cameraready.pdf

Laliker, M. K., & Lannutti, P. J. (2014). Remapping the topography of couples' daily interactions: electronic messages. *Communication Research Reports*, 31, 262–271.

Leary, M. R., Springer, C., Negel, L., Ansell, E., & Evans, K. (1998). The causes, phenomenology, and consequences of hurt feelings. *Journal of Personality and Social Psychology*, 74, 1225–1237.

Ledbetter, A. M., & Kuznekoff, J. H. (2012). More than a game: Friendship relational maintenance and attitudes toward Xbox LIVE communication. *Communication Research*, 39, 269–290.

Linderoth, J., Björk, S., & Olsson, C. (2014). Should I stay or should I go? A study of pickup groups in *Left 4 Dead 2*. Special Issue, *Nordic DIGRA 2012*, 1 (2). Retrieved from: http://todigra.org/index.php/todigra/article/view/15.

McManus, C. (2012, Oct. 12). *League of Legends* the world's 'most played video game'. *CNet*. Retrieved from: http://news.cnet.com/8301-17938_105-57531578-1/leagueof-legends-the-worlds-most-played-video-game/

McWhertor, M. (2012, Oct. 13). The *League of Legends* team of scientists trying to cure 'toxic behavior' online. *Polygon*. Retrieved from: www.polygon.com/2012/10/17/3515178/the-league-of-legends-team-ofscientists-trying-to-cure-toxic

Meng, J., & Williams, D. (2012). Channel matters: Media multiplicity and social capital for multiplayer online battle gamers. In *Proceedings from International Communication Association Conference*. Phoenix, AZ.

Meng, J., Williams, D., & Shen, C. (2012). Who do you play with? Social capital and media multiplicity for online gamers. In *Proceedings from International Communication Association Annual Conference*, Phoenix, AZ.

Merolla, A. J. (2010). Relational maintenance during military deployment: Perspectives of wives of deployed US soldiers. *Journal of Applied Communication Research*, 38, 4–26.

Messman, S. J., Canary, D. J., & Hause, K. S. (2000). Motives to remain platonic, equity, and the use of maintenance strategies in opposite-sex friendships. *Journal of Social and Personal Relationships*, 17, 67–94.

Mitchell, E. (1985). The dynamics of family interaction around home video games. *Marriage & Family Review*, 8, 121–135. Retrieved from: http://dx.doi.org/10.1300/J002v08n01_10

Murray, J. M., Arns, D. C., Chesney, T., de Castell, S., Jenson, J., & Taylor, N. (2012). *Reynard Verus Final Report*. Prepared by SRI International for the Air Force Research Laboratory (AFRL-RY-2012-0286).

Nardi, B. (2010). *My life as a Night Elf priest: An anthropological account of* World of Warcraft. Ann Arbor, MI: University of Michigan Press.

Park, M. R. (2006). *Personal relationships and personal networks*. Mahwah, NJ: Lawrence Erlbaum Associates.

Patton, M. Q. (2002). *Qualitative research and evaluation methods*. Thousand Oaks, CA: SAGE.

Pearce, C. (2009). *Communities of play: Emergent cultures in multiplayer games and virtual worlds.* Cambridge, MA: MIT Press.

Ratan, R., & Tsai, H. S. (2014). Dude, where's my Avacar? A mixed-method examination of communication in the driving context. *Pervasive and Mobile Computing.* doi: 10.1016/j.pmcj.2014.05.011

Shulman, N. (1975). Life-cycle variations in patterns of close relationships. *Journal of Marriage and the Family*, 37, 354–356.

Sicart, M. (2011). Against procedurality. *Game Studies*, 11(3). Retrieved from: gamestudies.org/1103/articles/sicart_ap

Sidelinger, R. J., Ayash, G., Godorhazy, A., & Tibbles, D. (2008). Couples go online: Relational maintenance behaviors and relational characteristics use in dating relationships. *Human Communication: A Publication of the Pacific and Asian Communication Association*, 11, 341–356.

Stafford, L. (2005). *Maintaining long-distance and cross-residential relationships.* Mahwah, NJ: Lawrence Erlbaum Associates.

Stafford, L. (2011). Measuring relationship maintenance behaviors: Critique and development of the revised relationship maintenance behavior scale. *Journal of Social and Personal Relationships*, 28, 278–303.

Stafford, L., Dainton, M. A., & Hass, S. (2000). Measuring routine and strategic relational maintenance: Scale revision, sex versus gender roles, and the prediction of relational characteristics. *Communication Monographs*, 37, 306–323.

Tassi, P. (2014a, Jan. 27). Riot's *'League of Legends'* reveals astonishing 27 million daily players, 67 million players monthly. *Forbes.* Retrieved from: www.forbes.com/sites/insertcoin/2014/01/27/riots-league-of-legendsreveals-astonishing-27-million-daily-players-67-million-monthly/

Tassi, P. (2014b, July 19). *'World of Warcraft'* still a $1B powerhouse even as subscription MMOs decline. *Forbes.* Retrieved from: www.forbes.com/sites/insertcoin/2014/07/19/world-of-warcraft-still-a-1b-powerhouse-even-assubscription-mmos-decline/

Taylor, N., de Castell, S., Jenson, J., & Humphrey, M. (2011). Modeling play: Re-casting expertise in MMOGs. In *Proceedings of the SIGGRAPH2011 Conference*, Vancouver, BC, August 8–10.

Taylor, N., Jenson, J., de Castell, S., & Dilouya, B. (2014). Public displays of play: Studying online games in physical settings. *Journal of Computer-Mediated Communication*, 19, 763–779.

Taylor, T. L. (2006a). Does WoW change everything? How a PvP server, multinational player base, and surveillance mod scene caused me pause. *Games and Culture*, 1, 318–337.

Taylor, T. L. (2006b). *Play between worlds: Exploring online game culture.* Cambridge, MA: MIT Press.

Taylor, T. L. (2009). The assemblage of play. *Games and Culture*, 4, 331–339.

Vangelisti, A. (2011). Interpersonal processes in romantic relationships. In M. L. Knapp & J. A. Daly (eds.), *Handbook of interpersonal communication* (pp. 527–562). Thousand Oaks, CA: SAGE.

Williams, D., Consalvo, M., Caplan, S., & Yee, N. (2009). Looking for gender (LFG): Gender roles and behaviors among online gamers. *Journal of Communication*, 59, 700–725.

Williams, D., Ducheneaut, N., Xiong, L., Zhang, Y., Yee, N., & Nickell, E. (2006). From tree house to barracks: The social life of guilds in *World of Warcraft*. *Games and Culture*, 1, 338–361.

Yee, N., Ducheneaut, N., Yao, M., & Nelson, L. (2011). Do men heal more when in drag? Conflicting identity cues between user and avatar. In *Proceedings of ACM CHI '11 Conference on Human Factors in Computing Systems* (pp. 773–776).

PART II

Groups: Norms, Leadership, and Virtual Organizations

5

Virtual Team Communication Norms: Modeling the Mediating Effects of Relational Trust, Presence, and Identity on Conversational Interactivity, Openness, and Satisfaction

JOHN C. SHERBLOM, LESLEY A. WITHERS,
LYNNETTE G. LEONARD, AND JEFFREY S. SMITH

5.1 Introduction

For individuals who work or game together online, the difference between a successful collaboration and disappointment often hinges on the quality of a virtual team's communication. Over time, teams develop communication norms of conversational interactivity, openness, and satisfaction. These norms are often unstated, but become part of the team's routine ways of communicating, including participants' ideas about appropriate topics of conversation, expectations of feedback, appropriate turn-taking behaviors, openness to self-disclosure, and satisfaction with the ongoing interaction among group members.

In virtual teams, developing and maintaining effective communication norms for conversational interactivity, openness, and satisfaction are often difficult. Several aspects of participant computer-mediated communication (CMC) competence, such as skill, efficacy, and confidence, influence the development of these norms (Sherblom, Withers, & Leonard, 2013; Sundararajan, 2009, 2010). Relational attributes, such as trust, presence, and identity also have an effect on virtual team communication (Leonard et al., 2015). Managing these various influences is essential to effective virtual team collaboration.

Developing an effective collaboration within a virtual environment is particularly important to teams whose members are geographically dispersed. The ability to share ideas freely, strategize together, be understood by other team members, and feel connected to other participants through their avatar representations is important to constructing a shared virtual team relational space in which to interact (Leonard & Withers, 2009). Developing this shared virtual space in which members feel a sense of togetherness builds team cohesion and facilitates effective communication.

The purpose of the present study is to examine two types of influences on virtual team collaboration. We analyze these influences by surveying participants at universities in the United States and eastern Europe after they have engaged in team problem-solving projects in the virtual environment of *Second Life*®. Our survey measures the personal competence of participants in using the CMC medium, the relational attributes among team members, and the norms of team conversation that develop. The study then models the influences of personal competence and relational attributes on these team conversational norms. We predict that personal competence, as measured through each individual's level of skill, efficacy, and confidence in using the CMC medium, is necessary but not sufficient to facilitate interactive, open, and satisfying virtual team communication. In addition to this personal competence, team members must develop the relational attributes of trust, presence, and identity to facilitate interactive, open, and satisfying communication.

5.2 Background

This study is grounded in three eras of CMC theory development that inform the understanding of computer-mediated communication (Houtman Makos, & Meacock, 2014; Oztok & Brett, 2011). The first era focuses on the influence of the medium. The second describes the communication competencies of the people engaging in CMC. The third analyzes the relationships that develop among those people in their interpersonal relationships, virtual teams, and communities.

Theories representing the first era, such as media richness, emphasize the role of the medium as a major influence on communication, in a way that is sometimes referred to as technological determinism (Daft & Lengel, 1986; Lengel & Daft, 1988; Trevino, Daft, & Lengel, 1990). Walther and his colleagues provide reviews and critiques of these early perspectives (Walther, 2004; Walther, Loh, & Granka, 2005; Walther & Parks, 2002). The more recent theories of the second era, such as social information processing and media naturalness, focus on how communicators develop personal competence in using the medium (Kock, 2004, 2005; Walther, 2009, 2010). This personal competence is often measured in an individual's perceived skill, efficacy, and confidence in communicating with others through the medium. The third era is represented in theories such as the hyperpersonal perspective and theories of virtual community that analyze the relational influences that shape CMC and the development of relationships in virtual environments (Walther, 2010; Willson, 2006).

Taking this third perspective, Leonard et al. (2015) argue that personal competence with a CMC medium is necessary, but not sufficient, for effective virtual team communication. They suggest that competence with the medium is required but, in addition, virtual team members must develop a sense of relational trust, presence, and identity for the team to achieve interactivity, openness, and member satisfaction in its conversations. Only with the development of relational trust, presence, and identity, in addition to personal skill, efficacy, and confidence, can a virtual team achieve conversational interactivity, openness, and satisfaction. Their study shows that these relational attributes can be developed through participant training programs, but they do not directly test the relationship of these relational attributes to team member conversational participation.

The present study compares two path analysis models. The first model examines the influence of personal competence, as measured in an individual's skill, efficacy, and confidence, on virtual team conversational norms. The second model includes the relational influences of trust, presence, and identity on the virtual team's conversational interactivity, openness, and satisfaction. The goal of the study is to test whether these relational attributes contribute substantially to the personal competence influences described by Leonard et al. (2015).

5.3 Personal Competence: Skill, Efficacy, and Confidence

Several lines of research describe the influence of CMC competence on virtual team communication. One line identifies participant skill with using the CMC medium as a primary influence (Bubas, Radosevic, & Hutinski, 2003). A second focuses on how a person's sense of efficacy in using the medium affects communication (Kelly et al., 2010; Wrench & Punyanunt-Carter, 2007). A third examines the confidence of participants in being able to express themselves appropriately, interpret the meanings of others, engage in smooth virtual conversations, and develop social relationships as a major influence (Spitzberg, 2006). These three lines of research indicate that skill, efficacy, and confidence each play an influential role and each competency must be developed over time, through individual effort and experience with the medium, for effective team communication to occur.

Media naturalness theory predicts that virtual communication initially requires more time, cognitive effort, and experience to develop these skills. It argues that humans have become adapted through evolution with neurologically optimized brains designed to function most efficiently in synchronous face-to-face communication, with its auditory and visual cues that assist in the interpretation of another person's meaning (Kock, 2004, 2005). The less a communication medium incorporates colocated, face-to-face, synchronous speech, the greater the cognitive effort required for a person to both convey and under-stand meaning. Over time, people can develop the cognitive schemas and social skills needed to communicate effectively in a virtual environment, but devel-oping these schemas and learning the appropriate skills requires substantial cognitive effort and practice (DeRosa et al., 2004; Kock, 2008; Kock, Verville, & Garza, 2007). Once people develop the cognitive schema and social skill to communicate effectively through a medium, however, the virtual environment begins to feel more natural and participants experience greater cognitive ease in coordinating and managing their meanings with others (Kock, 2004, 2005). Hence, personal skill, efficacy, and confidence are important to communicating effectively in a CMC medium.

5.3.1 Skill

Skill with communicating in a CMC medium develops through repeated inter-action with others and is a major influence on a person's ability to be expressive, attentive to others, and engage in smooth conversational coordination (Bubas et al., 2003). Expressiveness recognizes the ability to create messages that seem alive and animated to others. Attentiveness shows in a person's interest, con-cern, affection, and adaptability to others. Coordination means being able to achieve smooth conversational transitions, timing, topic initiation, and conver-sational repairs as needed (Bubas et al., 2003).

5.3.2 Efficacy

Efficacy describes the belief among participants that they have the necessary cognitive schema and social abilities to communicate effectively through a medium. Some communicators experience CMC reticence, apprehension, anx-iety, and inhibition, which can reduce their ability to express their meanings and emotions effectively (Kelly et al., 2010). Hence, anxiety, apprehension, and ret-icence affect a person's ability to communicate effectively in a virtual medium (Wrench & Punyanunt-Carter, 2007).

5.3.3 Confidence

Confidence is the sense that one has the social knowledge and skill to commu-nicate, and the ability to accurately interpret the meanings of others (Spitzberg, 2006). A virtual environment has particular communication constraints and affordances, and a participant must develop an ability to communicate effec-tively within them (Erhardt et al., 2016). A person's confidence in having the ability to perform competently within a virtual environment affects the willingness and motivation to participate. Confidence builds over time as a person experiences successful virtual conversations and develops relationships with others (Spitzberg, 2006). These positive experiences orient a person toward increased attentiveness, expressiveness, and willingness to engage in future conversations. This confidence facilitates conversational interactivity, openness, and the likelihood of satisfaction (Spitzberg, 2006).

5.3.4 Importance of Skill, Efficacy, and Confidence

Sherblom et al. (2013) use regression analysis to examine the influence of skill, efficacy, and confidence on virtual team communication. They conclude that increased skill, efficacy, and confidence, as represented in a lack of apprehension, positively affect virtual team conversations. They do not, however, investigate the potential of relational influences.

Leonard et al. (2015) do examine the relational influences of trust, presence, and identity on virtual team conversation. Their qualitative analysis indicates that relational trust, sense of presence, and development of an online identity all affect virtual team interactivity, openness, and satisfaction (Leonard et al., 2015). Building on their findings, the present study examines these influences: first by modeling the effects of personal skill, confidence, and efficacy, and then by modeling the additional influences of relational trust, presence, and identity.

5.4 Relational Attributes: Trust, Presence, and Identity

5.4.1 Trust

Trust is a complex relational attribute that influences both face-to-face and virtual team communication (Feng, Lazar, & Preece, 2004; Henderson & Gilding, 2004; Himelboim et al., 2012; Sarker et al., 2011). Trust between communicators builds over time. It is assessed as reputations develop among participants who judge each other to be trustworthy, or not, based on patterns of behavior that fulfill or disappoint expectations. Trustworthiness is the perception that a person possesses a set of relational communication characteristics such as responsiveness, benevolence, cooperation, and integrity that are beneficial to the team (Beldad, de Jong, & Steehouder, 2010; Cheng & Macaulay, 2013; Henderson & Gilding, 2004; Jarvenpaa & Leidner, 1998; Morrison, Cegielski, & Rainer, 2012; Schiller, Mennecke, Nah, & Luse, 2014).

Some characteristics of a virtual environment, such as the reduced social cues, perception of anonymity, and asynchronous communication, can create interpersonal uncertainty that hinders the development of trust and assessment of trustworthiness (Beldad et al., 2010; Henderson & Gilding, 2004; Jarvenpaa & Leidner, 1998; Nam, 2014; Turilli, Vaccaro, & Taddeo, 2010). It is possible, however, for communicators to compensate for these reduced social cues, increased anonymity, and asynchronous communication through clear, specific, frequent verbal statements and development of a social presence (Jarvenpaa & Leidner, 1998). Communicating with others through avatars provides adequate social information for participants to both express and assess trustworthiness over time (Henderson & Gilding, 2004; Turilli et al., 2010). Additionally, online relational trust builds as a participant's sense of presence. With that presence, participant feelings of connectedness, openness, and commitment to the group task increase (Beldad et al., 2010; Green-Hamann & Sherblom, 2014; Hains, 2014; Himelboim et al., 2012; Morrison et al., 2012).

5.4.2 Presence

Presence represents a person's subjective psychological state in which the individual does not perceive the technology as mediating the interpretation of sensory stimuli (Aymerich-Franch, 2010). Instead, the individual overlooks the technology as an influence on the interpretation of that experience (International Society for Presence Research, 2000). This conception of presence has moved away from a focus on the media richness or capacity as affecting a person's thoughts and feelings about the ongoing social, relational, and contextual processes in a virtual environment. Recent conceptualizations of presence focus more on how virtual community participants use the affordances of the medium to build relationships with other team members (Erhardt et al., 2016; Houtman et al., 2014; Kehrwald, 2008; Sherblom, 2010; Tu & McIsaac, 2002).

Thus, presence is a subjective, relational phenomenon that is dependent on the ability and willingness of participants to achieve interpersonal relationships with others. It represents a dynamic phenomenon rather than a simple learned behavior or skill (Kehrwald, 2008). Individuals must participate in an ongoing performance of presence that demonstrates to others that they have a willingness and ability to communicate within the virtual environment and to engage in interpersonal relationships (Kehrwald, 2008). This idea of presence places agency in the individual, rather than in the medium, and adds a relationally performative component. Participants must negotiate the medium, establish their presence through self-disclosure, and actively demonstrate that presence through ongoing relational cues that show an attentiveness, trust, empathy, rapport, and emotional expressiveness (Kehrwald, 2008; Sherblom, 2010).

The ability of individuals to effectively negotiate the virtual environment and construct this performative sense of presence in their conversations influences their ability to actively participate in the conversations of a virtual team and build personal satisfaction with those interactions (Houtman et al., 2014; Kehrwald, 2008).

The realism of the virtual environment, sophistication of avatar designs, and avatar-mediated communication facilitate this sense of presence (Jin & Bolebruch, 2010). Virtual team members frequently report experiencing high levels of presence in the vivid, immersive, three-dimensional spaces of virtual environments (Aymerich-Franch, 2010; Biocca, Kim, & Choi, 2001; Jin & Bolebruch, 2009; Leonard et al., 2015). Within this virtual environment, presence is associated with feelings of connectivity, immediacy, intimacy, warmth, mutual social awareness, involvement, and emotional accessibility (Green-Hamann, Eichhorn, & Sherblom, 2011; Jin & Bolebruch, 2009; Lee, 2004; Nowak, 2001; Sivunen & Nordbäck, 2015). These feelings produce important influences on a team's communication in the virtual environment, affecting team member interactivity, openness, and satisfaction.

5.4.3 Identity

The use of a screen name, or pseudonym, and consistently recognizable avatar appearance establishes a person's identity within a virtual community and helps develop an online reputation (Leonard & Toller, 2012). This identity contains both internal (personal) and external (social) components. The internal component is a person's self-belief, such as perceiving oneself to be honorable, competent, or funny. The external aspect represents how a person talks to and connects with others, and the types of social interactions that person participates in, such as belonging to and identifying with a particular group or maintaining friendships with certain types of individuals (Cheek & Briggs, 1982; Leary, Wheeler, & Jenkins, 1986). "Through their avatars and associated profiles, virtual world residents can establish their virtual identities, which can be molded according to their desires and expectations" (Nagy & Koles, 2014, p. 279). These virtual identities often represent a duality of self, similar to the dichotomy described by Cheek and Briggs (1982) and Leary et al. (1986). That is, a person's virtual identity embodies a self-representation made by the participant and an external representation that marks the choices made when communicating with others in the virtual environment (Seung-A, 2012). These internal and external choices are influenced by the person's knowledge of that virtual environment and affect the participation within it (DeGrove, Courtois, & Van Looy, 2015; Leonard, Withers, & Sherblom, 2010).

The relational attributes of trust, presence, and identity are essential to the development of successful virtual team communication. These attributes, along with personal competence, as measured in skill, efficacy, and confidence, influence communication norms that a team develops. Three measures of these norms are participant interactivity, openness, and satisfaction.

5.5 Team Conversational Norms: Interactivity, Openness, and Satisfaction

5.5.1 Interactivity

Interactivity includes the communication rate, feedback, turn-taking, timeliness, responsiveness, immediacy, and synchronicity that participants experience in a conversation (Karimi, Ramenzoni, & Holme, 2014; Tu & McIsaac, 2002). This interactivity is generally greater in a synchronous communication medium, such as in face-to-face discussion. In these face-to-face discussions the conversations are often more dialogic, open, and immediate, and the rate of information exchange is typically greater (Tu & McIsaac, 2002).

5.5.2 Openness

Openness describes an individual's level of comfort and ease with expressing personal thoughts, opinions, ideas, and emotions to others (Ayoko, 2007; Nam, 2014). This openness is reflected in a participant's willingness to self-disclose to the group (Goffman, 1959; Jourard, 1971). This self-disclosure is encouraged or discouraged by the interactivity norms established and implicitly maintained in the group. In a virtual team these openness cues may be communicated explicitly in words or demonstrated implicitly through such nonverbal cues as a person's avatar appearance, the topics discussed, or the verbal style of other participants (Gottschalk, 2010).

5.5.3 Satisfaction

Satisfaction is an affective response that represents an enjoyable, fulfilling experience (Hecht, 1978). Several factors affect an individual's level of satisfaction, including the communication climate of the group, amount of personal feedback received, and sociocultural expectations (Diener, 2000; Downs & Hazen, 1977). Participants who engage in group activities in a virtual environment often express satisfaction with the richness of the virtual environment, number of social cues available, sense of presence with others, and ease of participating (Hazel, Crandall, & Caputo, 2015; Nowak, Watt, & Walther, 2009;

Sherblom, 2010; Simon, 2010; Walther & Bazarova, 2008). The amount of feedback, complexity of information exchanged, and participant skill in using the medium all affect satisfaction (Walther & Bazarova, 2008). Adequate training and technical support positively influence participant satisfaction with a new CMC medium (Hiltz & Johnson, 1990; Leonard et al., 2015; Sherblom et al., 2013). The self-disclosure of other participants within that medium can increase a participant's communication satisfaction, as well (Morry, 2005).

5.6 Hypotheses

Following some early studies that focused mainly on media effects, a substantial amount of CMC research has shown the influence of personal competence, as measured in indices of skill, efficacy, and confidence, on virtual team conversational participation. In addition, much of this more recent CMC research suggests the influence of relational attributes such as trust, presence, and identity. At least one recent qualitative study of focus-group participants indicates that these relational influences affect the conversational participation of team members who meet in a virtual environment (Leonard et al., 2015). The present study examines whether these relational influences add substantially to the well-documented contributions of personal competence. The specific expectations of this study are stated in the following two hypotheses.

H1: The personal competence indices of participant skill, efficacy, and confidence predict virtual team conversational interactivity, openness, and satisfaction.

H2: The relational indices of trust, presence, and identity will add substantially to these personal competence indices in predicting virtual team conversational interactivity, openness, and satisfaction.

5.7 Method

5.7.1 Participants

The sample of 104 participants consists of seven relatively equal-size subsamples averaging 15 participants apiece. These subsamples were collected over the course of a year from three universities: an eastern US university, a midwestern US university, and an eastern European university. The total sample comprised 47 female and 57 male participants. Participant ages range from 18 to 40, with a mean age of 21.

5.7.2 Participant Training

The participants in this study were trained to use the *Second Life*® program over a period of several weeks. After an initial introduction to the use of the program, participants were given a set of team projects to complete before being invited to participate in the survey of their *Second Life*® communication experiences. These projects involved team discussion, decision-making, problem-solving, and report-writing assignments. Each team of four or five members had a specific meeting place in *Second Life*® to carry on these activities. For their first project, team members were required to interview *Second Life*® residents about their media use and develop a single group report of their findings. From this project participants learned about standards of media use in *Second Life*®, and faced the challenges of working and writing as a virtual team. For the second project, each team joined a virtual community in *Second Life*® and, after a period of observation and interviewing, reported on the community's values, goals, and ethics. These reports provided team members the opportunity to discuss and reflect on their assumptions about the purpose of virtual communities and the communication within them. In addition, writing together as a virtual team that met and communicated in *Second Life*® required group discussion, decision making, and problem solving to synthesize the results of each individual interview and experience into a single unified team report.

5.7.3 The *Second Life*® Virtual Environment

Second Life® is the largest three-dimensional, multiuser virtual environment created by users. There are 15.5 million registered participants in *Second Life*® and 900,000 of them are active each month. These users interact in a virtual space four times the size of New York City (Flowers, Gregson, & Trigilio, 2009; Kingsley & Wankel, 2009). Within this virtual space, participants communicate through symbolic visual representations of themselves called avatars, using both public and private forms of nearly synchronous text messaging (Sherblom, 2010).

These *Second Life*® participants engage in social activities and carry on business transactions, and numerous for-profit and nonprofit organizations operate and hold meetings in *Second Life*® (Sherblom, Withers, & Leonard, 2009). Among the most prominent of these companies participating in *Second Life*® are the American Cancer Society, Coca-Cola, Crescendo Design, Kraft Foods, IBM, Pepsi, Pizza Hut, and Starwood Hotels (Sherblom & Green-Hamann, 2013). The *Second Life*® currency, known as Linden dollars, has a real-world exchange rate and in 2015, *Second Life*® residents earned about 60 million US dollars through their business activities (Charara, 2016).

5.7.4 Procedures

The research procedures and survey questions used in this study were approved by all three university institutional review boards. Before beginning the survey, each participant was provided with an informed consent form detailing the study. Then participants responded to the survey that appears in the appendix. This electronically distributed survey took participants approximately 20 minutes to complete and participants were provided a small monetary incentive in Linden dollars for completing the survey.

5.7.5 Measures

Survey scales measure self-perceptions of skill, efficacy, confidence, trust, presence, identity, interactivity, openness, and satisfaction. Questions about participant biological sex and age appear at the end of the survey. Each measure consists of a series of statements to which participants respond on a five-point Likert-type scale. Response choices range from $1 =$ strongly agree to $5 =$ strongly disagree. Several items are reverse coded to reduce the likelihood of response-set bias.

Skill is measured using nine items. These items assess a participant's ability to engage in turn-taking, prioritize conversational responses, be articulate and expressive, display appropriate emphasis, and engage in a clear communication style. A Cronbach's alpha coefficient ($\alpha = .85$) shows an acceptable reliability for this measure.

Efficacy is measured with seven items. These items examine the extent to which respondents feel able to accomplish tasks, be productive, and be efficient in communicating with team members in *Second Life*®. Scales ask how much they use, rely on, and how useful they find this communication medium. A Cronbach's alpha coefficient ($\alpha = .79$) shows acceptable reliability for the efficacy measure.

Confidence is measured using five items. These items ask respondents to reflect on how capable, confident, knowledgeable, or nervous (reverse-coded) they feel, and how quickly they developed their ability in using this communication medium. A Cronbach's alpha coefficient ($\alpha = .81$) demonstrates acceptable reliability for confidence.

Trust is measured with seven items. These items ask participants how they present themselves to others, get to know others, and how much they trust others to be responsible, produce high-quality work, meet deadlines, and participate as productive team members. A Cronbach's alpha coefficient ($\alpha = .81$) demonstrates an acceptable reliability for trust.

Presence is measured using fourteen items. These ask how connected, immersed, and close participants feel to others when communicating through this medium. A Cronbach's alpha coefficient ($\alpha = .91$) shows an acceptable reliability for presence.

Identity is measured with seven items. These items ask about whether a participant's avatar looks, acts, and represents the participant adequately, and whether the participant feels able to make a true representation of self in *Second Life*.[®] A Cronbach's alpha coefficient ($\alpha = .84$) shows an acceptable reliability for identity.

Interactivity is measured using fourteen items. These items ask about the flow of the conversation, equality of participation among team members, ability to keep up with and follow the conversation, smoothness of turn-taking, and perceived willingness of other participants to respond quickly with relevant and on-topic contributions. A Cronbach's alpha coefficient ($\alpha = .91$) provides an acceptable reliability for interactivity.

Openness is measured using ten items. These items ask about whether participants feel like they are able to openly share their thoughts, feelings, ideas, and opinions; say what they really think and feel; and comment honestly on the ideas of others. A Cronbach's alpha coefficient ($\alpha = .80$) reveals an acceptable reliability for openness.

Satisfaction is measured with thirteen items. These items ask whether participants get what they want out of team interactions, achieve their goals, are able to express their ideas clearly, understand what others say, enjoy their interactions, believe their communication is effective, and feel good about their conversations. They also ask whether participants feel like they get to know people, can make friends easily, are pleased with their encounters, and are generally satisfied with their communication in this medium. A Cronbach's alpha coefficient ($\alpha = .94$) demonstrates an acceptable reliability for satisfaction.

5.7.6 Statistical Analyses

Three types of statistical analyses describe the relationships among these measures. Correlations describe the relationships among them. Regression analysis compares the influence of personal skill, efficacy, and confidence on team conversational interactivity, openness, and satisfaction found in the present study to the earlier results reported by Sherblom et al. (2013), who found that the personal competence measures of knowledge, skill, motivation, and lack of apprehension affect virtual team communication. Finally, structural equation modeling produces two path analysis models that provide tests of the research hypotheses. These two path analysis models more fully delineate the multiple direct and mediated regression relationships among personal skill, efficacy, and confidence, and of relational trust, presence, and identity, as influences on team conversational interactivity, openness, and satisfaction (Hayes, 2009).

The first path analysis model shows the influence of personal skill, efficacy, and confidence on team interactivity, openness, and satisfaction. The second path analysis model adds the relational attributes of trust, presence, and identity to the model along with these personal competence measures. To show an adequate fit to the data, a model must produce a nonsignificant χ^2 and a χ^2 to *df* ratio that is less than 5 (Marsh & Hocevar, 1985). In addition, an incremental fit measure such as the comparative fit index (*CFI*), which is relatively insensitive to model complexity, and a measure of absolute fit, such as the root mean square error of approximation (*RMSEA*), can be used to test and demonstrate an adequate model fit (Hair et al., 2006). The *CFI* is normed so that values closer to 1 indicate a better fit (Bentler & Bonett, 1980). A *CFI* value of .95 or greater indicates a model that has a good fit (Hayes, Slater, & Snyder, 2008). The *RMSEA*, with a built-in parsimony index that corrects for sample size and model complexity, provides an index of how well a model fits the population as well as the sample (Hair et al., 2006). An *RMSEA* value of .06 or less indicates a good model fit (Hayes et al., 2008).

In sum, a nonsignificant χ^2, χ^2 to degrees of freedom ratio of less than 5, *CFI* value of .95 or greater, and *RMSEA* of less than .06 indicate a good model fit (Hayes et al., 2008). See Tabachnick and Fidell (2013) for a fuller description of these indices and model fit criteria. In developing the path analysis model, weak links, that is, links producing a β value of less than .10, are dropped to produce a more parsimonious model. The examination of each model's fit statistics offers a good comparison for showing if the relational attributes of trust, presence, and identity provide a substantial contribution in addition to the personal skill, efficacy, and confidence effects on virtual team conversational interactivity, openness, and satisfaction.

5.8 Results and Discussion

Table 5.1 shows that skill has a weak correlation with efficacy ($r = .19$) and a moderate correlation with confidence ($r = .52$). Efficacy presents a weak correlation with confidence as well ($r = .15$). Trust has moderate correlations with both presence ($r = .53$) and identity ($r = .38$), and presence is moderately

Table 5.1 *Correlations*

	1.	2.	3.	4.	5.	6.	7.	8.	9.
1. Skill	1	.19	.52*	.46*	.52*	.34*	.50*	.50*	.57*
2. Efficacy	.19	1	.15	.19	.40*	.36*	.35*	.30*	.43*
3. Confidence	.52*	.15	1	.20*	.26*	.22*	.19	.33*	.47*
4. Trust	.46*	.19	.20*	1	.53*	.38*	.62*	.55*	.38*
5. Presence	.52*	.40*	.26*	.53*	1	.64*	.53*	.55*	.60*
6. Identity	.34*	.36*	.22*	.38*	.64*	1	.40*	.52*	.50*
7. Interactivity	.50*	.35*	.19*	.62*	.53*	.40*	1	.64*	.48*
8. Openness	.50*	.30*	.33*	.55*	.55*	.52*	.64*	1	.55*
9. Satisfaction	.57*	.43*	.47*	.38*	.60*	.50*	.48*	.55*	1

$N = 104$; * $p < .05$.

correlated with identity ($r = .64$). Interactivity is moderately correlated with both openness ($r = .64$) and satisfaction ($r = .48$), and openness is moderately correlated with satisfaction ($r = .55$). These correlations show that the measures are moderately correlated, but that each indexes a unique attribute.

Hypothesis 1 states the expectation that participant skill, efficacy, and confidence, as indices of personal competence, will predict virtual team conversational norms of interactivity, openness, and satisfaction. The linear regression analysis demonstrates that skill, efficacy, and confidence do combine to account for 33% of the variance in interactivity ($r^2 = .33$), 29% of the variance in openness ($r^2 = .29$), and 46% of the variance in satisfaction ($r^2 = .46$). These findings are similar to and corroborate the results reported by Sherblom et al. (2013). They found that the personal competence measures of knowledge, skill, motivation, and lack of apprehension accounted for 24% ($r^2 = .24$) of the variance in their virtual team communication.

Figure 5.1 provides a path analysis model that more carefully delineates these personal competence influences of skill, efficacy, and confidence on the virtual team conversational participation norms of interactivity, openness, and satisfaction. The model shows that skill predicts interactivity ($\beta = .46$) and satisfaction ($\beta = .33$). Efficacy predicts interactivity ($\beta = .27$) and satisfaction ($\beta = .31$). Confidence predicts openness ($\beta = .26$) and satisfaction ($\beta = .32$). In addition, interactivity also affects openness ($\beta = .54$).

Similar to the linear regression results, this model shows that the personal competence indices of skill and efficacy combine to account for a substantial amount of the variance in interactivity ($r^2 = .32$). Confidence, along with interactivity, accounts for variance in openness ($r^2 = .44$), and all three indices combine to predict satisfaction ($r^2 = .48$). This model, however, demonstrates

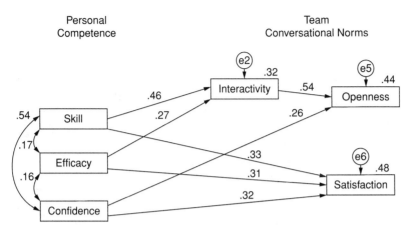

Figure 5.1 Model of personal competence influences on team conversational norms, with no relational attributes included. $\chi^2 = 14.32$; $df = 5$; $p = .014$; χ^2/df ratio $= 2.84$; $CFI = .82$; $RMSEA = .13$.

a relatively poor fit to the data. This poor fit is shown in the fit indices: $\chi^2 = 14.32$; $df = 5$; $p = .014$; χ^2/df ratio $= 2.84$; $CFI = .82$; $RMSEA = .13$. This relatively poor fit suggests that there are other predictors of these team conversational norms that are not recognized in this model. Hypothesis 2 predicts that the relational attributes of trust, presence, and identity will add substantially to the personal competence measures modelled in this first figure.

Figure 5.2 shows a path analysis model that includes these relational attributes of trust, presence, and identity as predictors of interactivity, openness, and satisfaction. The model fit indices of $\chi^2 = 10.11$; $df = 15$; $p = .813$; χ^2/df ratio $= .67$; $CFI = .99$; $RMSEA = .01$ demonstrate that this model provides a good fit to the data. The χ^2 value is nonsignificant, χ^2/df ratio is less than 5, CFI is greater than .95, and $RMSEA$ is less than .06. Each of these indices indicates a good model fit.

This model also shows that skill, efficacy, and confidence have both direct and indirect mediated effects on interactivity, openness, and satisfaction. Skill directly affects interactivity ($\beta = .22$) and satisfaction ($\beta = .22$). Efficacy influences satisfaction ($\beta = .22$). Confidence affects openness ($\beta = .17$) and satisfaction ($\beta = .22$). These effects show that the development of personal competence directly predict team conversational interactivity, openness, and satisfaction.

In addition, skill affects the relational attributes of trust ($\beta = .25$) and presence ($\beta = .46$). Trust affects openness ($\beta = .19$) and interactivity ($\beta = .42$), indicating that skill has an additional mediated effect, through trust, on team

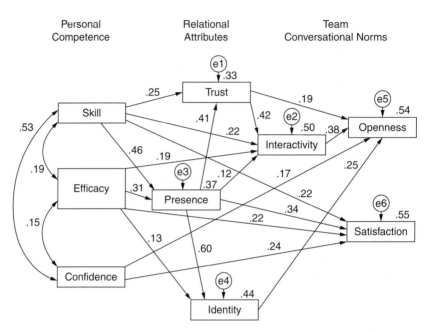

Figure 5.2 Model of personal competence and relational attribute influences on team conversational norms. $\chi^2 = 10.11$; $df = 15$; $p = .813$; χ^2/df ratio $= .67$; $CFI = .99$; $RMSEA = .01$.

interactivity and openness. Efficacy shows an additional mediated connection to interactivity and satisfaction through presence ($\beta = .31$). Presence is associated with both interactivity ($\beta = .12$) and satisfaction ($\beta = .34$). Efficacy shows a mediated association with openness through its connection with identity ($\beta = .13$), as well. Identity ($\beta = .25$) and interactivity ($\beta = .38$) are both associated with greater openness, as well.

This second model, which includes trust, presence, and identity, provides a much fuller picture and more complex description of the influences on team conversational norms. This model shows the direct and mediated relationships of personal skill, efficacy, and confidence, and the additional contributions of relational trust, presence, and identity to developing team conversational norms of interactivity, openness, and satisfaction. Including the relational attributes of trust, presence, and identity in this model not only provides a substantially better fit to the data, but also increases the amount of variance accounted in the team conversational norms.

Skill and presence combine to account for 33% of the variance in trust ($r^2 = .33$). Skill, efficacy, presence, and trust account for 50% of the variance in interactivity ($r^2 = .50$). Skill, efficacy, confidence, and presence account for 55% of

Table 5.2 *Model Fit Criteria Comparison*

Criteria:	χ^2	df	p of χ^2 > .05	χ^2/ df ratio < 5	CFI > .95	RMSEA < .06
Model (no relational attributes)	14.32	5	.02	2.84	.82	.13
Model (with relational attributes)	10.11	15	.81	.67	.99	.01

the variance in satisfaction ($r^2 = .55$). Confidence, trust, interactivity, and identity account for 54% of the variance in openness ($r^2 = .54$). That is, when the relational attributes are included in the model the variance accounted for in interactivity increases from 32% to 50%, in openness from 44% to 54%, and in satisfaction from 48% to 55%.

The superior fit and increased variance accounted for by this model shown in Figure 5.2 provide support for hypothesis 2. The relational attributes add substantially to the measures of personal competence in predicting virtual team conversational interactivity, openness, and satisfaction. Table 5.2 shows a comparison of the fit statistics for the two path analysis models. This comparison demonstrates that the model that includes the relational attributes of trust, presence, and identity provides a better fit to the data and a fuller picture of the relationships than the model that includes only the measures of personal competence.

In addition, a comparison of the residual correlation matrices associated with the two models shows a significant difference, $\chi^2 = 410.03$; $df = 42$; $p < .001$. The model that includes the relational attributes contains a smaller set of residual correlations ($M = .0008$, SD = .09) than the model without the relational attributes ($M = .032$, SD = .14). This indicates that the model containing the relational attributes of trust, presence, and identity does a better job explaining the observed relationships than the model containing no relational attributes. That is, including the relational attributes leaves less unaccounted correlations in the residual matrix (Anderson & Williams, 1992; Veit & Ware, 1983).

5.9 Conclusion

The literature review highlights two potential influences on virtual team communication. The first influence is each individual's ability to communicate competently within the medium. We measured this personal competence through indices of skill, efficacy, and confidence in the using the communication medium. Recent literature indicates that differences in the relational attributes of trust, presence, and identity also affect the virtual team communication. Our path analysis models examine and compare these two types of influences on virtual team conversational norms. Results of this comparison indicate that the relational attributes of trust, presence, and identity are associated with personal competence as measured in skill, efficacy, and competence, and contribute substantially to team conversational interactivity, openness, and satisfaction.

Virtual teams establish and enforce conversational norms of interactivity, openness, and satisfaction as they work together. The present results indicate that having team members who are competent in communicating in a virtual environment is necessary but not adequate to achieve effective norms of team conversational interactivity, openness, and satisfaction. To develop these norms requires relational trust, presence, and identity. Training programs designed to build effective virtual team communication should focus some attention on developing these relational attributes within the team, in addition to building the personal competence needed to use the medium. Media naturalness theory suggests that participants can develop these relational skills through mindful attention and cognitive effort.

Relational trust is built through the verbal and nonverbal communication in which one learns to trust another person and establishes that person's trust in oneself. Engaging in relational talk as well as task-oriented business, that is, offering personal information about oneself such as one's thoughts and feelings toward the project, and asking the other person for ideas and opinions can, over time, establish rapport and build relational trust. This trust-building process is not different than that engaged in by teams who meet face-to-face, but it may take longer and require more effort from virtual team members.

Presence is an ongoing dynamic process of being with the other person within the communication medium. It is built upon one's skill, efficacy, and confidence in understanding and be understood by the other person. Developing this relational presence with others through the medium comes with practice and experience, and forms the basis for an interactive, open, and satisfying task-oriented virtual team conversation.

Identity builds upon this sense of presence to define the participant's role expectations of others and of self within the group. This identity becomes an enduring attribute of a participant in the virtual team. It affects the roles a participant is given by the team, and the ones a person accepts and expects (Brandon & Hollingshead, 2004; Hollingshead, 2001). A participant's identity within the team affects conversational interactivity, openness, and satisfaction.

The model presented in Figure 5.2 shows that including these relational attributes of trust, presence, and identity provides a better model fit and a more complete description of the influences affecting a virtual team's conversational interactivity, openness, and satisfaction. Personal skill, efficacy, and confidence are necessary, but not sufficient, to generate conversational interactivity, openness, and satisfaction in a virtual team. In addition, team members must be able to form relationships that exhibit trust, presence, and identity with each other. These relational attributes of trust, presence, and identity build upon the personal competence influences of skill, efficacy, and confidence to affect the interactivity, openness, and satisfaction norms of the virtual team.

The present study shows the relationship between these relational attributes and a virtual team's conversational interactivity, openness, and satisfaction. A virtual team's conversational interactivity, openness, and satisfaction are associated with these relational attributes. Without relational trust, presence, and identity even team members who possess personal competence with the medium will have difficulty engaging in interactive, open, and satisfying conversations in a virtual environment.

Appendix: Communication in *Second Life*® Survey

Presence

1. I feel a bond with my avatar.
2. I feel connected with my avatar.
3. I feel immersed in the virtual world of *Second Life*.
4. I feel like I'm actually there in *Second Life*.
5. I feel like I'm a real person in *Second Life*.
6. I feel like the things that happen to my avatar are happening to me.
7. When people get too close to my avatar, I feel uncomfortable.
8. Someone bumping my avatar invades my personal space.
9. When my avatar falls and hits the ground, I feel it.
10. I don't notice the computer when I'm in the virtual space.
11. I often forget that there's a computer between me and others in *Second Life*.
12. The people I meet in *Second Life* seem real to me.
13. I feel connected to the people I meet in *Second Life*.
14. I feel like I'm actually in the virtual world with others.

Interactivity

15. There's a smooth flow of conversation.
16. The other members of my group are responsive in conversation.
17. People participate often in the conversation.
18. People participate equally in the conversation.

19. Someone reading the text of our group chat would be able to follow the conversation.
20. There's a lot of turn-taking in our conversation.
21. Taking turns is a smooth process in our conversation.
22. We reach a common understanding through our group discussion.
23. We come together as a team through our group discussion.
24. Through our conversation we stimulate new ideas.
25. Everyone is quick to jump into the conversation.
26. People respond quickly to my posts in the conversation.
27. Posts are on-topic with the rest of the conversation.
28. Posts are relevant to the ongoing conversation.

Identity

29. *Second Life* allows me to present my true self.
30. It's easy for me to deceive others about myself in *Second Life*. (reverse-coded)
31. My avatar looks like me.
32. My avatar acts like me.
33. My avatar accurately represents who I am.
34. My avatar represents the real me.
35. I can be my true self in *Second Life*.
36. *Second Life* gives me the opportunity to show who I really am.

Trust

37. I feel like I get to know others' real selves.
38. I am concerned that others can deceive me easily in *Second Life*. (reverse-coded)
39. I trust how others present themselves in *Second Life*.
40. I trust others to be responsible for their tasks in *Second Life*.
41. I believe that others will be responsible for doing their share of the work.
42. I trust that my group members will produce high-quality work.
43. I trust others will meet their deadlines.
44. I am confident that I can count on my group members.

Openness

45. I can openly express my feelings in *Second Life*.
46. I can share my feelings in conversations in *Second Life*.

47. I am comfortable sharing my thoughts with others in *Second Life.*
48. My team members express their ideas openly in *Second Life.*
49. I am willing to comment on others' ideas in *Second Life.*
50. I share my opinions with my group members.
51. My group members are supportive of each other's ideas.
52. I don't worry about offending group members with my comments.
53. I can say what I really think to my group members.
54. I tell my group how I really feel.

Confidence

55. I am capable of using *Second Life.*
56. I am confident in my ability to use *Second Life.*
57. I am nervous about my ability to use *Second Life.* (reverse-coded)
58. I quickly figured out how to use *Second Life.*
59. I know I can use *Second Life.*

Skill

60. I manage turn-taking in *Second Life* skillfully.
61. I am skilled in timing my responses to people who chat with me in *Second Life.*
62. I am skilled at prioritizing responses in my *Second Life* chat.
63. I am articulate and vivid in my *Second Life* messages.
64. I am expressive in *Second Life* conversations.
65. I display certainty in the way I write *Second Life* messages.
66. My objectives are emphasized in my *Second Life* messages.
67. My *Second Life* messages are written in a clear style.
68. I am skillful in revealing composure in *Second Life.*

Efficacy

69. I accomplish a tremendous amount in *Second Life.*
70. My *Second Life* interactions are more productive than face-to-face.
71. I am more efficient using *Second Life* than other forms of communication.
72. *Second Life* is a tremendous time saver.
73. I rely heavily on *Second Life* to communicate with my group.
74. I use *Second Life* for all of my communication with my group.
75. *Second Life* is very useful for group communication.

Satisfaction

76. I get what I want out of interactions in *Second Life*.
77. I achieve my goals in *Second Life* interactions.
78. My *Second Life* interactions are effective.
79. I get my ideas across clearly in conversations in *Second Life*.
80. I feel understood when I interact with others in *Second Life*.
81. I am generally satisfied with my *Second Life* communication encounters.
82. I enjoy my interactions in *Second Life*.
83. I feel good about my conversations in *Second Life*.
84. I am generally pleased with my *Second Life* interactions.
85. When I engage others in conversation in *Second Life*, they like me.
86. In *Second Life* conversation, people like to get to know me.
87. I make friends easily in *Second Life*.
88. People enjoy my company when interacting with me in *Second Life*.

Age: _____ years

Biological Sex: ___ Male ___Female ___Other: _____

Survey responses are available from the first author by contacting: john@maine.edu.

References

Anderson, S. E., & Williams, L. J. (1992). Assumptions about unmeasured variables with studies of reciprocal relationships: The case of employee attitudes. *Journal of Applied Psychology*, 77, 638–650.

Aymerich-Franch, L. (2010). Presence and emotions in playing a group game in a virtual environment: The influence of body participation. *Cyberpsychology, Behavior, and Social Networking*, 13, 649–654.

Ayoko, O. (2007). Communication openness, conflict events and reactions to conflict in culturally diverse workgroups. *Cross Cultural Management: An International Journal*, 14, 105–124.

Beldad, A., de Jong, M., & Steehouder, M. (2010). How shall I trust the faceless and the intangible? A literature review on the antecedents of online trust. *Computers in Human Behavior*, 26, 857–869.

Bentler, P. M., & Bonett, D. G. (1980). Significance tests and goodness of fit in the analysis of covariance structures. *Psychological Bulletin*, 88, 588–606.

Biocca, F., Kim, J., & Choi, Y. (2001). Visual touch in virtual environments: An exploratory study of presence, multimodal interfaces, and cross-modal sensory illusions. *Presence*, 10, 247–265.

Brandon, D. P., & Hollingshead, A. B. (2004). Transactive memory systems in organizations: Matching tasks, expertise, and people. *Organization Science*, 15, 633–644.

Bubas, G., Radosevic, D., & Hutinski, Z. (2003). Assessment of computer mediated communication competence: Theory and application in an online environment. *Journal of Information and Organizational Sciences*, 27, 53–71.

Charara, S. (2016, January 20). Virtual worlds reborn: Can Second Life's second life democratise VR? Retrieved from: www.wareable.com/vr/second-life-project-sansar-beta-2016

Cheek, J., & Briggs, S. (1982). Self-consciousness and aspects of identity. *Journal of Research in Personality*, 16, 401–408.

Cheng, X., & Macaulay, L. (2013). Exploring individual trust factors in computer mediated group collaboration: A case study approach. *Group Decision and Negotiation*, 23, 533–560.

Daft, R., & Lengel, R. (1986). Organizational information requirements, media richness, and structural design. *Management Science*, 32, 554–571.

DeGrove, F., Courtois, C., & Van Looy, J. (2015). How to be a gamer! Exploring personal and social indicators of gamer identity. *Journal of Computer-Mediated Communication*, 20, 346–361.

DeRosa, D. M., Hantula, D. A., Kock, N., & D'Arcy, J. (2004). Trust and leadership in virtual teamwork: A media naturalness perspective. *Human Resource Management*, 43, 219–232.

Diener, E. (2000). Subjective well-being: The science of happiness and a proposal for a national index. *American Psychologist*, 55, 34–43.

Downs, C., & Hazen, M. (1977). A factor analytic study of communication satisfaction. *The Journal of Business Communication*, 14, 64–73.

Erhardt, N., Martin-Rios, C., Gibbs, J., & Sherblom, J. (2016). Exploring affordances of email for team learning over time. *Small Group Research*, 47, 243–278.

Feng, J., Lazar, J., & Preece, J. (2004). Empathy and online interpersonal trust: A fragile relationship. *Behaviour & Information Technology*, 23, 97–106.

Flowers, A., Gregson, K., & Trigilio, J. (2009, April). Web interaction from 2D to 3D: New dimensions in company-stakeholder communications in Second Life. Paper presented at the Eastern Communication Association convention, Philadelphia, PA.

Goffman, E. (1959). *The presentation of self in everyday life*. New York, NY: Anchor.

Gottschalk, S. (2010). The presentation of avatars in Second Life: Self and interaction in social virtual spaces. *Symbolic Interaction*, 33, 501–525.

Green-Hamann, S., Eichhorn, K. C., & Sherblom, J. C. (2011). An exploration of why people participate in Second Life social support groups. *Journal of Computer-Mediated Communication*, 16, 465–491.

Green-Hamann, S., & Sherblom, J. C. (2014). The influences of optimal matching and social capital on communicating support. *Journal of Health Communication*, 19, 1130–1144.

Hains, R. (2014). Group development in virtual teams: An experimental reexamination. *Computers in Human Behavior*, 39, 213–222.

Hair, J. F., Black, W. C., Babin, B. J., Anderson, R. E., & Tatham, R. L. (2006). *Multivariate data analysis*. Upper Saddle River, NJ: Pearson Prentice Hall.

Hayes, A. F. (2009). Beyond Baron and Kenny: Statistical mediation analysis in the new millennium. *Communication Monographs*, 76, 408–420.

Hayes, A. F., Slater, M. D., & Snyder, L. B. (2008). *The SAGE sourcebook of advanced data analysis methods for communication research*. Los Angeles, CA: SAGE.

Hazel, M., Crandall, H. & Caputo, J. (2015). The influence of instructor social presence and student academic entitlement on teacher misbehaviors in online courses. *Southern Communication Journal*, 79, 311–326.

Hecht, M. (1978). The conceptualization and measurement of interpersonal communication satisfaction. *Human Communication Research*, 4, 253–264.

Henderson, S., & Gilding, M. *(*2004). "I've never clicked this much with anyone in my life": Trust and hyperpersonal communication in online friendships. *New Media & Society*, 6, 487–506.

Hiltz, S., & Johnson, K. (1990). User satisfaction with computer-mediated communication systems. *Management Science*, 36, 739–764.

Himelboim, I., Lariscy, R. W., Tinkham, S. F., Kaye, D., & Sweetser, K. D. (2012). Social media and online political communication: The role of interpersonal informational trust and openness. *Journal of Broadcasting & Electronic Media*, 56, 92–115.

Hollingshead, A. B. (2001). Cognitive interdependence and convergent expectations in transactive memory. *Journal of Personality and Social Psychology*, 81, 1080–1089.

Houtman, E., Makos, A., & Meacock, H. L. (2014). The intersection of social presence and impression management in online learning environments. *E-Learning and Digital Media*, 11, 419–430.

International Society for Presence Research. (2000). *The concept of presence: Explication statement*. Retrieved from: https://smcsites.com/ispr/

Jarvenpaa, S. L., & Leidner, D. E. (1998). Communication and trust in global virtual teams. *Journal of Computer-Mediated Communication*, 3, 791–815.

Jin, S. A., & Bolebruch, J. (2009). Avatar-based advertising in second life: The role of presence and attractiveness of virtual spokespersons. *Journal of Interactive Advertising*, 10, 51–60.

Jin, S. A., & Bolebruch, J. (2010). Virtual commerce (v-commerce) in Second Life: The roles of physical presence and brand-self connection. *Journal of Virtual Worlds Research*, 2. Retrieved from: http://journals.tdl.org/jvwr/article/view/867

Jourard, S. M. (1971). *The transparent self* (rev. edn.). New York, NY: Van Nostrand Reinhold.

Karimi, F., Ramenzoni, V. C., & Holme, P. (2014). Structural differences between open and direct communication in an online community. *Physica A: Statistical Mechanics and Its Applications*, 414, 263–273.

Kehrwald, B. (2008). Understanding social presence in text-based online learning environments. *Distance Education*, 29, 89–106.

Kelly, L., Keaten, J. A., Hazel, M., & Williams, J. A. (2010). Effects of reticence, affect for communication channels, and self-perceived competence on usage of instant messaging. *Communication Research Reports*, 27, 131–142.

Kingsley, J., & Wankel, C. (2009). Introduction. In C. Wankel & J. Kingsley (eds.), *Higher education in virtual worlds: Teaching and learning in Second Life* (pp. 1–9). Bingley, UK: Emerald.

Kock, N. (2004). The psychobiological model: Towards a new theory of computer-mediated communication based on Darwinian evolution. *Organization Science*, 15, 327–348.

Kock, N. (2005). Media richness or media naturalness? The evolution of our biological communication apparatus and its influence on our behavior toward e-communication tools. *IEEE Transactions on Professional Communication*, 48, 117–130.

Kock, N. (2008). Media naturalness theory: Human evolution and behavior towards electronic communication technologies. In S. C. Roberts (ed.), *Applied evolutionary psychology* (pp. 381–398). New York, NY: Oxford University Press.

Kock, N., Verville, J., & Garza, V. (2007). Media naturalness and online learning: Findings supporting both the significant and no-significant difference perspectives. *Decision Sciences Journal of Innovative Education*, 5, 333–355.

Leary, M., Wheeler, D., & Jenkins, T. (1986). Aspects of identity and behavioral preference: Studies of occupational and recreational choice. *Social Psychology Quarterly*, 49, 11–18.

Lee, K. M. (2004). Presence, explicated. *Communication Theory*, 14, 27–50.

Lengel, R. H., & Daft, R. L. (1988). The selection of communication media as an executive skill. *Executive*, 2, 225–232.

Leonard, L. G., Sherblom, J. C., Withers, L. A., & Smith, J. S. (2015). Training effective virtual teams: Presence, identity, communication openness, and conversational interactivity. *Connexions: International Professional Communication Journal*, 3, 11–45.

Leonard, L. G., & Toller, P. (2012). Speaking ill of the dead: Anonymity and communication about suicide on MyDeathSpace.com. *Communication Studies*, 63, 387–404.

Leonard, L. G., & Withers, L. A. (2009, November 14). The role of place in virtual environments. Paper presented at the annual meeting of the National Communication Association, Chicago, IL.

Leonard, L. G., Withers, L. A., & Sherblom, J. C. (2010). The paradox of computer-mediated communication and identity: Peril, promise and Second Life. In J. Park & E. Abel (eds.), *Interpersonal relations and social patterns in communication technologies: Discourse norms, language structures and cultural variables* (pp. 1–17). Hershey, PA: IGI Global.

Marsh, H. W., & Hocevar, D. (1985). Application of confirmatory factor analysis to the study of self-concept: First- and higher-order factor models and their invariance across groups. *Psychological Bulletin*, 97, 562–582.

Morrison, R., Cegielski, C., & Rainer, R. K. (2012). Trust, avatars, and electronic communications: Implications for e-learning. *Journal of Computer Information Systems*, 53, 80–89.

Morry, M. (2005). Allocentrism and friendship satisfaction: The mediating roles of disclosure and closeness. *Canadian Journal of Behavioral Science*, 37, 211–222.

Nagy, P., & Koles, B. (2014). The digital transformation of human identity: Towards a conceptual model of virtual identity in virtual worlds. *Convergence: The International Journal of Research into New Media Technologies*, 20, 276–292.

Nam, C. W. (2014). The effects of trust and constructive controversy on student achievement and attitude in online cooperative learning environments. *Computers in Human Behavior*, 37, 237–248.

Nowak, K. (2001). *Defining and differentiating copresence, social presence and presence as transportation.* Paper presented at Presence, Philadelphia, PA. Retrieved from: http://citeseerx.ist.psu.edu/viewdoc/summary?

Nowak, K., Watt, J., & Walther, J. (2009). Computer mediated teamwork and the efficiency framework: Exploring the influence of synchrony and cues on media satisfaction and outcome success. *Computers in Human Behavior*, 25, 1108–1119.

Oztok, M., & Brett, C. (2011). Social presence and online learning: A review of research. *International Journal of E-learning & Distance Education*, 25. Retrieved from: www.ijede.ca/index.php/jde/article/view/758/1299

Sarker, S., Ahuja, M., Sarker, S., & Kirkeby, S. (2011). The role of communication and trust in global virtual teams: A social network perspective. *Journal of Management Information Systems*, 28, 273–310.

Schiller, S., Mennecke, B., Nah, F., & Luse, A. (2014). Institutional boundaries and trust of virtual teams in collaborative design: An experimental study in a virtual world environment. *Computers in Human Behavior*, 35, 565–577.

Seung-A., A. J. (2012). The virtual malleable self and the virtual identity discrepancy model: Investigative frameworks for virtual possible selves and others in avatar-based identity construction and social interaction. *Computers in Human Behavior*, 28, 2160–2168.

Sherblom, J. (2010). The computer-mediated communication (CMC) classroom: A challenge of medium, presence, interaction, identity, and relationship. *Communication Education*, 59, 497–523.

Sherblom, J. C., & Green-Hamann, S. (2013). Public relations in a virtual world: A Second Life case study. In H. N. Al-Deen & J. A. Hendricks (eds.), *Social media and strategic communications* (pp. 137–155). Basingstoke: Palgrave Macmillan.

Sherblom, J. C., Withers, L. A., & Leonard, L. G. (2009). Communication challenges and opportunities for educators using Second Life. In C. Wankel & J. Kingsley (eds.), *Higher education in virtual worlds: Teaching and learning in Second Life* (pp. 29–46). Bingley: Emerald.

Sherblom, J. C., Withers, L. A., & Leonard, L. G. (2013). The influence of computer-mediated communication (CMC) competence on computer-supported collaborative learning (CSCL) in online classroom discussions. *Human Communication*, 16, 31–39.

Simon, A. (2010). Computer-mediated communication: Task performance and satisfaction. *The Journal of Social Psychology*, 146, 349–379.

Sivunen, A. & Nordbäck, E. (2015). Social presence as a multi-dimensional group construct in 3D virtual environments. *Journal of Computer-Mediated Communication*, 20, 19–36.

Spitzberg, B. H. (2006). Preliminary development of a model and measure of computer-mediated communication (CMC) competence. *Journal of Computer–Mediated Communication*, 11, 629–666.

Sueng-A, A. (2012). The virtual malleable self and the virtual identity discrepancy model: Investigative frameworks for virtual possible selves and others in avatar-based identity construction and social interaction. *Computers in Human Behavior*, 28, 2160–2168.

Sundararajan, B. (2009). Impact of communication patterns, network positions and social dynamics factors on learning among students in a CSCL environment. *Electronic Journal of e-Learning*, 7, 71–84.

Sundararajan, B. (2010). Emergence of the most knowledgeable other (MKO): Social network analysis of chat and bulletin board conversations in a CSCL system. *Electronic Journal of e-Learning*, 8, 191–208.

Tabachnick, B. G., & Fidell, L. S. (2013). *Using multivariate statistics*. Boston, MA: Pearson.

Trevino, L. K., Daft, R. L., & Lengel, R. H. (1990). Understanding manager's media choices: A symbolic interactionist perspective. In J. Fulk & C. Steinfield (eds.), *Organizations and communication technology* (pp. 71–94). Newbury Park, CA: SAGE.

Tu, C. H., & McIsaac, M. (2002). The relationship of social presence and interaction in online classes. *American Journal of Distance Education*, 16, 131–150.

Turilli, M., Vaccaro, A., & Taddeo, M. (2010). The case of online trust. *Knowledge, Technology & Policy*, 23, 333–345.

Veit, C. T., & Ware, J. E. (1983). The structure of psychological distress and well-being in general populations. *Journal of Consulting and Clinical Psychology*, 51, 730–742.

Walther, J. B. (2004). Language and communication technology. *Journal of Language and Social Psychology*, 23, 384–396.

Walther, J. B. (2009). Theories, boundaries, and all of the above. *Journal of Computer-Mediated Communication*, 14, 748–752.

Walther, J. B. (2010). Computer-mediated communication. In C. R. Berger, M. E. Roloff, & D. R. Roskos-Ewoldsen (eds.), *The handbook of communication science*, 2nd edn. (pp. 489–505). Thousand Oaks, CA: SAGE.

Walther, J., & Bazarova, N. (2008). Validation and application of electronic propinquity theory to computer-mediated communication in groups. *Communication Research*, 35, 622–645.

Walther, J. B., Loh, T., & Granka, L. (2005). Let me count the ways: The interchange of verbal and nonverbal cues in computer-mediated and face-to-face affinity. *Journal of Language & Social Psychology*, 24, 36–65.

Walther, J. B., & Parks, M. R. (2002). Cues filtered out, cues filtered in: Computer-mediated communication and relationships. In M. L. Knapp and J. A. Daly (eds.), *Handbook of interpersonal communication*, 3rd edn. (pp. 529–563). Thousand Oaks, CA: SAGE.

Willson, M. A. (2006). *Technically together: Rethinking community within techno-society*. New York, NY: Peter Lang.

Wrench, J. S., & Punyanunt-Carter, N. M. (2007). The relationship between computer-mediated-communication competence, apprehension, self-efficacy, perceived confidence, and social presence. *Southern Communication Journal*, 72, 355–378.

6

Toxic Allies and Caring Friends: Social Systems and Behavioral Norms in *League of Legends* and *Guild Wars 2*

MAUDE BONENFANT, LAURA ISEUT LAFRANCE
ST-MARTIN, FÉLIX PRÉGENT, AND LUCILE CRÉMIER

6.1 Introduction

Video games offer diverse gaming experiences (Corneliussen & Rettberg, 2008; Ducheneaut et al., 2006; Ensslin & Muse, 2011; Pearce & Artemesia, 2009; Sicart, 2009; Taylor, 2006, among others). Far from being neutral, these technological platforms are sociotechnical apparatuses that shape social interactions through the institution of relationships of power (Foucault, 1976, 2001 [1971]). Based on the approach of soft technological determinism (Chandler, 1995; Smith & Marx, 1994), we suggest that online video games not only influence players' experience within the apparatus, but also inform the production of collective identities, as each game elaborates a specific form of video game community through which players recognize each other, communicate, and normalize behaviors and social practices. In other words, video games are contexts in which social systems develop through behavioral norms, that is to say, "standard[s] of appropriate behavior for actors with a given identity" (Finnemore & Sikkink, 1998).

While the online gaming community of *Guild Wars 2* (GW2) (ArenaNet, 2012) is reputed to be "welcoming, respectful and peaceful," the *League of Legends* (LoL) (Riot Games, 2009) community is instead viewed as being "toxic, competitive and harsh." We argue that structural parameters within each game may allow, encourage, or prevent certain behaviors, and therefore participate in the production of identities and social norms that reproduce game-specific behavioral patterns. More precisely, some elements of both game design and gameplay mechanics may encourage either self-interest (LoL) or sharing (GW2), which informs players' socialization practices. While the reasons why these two games were selected will be explained in the first section of this chapter, we would like to insist on the goals of this research. Indeed, we undertook two distinct case studies, using the same set of methodological tools

130

and the same theoretical perspective, in order to expose observable similarities in our results rather than proceed to a comparative analysis. In other words, if the two games are in many ways diametrically opposed, our objective was to highlight their significant intersections and the existing parallels between them. This approach provides crucial insights into the direct effects of game design choices on communicational and social practices in video game communities. In this way, this does not constitute game analysis in its strictest sense, but rather an analysis of gaming communities from the consideration of the effects that the game platform has on social relationships.

Some researchers have studied GW2 (Scott, 2012) and LoL (Kou, 2014; Kou & Gui, 2014; Kwak & Blackburn, 2014) in the past, yet only few works look into these two highly popular games. Therefore, this chapter presents the results of our analysis of the production of social norms within these two games' communities of players based on a semiotic study of their main organizing principles. To identify how the two communities differ, we exhaustively describe signs and sign systems that constitute the two interfaces as well as the representations and features that further or impede specific actions in-game. We propose that analyzing in-game social attitudes implies observing the specific features, tools, and mechanics from which they emerge, such as the modes of avatar selection, the abilities and complementarity of avatars, the modes of group formation, the stability or instability of groups, the modes of communication, the sharing of rewards, the relationship to competition, the types of relationships between players, and the types of sanctions. Subsequently, we highlight the ways in which social dynamics are performed and normalized in each video game.

In addition to the semiotic study of the production of signification resulting from the interaction of players with game platforms, we analyze both video games' vocabulary, as well as the discourses used in the two companies' official documents. Semistructured interviews with GW2 and LoL players, whether they frequently play one or both games, come to complement our research. Players' gaming experience are taken into account so that we may not only identify how game design affects social relationships, but also observe how the community's culture is coconstructed within this environment.

We will first introduce our conceptual approach and the methodology of this research. We will then go through the main results of our research, which successively look at learning curves, expectations toward players, collective and personal goals, perceptions of competition and metrics, the intensity of playing practices, consequences of players' actions on other players, the management of toxic behaviors, stability in social relationships, and modes of communication. The structure of this chapter follows a typical player's progression in gaming practice. First, we focus on players' learning processes from their first gaming session to intensive practice. Second, we describe the key types of in-game social relationships. Third, we examine the ways in which practice is maintained through social groups and modes of communication. To conclude the chapter, we present a synthesis of our main arguments and offer some food for thought regarding our thesis that soft technological determinism does not entirely condition the development of video game communities, as appropriative and subversive practices remain central to the evolution of gaming practices.

6.2 Background: Semiotic Approach and Soft Technological Determinism

According to a semiotic approach to research, human beings are surrounded and immersed in signs that they interpret through the endless process of semiosis (sign-making). In that sense, reality is always already mediated by representations that shape the world in which humans socialize and form a sense of individual and collective identity. Although individual and social representations are organized in different ways and through different media, they always result from a process of interpretation that unfolds through a variety of human and technical productions. Human productions are effects of a cultural, ideological, institutional, and normative context, but they also elaborate their own cultural, ideological, institutional, and normative content. Studying the interactions between semiotic objects' conditions of production (engendering) and conditions of reception (recognition) forms part of the sociosemiotic approach to research, in which processes of signification are analyzed through the lens of specific human productions considered in their social context (Cobley & Randvir, 2009; Landowski, 1993; Veron, 1987).

One kind of human production that has been largely addressed by the literature is technology, which has transformed our societies since the emergence of language and tools (Leroi-Gourhan, 1964, 1965). Indeed, many important authors have shown the scope of technology's influence on human becoming as well as human activity's increasing subordination to technological processes (Ellul, 1954; Mumford, 1967, 1970; Simondon, 1958; Stiegler, 1994, 1996, 2001). Yet, some thinkers have argued that individuals may develop transformative strategies that circumvent, subvert, and defy hegemonic technological practices, thus changing power dynamics between humans and technology (De Certeau, 1980; Maigret, 2003). In that sense, while it shapes the world we live in and affects both individuals and societies in many ways, one must keep in

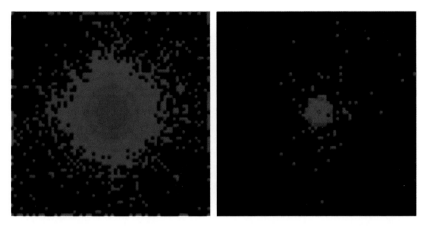

Figure 1.3 Step entropy histograms for two players: (left) higher entropy, (right) lower entropy.

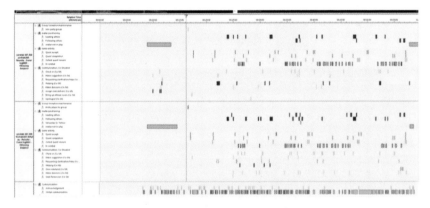

Figure 7.1 Leadership-related communication for Sfulab207 and Sfulab208.

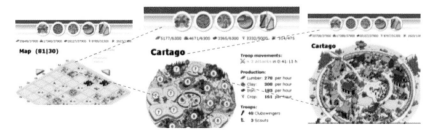

Figure 8.1 The virtual world of *Travian*.

Figure 9.3 The virtual funfair *Sherwood* (top) and the pop-up Duck Shoot interface (bottom).

Figure 10.1 A cluster of buildings constructed by players at a Nile crossing point.

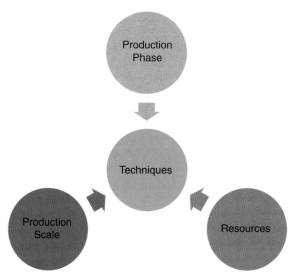

Figure 13.1 The techniques available for behavioral profiling in games rest on a variety of factors, notably: (1) the active production phase of a game, which determines what kinds of data are available; (2) the production scale, which determines the variety of data available, from a few key features to hundreds or more; and (3) the overall level of resources dedicated to analytics in the company and the active production.

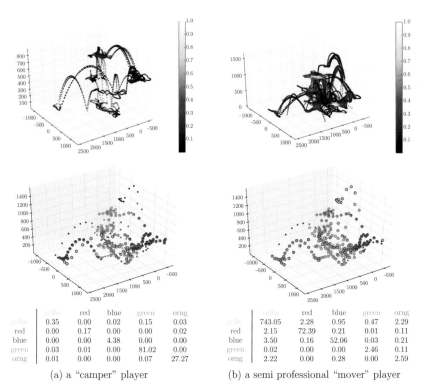

	yellw	red	blue	green	orng
yellw	0.35	0.00	0.02	0.15	0.03
red	0.00	0.17	0.00	0.00	0.02
blue	0.00	0.00	4.38	0.00	0.00
green	0.03	0.01	0.00	81.02	0.00
orng	0.01	0.00	0.00	0.07	27.27

	yellw	red	blue	green	orng
yellw	743.05	2.28	0.95	0.47	2.29
red	2.15	72.39	0.21	0.01	0.11
blue	3.50	0.16	52.06	0.03	0.21
green	0.02	0.00	0.00	2.46	0.11
orng	2.22	0.00	0.28	0.00	2.59

(a) a "camper" player (b) a semi professional "mover" player

Figure 13.5 Comparative analysis (derived from Bauckhage et al. (2014)) of movements of two different players on the *Quake III* map *q3dm17*. From top to bottom, each part of the figure respectively illustrates a heatmap indicating the frequently visited areas on the map, waypoints (in black) and DESICOM clusters (shown in color), and, finally, automatically determined affinities between the identified clusters.

mind that technology is elaborated by individuals acting as socialized subjects, that is to say, within the context of a given society's norms and customs.

Asserting technology's role as a mode of human production and a means of social reproduction and taking the context of emergence and use of technology into account while analyzing specific case studies characterizes the soft technological determinism approach. Bearing in mind the numerous critiques raised against technological determinism, one may argue that soft determinism does not presuppose that an ineluctable force imposes its rule on the whole of humanity – upholding technology as a primary catalyst of social and cultural change – but rather asserts that technology's tangible effects on humans can be studied within a social context: "Instead of treating 'technology' *per se* as the locus of historical agency, the soft determinists locate it in a far more various and complex social, economic, political, and cultural matrix" (Smith & Marx, 1994, p. xiii). Chandler (1995) refines this idea while arguing that

> [t]echnology is one of a number of mediating factors in human behaviour and social change, which both acts on and is acted on by other phenomena. Being critical of technological determinism is not to discount the importance of the fact that the technical features of different communication technologies facilitate different kinds of use, though the potential applications of technologies are not necessarily realized.[1]

Within this context and according to our sociosemiotic approach, soft technological determinism considers the development and use of technology as a site for relationships of power to unfold and produce social norms that will in turn reinforce or transform power dynamics (Foucault, 1971, 1976). As argued earlier, we consider technology as the effect of a cultural, ideological, institutional, and normative context, but we also acknowledge that it engenders cultural, ideological, and institutional content as well as social norms. "The important task [for the researcher] becomes . . . evaluating the material and social infrastructures specific technologies create for our life's activity" (Winner, 1986, p. 55). In that sense, we chose to study two online video games as technological artefacts, in order to highlight not only their impacts on their respective video game communities but also the development of specific cultural practices on each one of these digital platforms.

To this end, we adopt Charles Sanders Peirce's approach to the sign and its model, in which the sign is understood by means of its referential function. According to the pragmaticist and philosopher, the sign is defined as a relation between (1) a representamen, that is, how the sign appears to the senses, (2) an object, which is the thing being referred to as it is in the world and to the

---

[1] http://visual-memory.co.uk/daniel/Documents/tecdet/tdet13.html (accessed July 11, 2016).

mind, and (3) an interpretant, which is the (logical, kinetic, etc.) effect of the relation between representamen and object, that is to say, its contingent and specific signification. An interpretant is an always-already partial and circumstantial result of an interpretative process through which a particular mind (the interpreter) produces a relation among what it perceives, the object of that perception, and a resulting meaning or action. The stabilization of an interpretant implies that the sign's meaning has become a semiotic habit, that is to say, a habit of signification: "... what a thing means is simply what habits it involves" (Peirce, 1878, p. 131). More precisely:

> ... the identity of a habit depends on when and how it might lead us to act, not merely under such circumstances as are likely to arise, but under such as might possibly occur, no matter how improbable they may be. What the habit is depends on *when* and *how* it causes us to act. As for the *when*, every stimulus to action is derived from perception; as for the *how*, every purpose of action is to produce some sensible result. Thus, we come down to what is tangible and practical, as the root of every real distinction of thought, no matter how subtle it may be; and there is no distinction of meaning so fine as to consist in anything but a possible difference of practice. (Peirce 1878, p. 131)

Thus, as semioticians, our task is to characterize video game players' different practices, based on an analysis of the semiotic habits that emerge from sign-making processes. In other words, we start from what is perceived by players in order to make inferences about the establishment of specific interpretants, which allows us to deduce semiotic habits as well as the practices they entail, depending on pragmatic contexts of interpretation. To ensure the credibility of such an approach, researchers must collect a significant corpus of signs that strengthen their analyses: the more "examples" there are, the more solid their "argument" will be. To this end, they can count on a number of semiotic tools (typologies of signs, levels of interpretation, sign-making models, etc.) that are rigorously organized, for instance, in analysis grids to be systematically filled in.

The rigorous character of this semiotic approach secures the validity of the analyses and interpretations that it yields. Indeed, this approach to the production of knowledge means that one researcher alone can produce accurate analyses. While this could be seen as a weakness of the semiotic approach, collaborative work and the cross-referencing of results can minimize the biases intrinsic to individual research, as intersubjectivity fosters a sense of objectivity. In that sense, reception analysis or audience-focused studies (i.e., research based on the inquiry into a set of interpreters via questionnaires, interviews, etc.) are not necessary to establish the validity of semiotic research. Hybrid research methods that articulate both reception-focused and meaning production-focused studies remain possible, which can serve to validate semiotic observations or enrich findings with other information sources.

6.3 Case Studies

As mentioned earlier, our two case studies were independently selected, and we do not aim to compare them in any systematic way. Rather, our choice was informed by a focus on the degree of clarity with which the community's identity is defined, so as to be able to highlight sign systems that inform that community's semiotic habits and resulting practices. Several criteria structured our choice of case studies. First of all, we considered the reputation of individual games' communities, and the nature and tone of in-game exchanges between players. Second, we sought two cases in which players have the possibility to interact via avatars and communicate through chats. Moreover, case studies had to be both popular and recent enough to gather a significant number of players in stable online gaming communities with established and recognized characteristics. Finally, selected games had to provide players with the opportunity to play with new players at all times, through ad hoc temporary groups, for instance. These criteria influenced our choice of *League of Legends*, which was developed by Riot Games and released in 2009, and *Guild Wars 2*, developed by ArenaNet and released in 2012. According to the companies' official statistics, the former gathered a community of 67 million players in 2014[2] while the latter had sold 3.5 million copies one year after its release, in 2013.[3]

The *League of Legends* (LoL) community quickly became reputed for demonstrating toxic and harsh behaviors as well as making widespread use of slurs and insults. Meanwhile, the *Guild Wars 2* (GW2) community acquired a positive reputation for its friendliness and its welcoming and helpful attitude toward newcomers.

> [LoL] is a really weird community. High levels are thoroughly encouraged. You have to follow better players everywhere. If you don't play well enough, you can really get into deep trouble. In *Guild Wars 2*, there's more of a feeling of "let's help the community". In *League*, I think everything is highly capitalist. In the end, it's just "every one for themselves", may the best player win. And if others slow you down, it's their problem and it's their fault, ok?" (LG03_M_18[4])

---

[2] www.riotgames.com/articles/20140711/1322/league-players-reach-new-heights-2014 (accessed July 11, 2016).

[3] www.guildwars2.com/en/news/guild-wars-2-the-first-year/ (accessed July 11, 2016).

[4] Pseudonyms are codified as follows: game(s) played interviewee number_sex_age. *League of Legends* is abbreviated as "LG" and *Guild Wars 2* as "GW."

While some of the players we interviewed play both games regularly and adopt an either toxic or friendly attitude depending on the game, one may ask the following question: How do specific signifying practices encourage toxic or friendly behaviors in these two communities?

At first glance, the difference in type between the two games could seem to answer that question. While LoL is a multiplayer online battle arena (MOBA), GW2 is a massively multiplayer online role-playing game (MMORPG). On the one hand, LoL is mechanic driven. It consists in a fighting arena in which two five-player teams cooperate with and confront each other in order to destroy the enemy base. Players perform as individual avatars called "champions." On the other hand, GW2 is lore driven. Different types of individual or group activities are proposed around the elaboration of avatars in a persistent world, such as accomplishing goals through events,[5] exercising professions, doing dungeons, exploring the lore, etc. One could infer that LoL attracts primarily gamers who are used to first-person shooters (FPS) while GW2 massively appeals to role players. If our analysis of the two video game communities explains many but not all of their differences, then it offers only a partial answer to our question. Indeed, some MOBAs such as *Heroes of the Storm* (Blizzard Entertainment, 2015) present welcoming environments, while certain MMORPG communities can be aggressive, as the case of *World of Warcraft* (Blizzard Entertainment, 2004) shows. In that sense, if game types and target audiences are decisive factors in the making of video game communities, they certainly do not account for the social discrepancy between the so-called "toxic" LoL community and its purportedly "welcoming" counterpart that is the GW2 community. Therefore, game type was not a significant criterion in the selection of our two case studies, and we preferred to focus specifically on empirically observable social dynamics and gaming atmospheres.

6.4 Methodological Considerations

In order to diversify the approach to our question, we collected data following specific protocols across a 12-month time period (autumn 2014–summer 2015). Although our work is based on a semiotic approach, we gathered data that we proceeded to encode in an observation table (color, shape, location, size, function, etc. of observed signs) before codifying them in an analysis grid based on such criteria as the Peircean typology of signs (icons, indexes, symbols,

---

[5] "Events" are relatively small-scale quests. Reaching an objective gives all participating players rewards and experience points (xp).

etc.), the level of analysis (syntactic, semantic, pragmatic, etc.), and the semiotic paradigm being used (linguistic, rhetorical, semiopragmatic, sociosemiotic, etc.). Elements or documents that were considered as data are screenshots of gaming interfaces (all windows, features, tools, and main gaming experiences), screenshots of the games' official websites and forums, as well as official documents produced by the companies (websites, legal documents, ads, conferences). We focused on the organization of visual signs, on the presence or absence of features and tools, game mechanics, vocabulary and lexical fields used, etc. We also mapped the main websites on which players in the two video game communities can be seen.

To complete our observations and analyses, we organized 30- to 60 minute-long semistructured interviews with adult players (19–37 years old), most of whom were men (16 out of 18). Six subjects only played GW2 and another six only played LoL; the remaining six were well acquainted with both games. This stratified sample consisted of a homogeneous group of adults who speak French or English, who live in Quebec, and who have been playing for more than one year and practice at least five hours per week. A random sample was then drawn from that original sample. This random sample is obviously not likely to be representative of all players' opinions or illustrate the games' respective communities in a comprehensive way and hence cannot be generalized. However, we considered only one specific type of player and interviewed relatively few players because this kind of data collection was not our main source of information. Indeed, according to the semiotic approach described earlier, which we adopted in this study, reception analysis is not necessary to ensure the credibility of results. In that sense, we merely wanted to complement our observations with players' own opinions and voices at the end of the data collection stage. We wanted to hear from players about their perceptions of the games and their experiences, preferences, and critiques, as well as what they thought of their community's culture. Against the objectifying tendency of the semiotic approach, semistructured interviews made space for subjective interpretations of gaming experiences. Furthermore, data collection and interviews were facilitated by our research team's extensive experience with both games.

Finally, it should be mentioned that this research looks only at behaviors that are generally prescribed by the apparatus and its culture, that is to say, the "normalized" use of the two gaming platforms. Indeed, according to our soft technological determinist approach, subversive and deviant behaviors that transgress established norms, be it on a smaller or larger scale, always remain possible. Playing exclusively with friends, for instance, is one way in which one can have a fundamentally different gaming experience. However, within the scope of this chapter, only mainstream behaviors are discussed; we will not be extensively addressing transgressive behaviors. For the purpose of clarity and legibility, we also bypass a number of details and nuances. Furthermore, one must highlight that we do not aim to make any value judgments about either of the games under study. We do not claim, for instance, that GW2 is a "better game" than LoL. We believe that the value of any game experience depends on players' motivations. One cannot assess the ethical value of a game based solely on whether a game rewards behaviors driven by the principle of mutual aid (GW2), or promotes individualistic attitudes (LoL). All in all, we rather aim to show that while social experiences offered in each game vary greatly, such variety responds to different desires in terms of gaming experience.

6.5 Summary of Results

6.5.1 Learning Curves and Mutual Expectations among Players

To structure the presentation of our results, we follow players' progression in a game, starting with his or her learning of the game's fundamental rules, after being introduced to a game. On the one hand, our analysis reveals that GW2's soft learning curve is one of the main reasons for the community's welcoming attitude. Indeed, up to level 20, the game consists of a tutorial through which players are progressively introduced to different modes and activities. New elements are added to players' interfaces along the way, allowing them to steadily adapt to new gameplay features. Each new element (all new instances, mini-games, etc.) are explained by blocks of text. In this way, players progressively come to understand what is expected of them. Given the explicit presentation of information, the game effectively looks after a large part of players' learning process.

On the other hand, since its release, LoL has offered a tutorial to new players. The tutorial was improved in 2010 with the addition of battle training, which explains the game's basic principles, from minions, objectives, and champions to items and the importance of rounds. It was enhanced in 2011, and once again in 2012 with the *Coop vs AI* mode. In spite of these improvements to the original version, space for in-game learning is rather limited. Few strategies are taught and the tutorial does not reflect an actual experience of the game's competitive mode. Indeed, the gameplay is much more complex than what is revealed in the tutorial, and simulations differ greatly from games with real players. The gap between simulated practice and "real" games makes for a steep learning curve for new players, especially considering that metagaming is not taught in the tutorial.

Metagaming designates the norms and strategies that dictate the way in which players should navigate through the game. Although it is entirely defined by players, it can seem arbitrary. Yet, metagaming rules are highly elaborated, as their function is to optimize the efficacy of champions' actions and team efficiency during games. For instance, in a five-player team, there is always a tank/bruiser in the toplane, an apcarry in the midlane, an adcarry and support couple in the bottom lane, and a player in the jungle.[6] Any changes in the established organization of players' roles and champion types on the map can lead to the team's defeat. All advanced players expect others to master these implicit rules defined by the metagame system. However, a champion could be assigned a top role by Riot Games even if players judged that he or she would be more useful as support based on experience. Once he or she becomes support, that player is expected to take a combination of support-related items, the knowledge of which is also implicit in the metagame system. Players must learn those numerous and highly specific rules in advance, either by playing with the help of a more experienced friend, or by finding the information on external platforms such as wikis and forums, which are most often very well developed. It is the player's responsibility to seek the information on these platforms, especially regarding their player's builds, which are often complex. While everyone takes for granted that all players study gameplay mechanics on their own, players will rarely help each other in-game, and conflicts can emerge from a player's failure to optimize his or her build. Within this context, mutual expectations among (both new and experienced) players are very high, and it seems that players must know how to play well before they even start actually playing the game.

This phenomenon is all the more evident given that more experienced players can invest lower level categories, thus complicating new players' integration in LoL. While these "smurfs" are much more efficient in lower level categories, they may throw the gameplay off balance and put pressure on new players.

---

[6] The tank/bruiser is a powerful champion (thanks to a great quantity of life points or strong armors or both). He is usually placed at the top of the map. His main goal is to initiate fights thanks to his crowd control abilities, as well as protect the top lane and perform split pushes (i.e., destroy another line while adversaries are not trying to kill him). He is also a significant target for the team's opponents. Tanks and bruisers are mostly alike; however, if a bruiser performs too well too fast, he can become the team's main engine (carry).

The adcarry (attack damage carry) is a champion whose goal is to deal high amounts of sustained damage with regular attacks.

The apcarry (ability power carry) is typically a mage whose goal is to quickly inflict important damage (burst damage) to the team's opponents.

The support's goal is to protect the adcarry while giving him bonus points and kills. He may also support the whole team while healing teammates and incapacitating adversaries.

The jungle occasionally supports other champions in the team while carrying out surprise attacks.

> There's actually a lot of smurfing, so if you're a newcomer, you're not going to feel welcomed. Increasingly, you'll be seeing fewer and fewer new players. Like if you try to start playing LoL, you realize right away that many high level players create new accounts either because their original one was banned or because they're tired of playing at their level, as they don't find themselves good enough. They just want to get that feeling of victory so they create another account at a lower level. And that doesn't make for a pleasant atmosphere, as you never get the impression that you're making progress in *League of Legends*. (GWLG05_M_24)

This added difficulty in the learning curve is not compensated by any help feature: no in-game structure allows players who are new to the game or ignorant of some information to find help. In other words, in LoL, the elaboration of collective representations and the acquisition of semiotic habits is not performed *in-game*, as many rules and norms (the game mechanics and metagaming) have to be learned elsewhere.

In contrast, mutual help features and tools are numerous in GW2, the first of which is the "Looking for group" feature that allows players to not only ask for but also offer help. While some guilds give tutorials for new players within their group, guild structures also offer great support (as we show in the text that follows). Moreover, features such as guild inventories incite players in each guild to drop and take items or currency at will according to their needs and possessions. This promotes sharing within the community as well as a collaborative early experience for new players, as they get access to common inventories only three days after admission in the guild.

The sharing of loot, experience points, and resources through duplication is another feature of gameplay mechanics that encourages mutual aid. Instead of being equally or unequally distributed among players, resources and rewards are simply duplicated for all players who participated in a fight or gathered items.[7] Hence, players do not compete for resources and rewards, and the number of players involved in an action does not negatively impact their chances of amassing loot and resources. In addition, difficulty levels are always proportional, as the level of avatars to attack varies according to the number of involved players. The more players there are in a group, the harder it will be to kill a "monster," and the higher the quality of rewards. From the perspective of gameplay mechanics, playing as a team does not present any disadvantage and can even be advantageous as far as rewards are concerned.

Likewise, in GW2, the level of players' avatars depends on region levels, that is to say, that whatever a player's level, his or her power can be adjusted

---

[7] Duplication does not function as identical copy but rather depends on randomized attribution, that is to say, that all players may access rewards or resources, the value or quantity of which is randomized at any time for each player.

by the game system (and most often brought down) according to the general level in a given zone. Therefore, power leveling does not impact other players and new players can be as powerful as others in a specific zone, which makes their integration and learning experience easier and favors more convivial gaming practices. Also, in player versus player (PvP) mode, all players have similar stats and may access identical weapons and armors: this makes overpower impossible and facilitates a balance in gameplay.

The peculiar relationship to random elements and randoming also illustrates the absence of overpower in GW2. Indeed, all skills have a large range of efficiency: exact calculations of damage, for instance, are more difficult because there can be an up to a 200-point difference in range at any given time, that is, an 18% difference (between 900 and 1,100 damage points). Therefore, it is difficult to entirely predict and optimize one's performance, as part of it is left to chance. As a portion of the outcomes is out of players' control, individual responsibility is somehow minimized in case of failure on the part of players.

In contrast, LoL seeks to minimize random factors so that all parameters may be calibrated and measured. This complete absence of random elements, except for critical chance that remains random, partly explains the positive valuation of optimization. Indeed, the community puts great emphasis on optimal builds as well as complex and accurate calculations. In an environment where all game mechanics are, in theory, under players' complete control, players are made responsible for optimizing their performances. This sense of individual responsibility is one of the main triggers for conflict and disrespectful dynamics between players (slurs, insults), whatever their level of experience with the game.

6.5.2 Collective and Personal Goals

The dynamics of individual or shared responsibility are also manifest in the games' objectives. Whereas goals are mainly individual in LoL, they are collective in GW2. First of all, it should be noted that GW2 offers numerous objectives, a great diversity of experiences, and a large game space. Even if it is possible to play alone in some cases, most activities require teamwork, which means that individual players' actions are often motivated by common objectives that guide the whole group. Moreover, common objectives are actually defined while groups are being set up, which promotes social cohesion within groups. In addition, as argued earlier, collective actions are encouraged as resources or rewards are obtained through duplication rather than (equitable or inequitable) division among players. All players involved in a fight randomly receive rewards after it ends.

Furthermore, in player versus environment (PvE) mode, giving life to other players is rewarded, as resuscitating an avatar (rez) gives experience points. In this way, players have a direct personal interest in helping other players during fights, whether they are strangers or friends: not only do they all receive rewards, but also no part of the operation deprives any player of his or her rewards. Such mechanics effectively prevent unpleasant behaviors such as kills theft (striking the final stroke in order to obtain rewards), "camping" (hiding during a fight so as to come out only for the final shot and collect rewards) and "ninja looting" (stealing a resource from a player while he or she fights near that resource).

If, in LoL, the main goal (winning the fight) is common to all players involved in a team, many subobjectives or more global objectives are individual, which encourages an individualistic outlook in-game. Indeed, objectives are shaped by a limited game space and repetitive patterns in gameplay. This repetitive structure allows players to perfect their abilities round after round, and players' progress is reflected in the game's ranking system. Whether or not one plays in ranked mode, the matching system is based on rank (match making rating). The exact Elo system, which is a normalized mode of ranking used in checks, for instance, is not made available to players. Yet, it is based entirely on a specific ratio between games won, games played, defeated players' strength, and other factors. The matchmaking rating is a modified version of the Elo. It is based on the same system of point attribution, but it also considers whether players play alone or in teams.

This ranking system means that players are in constant competition against each other. However, players do not value all games equally: one game might be simultaneously crucial for one or two players and ordinary for others. This is especially the case for "promo" games, in which players attempt to go from one rank to another. They must obtain a 2 out of 3 or a 3 out of 5. If they fail, they will be sanctioned and will lose a few ranking points. This discrepancy between players' perceptions of the stakes in a given game constitutes another source of conflict. Indeed, some players might put pressure on others in the team given the importance of that game for their individual progression, while others might be rather detached; this situation can be frustrating for both parties.

In addition, resources are unequally shared among players, as each player accumulates his or her own rewards. This means that individual goals in LoL can become greatly dissimilar, if not incompatible. For instance, even if all players receive rewards after attacking the tower, the baron, and the dragon, the player who reaches the objective will obtain the most rewards. As far as kills are concerned, experience is shared among all players, yet assists receive between 0 and 150 points while the player who performs the kill receives around

300 points depending on several factors, such as first blood. Kills are extremely important in quantifying performances, so that the imbalance in reward points motivates kill "thefts," which are even more obvious when smurfs take advantage of less experienced players' lower performance level. This phenomenon is exacerbated by the snowball effect, in which all actions have repercussions for the duration of the game and come one after the other in an exponential way. This means that the more a player wins, the more powerful he or she becomes, and vice versa. Finally, although specific items allow some champions to heal, players cannot resuscitate (rez) each other and all players must deal with the penalties resulting from their avatar's death on their own.

6.5.3 Relationship to Competition and Metrics

If, at first glance, all five players in an LoL team seem to share a similar objective, that is, to coordinate the roles of each champion in order to destroy the opponent's base, other goals transcend each particular game, such as the optimization of one's position in the ranking system. This keeps players in competition against each other, inciting them to navigate gameplay mechanics with their self-interest rather than the group's collective interest in mind. Other personal objectives in the game can also justify an individualistic attitude, which can easily create imbalances in teamwork efforts. In contrast, although all players remain relatively equal in GW2, they are encouraged to help each other through gameplay mechanics that reward teamwork. So, they may compete only against themselves. Therefore, players have an interest in collaborating throughout their progress in the game.

These two very different ways of framing competitiveness and competition, be it against oneself or against others, are also revealed by the games' use of qualitative and quantitative representations. Indeed, while it greatly reduces the importance of metrics, GW2 prioritizes a qualitative relationship to the game, which is unusual in MMORPGs. Players cannot access any statistics regarding their performances and the effects of one's build are not clearly identified; hence, it is difficult to significantly optimize one's avatar. Likewise, there are no statistics regarding other players' abilities, builds, or profiles. This means that players must trust each other on what they claim about their build in order to ensure balance and cohesion within the team.

What is the specificity of GW2? I would say that what really struck me is the lack– the absence of competition between players. This community is more interesting because, in WoW, everything you do is measured, and it's the same in League: the kills you do, the gold you amass, your creep score . . . everything is displayed. If you're low on something, people will come and mess with you. In GW2, there's no

> damage meter, nothing like that... You don't know whether you're good; you don't
> even know who's good. Obviously, you notice that when you see someone strike,
> you see if they inflict damage or keep dying, but there really isn't a metric to
> measure that" (GWLG02_M_32)

Unlike many games of its type, GW2 does not make weapons and armors identifiable status symbols, that is to say that the "quality" of a player's stock is not necessarily indicative of a player's level. Weapons and armors are not necessarily linked to any statistics and only serve an aesthetic purpose. Incidentally, endgame stock is relatively easy to obtain through crafting, for instance. Players "dress" their avatars according to looks rather than power, as this player of both LoL and GW2 testifies:

> In a way, the OP [overpower] tendency of the power gamer in me was a little
> disappointed by the fact that there were no metrics [in GW2]. Perhaps it was a good
> thing though. It's what makes the game what it is. It forced me to focus less on stats
> and more on other things like my avatar's look. I had never – I didn't *care*, I just
> wanted to be as powerful as possible. Well, oddly enough, I found myself wanting
> my avatar to look good." (GWLG02_M_37)

Furthermore, apart from level ranking, which is relative to the space in which players evolve, there is no ranking system in GW2. While all players may gain access to the top, which is not hierarchically defined, there is no sense of competition among players to reach first place. This means that players share a common interest in collaborating to reach their objectives rapidly.

Meanwhile, metrics are crucial in LoL, as game dynamics are almost entirely structured by its complex ranking system. Statistics regarding performances, one's own build, as well as other players' skills and builds are clearly identified. Players may easily access other players' profiles and evaluate their power based on the quantification of performances; hence, profiles become identifiable marks of player status.

> Want it or not, [in LoL] you fall into a sort of playground mentality that requires
> you to perform better than others, to be tougher than others and show it. It's a
> bit hard to make friends and have fun interactions in that kind of environment.
> (GWLG01_M_23)

Each player's kill, death, and assist counts are visible in-game in real time. Hence, everyone may judge others' performances in each game. Even the honor banner system, introduced in 2012 to encourage "good" behaviors, quantifies players' positive impact. This system, which was popular in the early days of LoL but then quickly became obsolete, offered honor banners to players based on a specific ratio determined by the number of honors they received from other players as well as the number of games they played. Therefore, in LoL, even behaviors that are qualitatively perceived as "good" are quantified and inscribed in the game's complex metrics system.

6.5.4 Practice Intensity

In LoL, both the ranking system and the important role of stats in judging others' as well as one's own performance encourage an intensive gaming practice. Indeed, playing very regularly furthers one's chances to move upward in the ranking system and eventually get from one league to another. Whereas pointing to a player's presence in a lower league (e.g., bronze) is a common means to put other players down and often stands for a proper insult, it is clear that vertical mobility (moving upward from one league to another) is highly valued and induces respect. Also, when players progress from league to league, their margin of error shrinks as they compete with increasingly expert players. Showing off one's skills and level thus becomes all the more difficult and requires intensive practice. This explains the development of e-sport leagues such as Master and Challenger, assuming that Challenger players qualify as e-sport–level players.

The fact that players have to start from scratch and rebuild their avatar for each game also incites repetitive practice. Players may rebuild the same champion(s) with a similar build in order to improve it as much as possible. The complexity of each build and the quantity of champions (more than 120) justifies practice intensity as well, considering not only players' genuine desire to master the game but also that constant changes brought into gameplay mechanics demand a high level of adaptability on the part of players. One player explains: "You constantly have to adapt to new metagaming rules, new patches, because they nerfed this guy and buffed that one. In this game, if you stop playing for a week, you're already rusty, you've already lost your skills" (GWLG04_M_30). Indeed, the longer a player is absent from the game, the harder it will be for him or her to come back to it. For instance, while seasons last for about 12 months, leaving during one season and coming back during the next entails copious amounts of reading in order to learn all the new mechanics and metagaming rules. It is just as if one had to learn how to play an entirely new game.

Such incentives for players to practice more intensively result in an increase in the number of games played, which can minimize the relative importance of each game (promo games set aside). Such trivialization of individual games can be correlated to the banalization of relationships with other players. As the quantity of games makes events and interactions within a particular game less meaningful than outcomes and resulting rankings, appreciating the quality of one's interactions with other players becomes more difficult or less obvious. In this way, players may dismiss their own toxic behaviors as being rather infrequent, or determined by rather insignificant particular circumstances. The tendency to interpret toxic behaviors as minor incidents given the important number of games played was confirmed by Jeffrey Lin, LoL's lead social systems designer, in his conference entitled "The Science behind Shaping Player Behavior in Online Games" (2013).[8] Indeed, he asserts that although 98% of LoL players show nontoxic behavioral profiles, great majority of players does "have [its] own toxic behaviors, but it's not too severe, it's not too frequent. And this makes sense: all of us have our bad days."[9] In other words, millions of LoL players generally show good behaviors. Yet, out of any 10 players present in a game, it is quite probable to meet at least one who is going through a "bad day." This would explain LoL's reputation for the toxicity of its social interactions. Yet, according to the company's argument, it is "normal" for negative behavioral patterns to manifest in players' interactions with other players.

6.5.5 Consequences of Players' Actions on Other Players

One player's behavior may significantly affect other players' gaming experience. Once more, major differences can be observed between the ways in which players' actions impact others in the two games under study. First of all, with regard to avatar complementarity, one may notice that the threshold of complementarity is very low in GW2. Except for exceptional cases, specific team compositions according to predetermined roles are not required for events and dungeons. In this way, players may progress in the game and form teams as they please. Also, players may temporarily leave one thread of action and change avatars without missing out on the event their team is working on. Moreover, leaving a group never results in negative consequences for oneself or for other players, as there are no sanctions for leaving and players who have left are easily replaced thanks to the "looking for group" feature. Conversely, groups can decide to dismiss players when their unpleasant or harmful attitude warrants it: guild leaders can directly expel players from their guild, and players can use the "kick" feature through a democratic vote within the group.

In contrast, in LoL, the high degree of complementarity between avatars pushes players to select a champion according to its coherence with team strategies. As explained earlier, in the absence of one of the roles prescribed by

---

[8] http://gdcvault.com/play/1017940/The-Science-Behind-Shaping-Player (accessed July 11, 2016).
[9] http://gdcvault.com/play/1017940/The-Science-Behind-Shaping-Player, 3:48 to 3:56 (accessed July 11, 2016).

metagaming rules, team imbalances can lead to defeat. So, players are implicitly compelled to make choices in line with other players' decisions. Players "call" their role on the lobby's chat room, and then go on to choose their champion bearing in mind the role that they announced. All five players in a team usually participate in deciding each role's composition so as to ensure proper balance between roles. Choices are then locked using the "lock" feature. If one player locks his or her own choice of champion before collective decision making has taken place ("insta-lock"), the rest of the team must then take decisions according to the insta-locker's choice. Such individualistic behavior is detrimental to the whole team, as it increases the likelihood of defeat and undermines other players' freedom in building their champions. Therefore, before the game even starts, champion selection is a significant source of conflict between players.

Furthermore, in LoL, leaving a group can bear dire consequences for both oneself and other players. Indeed, players who leave a group during a game are sanctioned: they may not play until the game is over. Also, if the behavior is recurrent, warnings may be issued, potentially leading to a ban. This system puts considerable pressure on players to stay in their team, even when the atmosphere in a game becomes nasty. While players are "obliged" to go through such unpleasant gaming experiences, they may be more likely to vent their frustration in the next game, hence causing negative affects in other players, and so on. While players may not be replaced halfway through a game, one player's decision to leave a game regardless of sanctions destabilizes the team. This has considerable consequences for other players, as it leads to an important power differential in the fight (four against five) and, most likely, to defeat. Surrendering is the only way in which players may stop a fight using game features. This requires that the team take a collective decision to end the fight and grant victory to their opponents. However, this feature is made available only 20 minutes into a fight, which seems like a long time if the atmosphere quickly becomes belligerent and escalates into toxic behaviors.

6.5.6 Managing Toxic Behaviors

ArenaNet relies on managers to deal with unpleasant behaviors. In GW2, managers' presence is visible through clearly identifiable avatars that travel across the game, giving information, registering complaints, and helping players. The company is also very present on GW2's official forum to make sure to offer as much support to players as possible. Furthermore, the "report" feature allows anyone to flag toxic behaviors and ArenaNet has the ability to ban perpetrators from the game if and when incidents are found to be serious or recurrent.

However, the company's unorthodox methods of reprisal against one player caused controversy in a 2015 case. The player in question had discovered a loophole in the structure of the game, and took advantage of it so as to "terrorize" a large number of players during a *World versus World* (WvW) game. The incident lasted for weeks. While the player's behavior was deemed unacceptable according to the software's rules, ArenaNet proceeded to an in-game "public humiliation" in May 2015. The company took control of the player's avatar, undressed it, and forced it to jump from a high floor of Divinity's Reach, hence precipitating its symbolic "death."[10] While it was reclaimed by the GW2 community, this kind of sanction remains exceptional, as its ethics are, to say the least, debatable. Nonetheless, this incident shows that the company took responsibility in the management of such toxic behavior.

Likewise, Riot Games is also very active on forums and encourages positive modes of interactions between players in LoL, especially through its code of conduct, which is available online.[11] The company also produced an ad campaign to encourage good gaming practices and promote cooperation in-game, arguing that this approach leads to success and victories just as well as confrontation.[12] However, Riot Games counts primarily on a "tribunal" with regard to the management of toxic behaviors. This tribunal, which was set up in 2011 (and disabled in 2014), is a self-managed institution run by and for players. It operates via a social voting system: any player can log into the tribunal, examine cases under scrutiny by reading the game's chat, and recommend appropriate sanctions. If the player whose behavior is being examined is found guilty, the tribunal pronounces an official sanction, which is adjusted according to the nature of the fault as well as the number of counts. This means that Riot Games places responsibility for handling harmful attitudes and actions between the hands of players themselves. In other words, players have to self-manage behaviors within their community. In this way, the company delegates responsibility for the task. Aside from the ethical questions that this form of mob justice raises, one may highlight the possibility of false reports and the banalization of harm in such a system. Some toxic behaviors might well be minimized, if not tolerated, especially in cases in which insults would seem

---

[10] www.engadget.com/2015/05/07/guild-wars-2-cheater-humiliation/ ; www.polygon.com/2015/5/6/8559503/guild-wars-2-cheater-banned-video ; www.idigitaltimes.com/cheating-hackers-guild-wars-2-character-stripped-naked-killed-banning-watch-hilarious-439031 (accessed July 11, 2016).

[11] http://gameinfo.na.leagueoflegends.com/en/game-info/get-started/summoners-code/ (accessed July 11, 2016).

[12] http://na.leagueoflegends.com/en/news/game-updates/player-behavior/does-teamwork-win-more-games; http://na.leagueoflegends.com/en/media/art/teamwork-op (accessed July 11, 2016).

justifiable. There is a significant possibility that one may be judged according to criteria that lie outside of the scope of justice.

6.5.7 Social Stability

Social structures in LoL also explain such banalization of in-game toxic behaviors. Players seldom stick to a single team and often prefer to follow their own trajectories, as shown by the solo queue mode. The standardized format of players' representation through champions may encourage players to instrumentalize other players, or even forget about the fact that other players are human subjects, as their multifaceted subjectivity as human agents is barely visible through the singular plane of their avatar identity. One player confirms that trend:

> In the end, you end up not really caring who is and who is not in your team, it continually changes, unless you play in a premade team. If you are in a premade team, you have to play with people you already know. So, putting such cases aside, you really don't care about who you're playing with. So you don't need [to interact with them] – like I'm not chatting while I'm playing League. People will rarely say nice things; sometimes, most times, they will say irritating things. I ignore them, I play my game." (LG06_M_26)

The stability of relationships between players, illustrated by the recurrence and intensity of contact between players, is a crucial element in furthering harmonious gaming experiences and behaviors in any video game. Chances for the development of mutual respect, or even friendship, increase as players spend more time playing together. Both games under study offer different means to form groups, be it through team building and the "looking for group" or "squad" feature in GW2, or group formation in ranked solo/duo, ranked team, team builder, or normal mode in LoL. Yet, it is significant that GW2 encourages teaming up with "known" players first and foremost, even if it remains possible to engage in games with complete strangers.

In GW2, guilds are stable groups of players that make certain features available to their members and organize players' socialization. In this way, guilds promote stability in social relationships. As hierarchized tribes, guilds provide support to all members on both functional and symbolic levels. Aside from guild inventories, several features promote cohesion within the group, such as an exclusive chat box, an open list of online members, guild-specific quests and puzzles, and guild points that allow members to unlock content in the game. Furthermore, guild membership is made clearly legible, as bracketed acronyms next to avatars' names signal players' affiliations. Such signs thus provide evidence for social position but also produce contextualized identities. One GW2 player explains how the features of his avatar impact his gaming practice:

> There are 260 members [in my guild]: I'm pretty sure to find someone who's already visited a certain region and knows it better than I do. I'm pretty sure that I'll have resources in a region that I'm not sure how to use, or resources for an event that I don't know how to finish. Because I acquired the resource in World versus World [WvW], I act as a resource for a lot of people. Helping and guiding people is very time-consuming. (GW06_M_25)

Moreover, gameplay mechanics increase one's chances to come across the same players during group formation thanks to guild membership, automatic teaming up by megaservers, and the friends list. Players may choose whom to add in their friends list and can also be added by other players. Also, friends lists are linked to the user's account rather than a specific avatar. Conversely, GW2 also proposes a blocking feature that allows players to mute disruptive players' accounts. Therefore, it is important to mention that team making is influenced not only by such features as friends lists, but also by the matching algorithms producing those friends lists. In other words, if in-game identity signaling significantly impacts communication and practices such as mutual help, the automated mode of team "suggestion" (e.g., processes involving megaservers) also play a role in determining players' choices. This means that technological mediation itself contributes to shaping specific socialization practices.

Identity recognition is another factor promoting stable social relationships. In GW2, playing as different avatars is common, as a regular account allows for five avatars, but the account name is clearly indicated and accessible to other players at all times. The visual predominance of pseudonyms over avatars, that is to say the ability to see players' names more easily than avatar names, means that players use each other's names instead of avatar names when communicating with each other. The fact that players refer to each other in this way furthers a more complex sense of identity in processes of mutual recognition as well as self-reflective identity formation. Also, avatars can be personalized in different ways: players may modify some features of their physical appearance, elaborate on their background, and customize their appearance through accessories and gear. Also, as power discrepancies do not affect actual gameplay, the fact that avatars in each region are leveled encourages players to practice with friends, be it out-game acquaintances or users known through other avatars. Hardcore gamers can play with less experienced players in a harmonious way. It is even possible to choose one's avatar according to whom one wants to play with, which allows selecting a lower level avatar for games with friends who practice on a more occasional basis, for instance.

Meanwhile, LoL encourages two types of gaming practice. On the one hand, in nonranked mode, players may team up on the spot with as many "friends" as they want or form new teams with strangers before each game. On the other hand, in ranked mode, one may play solo or duo, or form stable teams provided that one plays regularly enough to ensure constancy. Although it is always possible to play in stable teams (premade teams), that is to say, with the same players (e.g., friends from real life), organizing regular practices with other players is a substantial logistic challenge. Besides, ranked teams start out at the Bronze 5 level, and (five-player) team-ranking functions in the same way as solo player ranking. Therefore, the stakes in team building are considerably high: if a player is less efficient than his or her teammates, he or she might become a "weak link," which may create tensions and conflicts within the group and lead to the player's exclusion. Therefore, while friendship and competition make for stronger social ties, stable teams remain the best way to prevent toxic behaviors nonetheless.

> I try to stick to the same group of people. I don't mind playing with other Quebeckers, I can Skype with them sometimes, which is cool, but when I talk to a random stranger, it's pretty rare that they try to be even remotely sympathetic in-game or that they attempt to do anything apart from dissing others. (LG03_M_18)

Nevertheless, in LoL, the fact that players have to form a new team at the beginning of each game (assisted by the Elo system) does not favor stability in social ties. Without a conscious intention and effort to do so, one may never play with the same players twice. Such dynamics are confirmed by the sheer size of the community. Harmful behaviors might be further banalized given that players are almost completely anonymous.

Moreover, in LoL, emphasis is put on champions' rather than players' identity. Champion names are more visible than pseudonyms on the interface and players use champion names to call out to each other during fights. This means that the identity of players themselves is only secondary, if it is considered at all, given that avatars' capabilities are determined by the characteristics of champions. Champions may be personalized with skins, which are identical for all players and come at a (monetary) cost. Owning rare and expensive skins enhances social status and destandardizes players' identity to a certain extent, as a majority of players are not willing to spend money on their avatar's appearance. Even if specific abilities such as runes, skills, and summoner abilities make avatars more personalized, champions' abilities are generally stable and even come to define players' roles in the metagame. While profile metrics define players' sense of identity more so than visual signs, the preeminence of quantitative individuation and player interactions leaves relatively little space for in-game social recognition.

6.5.8 Communication

Lastly, communication should also be considered as a crucial catalyst of social relationships. Even if it is possible to play without verbally communicating with other players and to "mute" unhelpful players in both games, there are observable differences in the way each game produces the conditions for communication. Whereas in GW2 communicating with other player is not compulsory as long as the required actions are performed within the framework of the group's objectives, it is crucial in LoL. Indeed, a failure in communication can result in defeat if players do not convey what is expected of them. As argued earlier, mutual expectations among players are high in LoL, as players' individual success depends on other players' actions. For instance, the "vision" of each individual player coconstitutes the team's general "vision," that is to say, the visual identification of enemies on the game's map depends on the combination of active avatars' positions on the map. If one player loses sight of an opponent, the latter will disappear from the map, which is called the "fog of war." Players must rapidly inform their teammates in that situation.

It is important to stress that communicational tools in LoL are very efficient owing to the specificity of their function. Therefore, conversational content is mostly instrumental and seldom requires politeness or decorum, which means that communication is not a catalyst for social relationships in and of itself. For instance, "pings" are used extensively during games. They consist of five clearly identifiable icons, which can be placed on the playing ground to signal simple information to other players: "need help," "on my way," "missing enemy," "danger," as well as a red sign, the signification of which changes depending on its position on the playing surface. Transmission must be quick. The function of these signs is not to engage in elaborated discussions but to trigger action, as shown by the fact that they are predominantly indexical (action-inducing rather than reflexion-inducing). Putting aside the red sign's contextual interpretation, pings' signification must be univocal, which stresses the importance of a quick and unambiguous semiotic process motivated by a signaling rather than communicational purpose: "I go 'ping,' to talk to them and say 'we do this and this and that.' Sometimes I'll swear as well, but that's rare" (LG03_M_18).

Pings also emit clearly audible sounds at each activation, which further draws teammates' attention to the message, thus amplifying their communicational effect. However, although pings are difficult to ignore, they become omnipresent in one's gaming experience, and can even be used to bother other players. Similarly, the (written) chat box, which is the other main means of communication in LoL, consists of a large and very visible window, which means that toxic verbal content is hard to ignore. Therefore, both pings and the chat room can act as invasive and disruptive signs rather than helpful communicational tools in the context of their purportedly detrimental use.

Conversely, in GW2, different types of chat rooms structure group interactions: the guild, proximity, map, party, squad, team (in both PvP and WvW modes), and private chat rooms. The written chat window is adjustable in size; it can also be made transparent, and thus almost invisible. In this way, it is easy to ignore unpleasant conversations.

> It feels like playing and being on a forum simultaneously, but the chat interface is so discreet that you can hardly notice it, even when you play for hours. If you want to talk about something, whatever it is, then just do it, but if that doesn't appeal to you, you really don't get the impression that you're missing out on anything. (GWLG01_M_23)

Besides, while the gameplay does not require players to interact directly through conversation, GW2 produces the general conditions for extensive communication, from interpersonal communication about topics beyond the scope of the game itself to, most importantly, mutual aid in the form of requests for help or information. For instance, it is common for more experienced players to ensure that other players understand how to reach an objective before starting a quest or a fight, which is a very rare behavior in LoL.

In that sense, although communication habits and patterns greatly differ between LoL and GW2, they constitute pertinent indicators of cultural norms within the two communities. In GW2, players try to maintain friendly social relations, as shown by the widespread expression of gratitude, thanks, and congratulations when objectives are met. Also, if the term "noob" is generally understood as a derogatory term in LoL, even by players in the lower levels (who are "new" to the game themselves), the word is rather used to ask for advice and help in GW2. As a matter of fact, such requests rarely remain unanswered in GW2, as mutual help is one of the community's main identity traits. "There is always a positive state of mind in GW2. There will always be people who are ready to participate and help out. But I would say that it is not surprising at all, as this is something that is deeply engrained in the game's functioning" (GWLG03_M_37). Indeed, one may add that the GW2 community has successfully appropriated game features in order to further its ethics of mutual aid. For instance, the "looking for group" feature is often used as a transportation tool, allowing players to guide others through a map.

While it is common practice in GW2, mutual assistance can still be observed in LoL, yet almost exclusively on external websites such as the League of Legends Wiki, Mobafire, LoLPro, LoLKing, and solomid.net, where the community shares an array of information, resources, and build optimization tools. The impressive quantity of cultural productions, ranging from fanart,[13] parodies,[14] and streaming[15] to music,[16] fanfilms,[17] cosplay,[18] and more, reflects the active, prolific, and passionate temperament of the LoL community. Nevertheless, this culture of sharing seems to be most often set aside while in-game, as it is replaced by the adversarial use of slurs as well as vulgar and harsh language, sometimes right from the outset (at one's entry in the lobby) before any action is even performed.

It seems important to stress that there are many ways to negatively impact other players' gaming experiences in LoL: for instance, using the insta-lock feature during players' choice of a champion, harassing players in chat windows both in the lobby and during games, using "pings" excessively, stealing enemies' or minions' kills, voluntarily letting oneself die, putting oneself away from keyboard (AFK), rage quitting, refusing to follow team tactics or basic strategies (established by the metagame), or smurfing in lower categories. Also, subscription to the game is free and requires only an email address. Hence, it is easy to open several accounts on LoL, which makes banning users less efficient. Conversely, GW2 players pay a membership fee,[19] which deters users from opening more than one account and may even dissuade certain types of players from subscribing at all. This also permits decreasing the recurrence of bans. In addition, GW2 greatly limits opportunities to harm others. Remaining passive, that is to say, not helping (not healing, not resuscitating [rez], not participating during fights), may well be the worst possible attitude. However, passivity yields no results, as passive players do not earn experience points; neither do they obtain rewards that they would have obtained had they helped their teammates. Harassing players in chat rooms is still possible, yet the fact

---

[13] http://na.leagueoflegends.com/en/media/art/Fan%20Art (accessed on July 11, 2016).

[14] www.youtube.com/watch?v=Idz7MZz9-vc&feature=youtu.be (accessed July 11, 2016).

[15] www.solomid.net/streams (accessed July 11, 2016).

[16] www.youtube.com/watch?v=0xk6OyJii4E (accessed July 11, 2016).

[17] www.youtube.com/watch?v=k8UdPiZaP2U (accessed July 11, 2016).

[18] www.lolcosplay.com/ (accessed July 11, 2016).

[19] A free mode was introduced on August 29, 2016. However, this change in accessibility does not seem to have significantly affected the identity of GW2's community.

that the chat window may be minimized or made transparent makes it easier for targeted players to overlook slurs and insults.

6.6 Discussion

Our observations highlight the fact that while video games allow, encourage, or prevent certain actions and strategies, they normalize specific behaviors and influence cultural elaborations in each video game community. Indeed, we have identified a number of signs and sign systems, the effects and recurrence of which foster the elaboration of interpretative habits. While such habits come to influence the way players not only adapt to game mechanisms but also shape collective meaning-making practices, our semiotic analysis has allowed us to better understand the construction and reinforcement of "a standard of appropriate behavior for actors with a given identity" (Finnemore & Sikkink, 1998, p. 891). In other words, we have highlighted a set of in-game representations and we have shown how these representations, once their meaning is collectively stabilized, both influence and directly trigger specific actions and behaviors. Accumulating evidence for the strong link between such observable signs and "toxic, competitive and harsh" or "welcoming, respectful and peaceful" behavioral patterns has helped us understand better the two games' respective reputations as well as the reasons why certain behaviors and types of interpersonal relationships are promoted or discouraged. The way in which new players are introduced to games has provided meaningful insights in this regard: if GW2 players' habits are first and foremost influenced by the technological apparatus and writers' design choices, new LoL players rather rely on the community's preexisting interpretative habits in order to define their own gaming practices. This partly explains why expectations toward players are so high in LoL. Indeed, players must demonstrate knowledge of many facts and features that are often not introduced in the game. The opposite can be found in GW2, where expectations are rather low given that players may remain in the initial tutorial section and move up toward interpersonal interactions once their knowledge of the game has stabilized. Therefore, following Umberto Eco's semiotic terminology (1984), one may argue that LoL players' encyclopedias largely depend on knowledge and experiences developed through the community, whereas GW2 players' are, to a certain extent and up to a certain level of practice, elaborated on an individual learning process.

Such reliance on collective knowledge and experiences in LoL is reinforced by avatar complementarity. Indeed, the important interdependence of avatars exacerbates expectations toward other players, as failure on the part of one

player can have repercussions on the team as a whole. In that sense, consequences of players' actions on other players are very important and it is impossible not to take others into account. In contrast, although it is possible to play
alone or go solo in GW2, consequences of other players' actions are minimized
by many different mechanics, including the "looking for group" feature. In
this way, GW2 players' encyclopedias, which determine their semiotic habits
and their actions, are allowed to develop gradually and relatively free of peer
pressure.

Moreover, common objectives, which are shared by all players within a
group, as well as reward duplication among all players participating in an
action, promote harmonious relations between members of a group and can
even stimulate teamwork in GW2. Meanwhile, personal objectives in LoL,
which are articulated mainly around ranking and Elo, encourage individualistic
behaviors that are all the more present in-game, as rewards are not equitably
distributed. Metrics, as a specific mode of information visualization, produce
highly connoted signs, as numbers and stats are usually associated with rigor
and accuracy and have thus come to possess relatively unquestioned truth value
and authority. In this sense, expectations among players in LoL are incredi-
bly high given that performances are perceived to be rigorously and accurately
recorded. Therefore, the predominance of metrics in LoL contributes to the
dynamic of competition between players. Conversely, in GW2, players only
compete against themselves, as overpower is nonexistent. Also, performances
cannot be quantified; hence, evaluation remains qualitative and vague. While
avatars are leveled out according to playing fields (zones), significant power
imbalances cannot arise. Such imbalances are visible in LoL, as seen in the
case of "smurfs," in which some key signs (representamens) referring specifically to involved agents fail to convey useful information. Indeed, an avatar's
appearance should normally signal the player's level, which is supposed to be
lower in lower leagues. If a smurf invests a lower league, other players cannot
trust the available information (visual and textual signs) about other players
anymore: the meaning of those signs is unstable and latent, which may cause
not only distrust but also anxiety in the interpreter, who can't grasp what signs
really stand for or who or what they really refer to. This justifies the view that
LoL is a "jungle" in which only the fittest survive.

This "every one for themselves" mentality, which reflects differently for
every LoL player according to their pragmatic context, is also revealed by the
difficulty to maintain a team or play with the same players game after game.
Although temporary groups are commonplace in GW2, within the context of
specific quests for instance, and could very well trigger aggressive and toxic
behaviors, such patterns are rarely seen because key game features (described

earlier) prevent them, and because pragmatic contexts of interpretations are most often the same for all players involved in a common objective. Besides, the social structures prescribed by guilds and communicational habits promote harmonious relationships: the stability of groups in which social ties are solid and based on the recognition of others prevents many forms of toxic behavior. Although stable teams in LoL may work toward common objectives, teams are still difficult to maintain because all players must have roughly the same amount of practice in order to be ranked closely enough to each other. Without such conditions, harmonious practice is not easy to achieve, as individual players' pragmatic contexts diverge.

Furthermore, in LoL, communication between players is both limited by pings and highly present in the form of text chat windows, and plays a specific role in the proliferation of toxic behaviors. The signaling function of pings requires not only quick, processual interpretation on the part of individual players, but also entirely conditioned triggers for action, which puts pressure on less experienced players. Within a general context of toxicity, opportunities for expressing dissatisfaction or frustration are numerous and even promoted by the important space taken by chat boxes, which then become places of individualist self-expression more so than spaces for sharing and reciprocal exchanges.

Such toxic behaviors are handled differently in GW2 and LoL: in the former case, one witnesses direct interventions in the game, while in the latter case, incidents are to be addressed by a self-managed tribunal. Therefore, in the face of behaviors that deviate from the norm of acceptable interactions and negatively impact the game's optimal functioning, we witness two different systems with similar *objects* yet diverging sets of *criteria* put in place to address them, as the *agents* in charge of the interpretation process are different. On the one hand, in GW2, administrators and game creators are responsible for the normalization of practices, and influence semiotic habits and social practices in this way. On the other hand, in LoL, players are responsible for establishing appropriate standards of practice in-game. This puts the weight of ethical decisions on their shoulders, which can either be an advantage or an inconvenient depending on the way in which such power is managed. In the specific case of LoL, the tribunal does not seem to have fulfilled its function: the institution had to be disabled so that irresponsible tendencies would stop happening.

Nevertheless, all of these factors do not entirely and univocally determine behaviors and attitudes, as harmful dynamics can be witnessed in GW2 and as fights devoid of toxic interactions can lead to harmonious experiences in LoL. Indeed, LoL is exploited by many as a free socialization platform conducive to mutually helpful practices and enduring friendships between passionate gamers.

I didn't know everyone in real life, but I made great friends that I then met in real life. I knew our mid laner when we were younger, then we lost touch when my family moved out, but then we started speaking again and started playing League together. Then he introduced me to new worlds that we played together. We often talk on Skype nowadays. I met them in real life and I've been to their place several times and they've become great friends. I really met some people *through the game*. (LG03_M_18)

The option to form teams with friendly players always remains available and one can always check who is online at any given time on the friends list. Furthermore, while certain mechanics encourage intensive practice in LoL, the game may be played off-ranking (casual game) and thus on an occasional basis. Also, the ARAM (all random all mid) mode allows quicker rounds that minimize the possibility of substantial harm to others. Game custom tools allow players to choose the number and identity of players to be involved, the number of bots, etc. Therefore, harmonious experiences in LoL remain entirely possible.

Also, one should highlight the importance of LoL's active and collaborative fanbase, which exists, in part, because of the high intensity of many players' practice as well as players' dependence on the community for the definition of their encyclopedias. While players are highly invested in their community, they demonstrate a rich and diversified culture through numerous cultural productions. The community appears passionate and dedicated, as shown by its welcoming attitude on these external cultural platforms where players share a large amount of material. One may note that there are many more websites about LoL than GW2, for instance. Such diverse cultural elaborations around LoL are an important factor of social cohesion, as players share common norms and referents, be it in their vocabulary, jokes, or imaginary. Moreover, e-sport is extremely developed around commissioned and highly spectacular international contests,[20] which encourages a very active collective life. That type of activities contributes to various degrees of social recognition among players.

Finally, all of these observations illustrate the fact that the production, use, and evolution of signs have a direct and very real impact on both individual and collective gaming practices. For instance, throughout this chapter, we have highlighted the efficiency (or lack thereof) of specific signs that intervene in-game, such as quantitative and qualitative markers of performance, communicational conventions, and status symbols. The example of the term "noob," which is often used as an insult in LoL but rather functions as a referent for help-seeking in GW2, showed that identical representamens can lead to different interpretations and courses of action according to the identity of interpreters

[20] www.lolesports.com/en_US/ (accessed July 11, 2016).

and their communities, as well as the pragmatic contexts of interpretation. Similarly, the evolution of the honour banner system in LoL illustrated the contingent and malleable nature of signs and their impact on pragmatic changes in gaming habits. The honor banner system quickly became obsolete because its qualitative markers of performance did not really fit in with the game's highly quantified and complex metrics system. In other words, the conventional organization and visualization of signs in LoL contributed to preventing such qualitative signs from enduring as semiotic habits. This also conveys the importance of ethical valuation in the stabilization of interpretants: as honor banners failed to be valued as significant social cues, their use was less and less motivated, and they gradually lost relevance.

Therefore, not only do signs' *functions* determine specific uses, but beliefs and feelings about the *value* of signs also influence their efficiency. Some signs are not always used in the same way depending on the value system of the community under study (as shown in the case of the term "noob"). Specific signs are not actualized by video game communities the way game designers intended, as seen through our last example. In that sense, semiosis and the (de)stabilization of meaning-making habits appear to be intrinsically adaptive processes in which intersubjective experiences and learning are central: no social and cultural dynamics can be entirely and unambiguously *determined* by prescribed game mechanics or video game infrastructure because interactions with the platform and with other players always depend on semiotic processes that are multipolar (involving several interpreting minds), affected (subject to individual and collective beliefs and feelings), and contingent (subject to pragmatic contexts).

6.7 Conclusion

All in all, while one may identify many signifying practices and modes of representation that encourage or discourage certain behaviors and influence the development of cultural norms, video games cannot entirely constrain gaming experiences. According to soft technological determinism, behaviors are normalized through players' interaction with video games. Yet transgressive and appropriative behaviors maintain the possibility for gaming practices that subvert and surpass technologically and culturally prescribed experiences. Nevertheless, if we started this chapter by recognizing that relationships of power are embedded within world views, modes of intersubjectivity, and actions and values that are prescribed within particular communities, this research has also shown how power dynamics are intrinsic to semiotic processes and uses of signs like specific game features, mechanics, and procedures. In other words, relationships of power and semiotic practices are mutually informed and shaped: not only does analyzing specific social, cultural, and political practices entail a need to pay attention to sign production, but there also are crucial political stakes in the way communities produce meaning. Therefore, as objects of semiotic study, video games can be analyzed as effects of specific cultural, ideological, and institutional contexts, but they also produce cultural, ideological, and institutional norms. As such, they can never be ethically and politically neutral. In light of the analyses presented in the preceding text, it seems hard not to consider LoL as the mirror of neoliberal individualism, and view GW2 as the fantasy of socialist collectivism.

References

Chandler, Daniel. (1995). Technological or media determinism. Retrieved from: http://visual-memory.co.uk/daniel/Documents/tecdet/tecdet.html (accessed July 11, 2016).

Cobley, Paul, & Randvir, Anti (2009). Introduction: What is sociosemiotics? *Semiotica*, 2009(173,).

Corneliussen, Hilde-G., & Rettberg, Jill Walker (eds.) (2008). *Digital culture, play, and identity: A World of Warcraft reader*. Cambridge, MA: MIT Press.

De Certeau, Michel. (1980). *L'Invention du quotidien*. 2 tomes. Paris: Gallimard, Folio essais #146.

Ducheneaut, Nick, Yee, Nick, Nickell, Eric, et al. (2006). Building an MMO with mass appeal: A look at gameplay in *World of Warcraft*, games and culture. *Games and Culture*, 1(4), 281–317.

Eco, Umberto. (1988). *Sémiotique et philosophie du langage*. Paris: Presses Universitaires de France,

Ellul, Jacques. (1954). *La technique ou l'enjeu du siècle*. Paris: Armand Colin.

Ensslin, Astrid, & Muse, Eben (eds.). (2011). *Creating second lives: Community, identity and spatiality as constructions of the virtual*. London: Routledge.

Finnemore, Martha, & Sikkink, Kathryn. (1998). International norm dynamics and political change. *International Organization*, 52 (4), 887–917.

Foucault, Michel. (2001 [1971]). *Dits et écrits I, 1954–1975*. Paris: Gallimard, Quarto.

Foucault, Michel. (1976). *Histoire de la sexualité I. La volonté de savoir*. Paris: Gallimard.

Kou, Yubo. (2014). Governance in *League of Legends*: An hybrid system. In *Foundation of Digital Games 2014*, April 3–7, Fort Lauderdale, FL.

Kou, Yubo, & Gui, Xinning. (2014). Playing with strangers: Understanding temporary teams in *League of Legends. CHI PLAY '14*. New York, NY: ACM Publications.

Kwak, Haewoon, & Blackburn, Jeremy. (2014). *Linguistic analysis of toxic behaviour in an online video game* (pp. 209–217). Social Informatics, Vol. 8852. Barcelona: Springer.

Landowski, Éric. (1993). *L'esprit de la société*. Liège: Margada, Philosophie et Langage.

Leroi-Gourhan, André. (1964, 1965). *Le geste et la parole*. 2 tomes. Paris: Albin Michel.

Maigret, Éric. (2003). *Sociologie de la communication et des medias*. Paris: Armand Colin.

Mumford, Lewis. (1967, 1970). *The myth of the machine*. 2 vols. New York, NY: Harcourt Brace Jovanovich.

Pearce, Celia, & Artemesia (2009). *Communities of play. Emergent cultures in multiplayer, games and virtual worlds*. Game Studies. Cambridge, MA: MIT Press.

Peirce, Charles Sanders. (1878). How to make our ideas clear. *Popular Science Monthly*, 12, 286–302. *Essential Peirce*, Vol. 1, p. 131.

Scott, Michael. (2012). A monument to the player: Preserving a landscape of sociocultural capital in the transitional MMORPG. In *New review of hypermedia and multimedia*, Vol. 18(4), pp. 295–320. Boca Raton, FL: Taylor & Francis.

Sicart, Miguel. (2009). *The ethics of computer games*. Cambridge, MA: MIT Press.

Simondon, Gilbert. (1958). *Du mode d'existence des objets techniques*. Paris: Aubier.

Smith, Merritt Roe, & Marx, Leo. (1994). *Does technology drive history? The dilemma of technological determinism*. Cambridge, MA: MIT Press.

Stiegler, Bernard. (1994, 1996, 2001). *La technique et le temps*. 3 tomes. Paris: Éditions Galilée, La Philosophie en Effet.

Taylor, T. L. (2006). *Play between worlds: Exploring online game culture*. Game Studies. Cambridge, MA: MIT Press.

Veron, Eliseo. (1987). *La sémiosis sociale: Fragments d'une théorie de la discursivité*. Saint-Denis: Presses Universitaires de Vincennes, Sciences du Langage.

Winner, Langdon. (1986). *The whale and the reactor: A search for limits in an age of high technology*. Chicago, IL: University of Chicago Press.

7

Management (Im)Material: Negotiating Leadership in Virtual Worlds

NICHOLAS TAYLOR, SUZANNE DE CASTELL,
JENNIFER JENSON, AND RYAN HURLEY

7.1 Introduction

In a recent article in *CNN: Money*, Stephen Gillett, COO of Symantec (maker of computer security software), explains why he put "*World of Warcraft* guild master" on his resume when moving his way up the corporate ladder. According to Gillett, the experiences of "organizing dungeon raids" and managing the collective online assets of his guild are transferable to other contexts – particularly, as he alludes to, as consumers and corporate workers alike see their environments becoming more game-like (Pagliery, 2014).

At the same time, academic research has begun to chart the leadership activities cultivated by players in commercial massively multiplayer online games (MMOGs) such as *World of Warcraft* (WoW) and *EVE Online*. Players form into groups, ranging from temporary small teams to large-scale, long-term associations numbering in the hundreds, in order to carry out goal-driven activities. Directing these activities requires an array of communicational and interpersonal competencies, from establishing and communicating short-term and long-term priorities (Schrader & McCreery, 2008); recruiting new players (Goh & Wasko, 2011); resolving conflicts between players (Chen, 2009); allocating resources (Silverman & Simon, 2009); negotiating interactions with other player associations (Taylor, 2006); and choreographing the actions of other players whose avatars have specific roles, skill sets, and weaknesses (Bardzell et al., 2008).

The potential benefits of these activities to players outside of virtual environments have been the topic of discussion among various MMOG communities for some time (see, e.g., Sorden, 2008). The notion here, as the COO of Symantec attests to, is that effective leaders in goal-driven virtual environments can make for effective leaders in other domains, and that leadership skills gained from activities undertaken as a "WoW guild leader" (for example) translate to

162

very real, and valuable, real-world skills (Rubenfire, 2014). Researchers in both educational and managerial-related fields echo this enthusiasm, asserting that leadership competencies developed through MMOG play might carry over into other contexts (Ee & Cho, 2012; Lisk, Kaplancali, & Riggio, 2012; Mysirlaki & Paraskeva, 2012; Xanthopoulou & Papagiannidis, 2012; Yee, 2006).

This research presumes that leadership behaviors and propensities exhibited in games are indicative either of players' real-life leadership qualities, and/or of the capacity of games to operate as "leadership labs" (Reeves, Malone, & O'Driscoll, 2008). What this work lacks, however, is a more rigorous account of the relationships between players' real-life characteristics, the conditions of their play, and their online behavior – including the ways this behavior is compelled and coproduced by a game's specific rules, narratives, and community. Seen in this light, the forms leadership takes in MMOGs might well be contingent on the specific objectives and mechanics of a given game, making their usefulness as "leadership labs" anything but transparent or the resultant behaviors easily transferable to other contexts. In fact, it may even be the case that leadership in some online game contexts involves behaviors and practices that are undesirable or untenable in other domains.

This chapter offers an empirically driven account of the (dis)connects between players' dispositions and the embodied experiences of their play, and their propensity for and enactment of leadership in MMOGs. We do so by drawing from both quantitative and qualitative data gathered as part of a three-year study (2009–2012) of gameplay practices and player communities across multiple MMOGs, including WoW, *EVE Online*, and *Rift*. We focus primarily on observations of small-group play in lab-based settings, in the opening stages of the MMOG *Rift*, supplementing these microanalyses of emergent leadership and group management with surveys solicited from players across multiple MMOGs, as well as observations of online gameplay in naturalistic settings such as LAN parties and internet cafes. This mixed-methods data set gives us a chance to examine, in a granular way, the formation (and dissolution) of leadership in a controlled setting, while also testing insights derived from these close observations against the larger population of players who took our survey.

We offer an inductively derived scheme for classifying leadership performances: *autocratic* leadership, in which a single player issues commands and offers help to group members, and communicates the best course of action; *self-interested* leadership, in which a player issues commands to others, does not offer them help, and seeks to guide the group toward his or her own objectives; and *networked* leadership, in which leadership is distributed across players as well as the game's nonhuman agencies. With this categorization, we contribute a theorization of leadership as a dynamic phenomenon that emerges through the contingent relationships between players' embodied identities, game mechanics, and genre conventions, and players' varying levels of expertise with(in) these virtual, fantasy-themed environments. The microanalytic work we outline supplements rather than detracts from work that looks at more established, long-term leadership in games (Siitonen, 2009; Williams, Kirschner, & Suhaimi-Broder, 2014), illustrating the various mechanics and processes through which leadership is negotiated from moment to moment.

Our approach offers important insights into the crucial connection between competence in a particular MMOG and propensity for leadership. More experienced players are more likely to take on leadership roles when playing with others less experienced (regardless of any leadership status/authority in their everyday lives), but analyses of *networked* leadership reveal that among players of roughly equal competence, leadership all but vanishes from players' actions. In these instances, we can see how leadership transfers from human to nonhuman actors: when competent players are able to read and take their cues from the game, the need for explicit direction among players disappears.

In the next section, we review the literature to date on leadership and virtual environments (including MMOGs). We trace the underlying conceptions of leadership, and assess claims and evidence for its transfer from MMOGs to real-world contexts. We then describe our study, focusing first on the qualitative microanalyses of twelve female and twelve male players in *Rift*. We then turn to our survey data, asking whether insights gleaned from our qualitative observations apply to our broader survey population. We conclude by pointing out the contributions our chapter makes to the ongoing efforts of exploring connections between players' gaming experiences and their lives outside of games. Along this vein, we assert that if MMOGs are indeed windows into human behavior, we need to better understand the ways these windows – like any other medium – do not simply reveal, but transform. In other words, our account of MMOG leadership understands that virtual worlds are not only expressive of culture, but also generative of it. After all, can we seriously consider the question of how leadership in MMOGs might transfer to other domains if we do not acknowledge, at some level, the ways certain game logics and practices – digitized surveillance, incentivized labor, and the increasing role of algorithms in predicting and governing human behavior – are remaking our everyday lives?

7.2 Related Literature

Our starting point for research on leadership and MMOGs is the early work on leadership in virtual environments. Pioneered by Avolio, Kahai, and Dodge

(2001), research on leadership in geographically distributed, digitally mediated teams – or "e-leadership" – is highly relevant to this study of small-group–based play in game-based environments. Studies of virtual teams provide useful examples of how different communications media (videoconferencing, text chat, VOIP, etc.), shape what leadership styles are most effective in a given scenario. In particular, studies by Hambley, O'Neill, and Kline (2007), Purvana and Bono (2009), and Ruggieri (2009) provide empirical insights into the dynamics of small groups collaborating through different media, drawing on the distinction between "transactional" and "transformational" leadership styles to map these dynamics. Both Hambley et al. (2007) and Purvana and Bono (2009) report that transformational (or "charismatic") leadership becomes increasingly more effective than transactional (or "managerial") leadership, in terms of both team success and reported satisfaction among group members, as the platform for communication becomes more abstract. In other words, as cues like nonverbal gestures and verbal intonation are lost, the importance for leaders to create and maintain an emotional connection through textual communication increases.

These studies demonstrate how transformational and transactional leadership styles operate in virtual contexts; however, the group collaborations they study are based around artificially designed experiments in non–game-based virtual environments, with designated leadership roles established at the outset. We turn next to studies of leadership in MMOGs.

7.3 Leadership and MMOGs

While much attention has been paid to e-leadership over the last decade in recognition of the changing nature of work, comparatively fewer studies have looked to the leadership competencies developed and rehearsed through collaborative play in game-based virtual environments. These games remain highly popular; WoW, for years the most popular MMOG, still had more than 5 million subscribers globally as of November 2015 (Kollar, 2015), and *Guild Wars 2* reached more than 7 million at the same time (Karmali, 2015). These figures indicate a massive amount of time, energy, and thought invested in MMOGs; as social scientific research on MMOG communities continues to demonstrate, these are leisure-oriented activities in which players nonetheless spend large amounts of time (Yee, 2006) and take very seriously (Chen, 2009; Taylor, 2006; Williams et al., 2006).

MMOGs offer players multiple and varied opportunities to take on leadership roles, from small, informal teams working together on short-term in-game goals to much larger, longer-term guilds, clans, or corporations of players organized around a shared set of priorities, gameplay preferences, or "real-life" orientations (as in the case, for example, with queer-friendly guilds in WoW; see Sunden, 2009). As many have pointed out (Contractor et al., 2012; Goh & Wasko, 2011; Lisk et al., 2012; Reeves et al., 2008), this makes online games compelling sites in which to study leadership. MMOGs, these authors suggest, may serve as training grounds for twenty-first-century civic and business leaders. Overall, research on leadership in MMOGs falls into one of four categories, outlined in the text that follows.

7.3.1 "Leadership Labs" and Their Application to Business

A small number of reports, primarily from business and management-related fields, are concerned with exploring the potential of MMOGs to act as training grounds for the next generation of business leaders (Guthrie, Phelps, & Downey, 2011; Reeves & Malone, 2007). This work is based primarily on informal observations, first-hand experiences of play in MMOGs, and/or references to recent social science research on networked games. The operating assumption is that to the extent that twenty-first-century organizations are becoming more like MMOGs, in their increasing reliance on geographically distributed team-based collaboration and in the incentivization of worker performance, the opportunities for MMOG-based leaders to transfer their skills to workplace contexts increases. For instance, the intensive eight-month study of Reeves et al. (2008) of "a half-dozen veteran players, with more than 50,000 hours of cumulative experience," argues that games have the "potential" to cultivate leadership qualities in players that are applicable to real-life workplaces, particularly if workplaces themselves "begin to feel more gamelike" – which they equate (problematically) with "fun" (2008). Ee and Cho (2012) complicate this picture, finding in their interviews with WoW guild leaders only limited evidence that their activities cultivate the kinds of leadership competencies deemed desirable for real-life work contexts, regardless of whether such competencies transfer from gameplay to other domains.

7.3.2 Ethnographies of MMOG Communities

Ethnographies by Chen (2009), Reeves and Malone (2007), Taylor (2006), and Silverman and Simon (2009) examine communicative practices and social norms in MMOG play. Although not all focusing explicitly on leadership, these studies provide in-depth analyses of the ways players' activities are shaped by the designed affordances and constraints of specific games, including opportunities for formal and informal, temporary, and long-term leadership roles. This research also highlights the role that players assume in collectively establishing norms and protocols for group collaboration, where and when no such structures are provided by the game (see, for example, Silverman and Simon's discussion of "Dragon Kill Points" in WoW, a community-engineered system for distributing loot).

7.3.3 Quantitative Research on Leadership Transfer

Quantitative studies by Lu, Shen, and Williams (2014), Yee (2006), and Xanthopoulou and Papagiannidis (2012) draw primarily on self-report survey data to explore whether leadership-related behaviors acquired through MMOG play transfer to offline contexts. These studies suggest a correlation between players' experiences with MMOG-based leadership and either their self-efficacy in other aspects of their lives (Xanthopoulou & Papagiannidis, 2012), or their involvement in voluntary organizations (Lu et al., 2014). Taken as a whole, this work is ambivalent on whether leadership "travels" from MMOGs to business contexts; leaders in these domains might share similar qualities, but this does not indicate that one can or does serve as a training ground for the other.

These strands of research – business-oriented reports of MMOG players' leadership potentials, ethnographic player studies, and quantitative research on players' (self-reported) capacities for real-world leadership – all look primarily to *formalized* leadership roles, concretized through the hierarchically based social mechanics of in-game guilds. Leadership in these positions consists substantially of managerial tasks across multiple play sessions (and indeed, months and years): moderating guild message boards, distributing guild resources, establishing and communicating both short- and long-term goals, scheduling events, and recruiting and training new players (Goh & Wasko, 2009). This work also points to features of both players and avatars that tend to enable (or disable) their capacity to take on leadership positions: for example, male avatars and players from classes on the "front lines" of in-game combat, such as warriors and paladins, are more likely to occupy formal leadership roles (Lehdonvirta et al., 2012).

These studies presume that the managerially focused work of guilds is where the greatest potential lies in terms of examining the relevance of MMOGs to contemporary work practices. But increasingly, as is acknowledged in the research on e-leadership, the twenty-first-century workforce – and in particular, the IT sector – is characterized less and less by rigid and formalized hierarchies, and more by temporary collaborations between geographically distributed specialists (Avolio et al., 2014; Bidwell & Briscoe, 2009; Carte,

Chidambaram, & Becker, 2006; Muethel & Hoegl, 2013), often working as self-employed contractors. These forms of digitally mediated work certainly have their corollaries in games – though not in the stable, hierarchical arrangement of guilds, but in the form of "pick-up groups," players who coalesce around shared short-term goals and who may or may not have prior, or even subsequent, contact with one another (Linderoth, Björk, & Olsson, 2014). It should be noted that such small-group scenarios are not unique to MMOGs, but characterize much of the networked play in highly popular first-person shooter (FPS) and multiplayer online battle arena (MOBA) genres, in which leadership is continually renegotiated from game to game, and even in response to changes in game state.

7.3.4 Case Studies of Emergent Leadership

A small number of case studies address these dynamics of small-group play in MMOGs. Lisk et al. (2012) discuss a study in which undergraduate students carried out collaborative small-group tasks in a specially designed online environment called *INFINITEAMS*. The authors state that players' self-reported leadership behavior was strongly linked to team performance, but note that strong team performance could have informed players' self-report (p. 140). Like the study reported by Lisk et al. (2012), Siewiorek and Lehtinen (2011) make use of empirical evidence from participants' gameplay; their study involved nine undergraduate students playing *Build-a-lot*, a resource management game designed for single players but played, here, in groups of three (with one player at the controls). The focus of the study was to see which leadership styles emerged in each of the three groups over the course of play. The authors report that the most successful team, as measured by the efficiency of in-game task completion, developed a shared (or "democratic") leadership style, while the two less effective teams featured a single, transformational leader whom they described as "autocratic" (p. 366). Van Dijk and Broekens (2010) also propose a distinction between formalized, or "authoritative," leadership, and "distributed" leadership where leadership roles and responsibilities are constantly negotiated and shared depending on specific in-game situations.

In contrast to examinations of formal leadership roles, the case studies view leadership in relational and dynamic terms, rather than as a set of attributes pertaining to individuals (Uhl-Bien, Marion, & McKelvey, 2007). Leadership is understood to be contingent, a product of what is needed in different situations; leader and follower hierarchies are more fluid and organic than in traditional scenarios where leadership is assigned based on top-down decision making.

As Reeves et al. (2008) state, "leadership in games is a task, not an identity- a state that a player enters and exits rather than a personal trait that emerges and thereafter defines the individual" (p. 62).

This leads us to ask:

If leadership is not an inherent trait but an emergent phenomenon, under what circumstances is effective leadership produced?

7.4 Theoretical Framework

Leadership in such dynamic and contingent contexts as pick-up groups and, increasingly, twenty-first-century workplaces, is often described as "distributed" across practitioners (Day, Gronn, & Salas, 2004; Gronn, 2002). This perspective is theoretically rooted in cultural-historical psychology (Vygotsky, 1978; Wertsch, 1998) and sociocultural activity theory, as developed and articulated by Engeström (1987, 1990). It frames social practice as the product of historically and contextually relationships between other humans, technologies, institutions, and activities; the emphasis on the inseparability of human thought and action from sociocultural and technological contexts makes this perspective ideally suited to studies of group collaboration in digitally mediated environments (Mysirlaki & Paraskeva, 2012; Nardi, 1995).

Our own research on small-group play in MMOGs acknowledges and extends this perspective on distributed leadership in virtual environments – specifically, we suggest that leadership is not only distributed across members of a team, but across software and hardware agencies as well. As we report on in the text that follows, at times we observed small-group play where no human leadership seemed apparent; in those instances, players' shared expertise in MMOGs meant that little work had to be done identifying goals and articulating or correcting strategies. To adopt an actor–network theory perspective, leadership does not disappear in these moments, but is "delegated" (Latour, 2005) across the various systems and mechanics – conventions of genre and platform that experienced MMOG players readily perceive – that the game employs to guide players toward challenges and rewards. This theoretical framework is a marked departure from the majority of research in this field, which tends to view leadership as an inherent trait that can (potentially) transfer from one domain to another.

The next section provides an overview of our study. Specifically, we describe the methods used to gather both microanalytic accounts of emergent leadership in small-group play, and self-report survey data of players' leadership roles in game-based and other, more mundane domains.

7.5 Study Description

This work is part of a larger study of social interactions in MMOGs, carried out between 2009 and 2012. The Virtual Environment/Real User Study (VERUS) involved collaborations between researchers at SRI International, Simon Fraser University, York University, and Nottingham University, to document and analyze MMOG-based behaviors in university laboratory play sessions and public gaming contexts (including LAN parties, internet cafes, and e-sports events). In this chapter, we report on the second half of the study (late 2010–early 2012). Our data set includes video data collected in campus-based experiments and a larger survey of player demographics, practices, and preferences.

7.5.1 Microanalyses of Dyad Play

For the purpose of this analysis, we rely primarily on qualitative analyses of video recordings of twenty-four participants' progression through the opening quests of the MMOG *Rift*, played in pairs and recorded in a university laboratory setting. *Rift* was selected for the experimental virtual environment as it was relatively new at the time of the study – none of our participants had played it – but similar enough in its narrative and representational and ludic conventions to established MMOGs like WoW and *Guild Wars* to afford experienced players a relatively familiar experience.

The "microethnographic" methodology we applied to the qualitative aspect of our study is now firmly established within studies of digital play (de Castell, Boschman, & Jenson, 2008; Giddings, 2008). Operating broadly from a Goffmanian perspective on the role played by minute social interactions in the reproduction of social orders, it is particularly suited to studies of multi-participant play in virtual worlds, as it is capable of illuminating the complex "choreographies" between human participants and the many technological agencies that coproduce digital play (Taylor, Kampe, & Bell, 2015).

Our process for generating this audio-visual data set began with the development of a qualitative coding scheme based on observations from play sessions, and from existing literature on leadership in digitally mediated, small-group settings. The items in our coding schema combined indicators of in-game progression and events (quests completed, areas explored, avatars dying or leveling up) with verbal utterances between players, understood to be expressive of leadership or its negotiation (such as giving commands, requests for clarification and help, deferrals, suggestions, and statements of avatar position or status). Applying the finalized version of the coding scheme to a test session video, implemented in Noldus: The Observer XT (Noldus), two research

Table 7.1 *Study design for the microanalysis of leadership*

	Male	Female
MMOG novice	4	4
MMOG expert, non-leader	4	4
MMOG expert, leader	4	4
Total	12	12

assistants obtained an interrater reliability score of 74%, which we deemed acceptable.

Given that the literature on leadership in MMOGs indicates correlations between leadership roles and players' age, sex, and expertise level, our design for this exploratory study incorporated each of these variables; we conducted microanalyses of the play sessions of twelve male and twelve female players, including in each four novices, four expert players who had not held formal in-game leadership roles, and four expert, self-identified guild leaders (Table 7.1).

7.5.2 Survey

To understand whether insights into leadership and expertise, generated from our qualitative observations, can be generalized to the broader study population, we draw on surveys collected from study participants in both university and public gaming settings over the course of the second half of the VERUS study. The survey asked for participants' demographic information, their MMOG practices, preferences, and levels of engagement, and their self-efficacy regarding leadership in both game-based and non–game-based contexts, using a set of questions based on the Sloan Leadership Model (Ancona et al., 2007).

As with the qualitative, audio-visual data, we are less concerned here with determining whether participants occupying formal leadership roles in online games also occupy leadership roles in their work contexts. The claim that guild leaders and related in-game responsibilities serve as training grounds for twenty-first-century business leaders is largely undersupported in recent research (see Lu et al., 2014), with no correlation found between game-based positions of leadership and the cultivation of "managerial" or "transactional" leadership in professional work contexts, and only limited correlation between games and "transformational" leadership in voluntary organizations. We argue, furthermore, that truly understanding whether and how leadership *transfers* across domains (rather than simply pointing to a correlation) requires a rigorous, in-depth comparison of the institutional/structural similarities and differences between specific virtual environments and specific organizational contexts. A comparison of this kind has not yet been undertaken and is beyond the scope of this chapter. Instead, our survey questions – primarily the Likert-style questions, "I feel like a leader in MMOGs" and "I feel like a leader in everyday situations" – reflect an understanding that leadership is not only enacted through long-term, formalized hierarchies but is called for, and emerges in, contingent, short-term situations.

In what follows, we provide an overview of our qualitative data and explore its potential implications, before turning to our quantitative survey to see whether insights derived from our microanalytic observations "play out" in our broader study population.

7.6 Microanalytic Observations

The twenty-four video observations that we coded in Noldus allowed us to generate inductive understandings of leadership as it is negotiated by pairs of participants playing through the opening stages of *Rift*. Alongside researchers' field notes from each of the laboratory-based sessions included in this study design, these observations provide an empirical basis from which we developed characterizations of specific leadership styles. In what follows, we give a brief account of participant pairs whose interactions most clearly demonstrate the three broader patterns of leadership behaviors we identified across observations: *autocratic*, *self-interested*, and *networked*.

7.6.1 Autocratic Leadership

"Sfulab207" (white man) and "Sfulab208" (white woman), both aged 34, were in a romantic relationship at the time of the study. In talking with one of the research session facilitators while the participants finished customizing their avatars, Sfulab207 explained that he is a unit leader in the Canadian Armed Forces, and leader of a clan that plays multiple online games together, made up primarily of his military subordinates and colleagues (and not including Sfulab208). The couple evinced a dramatic difference in expertise, with Sfulab207 describing his extensive involvement in both online MMOG and FPS games, while Sfulab208 described herself as a novice. As indicated in the observation notes, Sfulab207 acted in charge of their play session even prior to its start, speaking on both their behalf to the researchers, and instructing Sfulab208 as to what race and faction to select for her avatar (all *Rift* avatars

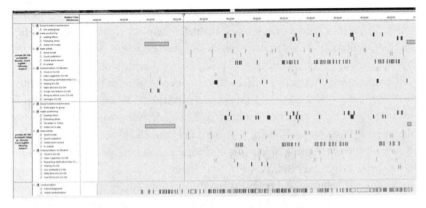

Figure 7.1 Leadership-related communication for Sfulab207 and Sfulab208.
(This image is shown in full color in the Color Plates section.)

must belong to either "Guardian" or "Defiant"), as opposed to deciding collaboratively.

Sfulab207's interactions with Sfulab208 are characterized by a strongly authoritative approach to managing her play; he begins by "making suggestions" to her as they both explore the game's environment and interface, then as he grows more familiar (and at a faster rate than she, owing to his knowledge of genre conventions), begins to "give commands" more frequently. Figure 7.1 illustrates how many times particular verbal behaviors occurred per minute over the session duration – showing, for instance, that Sfulab207 gives an average of one command per minute of play. Both players "check-in" numerous times (Sfulab207 22 times, Sfulab208 23 times); this code was used to indicate players' status reports to each other. For Sfulab208, the majority of these check-ins serve to indicate the location of quest-related monsters and items; she is filling him in on her progress toward their shared goals. By comparison, the majority of Sfulab207's check-ins serve to report on the status of their group, indicating his concern for engineering their progression through quests.

Sfulab207 is managing their play, leveraging his greater expertise with MMOGs to set goals for his partner's actions and provide her with explicit directions. At the same time, he describes his actions as selfless; he chooses a healing character for himself so that he can ensure her safety, thereby (in his own words) "allowing her to do all the fun stuff." The "helping" behaviors in this pair are completely one sided, with Sfulab207 giving and Sfulab208 receiving all the help – as we would expect given the differences in expertise.

In-game, Sfulab207 rarely leaves Sfulab208's side, with the exception of one minute-long stretch in which her game software freezes and she has to relaunch the application. During this time, Sfulab207 does not progress in the game, and when his partner appears back in, he rushes to help her fight off enemies. For her part, Sfulab208's communication during their play session is characterized by "Requesting help/clarification," and "Seeking permission" – as well as by self-disparaging comments, which we did not code. We see this as the cultivation of a kind of learned helplessness toward Sfulab208's gameplay, wherein Sfulab207 actively works to maintain a preestablished position of leadership that derives from his familiarity with the game. This is reflective of the broader gender dynamics shaping men and women's access to, enjoyment of, and familiarity with, these and other types of time-intensive online games (particularly in the case of heterosexual couples; see Ratan et al., 2015).

While Sfulab207 and Sfulab208 represent the most marked instance of *autocratic* leadership, where the more expert player assumes control of the group's goals and actions, we saw it play out in other pairs as well, including one in which a younger, expert female player authoritatively directed the actions of her older, novice play partner. The particular example provided by Sfulab207 and Sfulab208 is of a male/female pairing; more significant is the fact that they have drastically different levels of prior experience and familiarity with MMOGs, as leadership in this instance is as much a function of expertise as it is gender.

7.6.2 Self-Interested Leadership

The second style we identified is what we call *self-interested leadership*, exhibited most clearly in the interactions of two Southeast Asian male participants, dubbed "Yorklab244" and "Yorklab245." They played with a third Southeast Asian male participant, "Yorklab246," who spent much of the play session logged out of the game, and whose video was not coded in this study design. "Yorklab244" and "Yorklab245" are roughly the same age (25 and 26, respectively, at the time of the study); all three players were self-professed MMOG novices, but expert FPS players. They regularly played the competitive FPS *Counterstrike* together, with Yorklab244 professing that he avoided taking on leadership roles in that game, while Yorklab245 stating that he did so when the situation called for it. In their *Rift* session, the two participants did not party together until a research assistant suggested they do so. They made no attempt to select complementary roles, as Sfulab207 and Sfulab208 had done (at Sfulab207's behest) in selecting a healer and warrior. Though they ended up spending the majority of the session in the same party, sharing experience points and quest progress, their play was marked by long bouts of solo exploration punctuated by short, usually incidental, and often unproductive periods of collaboration.

Yorklab244 selected a rogue, a character who uses a bow and arrows, and spent the first half of the hour-long session experimenting with different tactics for fighting enemies. These tactics seemed informed by his FPS expertise: strafing in circles to avoid enemy attacks, standing on top of buildings and tree stumps to attack enemies from above, and hitting the attack button repeatedly. Like most other fantasy-themed, tabletop gaming-inspired MMOGs, however, combat in *Rift* is governed less by these kinds of positional and reflex-driven actions and more by the underlying statistical properties of an avatar's attack and defense ratings, rendering Yorklab244's FPS-like play largely ineffective.

Midway through the session, to aid in his attempts to fight a particular group of enemies, he repeatedly tries to enlist the help of Yorklab245 through direct assertives (repeatedly saying "I'll tell you what to do"). Yorklab245, playing as a mage, locates his coparticipant; instead of helping, he tries unsuccessfully to fight Yorklab244, asking "can I kill you?" (they were playing on a server in which player versus player combat is prohibited outside of dedicated arenas). Yorklab244 soon dies, neither getting the help he needed nor adapting his attack strategy. Minutes later, they team up again; this time Yorklab244 lets Yorklab245 engage enemies first, and only then starts shooting them from a safe distance. On killing his first enemy, he high-fives Yorklab246 (sitting next to him) and demands that Yorklab245 replicate this tactic; instead, Yorklab245 again moves on once more to explore the world on his own.

Near the end of the session, Yorklab244 instructs Yorklab245 to follow him to an area with more powerful enemies, into which he had wandered and promptly died, instead of remaining to finish quests in their current area. Again, Yorklab245 ignores his command, and consistent with his behavior throughout the session, seems more concerned with reading NPC dialogue and learning controls while exploring the environment on his own.

Yorklab244 and Yorklab245's session has very few instances of collaboration, as the players were often wandering, exploring, and playing separately. Their lack of coordinated play is reflected in their communication (see Figure 7.2), with Yorklab244's largely unsuccessful attempts to enlist Yorklab245's aid illustrated in the instances of "requesting help" and "assigning actions," though these are in the service of an individual rather than group goal (attacking the enemies threatening him). His attempts to "give commands" are likewise carried out for individualistic ends – to compel Yorklab245 to support him toward aims that he has not actually communicated.

There is a general absence of helping in this play session, either solicited or unsolicited, despite the high incidences of Yorklab245's "requesting help." As a result, their few attempts at collaboration were mostly unsuccessful; both players were more concerned with pursuing individual, and discordant, goals,

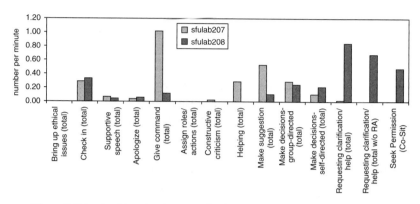

Figure 7.2 Leadership-related communication for Yorklab244 and Yorklab245.

as opposed to Sfulab207's micromanaged coordination of his partner. We see this discordance largely as a product of their lack of experience in MMOGs; without knowledge of genre conventions and mechanics, they are largely left to their own, unaligned, devices.

7.6.3 Networked Leadership

We refer to the third style of leadership we identified in our observations as *networked*, as it involves a distribution of leadership across both human players and software agents, and arises under conditions of roughly equal expertise between players. Here, both players' emphasis is on facilitating efficient play rather than on micromanaging a less capable teammate or demanding help from one similarly unskilled. "Yorklab207" (white woman, 36 at the time of the study) and "Yorklab208" (white man, 31 at the time of the study) best exemplify this relationship. Yorklab207 was leader of her WoW guild, while Yorklab208 described himself as a "follower" and claimed he generally tries to avoid positions of responsibility in online games, despite also being an avid WoW player. Like Sfulab207 and Sfulab208, these players were in a romantic relationship at the time of the study, and often played WoW together. They required very little help from the research assistants to get started, and teamed up almost immediately on finishing avatar creation and entering the gameworld; in fact they joked about who invited who to team up first.

Throughout the session, Yorklab207 talks a great deal, but much of it is narrating her play, rather than "giving commands" or "assigning roles / actions" – the types of utterances that most characterize our *autocratic* and *self-interested* leadership styles – or even, for that matter, "Make suggestion", which appears

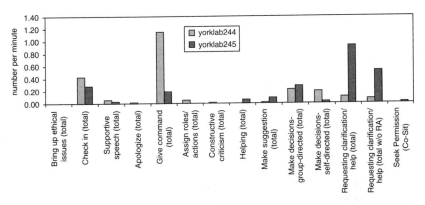

Figure 7.3 Leadership-related communication for Yorklab207 and Yorklab208.

frequently in Sfulab207's management of Sfulab208. Figure 7.3, visualizing their leadership-related interactions, shows a general lack of communication. This is because our coding scheme, with its emphasis on capturing overt attempts to guide or manage others' play, does not catalog other forms of communication. Figure 7.4, by contrast, displays a screenshot of the Noldus coding environment, comparing their relatively sparse leadership-related communication (above) with a visualization of their total verbal utterances (below), during the same session. As this shows, they are in near-constant communication, but little of this is visible in terms of overt leader–follower dynamics.

In terms of coded verbal interactions, the most frequent for this pair are check-ins, used mainly to coordinate their highly efficient play. Rather than instructing each other in how to complete quests and advance in the game, both

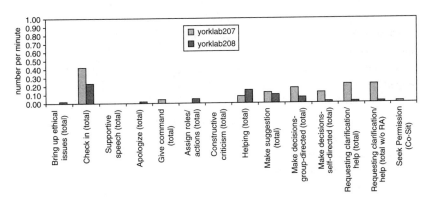

Figure 7.4 Screenshot of Yorklab207 and Yorklab208's session as coded in the Noldus environment, with near-constant communication visualized at the bottom.

players recognize how to go about doing this in the most expedient way (which enemies to fight and which to avoid in order to meet certain quest criteria, where to find quest items, etc.), based on their shared familiarity with MMOG conventions. Their check-ins are used to establish location, and note which quests they are working on at any given time. In contrast to both the imbalance of "helping" between Sfulab207 and Sfulab208, and the near-lack of any "helping" between Yorklab244 and Yorklab245, Yorklab207 and Yorklab208 reciprocate help. Overall, their play is highly coordinated despite the comparatively low amount of overtly leadership-related communicative exchanges. This *networked* leadership is a by-product of two participants with matching high levels of experience playing together, wherein the work of establishing and communicating goals is delegated almost exclusively to the game's interface and quest structure, a delegation made possible by players' operational knowledge of the logics and genre conventions underlying MMOGs. Yorklab207 and Yorklab208 have no need of a leader–follower dynamic, as they are collectively led by the game. It is important to note that we observed this leadership style in male–male dyads as well, suggesting that, like autocratic leadership, it reflects a relationship of expertise rather than gender.

7.7 Discussion of Microanalytic Observations

Our microanalytic observations demonstrate the central role that expertise – understood as operational competency with input devices, and a familiarity with MMOG genre conventions, particularly around class-based combat and quest-based progression systems – plays in the emergence of particular leadership behaviors. In our analysis, differences in expertise may be as germane to understanding how and why leadership emerges in particular ways than whether any given player occupies a formal leadership role in either virtual and/or "real-life" contexts.

Conventional models of leadership lack a theorization of how participants' expertise in a given domain shapes leader–follower dynamics. Following Giddings and Kennedy (2008), we understand gaming expertise less in terms of mastery *over* the hardware and software apparatus, and rather as a matter of enmeshing oneself *within* this apparatus, recognizing, and efficiently reacting to, what the game requires in order to reach a certain state. Virtuoso displays of gaming, then – such as completing *Fallout 3* in fifteen minutes, single-handedly achieving a "Pentakill" in *League of Legends*, or playing "blind" *Tetris* in which the blocks have disappeared – are best understood as instances in which the player has seamlessly melded her embodied activities into the

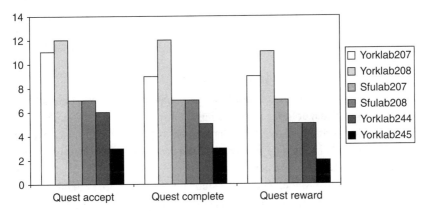

Figure 7.5 Progression through quests over the first hour of *Rift* play.

game's machinic and computational "circuits" (Giddings & Kennedy, 2008). This posthumanist understanding of expert gameplay is more equipped than conventional models of leadership used in MMOG studies to account for the differences in leader–follower dynamics we observed. From this perspective, the dissonant play of Yorklab244 and Yorklab245 reflect an almost total lack of competence between them regarding MMOG mechanics, and while Yorklab244 insists on applying FPS-based tactics to the game and unsuccessfully calling on Yorklab245 for help, Yorklab245 spends his time scrolling through tutorial and NPC dialogue in an effort to learn the game on his own. Sfulab207 and Sfulab208's mixed-expertise pairing represents the clearest instance of transactional leadership, as he micromanages her play toward game-defined goals that he has identified. Their difference in experience helps create a dynamic of learned helplessness, in which she has little opportunity to cultivate competence, ensuring his continued control. Finally, Yorklab207 and Yorklab208, as an expert–expert pairing, share a dynamic that seems at once more harmonious and more productive than the other two pairs. Both have learned how to imbricate themselves into the rhythms common to most fantasy-themed MMOGs, accepting multiple quests at one time, progressing through quests in the most expedient ways, and "cashing in" before moving on to the next area, all without little instruction or guidance from each other. This is "distributed" leadership, if we accept that leadership can be distributed – or in our words, *networked* – across nonhuman agents as well as players.

These dynamics are reflected in Figure 7.5, showing each participant's in-game progress over the first hour of play, expressed in terms of quests accepted, completed, and turned in for rewards – the most efficient way of advancing both the game's narrative and an avatar's experience levels. Dyads are color coded. As the figure shows, Yorklab207 and Yorklab208 made the most progress, despite the lack of overt leadership-related utterances. Sfulab207 and Sfulab208 show the most degree of synchronicity in terms of quests accepted and quests completed, reflecting Sfulab207's close micromanagement of group progress. Finally, Yorklab244 and Yorklab245 have the two lowest numbers of quests accepted and completed, as well as a low degree of synchronicity.

Sfulab207 certainly stands out as an example of a participant who takes on a leadership role in his play session, and who also fulfills leadership roles in both real-life and virtual contexts. That said, he is one of only three participants out of the twenty-four included in this study design who were both in a formalized leadership role in their online guild and who clearly exhibited leadership behaviors in their play sessions. More salient, for us, is the fact that differences in expertise between players in a given dyad more often determined who would lead than did players' positions as guild or clan leaders in other MMOGs; in our observations, leadership defaulted de facto to players with greater expertise more consistently than it did to players who came into the study already occupying positions of guild leadership de jure in their respective games.

This apparent disconnect is possibly a reflection of the different kinds of work required to manage a guild versus orchestrating small-group play. Guild leadership, as other scholars point out (Chen, 2009; Goh & Wasko, 2009; Reeves & Malone, 2007), is a matter of incentivizing recruitment and participation in the guild through regular group activities and the distribution of rewards; this kind work seems to parallel the "transactional," or "task-oriented" style of leadership articulated by Bass (1985) and applied to MMOGs by Lu et al. (2014). Also described as "managerial," this approach is often associated with stable, longer-term organizations where matters of recruitment, retention, and promotion or demotion – "keeping the lights on" – take priority. Conversely, "transformational" or "relationship-oriented" leadership (Bass, 1985) may be more appropriate for describing the kind of work required to successfully guide players through their first forays into a new game environment. In this model, leadership is often enacted through encouragement, aid, and emotional support – something we saw carried out consistently by Yorklab207 (though not explicitly coded as "leadership"), less consistently by Sfulab207, and nonexistent in the exchanges between Yorklab244 and Yorklab245.

In examining play situations in which formalized leadership positions are not preestablished, then, our microanalytic observations offer a provisional foray into how leadership emerges out of a context that is more dynamic, temporary, and precarious than has been considered thus far in studies of MMOG leadership. As we argue in the preceding text, this configuration is analogous to the forms of short-term collaboration between independently contracted workers that scholars in the fields of business management and e-leadership increasingly see as emblematic of twenty-first-century work, particularly in IT fields (Carte et al., 2006; Contractor et al., 2012). Of equal relevance to us, as media scholars, is its application to other forms of highly popular and increasingly lucrative online gaming, such as the short rounds of small-group play in MOBAs such as *League of Legends* and *Defense of the Ancients 2*, or in team-based FPS games such as *Counterstrike* or *Overwatch*. The implication here is that players in these games can be likened to independent IT specialists – a characterization that, according to scholars studying the labor required for professional competitive play, is quite apt (Taylor, 2012).

We now turn to our survey data to see whether and how these observations about the crucial interplay between leadership and expertise apply to our broader population of survey respondents ($N = 389$). We should note that all of the participants in the microanalytic study took an earlier version of the VERUS survey, one that did not include questions about leadership specifically. Thus, for the purpose of this analysis, our two study populations are wholly separate.

7.8 Survey Results

To untangle the relationship between participants' self-perceptions of in-game leadership and expertise, on one hand, and in-game leadership and leadership opportunities in everyday life, on the other, we considered the Likert-style survey questions, "I feel like a leader in MMOGs" and "I feel like a leader in everyday life" (with possible responses for each consisting of "All of the time," "Most of the time," "Some of the time," and "None of the time"). To account for expertise, we considered the Likert-style question "Please indicate your level of expertise in the MMOG you play the most," with responses consisting of "Expert," "Advanced," "Intermediate," "Novice," and "Newb." Additionally, our measure of expertise also includes the Likert-style question "How many of the people you interact with in MMOGs do you know offline?", with responses ranging from "All of them" to "None of them." Based on previous work, this is a strong predictor of gaming commitment as it indicates the degree of overlap between one's online and offline peer groups (Taylor, 2006; Williams et al., 2006). In addition, in order to examine possible correlations between participants' self-perceived leadership responsibilities and other salient demographic information, we considered participants' sex, self-reported level of household income (on a five-point Likert scale from "High" to "Low"), and highest level of education attained (on an eight-point Likert scale from "Doctorate" to "None").

Table 7.2 *Bivariate correlations for "Feel like a leader in MMOGs (all or most of the time)"*

	Feel Like a Leader in Everyday Life	Level of MMOG Expertise	In-game Contacts Known Offline	Household Income	Highest Level of Education Attained
Feel like a leader in MMOGs, "all" or "most" of the time (N = 55) Pearson correlation	.122	**.345**	−.007	.125	.137
Significance (two-tailed)	.374	**.010**	.962	.363	.320

We undertook three sets of queries. For the first, we grouped together participants who claimed to feel like a leader in MMOGs either "all of the time" or "most of the time" (N = 55, 48 men and 7 women), and conducted bivariate correlations with our other considerations (Table 7.2; significant correlations in bold).

As Table 7.2 indicates, the only significant relation here is between participants' self-efficacy with regard to leadership and expertise.

For the second query, we involved the entire survey population (N = 389, 284 men and 105 women) in the same bivariate analysis (Table 7.2), again limiting the results in terms of correlations with "Feel like a leader in MMOGs."

Table 7.3 illustrates more significant correlations, both in number of correlations and in strength. Although there is a minimal correlation between "feeling like a leader in MMOGs" and "in everyday life," the correlations between "feeling like a leader in MMOGs" and our two measures of expertise – self-reported expertise and number of in-game contacts known offline – become much more substantial. Notably, self-reported level of household income and highest level of education attained are not significantly correlated with feeling like a leader in MMOGs.

These tables indicate only weak correlations (if any) between "feeling like a leader" in MMOGs and in everyday life. Our third query (Table 7.4) focuses on "feeling like a leader in everyday life" to see which (if any) attributes are correlated.

The strongest interaction here is between "feeling like a leader in everyday life" and "household income," which is not a surprise, given the importance of

Table 7.3 *Bivariate correlations for "Feel like a leader in MMOGs," using total survey population*

	Feel like a leader in everyday life	Level of MMOG expertise	In-game contacts known offline	Household income	Highest level of education attained
Feel like a leader in MMOGs, total (*N* = 389) (Pearson correlation)	.153	.845	.793	.035	−.092
Significance (two-tailed)	.002	.000	.000	.497	.069

socioeconomic status to self-efficacy (Li et al., 2011). Perhaps not surprisingly, there is no correlation between leadership self-efficacy in everyday life and participants' level of expertise with MMOGs.

7.9 Survey Discussion

We think these survey results demonstrate the broader applicability of our qualitative insights: that participants' self-perceptions of their in-game leadership are more closely contingent on their mastery of the given virtual environment

Table 7.4 *Bivariate correlations for "Feel like a leader in everyday life," using total survey population*

	Feel like a leader in MMOG	Level of MMOG expertise	In-game contacts known offline	Household income	Highest level of education attained
Feel like a leader in everyday lives, total (*N* = 389) (Pearson correlation)	.153**	.029	.047	**.294**	.071
Significance (two-tailed)	.002	.567	.359	**.000**	.159

and their level of social involvement in it, more so than any perceived efficacy in everyday life leadership situations. Conversely, we see, at least provisionally, that "feeling like a leader in everyday life" is contingent upon other "real-life" indicators such as household income (which itself was not significantly correlated with in-game leadership in our study). Perhaps leadership capabilities in MMOGs grow out of different experiences and material conditions than does leadership opportunities in everyday life, particularly work related; as we see in our analysis, the former is closely tied to MMOG expertise, which itself is contingent on access to leisure time and intensive involvement in gaming communities.

When read alongside our microanalytic accounts of how leadership emerges in short play sessions, our quantitative data regarding whether players with formal, in-game leadership roles take on positions of authority in other domains confirms what we argue in our review of existing research on leadership and MMOGs: conventional notions of leadership as an inherent trait can take us only so far in understanding the dynamics of temporary, small-group collaborations. For us, the question of whether "guild leaders make good management material," and the attendant focus on formal, long-term leadership roles in games, represents an instance of using outmoded theories to understand new phenomena (de Castell et al., 2014). Instead, recognizing the ways in which leadership is distributed – not just between players, but across features of the virtual environment – allows us to better theorize how smaller, digitally mediated teams accomplish tasks. To echo recent insights by posthumanist theorists of game-based interactions (Giddings, 2008), leadership is an accomplishment of both human and nonhuman "teamwork"; we collaborate not just *in*, but also *with* the virtual world.

7.10 Conclusion

Our study of game-based leadership styles and behaviors found that what we termed *self-interested* leadership proved least effective in terms of in game progression, *autocratic* leadership was next, and *networked* leadership was demonstrably most successful. We also determined, however, that considerations of in-game expertise may be far more salient to whether and how players took on temporary leadership roles than whether they occupy formal leadership positions in their regular MMOG play or their nongaming activities. To illuminate the relationship of game-based to "everyday life" leadership, we used survey data to look for significant relationships between "feeling like a leader" in game, level of gameplay expertise, and "feeling like a leader in everyday life." As would be expected, we found a correlation between feeling like a leader in MMOGs and level of gameplay expertise. The strongest correlation we found to "feeling like a leader in everyday life" was household income, with no correlation between MMOG expertise and leadership self-efficacy in everyday life.

As we have illustrated, the conventional notion of leadership as a trait that can be cultivated through carrying out formalized, de jure positions of authority in games and then "transferred" to work contexts represents only one – and we would argue, increasingly anachronistic – understanding of leadership. It reflects a modernist paradigm in which labor is organized predominantly via persistent, long-term, hierarchical organizations (wherein "managerial" leadership is most serviceable), rather than the contingent, short-term, entrepreneurial, task-driven, skill-based twenty-first-century forms of work for which networked leadership configurations are most desired.

The forms of collaboration that we focused on in our microanalytic observations and that we see exemplified by pick-up groups in many networked games, involves players coalescing around shared short-term goals rather than through longer-term, stabilized guild allegiances. We regard this networked play as more amenable to meeting twenty-first-century labour force requirements, particularly in the IT sector, characterized less and less by rigid and formalized hierarchies, and more by temporary collaborations between geographically distributed, often self-employed specialists.

7.10.1 "The Rules Are No Game"

We end with a brief commentary on the broader cultural logics that animate recent attempts to frame online games as "leadership labs." Such questions about skills transfer from game leadership to "real-world" leadership might begin to acknowledge and critically evaluate the extent to which work in contemporary professional, knowledge economy contexts – the twenty-first-century workplace – borrows increasingly from the logics of games, avoiding the presumption that more "game-like" must necessarily mean more enjoyable, fair, or rewarding. Some years ago, Lankshear (1997) drew critical attention to the ways and extents to which "new work orders" successfully appropriated and effectively mobilized discourses and value orientations – collaboration, empowerment, critical thinking, and teambuilding, for example – to bolster new forms of workplace organization that reduced worker autonomy, promoted deskilling, and discouraged critical rationality. We would argue that new workplace logics, particularly the gamification of work, has had similar results, individuating competition between workers and rewarding successful individuals with benefits and security that had traditionally been granted collectively (Dyer-Witheford, 2015). Incentivized in this way are precarity (intermittent and insecure employment), widespread surveillance, and a return to the piecework economy of "payment by results" that now extends well beyond the old factory floor to encompass executive roles and responsibilities, as an ethos of "entrepreneurialism" is encouraged across the board.

Our efforts to address how intensive online play might transfer to real-life work contexts should therefore, at a minimum, carefully attend to how those contexts adopt the logics of games, whether and how these changes benefit workers/players, and whether these changes might be wrought not in order to make the workplace more enjoyable or rewarding, but to make workers and work more amenable to globalized structures of regulation – contributing thereby to the further erosion of collective, localized labor movements.

A final question researchers can ask about prospects for developing leadership through digital gameplay, is whether, in this very way of posing the question, the biggest "boss battle" over leadership has already been relinquished. For to the extent that both efficient play in programmed gameworlds and successful workplace performance in real ones have devolved to the internalization and skillful mobilization preestablished rules, then seeking out forms of leadership in common between those two domains may have researchers duped into unwittingly presuming a thoroughly remediated conception of what leadership might be. Such a conception leaves far distant and well out of account precisely those virtues, such as creativity, charisma, originality, ingenuity, self-sacrifice, far-sightedness, fair play, and, indeed, even heroism, which have until the last few decades been central to an understanding of leadership and its worth in social and vocational life.

References

Ancona, D., Malone, T. W., Orlikowski, W. J., & Senge. P. (2007). In praise of the incomplete leader. *Harvard Business Review*, February 2007 (n.p.).

Avolio, B. J., Kahai, S. S., & Dodge, G. E. (2001). E-leadership: Implications for theory, research, and practice. *The Leadership Quarterly*, 11(4), 615–668.

Avolio, B. J., Sosik, J., Kahai, S. S., & Baker, B. (2014). E-leadership: Re-examining transformations in leadership source and transmission. *The Leadership Quarterly*, 25(1), 105–131.

Bardzell, S., Bardzell, J., Pace, T., & Reed, K. (2008). Blissfully productive: Grouping and cooperation in *World of Warcraft* instance runs. CSCW'08, November 8–12, San Diego, CA.

Bass, B. M. (1985). *Leadership and performance*. New York, NY: Free Press.

Bidwell, M. J., & Briscoe, F. (2009). Who contracts? Determinants of the decision to work as an independent contractor among information technology workers. *Academy of Management Journal*, 52(6), 1148–1168.

Carte, T., Chidambaram, L., & Becker, A. (2006). Emergent leadership in self-managed virtual teams. *Group Decision and Negotiation*, 15(4), 323–343.

Chen, M. (2009.) Communication, coordination, and camaraderie in *World of Warcraft*. *Games and Culture*, 4(1), 47–73.

Contractor, N. S., DeChurch, L. A., Carson, J., Carter, D. R., & Keegan, B. (2012). The topology of collective leadership. *Leadership Quarterly*, 23(6), 994–1011.

Day D. V., Gronn, P., & Salas, E. (2004). Leadership capacity in teams. *The Leadership Quarterly*, 15 (6), 857–880.

de Castell, S., Boschman, L., & Jenson, J. (2008). In and out of control: Learning games differently. *Loading*, 2(3), 1–16.

de Castell, S., Jenson, J., Taylor, N., & Thumiert, K. (2014). Re-thinking foundations: Theoretical and methodological challenges (and opportunities) in virtual worlds research. *Journal of Gaming and Virtual Worlds*, 6(1), 3–20.

Dyer-Witheford, N. (2015). *Cyber-proletariat: Global labour in the digital vortex*. Chicago, IL: University of Chicago Press.

Ee, A., & Cho, H. (2012). What makes an MMORPG leader? A social cognitive theory-based approach to understanding the formation of leadership capabilities in massively multiplayer online role-playing games. *Eludamos. Journal for Computer Game Culture*, 6(1), 25–37.

Engeström, Y. (1987). *Learning by expanding: An activity-theoretical approach to developmental research*. Helsinki: Orienta-Konsultit.

Engeström, Y. (1990). When is a tool? Multiple meanings of artifacts in human activity. In Y. Engeström (ed.), *Learning, working and imagining: Twelve studies in activity theory*. Helsinki: Orienta-Konsultit, 171–195.

Giddings, S. (2008). Events and collusions: A glossary for the microethnography of video game play. *Games and Culture*, 4(2), 144–157.

Giddings, S., & Kennedy, H. (2008). Little Jesuses and *@#?-off robots: On cybernetics, aesthetics, and not being very good at Lego Star, Wars. In M. Swalwell & J. Wilson (eds.), *The pleasures of computer gaming: Essays on cultural history, theory and aesthetics* (pp. 13–32). Jefferson, NC: McFarland.

Goh, S., & Wasko, M. (2009). Where's the leader? Identifying leadership candidates within virtual worlds. *MG 2009 Proceedings*. Paper 9.

Goh, S., & Wasko, M. (2011). Leader-member relationships in virtual world teams. In 44th Hawaii International Conference on System Sciences (HICSS), Kauai, HI.

Gronn, P. (2002). Distributed leadership. In K. Leithwood, P. Hallinger, K. Seashore-Louis, G. Furman-Brown, P. Gronn, W. Mulford, & K. Riley (eds.), *Second international handbook of educational leadership and administration*. Dordrecht: Kluwer.

Guthrie, K. L., Phelps, K., & Downey, S. (2011). Virtual worlds: A developmental tool for leadership education. *Journal of Leadership Studies*, 5(2), 6–13.

Hambley, L. A., O'Neill, T. A., & Kline, T. J. B. (2007). Virtual team leadership: The effects of leadership style and communication medium on team interaction styles and outcomes. *Organizational Behavior and Human Decision Processes*, 103(1), 1–20.

Hiller N. J., Day, D. V., & Vance, R. J. (2006). Collective enactment of leadership roles and team effectiveness: A field study. *The Leadership Quarterly*, 17(4), 387–397.

Karmali, L. (October 23, 2015). *Guild Wars 2* hits 7 million players as expansion launches. *IGN*. Retrieved from: www.ign.com/articles/2015/10/23/guild-wars-2-hits-7-million-players-as-expansion-launches (accessed January 12, 2016).

Kollar, P. (November 16, 2015). *World of Warcraft* team responds to shrinking subscriber numbers. *Polygon*. Retrieved from: www.polygon.com/2015/11/16/9731672/world-of-warcraft-legion-subscription-numbers-expansion-speed (accessed January 12, 2016).

Lankshear, C. (1997). *Changing literacies*. Bristol, PA: Open University Press.

Latour, B. (2005). *Reassembling the social: An introduction to actor-network theory*. Oxford: Oxford University Press.

Lehdonvirta, M., Nagashima, Y., Lehdonvirta, V., & Baba, A. (2012.) The Stoic male: How avatar gender affects help-seeking behavior in an online game. *Games and Culture*, 7(1), 29–47.

Li, W-D., Arvey, R. D., & Song, Z. (2011). The influence of general mental ability, self-esteem and family socioeconomic status on leadership role occupancy and leader advancement: The moderating role of gender. *The Leadership Quarterly*, 22(3), 520–534.

Linderoth, J., Björk, S., & Olsson, C. (2014). Should I stay or should I go? A study of pickup groups in Left 4 Dead 2. *ToDIGRA: Transactions of the Digital Games Research Association*, 2(1), 117–145.

Lisk, T. C., Kaplancali, U. T., & Riggio, R. E. (2012). Leadership in multiplayer online gamingenvironments. *Simulation and Gaming*, 43(1), 133–149.

Lu, L., Shen, C., & Williams, D. (2014). Friending your way up the ladder: Connecting massive multiplayer online game behaviors with offline leadership. *Computers in Human Behavior*, 35, 54–60.

Muethel, M., & Hoegl, M. (2013). Shared leadership effectiveness in independent professional teams. *European Management Journal*, 31(4), 423–432.

Mysirlaki, S., & Paraskeva, F. (2012). Leadership in MMOGs: A field of research on virtual teams. *Electronic Journal of e-Learning*, 10(2), 223–234.

Nardi, B. (1995). *Context and consciousness: Activity theory and human-computer interaction*. Cambridge, MA: MIT Press.

Pagliery, J. (June 19, 2014). Why I put World of Warcraft on my resume. *CNN: Money*. Retrieved from: http://money.cnn.com/2014/06/19/technology/world-of-warcraft-resume/ (accessed May 31, 2016).

Purvana, R. K., & Bono, J. E. (2009). Transformational leadership in context: Face-to-face and virtual teams. *The Leadership Quarterly*, 20(3), 343–357.

Ratan, R., Taylor, N., Hogan, J., Kennedy, T. L. M., & Williams, D. (2015). Stand by your man: An examination of gender disparity in *League of Legends*. *Games and Culture*. doi: 10.1177/1555412014567228.

Reeves, B., & Malone, T. (2007). *Leadership in games and at work: Implications for the enterprise of massively multiplayer online role-playing games*. Report prepared for IBM.

Reeves, B., Malone, T. W., & O'Driscoll, T. (2008). Leadership's online labs. *Harvard Business Review*, May 2008 (n.p.).

Rubenfire, A. (August 12, 2014). Can 'World of Warcraft' game skills help land a job? *Wall Street Journal*. Retrieved from: www.wsj.com/articles/can-warcraft-game-skills-help-land-a-job-1407885660 (accessed January 13, 2016).

Ruggieri, S. (2009). Leadership in virtual teams: A comparison of transformational and transactional leaders. *Social Behavior and Personality*, 37(8), 1017–1022.

Schrader, P. G., & McCreery, M. (2008). The acquisition of skill and expertise in massively multiplayer online games. *Educational Technology Research & Development*, 56(5–6), 557–574.

Siewiorek, A., & Lehtinen, E. (2011). Exploring leadership profiles from collaborative computer gaming. *International Journal of Leadership Studies*, 6(3), 357–374.

Siitonen, M. (2009). Conflict management and leadership communication in multiplayer communities. In H. Kennedy (ed.), *Proceedings of DiGRA 2009: Breaking new ground: Innovation in games, play, practice and theory*, Brunel University, London.

Silverman, M., & Simon, B. (2009). Discipline and dragon kill points in the online power game. *Games and Culture*, 4(4), 353–378.

Sorden, C. (May 12, 2008). Player vs. Everything: Putting raiding on your resume. *Massively*. Retrieved from: www.engadget.com/2008/05/12/player-vs-everything-putting-raiding-on-your-resume/ (accessed January 12, 2016).

Sunden, J. (2009). Play as transgression: An ethnographic approach to queer game cultures. In *Proceedings of DiGRA 2009: Breaking new ground: Innovation in games, play, practice and theory*. London: Brunel University.

Taylor, N., Kampe, C., & Bell, K. (2015). Me and Lee: Identification and the play of attraction in *The Walking Dead*. *Game Studies*, 15(1). Retrieved from: http://gamestudies.org/1501/articles/taylor (accessed January 12, 2016).

Taylor, T. L. (2006). *Play between worlds: Exploring online game culture*. Cambridge, MA: MIT Press.

Taylor, T. L. (2012). *Raising the stakes: The professionalization of computer gaming*. Cambridge, MA: MIT Press.

Uhl-Bien, M., Marion, R., & McKelvey, B. (2007). Complexity leadership theory: Shifting leadership from the Industrial Age to the Knowledge Era. *The Leadership Quarterly*, 18(4), 298–318.

van Dijk, N., & Broekens, J. (2010). Virtual team performance depends on distributed leadership. In *9th International Conference on Entertainment Computing*. Seoul, South Korea, September 8–11.

Vygotsky, L. S. (1978). *Mind and society: The development of higher psychological processes*. Cambridge, MA: Harvard University Press.

Wertsch, J. (1998). *Mind as action*. Oxford: Oxford University Press.

Williams, D., Ducheneaut, N., Xiong, L., Zhang, Y., Yee, N., & Nickell, E. (2006). From tree house to barracks: The social life of guilds in *World of Warcraft*. *Games & Culture*, 1(4), 338–361.

Williams, J. P., Kirschner, D., & Suhaimi-Broder, Z. (2014). Structural roles in massively multiplayer online games: A case study of guild and raid leaders in *World of Warcraft*. In M. D. Johns, S-L. S. Chen, & L. A. Terlip (eds.), *Symbolic interaction and new social media* (pp. 121–142). Bingley: Emerald Group Publishing.

Xanthopoulou, D., & Papagiannidis, S. (2012). Play online, work better? Examining the spillover of active learning and transformational leadership. *Technological Forecasting and Social Change*, 79(7), 1328–1339.

Yee, N. (2006). The demographics, motivations and derived experiences of users of massively-multiuser online graphical environments. *PRESENCE: Teleoperators and Virtual Environments*, 15, 309–329.

8

Virtual Organization and Online Games

ROLF T. WIGAND

8.1 Introduction

The virtual organization, often also called the network organization or adhocracy, has been of increased interest to firms as a new type of organization form and structure (Barnatt, 1995; Davidow, 1992; Malone & Rockart, 1993; Shekbar, 2016; Tapscott, 1996; Wigand, Picot, & Reichwald, 1997). Such network or virtual organizations have surfaced in a wide range of industries, from airlines to computer chips and aircraft manufacturing. Virtual enterprises manifest themselves as dynamic networks of organizational units. Single network nodes can be set up either by authorized individuals, by organization units, or by entire organizations. Connections among single nodes are established dynamically and in a problem-oriented fashion. Therefore, task-oriented assignments determine the structure of a virtual enterprise at any point in time. In spite of its often transitory nature, this organizational structure is not shapeless, as performance increases by means of virtuality within systems are attainable only if fundamental components are able to meet the demands of specific basic tasks.

8.2 Characteristics of Virtual Organizations

In accordance with the preceding discussion, we can isolate characteristics that are essential for virtual enterprises and their goal attainment:

Modularity
Heterogeneity
Time distribution
Spatial distribution
Transparency principle
Complementarity principle
The open–closed principle

191

These characteristics and design principles (Picot, Reichwald, & Wigand, 2008) seem at first to be very abstract, but they help us judge to what extent virtual enterprises may indeed be able to increase their performance based on virtuality as an organizational concept. The demarcation of organizational characteristics of virtual enterprises enables the scope of their applications.

8.3 Virtual Collaboration in Virtual Organizations

What are the distinguishing factors that separate information and communication technology (ICT)–enabled collaboration in a physical setting from a geographically dispersed setting? Can findings of previous ICT-enabled physical collaboration (e.g., Computer Supported Cooperative Work [CSCW] and Computer Mediated Communication [CMC] supported by some level of face-to-face communication) help us to understand virtual collaboration (e.g., CSCW and CMC for supporting geographically dispersed collaboration with no face-to-face communication)? How is the development and sustainability of trust different from ICT-enabled physical collaboration and ICT-enabled virtual collaboration? We address these questions below.

We define ICT-enabled physical collaboration as technology-based collaborative systems with the presence of some level of face-to-face communication (see Ludwig, 1999). It may also be referred to as electronically supported communication media ranging from telephone to internet to low-earth orbit satellite cellular technologies that organizations use to support linking individuals in electronically mediated communication (Adhikari, 1998; DiMartino & Wirth, 1990; Hiltz & Turoff, 1992; Kiely, 1993; Niederman & Beise, 1999; Papows, 1998; Shekbar, 2016). For example, McLeod's (1992) meta-analysis of twelve studies suggests that electronically supported face-to-face meeting tools such as group support systems influence decision quality, time to reach decisions, participation quality, and degree of task focus. In an empirical study, Fowler and Wackerbarth (1980) found that audio conferencing may be substituted for and can even outperform face-to-face meetings. However, face-to-face communication was found to be more effective than audio conferencing for tasks which rely on interpersonal communication and are more complex in nature (Fowler & Wackerbarth, 1980; Niederman & Beise, 1999).

In an empirical study in face-to-face versus virtual team settings, 411 subjects participated, communicating asynchronously via groupware technology. The results suggest that virtual teams are most effective in making decisions (Schmidt, Montoya-Weiss, & Massey, 2001). Other studies such as implementing electronic meetings at IBM (see Grohowski et al., 1990), computer systems for facilitating the quality improvement process at the IRS (see

DeSanctis et al., 1991), group technologies for supporting teamwork at Texaco (see DeSanctis et al., 1993), Group Support Systems (DeSanctis & Gallupe, 1987), and Retail Technology Consortium (see Palmer, 1996) also demonstrate perceived effectiveness of ICT for supporting teamwork. The claim that ICT is useful for supporting and improving collaborative work has also been addressed in the CSCW and CMC literature (Coleman, 1996; Dyson, 1990; Jirotka, Gilbert, & Luff, 1992; Jude-York, 1998; Townsend, DeMarie, & Hendrickson, 1998; Warkentin, Sayeed, & Hightower, 1997). For example, a study of three teams and their use of technology at two large US corporations with global extensions suggest significant improvement in collaborative work processes and business results (Jude-York, 1998). Furthermore, an exploratory investigation of the use of web-based conferencing indicates that virtual and face-to-face teams had similar levels of communication effectiveness (Warkentin, Sayeed & Hightower, 1997). However, a higher level of satisfaction was reported for the case of face-to-face communication when compared to virtual teams in this exploratory study.

8.4 ICT for Supporting Virtual Collaboration

Is virtual collaboration related to the application of ICT for supporting geographically dispersed collaboration with no face-to-face communication? Virtual teams may be differentiated from physical teams by time, space, and culture (Grantham, 1996; Paré & Dubé, 1999; Speier & Palmer, 1998). Therefore, these variables have the potential to influence communication, development of trust, and types of ICT required for supporting work activities. However, the direct relationship between the magnitude of physical distance and the tendency to use electronic mediation needs careful examination (Allen, 1977; Churchill & Bly, 1999; Grantham, 1996; Hart, 1999; Kraut, Egido, & Galegher, 1988; Niederman & Beise, 1999; Warkentin, Sayeed & Hightower, 1997).

We define virtual collaboration as ICT-enabled collaboration for geographically dispersed groups with no or very little face-to-face communication. Townsend et al. (1998) suggest that the virtual workplace relates to geographical dispersion of essential employees who are assembled using a combination of telecommunications and information technologies to accomplish an organizational task. By creating a virtual collaborative workspace, organizations may also realize the competitive synergy of teamwork, as well as exploit the benefits of ICT (Harasim, 1993; Igbaria, Shavo, & Olfman, 1999; Kock, 2000; Sproull & Kiesler, 1991). Townsend et al. (1998) further assert that there are five key considerations for organizations moving from face-to-face communication to virtual collaboration: (1) the increasing prevalence of flat or horizontal organization structures; (2) increased interorganizational cooperation, as well as competition; (3) increased accommodation to the changes in workers' expectation of organizational participation; (4) the shift from production to service or knowledge work environments; and (5) the increasing globalization of trade and corporate activity.

Churchill and Bly's (1999) investigation suggests that the text-based multiuser domain (MUD) is effective in supporting collaboration among dispersed groups. They note further that MUDs are powerful in filling the valuable communication niche for dispersed workgroups for both synchronous and asynchronous networks. It can be seen as a multiuser, end-user extensible, low-bandwidth, distributed network accessible environment designed to support collaboration among noncolocated individuals (see Curtis, 1995). MUDs were further found to be more reliable than technologies such as media services (Bly, Harrison, & Irwin, 1993), video conferencing (Finn, Sellen, & Wilbur, 1997), and distributed 3-D graphical environments (Churchill & Snowdon, 1998). MUD-based collaboration takes place within interconnected rooms wherein other users and texts are located.

However, in the virtual collaborative environment with geographically dispersed groups, traditional social mechanisms for facilitating communication and decision making are not present. Therefore, members must find new ways to communicate and interact and this has to be guided by business principles that promote trust among parties (Bandow, 1997; Handy, 1995). A precursor, even a precondition, for such activities undoubtedly is trust. Overall the relevant literature seems to suggest that without trust nothing too positive happens on virtual teams. Trust for managing virtual collaborative relationships is increasingly seen as an important and essential prerequisite in the information systems literature so that optimal use of ICT for supporting collaboration is ensured (Drescher et al., 2014; Hoffman, Novak, & Peralta, 1999; Hossain & Wigand, 2003; Jarvenpaa, Knoll, & Leidner, 1998; Jones et al., 2000; Kasper-Fuehrer, Ashkanasy, & Neal, 2001; Nayak, Bhaskaran, & Das, 2001; Ono et al., 2001; Piccoli & Ives, 2000; Ratnasingham & Kumar, 2000; Rittenbruch, Kahler, & Cremers, 1998; Whittaker, 1996). Studies also suggest that an electronic interface is not a substitute for face-to-face communication (Abel, 1990; Sproull & Kiesler, 1991). However, ICT may be used to support further relationships once teams have experienced some level of initial face-to-face communication. This has been documented in Abel's (1990) study, where it is suggested that teams and groups require face-to-face communication initially to establish common understanding, but ICT may be used to support future relationships. Thus trust is an essential prerequisite for developing and sustaining relationships for virtual collaboration.

8.5 Forming Virtual Organizations

Flexibility is the main goal when forming virtual organizations. It describes the capability of an organization to dynamically adapt to environmental changes. The more turbulent the environmental conditions and the higher the variability of demands, the more successful a flexibility strategy will be (Wigand et al., 1997). Modern ICT has an enormous influence on organizational flexibility, yet, as pointed out by Lucas and Olson (1994), this influence does not always appear to be beneficial. The flexibility paradox exists when deploying information technology that is based on the difference between organizational and technical flexibility. How can virtual organizations go about becoming flexible? They may want to aim at (Wigand et al., 1997)

Achieving "virtual largeness" in spite of "actual smallness"
Taking advantage of centralization within a decentralized structure
Abolishing the contradiction between generalization and specialization.

Firms tend to expect that a virtual organization is synonymous with a strategic organizational structure. It is questionable whether or not this works for every type of business. Any advantages of such strategies depend on the purpose of the task and the related requirements. It is too soon, that is, fundamentally we know too little, to discuss fully design strategies and their particular advantages as they may pertain to virtual enterprises. Therefore, it appears for now to be more meaningful to highlight characteristics and fundamental design principles of virtual enterprises.

Chesbrough and Teece observe that, "While there are many successful virtual companies, there are even more failures that don't make the headlines" (1996, p. 65). They conclude that the virtues of being virtual have been oversold. *Industry Week* reported that in the 1990s, the notion of virtual companies sparked extensive discussion without mentioning a fair amount of skepticism (Sheridan, 1996).

Before building a virtual organization, firms should consider the following questions:

What is the strength of the virtual organization in a given setting?
How does the virtual organization work for new business trends and environments?
What kinds of virtual organizations exist?
What are the advantages and disadvantages in existing virtual organizations?
Will the virtual organization become a core organization structure?

8.6 Boundaries of Virtual Organizations

Virtual organizations manifest themselves across many boundaries: across defined boundaries of time and space, across boundaries of a legally defined internal and external sphere of the organization or extending beyond long-range contractual boundaries pertaining to the membership or lack thereof of organizational participants. This organizational form, however, also has its limits stemming from the technical infrastructure. This infrastructure is considered the nerve center of an enterprise and determines the possibilities for participation (see Jarvenpaa & Ives, 1994).

There are also boundaries and limitations imposed on institutions by human behavioral patterns, for example, bounded rationality or opportunism. The theoretical bases of the role of information for markets and firms, as well as the insights of communication and information behavior enable us to discover initial problem areas with regard to the "boundary-lessness" of virtual organizations. Just two such problem areas are briefly addressed here:

1. Improved support of economic activities via *modern information systems* is a promising strategy for the expansion of human performance limits. Human beings have only limited capacity to process information. We try to compensate for this through the use of information systems. It is possible, for example, to disseminate requests for proposals with low costs and almost no waste of time, as well as worldwide online offers (see Benjamin & Wigand, 1995). It follows that, therefore, costs for economic transactions are reduced. The actual limits of appropriate dynamic technical arrangements are no longer generated by the cost for such arrangements, but by the quality of the electronically available information. The practicality of virtual organizations depends on the willingness to provide information and also on the readiness to use available information. Nevertheless, "No technology has yet been invented that can convince unwilling managers to share information or even to use it" (Davenport, Eccles, & Prusak, 1992, p. 56). One might raise the question and ask what are the consequences for a virtual organization as an institution for the processing of economic activity?
2. *Trust* counts as an essential and decisive coordination mechanism for virtual organizations (see Handy, 1995). Opportunistic human behavior, in the sense of pursuing self-interests at another person's expense, causes risks. Principal–agent theory might be helpful to describe how opportunistic usage of asymmetrical information influences the relationship between buyer and seller. Asymmetric information can cause a risk of delegation. The higher the uncertainty of behavior and the higher the risk of sustaining a loss, the

more someone wants to safeguard his or her actions. Likewise, the more complex and strategically important a performance, the higher the interest for contractual guarantees. Contracts are traditionally used to provide for performance guarantees. Virtual organizations, however, mostly renounce performance guarantees in order to ensure their dynamic features. Contracts in this case are based on trust (Luhmann, 1986, 1994). Blind trust, on the other hand, is definitely not recommended either. Short-lived and dynamic virtual organizations based on trust require, therefore, a long-term relationship including stable and informal confidence, an acceptable level of reputation, and reliable certification or "rules of the game." Only the long-range stability of the rules of the game ensures the necessary flexibility of organizations.

8.7 Today's Importance of Virtual Organizing

The virtualization of economic and societal processes is an ever increasing phenomenon (Overby, 2008). From an organizational perspective, this development is driven mainly by three major trends: first, the changing nature of the organizational environment; second, the innovation potential of ICT; and third, the dynamics of work and society in general (Picot et al., 2008). As a consequence, formerly self-contained and hierarchically integrated structures are becoming more open and permeable by incorporating innovative forms of virtual work arrangements (Martins, Gilson, & Maynard, 2004). Virtual teams are becoming the rule rather than the exception, as work processes, which were traditionally conducted through physical mechanisms, are increasingly being conducted electronically (Bell & Kozlowski, 2002; Overby, 2008; Picot et al., 2008). Furthermore, geographic dispersion is no longer a prerequisite for virtuality since colocated team members may also choose to employ virtual means for coordinating their actions (Kirkman & Mathieu, 2005).

Virtual organizing is increasingly seen as a power concept for understanding the interplay among ICT, organization structure, and geographically dispersed teams working on a common business goal (Venkatraman & Henderson, 1998). It focuses on the importance of knowledge and intellect to create value for organizations. Collaboration denotes communicating and working together across organizational boundaries (Baker, 1992). Virtual collaboration, on the other hand, refers to the use of ICT for supporting the collective interaction among multiple parties involved (Hossain & Wigand, 2003; Kock, 2000). It is suggested here that virtual organizing is an essential prerequisite for ensuring a higher level of virtual collaboration. Therefore, the development and sustainability of virtual collaboration have to be guided by common organizational goals (Picot et al., 2008; Wigand & Imamura, 1997; Wigand et al., 1997). This, in turn, will ensure the linkages among ICT, organization structure, and geographical dispersion (Hossain & Wigand, 2003). Understanding the implications of common organization and business goals for building trust may lead to higher levels of knowledge sharing and therefore help build and sustain collaboration.

Research on virtual organization and virtual teams faces some of the same challenges that research on traditional organization and teams does: Field studies are typically small in scale and often lack quantitative or objective data. Laboratory studies, while allowing for large-scale, well–controlled, and rigorous quantitative data collection, involve relatively short-lived simulations in which the participants have little psychological investment. In addition to these limitations, researchers working on virtual organizations and teams have to deal with the rapid development of new ICTs and the innovative usage thereof by a tech-savvy generation of digital natives (Beck & Wade, 2004). Single communication media cannot be analyzed by themselves or in comparison with one other medium anymore (e.g., email vs. instant messenger) but rather have to be considered as part of entire communication media repertoires (Watson-Manheim & Bélanger, 2007).

As mentioned earlier, the purpose of this chapter is to show that massively multiplayer online games (MMOGs) as research environments offer a unique opportunity to study virtual organizational structures such as virtual teams. They have the potential to overcome some of the limitations of previous research on virtual teams and therefore serve as a powerful extension of traditional research environments.

We begin by discussing the potential of MMOGs as research environments and illustrate how research in MMOGs can offset some of the limitations of research in traditional environments. We then describe a research example conducted by the author (and others) in MMOGs. Finally, we integrate these insights in the context of virtual organizations and present their implications for future research.

8.8 MMOGs as Research Environments

8.8.1 The Emergence of MMOGs

In general, an MMOG is an online game usually played simultaneously by hundreds of players constituting a virtual world. A virtual world can be defined as a "synchronous, persistent network of people, represented as avatars, facilitated by networked computers" (Bell, 2008, p. 2).

Over the past few decades, MMOGs grew from relatively simple text-based games with hundreds of players into complex 3-D environments with millions of players. In this process, teams and organizations within these virtual worlds have become increasingly important for the gameplay, especially since EverQuest introduced the raid mechanic to the genre in 1999, forcing players to cooperate and coordinate their actions in order to be successful.

The social dynamics of these teams and other organizational structures have increasingly attracted the attention of scholars from many disciplines (Bainbridge, 2007; Korsgaard et al., 2009). Researchers have begun to understand the potential of virtual worlds as research environments (Castronova & Falk, 2008) for the study of organizational phenomena: they tremendously increase the number of participants, transcend sociocultural boundaries, and allow for collecting standardized data of social and economic interactions (Bainbridge, 2007, 2009). Researching MMOGs offers new promising opportunities and previously undiscovered potential, and how such research expands the possibilities of social science researchers and for research in virtual organizations in particular (Korsgaard et al., 2009).

8.8.2 The Opportunities of Conducting Research in MMOGs

Like traditional research environments, MMOGs can be used to conduct both experimental and correlational studies. In the text that follows, we describe the most important opportunities in virtual team research using MMOGs.

One characteristic of MMOGs is that a broad variety of people are playing together and against each other in a virtual world. In contrast to common opinion, research shows that online gamers defy common stereotypes (Williams, Yee, & Caplan, 2008). Therefore, MMOGs offer researchers the opportunity to use research subjects from a much broader background (e.g., age, nationality, education, profession) than university students. This is a common limitation in many studies (Jarvenpaa et al., 1998; Jarvenpaa, Shaw, & Staples, 2004; Kanawattanachai & Yoo, 2007; Sarker & Sahay, 2003; Zhang et al., 2007), which reduces the extent to which findings can be generalized (Peterson, 2001; Reips, 2000).

Moreover, MMOGs tend to be highly engaging and psychologically meaningful to participants. Especially certain strategy games where teams compete against each other in pursuit of a certain goal resemble the competitive dynamics to be found in the business world. Often the relationship between players is compared to the relationship between co-workers in their real jobs (Williams et al., 2006; Yee, 2006). Therefore, few incentives are needed to motivate players. This presents a major opportunity since participants from studies with university classes usually receive incentives for their participation in experiments or surveys (most of the time credit points) (Heninger, Dennis, & Hilmer, 2006; Jarvenpaa et al., 1998; Kanawattanachai & Yoo, 2007; Sarker & Sahay, 2003).

Another advantage comes from the social dynamics within teams in MMOGs. The time investment of players in the formation, functioning, and development of the team is quite comparable to that of the members of a real virtual work team. Also, the tasks fulfilled within the games are highly complex and sometimes comparable to the task complexity that is predominant in the context of virtual work teams and organizations in the real world (Kanawattanachai & Yoo, 2007). As a result, online games are blurring the boundaries between work and play very rapidly, and the activities performed in such games are increasingly similar to the work performed in business corporations (Yee, 2006). Furthermore, in MMOGs, roles within teams can be self-allocated based on knowledge and experience rather than arbitrary assignment by an experimenter (Jarvenpaa et al., 1998; Kanawattanachai & Yoo, 2007).

Teams in MMOGs usually play together for a long time, often over several years. In contrast, laboratory studies for the most part have to manipulate ad hoc teams without future orientation or joint history, which can lead to a lack of commitment (Piccoli & Ives, 2003) as well as trust, and influence team cohesion and performance (Zhang et al., 2007). Along with this temporary setting in lab studies, the examination of team development, alternating roles of team leaders (Wakefield, Leidner, & Garrison, 2008), and interactions within the group (Piccoli & Ives, 2003) over longer periods is limited. Depending on the game, teams in MMOGs play together for months or even years, leading to high commitment, strong team cohesion as well as intensity among the members. Therefore, team development and alternating roles of team leaders can be studied here thoroughly and readily.

In terms of size, teams in MMOGs vary strongly and range from small three player teams to highly structured organizations with hundreds of members. Furthermore, manipulation can be introduced at the organization rather than just the team or the individual level. Some researchers even propose experiments at the societal level (Boellstorff, 2008). These teams could even overcome the problem that sample and team size of virtual team studies are mostly rather small, which constraints statistically confirmed results and generalizability (Bélanger & Watson-Manheim, 2006; Majchrzak et al., 2000). Studies in

MMOGs could answer the call for longitudinal data (Joshi, Lazarova, & Liao, 2009; Malhotra, Galletta, & Kirsch, 2008; Piccoli & Ives, 2003; Raghuram et al., 2001; Webster & Wong, 2008), allowing researchers to observe processes within teams, such as team formation, the formation of trust, and their influence on the teams' performance over time.

External effects can be controlled to a much greater extent in MMOGs than in field experiments, because these games are based on computer code that keeps the in-game environment constant over time. Furthermore, as field experiments often take place in companies, this environment also sets boundaries to manipulating participants (Malhotra et al., 2008). MMOGs, however, offer diverse opportunities for manipulations, as discussed in the subsequent experiment section. In addition, most games have a built-in objective performance measure, substituting for flawed perceptional performance measures and avoiding possible common method variance (Majchrzak, Malhotra, & John, 2005).

Another major opportunity is that MMOGs are played throughout the world. Hence, MMOGs allow researchers to conduct truly international and cross-cultural studies at very low cost. In traditional research environments the sample composition sometimes limits the possibilities for deducing differences between cultures, for example, values and conflict resolution styles (Hertel, Konradt, & Orlikowski, 2004; Wakefield et al., 2008). Teams from MMOGs could therefore reveal theoretical and practical implications improving, e.g., the leadership of virtual teams with regard to cultural differences.

Finally, companies examined in field studies usually permit only a certain set of communication channels whereas MMOGs do not constrain the selection of ICTs. This allows players to use any communication media as well as to adjust the communication media repertoires to their specific needs. Hence, the usage of ICT in MMOGs provides researchers with extraordinary insight on what future organizational communication as well as virtual organizations might look like.

In summary, many MMOGs resemble situations of firms in competitive economic environments since they involve complex team building and team management over a longer period of time as well as the management of scarce resources and the race for achieving something that can be reached only by one or few actors, for example, exploitation of a new market, winning an innovation race, and the like. At the same time, the situation of MMOGs is better under control than strategic competition in the real world, thereby allowing for the collection and alignment of subjective and objective data in surveys or experiments.

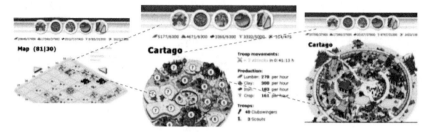

Figure 8.1 The virtual world of *Travian*. (This image is shown in full color in the Color Plates section.)

8.9 Conducting Research in MMOGs

8.9.1 The MMOG *Travian*

Here we present a popular browser-based MMOG called *Travian* that we used for conducting virtual team studies. *Travian* was first released on September 5, 2004 by Gerhard Müller with Travian Games GmbH in Munich. The game is written in PHP and is available in forty-one languages. There are more than 5 million players on more than 300 game servers worldwide. In 2006 *Travian* won the Superbrowsergame Award in the large game category. The advantages of this game are manifold: first, it is playable without subscription fees or initial costs. Second, being browser based, no special client software is needed. Thus, the entry barrier for new and casual players is low. Moreover, *Travian* can be played on different country servers run in the native language of the specific country and international servers open for players from any place in the world. These factors provide for a broad user base, making it particularly interesting and suitable for cross-cultural research by comparing countries on the one hand and multicultural teams on the other hand. Please see Figure 8.1 depicting the virtual world of *Travian*.

The game itself is a real-time strategy game. Players seek to gain natural resources, build armies, and expand their realms. Playing with up to 40,000 users on one server with scarce resources, actors soon find themselves in a social dilemma (Dawes, 1980). The actors have to cooperate with others in order to protect their territory and to successfully expand their reach. In the race to dominate, actors form teams of up to sixty members under a leader or a leadership team. The game lasts approximately one year, at which time one team is deemed the winner based on the fastest completion of a building called "Wonder of the World." Teams are equipped with a shared forum, a chat room, and an in-game messaging system. Furthermore, players can use all types of external communication media (e.g., self-administered forums, Skype). The leadership of a team can invite further members or dismiss current ones. Like virtual teams at work, teamwork and negotiation skills play a crucial role in this context.

8.9.2 Experiments in MMOGs

MMOGs offer great potential to conduct experiments as well as to study virtual organizations. Depending on the extent of interventions granted by the game provider, researchers can manipulate the entire gameworld. This section illustrates two possible concepts showing how to implement manipulations in a game context and gives an example realized in this research.

First, given the possibility to alter game code, researchers could manipulate all game processes. An example is communication: by providing certain communication channels exclusively to subpopulations researchers could analyze the impact of communication media (mixes) on several dependent variables such as performance or trust. This provides the opportunity to examine, for example, media usage, media efficiency, or communication content in a long-term virtual environment that usually is possible neither in laboratory experiments because of time restrictions nor in field studies because companies do not permit groups of employees to participate in experimental settings over lengthy periods of time. Second, manipulations can be introduced by task assignment, both game related and unrelated, fostering certain behaviors. The embodiment of tasks is at the discretion of the researcher. Tasks can refer to single players, teams, or the whole gameworld. Further, the duration of tasks is scalable according to the manipulations' needs: from single action tasks to assignments lasting over weeks or months.

The latter concept was used in a series of experiments conducted on an international *Travian* game server. The server lasted five months, with about 6,000 players and 120 teams from 30 nations. The gameworld was clustered into three geographic sectors after six weeks, when teams were established and stabilized. In each sector, teams were assigned to manipulations, namely coordination, cooperation, and communication. For example, teams in the coordination condition expected that at least 30% of the team members manage to attack each of the five villages within a timeslot of 60 seconds once per day. Depending on the geographic distance, troop speed, and team size this task required high coordination efforts of the teams and their leadership. After the five-day manipulation period, all teams were exposed to a trust manipulation leading to the final task after day 6, a public goods game with a threshold depending on team size. Additionally, all in-game interactions of the players stored in the server log-files (e.g., in-game communication, attacks, and trade) were tracked over the full duration of the server. The combination of experimental data, server log-files, and survey data provides a powerful instrument for researchers. It allows them to analyze experimental data with unobtrusively measured ratios and to observe the long-term development of manipulated teams. Of course, such experimentation has to meet all requirements of ethical research including that subjects must be at least 18 years old and that they receive an adequate debriefing.

8.9.3 Correlational Studies in MMOGs

MMOGs offer some great opportunities for correlational studies. First, combining survey data and log-files (e.g., objective individual and team performance) avoids possible common method variance. Second, server log-files can be used to derive structural data necessary for statistical analysis such as hierarchical linear modeling (HLM) or social network analysis (e.g., team membership, player interaction). Third, the log-files offer the opportunity to track the development of individuals and teams precisely over time and thereby allow researchers to conduct longitudinal studies. As an example, Picot et al. (2009) use survey data combined with structural log-file information in an HLM to examine the antecedents and consequences of trust of team members in virtual team leaders.

8.10 Discussion and Implications

This chapter set out to illustrate the potential of MMOGs as environments for empirical research. By identifying some of the major advantages of conducting research in MMOGs, we showed how these innovative environments can complement traditional research environments.

Research using MMOGs somewhat bridges the gap between laboratory studies and field studies regarding internal and external validity. For instance, findings from laboratory studies can be tested in MMOGs in a more general way. Vice versa, lab designs allow to confirm results obtained from MMOGs in a more controlled environment. Likewise, MMOGs offer the opportunity to test results from field studies in an environment that provides more control. Yet, it still includes a broad part of society as possible participants. Inversely, field studies constitute a research design that can potentially confirm findings obtained in MMOGs enhancing generalizability.

However, using MMOGs as research environments is still in its relatively early stages. The log files of these games could create thousands of potential variables (e.g., Webb et al., 1966). Many other metrics need to be developed.

Combining them with survey data or experimental stimuli bears the potential lead to a major realignment of social sciences (Castronova & Falk, 2008). Research shows that the social processes within teams can be linked to rankings of the games. This temporal separation of different data points by days, weeks, or even months is possible not only in *Travian* but in almost all MMOGs, such as *EverQuest II* and *World of Warcraft*.

These games are played worldwide. *Travian* even emphasizes this practice and runs servers in around fifty countries in the local language. Therefore, cultural effects can be explored on a national level first. Building on these results the international server can be used to explore any deviances from the national characteristics once a player is exposed to a multinational team.

Furthermore, by studying the usage of ICT in virtual teams within MMOGs it is possible to derive implications for future ICT usage in companies. In MMOGs, players range from newbies to highly experienced computer experts. As shown in the example, the appropriate choice of communication media, whether new or established, is critical to efficient team processes. In an ongoing process, teams with varying experience in ICT include new developments in their communication media mix. Foremost, tech-savvy players are the first to try out new communication applications. Applications that turn out to be superior replace traditional technologies and are incorporated into the players' communication media repertoire. In contrast to companies, the context of MMOGs allows virtual teams to experiment with new ICT developments without taking too much risk (Reeves, Malone, & O'Driscoll, 2008). After the selection process of new technologies by experts, less experienced players begin to use the new applications. This process, however, determines the future success of the technology. If a new channel turns out to be unable to transport information accurately or lacks usability for less tech-savvy players, it will be rejected by the community. Hence, the bandwidth of experience with ICT of players in MMOGs allows researchers to observe the early adoption of new ICT media as well as its diffusion in the community. Thus, findings obtained in MMOGs give practitioners valuable insights in application areas of new ICTs, for example, which communication channel(s) is(are) appropriate for which kind of information transfers, or for which team size.

Apart from the adoption process, players of MMOGs constantly search for new ways to share and conserve information. If nothing appropriate is available, they develop new tools in order to process and transfer information efficiently. In case of *Travian*, several online platforms emerged around the game (e.g., https://www.gettertools.com/en/). These platforms give players the opportunity to comprehend the enormous amount of public information available. Additionally, they provide the opportunity to track and coordinate team members' actions. By analyzing the emergence and the functionality of platforms around MMOGs, researchers can reveal practical implication for the usage and implementation of innovative ICT solutions in companies that can enhance efficiency in knowledge sharing and reduce cost at the same time (Bughin, 2008).

As with any research environment, there are some limitations that have to be considered. Even though gamers playing MMOGs develop a strong psychological involvement with the game, taking risks in the game essentially leads to fewer consequences than taking comparable risks in the real world. This fact yields the most serious limitation of MMOGs as a research environment, thereby reducing the extent to which obtained results can be generalized. However, it is worth noting that the long-term orientation of MMOGs strengthens the participants' engagement to succeed in the game. This improves the experiment's subjects'66 commitment compared to laboratory studies.

Furthermore, hierarchies within MMOGs differ from real-world virtual team hierarchies. Whereas globally dispersed teams within or between companies usually have clearly defined formal authorities, teams in MMOGs usually do not; in case of conflict, players can usually change team membership with one mouse click.

An additional concern is the honesty of the players within an MMOG. First, it is hardly possible to verify sociodemographic data. All the information they choose to disclose can be deliberately false. For instance, sometimes players even choose to switch their "online" gender (Huh & Williams, 2009). Second, players could try to cheat in the game to achieve an advantage over competing players and therefore potentially distort the collected log file data. Yet, MMOGs usually have very strong communities of honest players. Supported by incentives from the developers of MMOGs, players usually "police" their own game and report any suspicious activity. In *Travian*, so-called "Multihunters" are recruited from the game's community and trained to identify cheaters.

Another limitation might be that players of MMOGs do not necessarily represent the society as a whole because the social composition of these games is often biased (Kendall, 2002; Nakamura, 2009). Depending on the MMOG the bulk of players are usually predominately male. As the gaming industry is trying to develop new markets, games that specifically cater to the demands of female players will in the future potentially mitigate this limitation. Furthermore, most MMOGs need advanced hardware as well as a fast and stable internet connection, which restricts access almost solely to computer experienced players from countries with a decent internet infrastructure. However, recently, the gaming industry has been developing browser based games, both "simple" html-/php-based and sophisticated flash-based 3-D games. Thereby, less tech-savvy people from countries with less advanced infrastructure acquire the opportunity to participate in those virtual worlds.

The access to MMOGs is limited not only for players but far more severely for researchers. For the most part, scholars depend on the cooperation of providers of MMOGs to grant them access to their data and players. Even if a developer of an MMOG grants full access, the research design is still bounded by the game design of the examined MMOG. To date, researchers have not succeeded in developing an MMOG that caters to the need of researchers and establishes a committed player community at the same time to ensure the players' long-time personal and emotional involvement.

Next we explore limits and boundaries of virtual organizational forms.

8.11 Limits of Virtual Organizational Forms

Based on virtual organizational forms we need to ask ourselves which fundamental forms of spatial flexibility are easier and which ones are more difficult to implement. Moreover, which organizational forms promise strategic advantage for companies or meet the demands and expectations of coworkers most readily, which forms offer ecological and traffic flow-enhancing problem solutions or even enable regional or structure-political aims (cf., Englberger, 2000; Picot et al., 2008)? The implementation barriers for virtual and tele-cooperative work forms can be estimated to be the lowest where tele-cooperation corresponds directly with the competitive and strategic alignment of a company, customer closeness, customer integration, flexibility, and efficiency as well as the integration and reachability of business and cooperation partners. Mobile tele-work or tele-work on site at the location of the customer, supplier, or value-adding partner are therefore especially effective work forms. For the forms per se we find very little empirical research evidence. Their use, however, occurs without much furor, planned piloting, or scientific monitoring nor with associated research efforts, but with much apparent success. Virtual organizational work forms are bound to face high implementation barriers when, on the one hand, advantages for individual coworkers or the company as a whole can be realized, but when these, on the other hand, do not demonstrate calculable or in some way assessable efficiency or cost-effective advantages for the company.

Virtual organizations manifest themselves across many boundaries: across defined boundaries of time and space, across boundaries of a legally defined internal and external sphere of the organization, or extending beyond long-range contractual boundaries concerning the membership or nonmembership of organizational participants (Shekbar, 2016; Wigand et al., 1997). However, this organizational form naturally has its limits too. On the one hand, these are the limits and boundaries of the technical infrastructure. This infrastructure is considered to be the nerve center of an enterprise and decides on the possibilities to participate (cf., Jarvenpaa & Ives, 1994). But there are also boundaries and limitations imposed on institutions by human behavioral patterns (e.g., limited rationalism or opportunism). The theoretical bases of the role of information for markets and firms developed as well as the insights gained in communication and information behavior enable us, however, to discover initial problem areas with regard to the "boundary-lessness" of virtual organizations. Here we need to consider the following:

- Improved support possibilities of economic activities via *modern information systems* are a promising strategy for the expansion of human performance limits. Human beings have only limited capacity to process information. We try to compensate for this through the use of information systems. It is possible, for example, to disseminate requests for proposals with low costs and almost no waste of time, as well as to make worldwide online offers (cf., Benjamin & Wigand, 1995). Therefore, costs of economic transactions become lower and lower. The limits of appropriate dynamic technical arrangements are no longer generated by the costs for such arrangements, but by the quality of the electronically available information. The practicality of virtual organizations depends on the willingness to provide information and also on the readiness to use available information. Nevertheless, "No technology has yet been invented that can convince unwilling managers to share information or even to use it" (Davenport et al., 1992, p. 56; cited by Jarvenpaa & Ives, 1994). What are the consequences for a virtual organization as an institution for the processing of economic activities?
- *Trust* counts as a decisive coordination mechanism for virtual organizations (cf., Drescher, Korsgaard, Wigand, Welpe, & Picot, 2014; Handy, 1995; Hossain & Wigand, 2004; Ripperger, 1998; Wise, 2016). Opportunistic human behavior, in the sense of pursuing self-interests at other persons' expense, usually favors risk taking. Principal–agent theory might be helpful to describe how opportunistic usage of asymmetrical information influences the relationship between buyer and seller. Asymmetrical information can cause a risk of delegation. The higher the uncertainty of behavior and the higher the risk of sustaining a loss, the more someone wants to safeguard his/her actions. Likewise, the more complex and strategically important a performance, the higher the interest for contractual guarantees. Contracts are traditionally used to provide for performance guarantees. However, virtual organizations mostly renounce contractual guarantees in order to ensure their dynamic features.

Trust is their constituting element (cf., e.g., Drescher et al., 2014; Fukuyama, 1995; Hossain & Wigand, 2004; Kramer & Tyler, 1996; Luhmann, 1994, 2000; Ripperger, 1998; Wise, 2016). Contracts in this case are based on *trust* (Luhmann, 1989, 1994). Nevertheless, blind trust is definitely not recommended. Short-lived and dynamic virtual organizations based on trust require a long-term relationship including stable and informal confidence, generally accepted reputations, and reliable certifications or "rules of the game." Only the long-range stability of the rules of the game ensures the necessary flexibility of organizations (see Wigand et al., 1997).

In virtual organizing we are then concerned with cooperative problem solutions among loosely coupled cooperation partners. The structures within which such cooperative relations occur configure themselves dynamically and have only a temporary existence. What does a suitable provision of information for such organizations look like and what motivational problems need to be considered? How are the rights distributed for authority, decisions, and disposal within such structures and how does their assigning take place? How can we appropriately and effectively address the fundamental problems of the principal–agent relationship between the contractor and agent (hidden characteristics, hidden action, hidden intention) in this organizational form? How do the contractual relations have to be structured such that sufficient flexible and discretionary action is possible, but such that the danger of opportunistic shortchanging is limited?

Absolute and concluding answers to the questions cannot be provided. They address problem complexes, however, pointing toward one thing: the boundaries of virtual enterprises as a reputed "boundary-less" organizational form are not located solely within the realm of technical feasibility. Adequate information and communication-technical infrastructures are indeed a necessary, but not a sufficient condition for the successful realization of this innovative organizational strategy.

8.12 Conclusion

Future research may build upon our argumentation and fully explore MMOGs as research environments for virtual organizations. If researchers gain access to communication logs, advanced tools are needed to automatically categorize the content of these messages, code it, and finally analyze it. Furthermore, the use of ICTs in MMOGs to cooperate and coordinate team and other efforts offers intriguing opportunities.

In conclusion, as almost all work becomes virtual to some degree, the influence of virtuality on human behavior will continue to be on the research agenda of various academic disciplines. Research on the effects of the virtualization of organizational structures, on social dynamics, and on decision processes has made great progress in recent years, yet many questions are left unanswered. We firmly believe that research in MMOGs and other virtual worlds will help to answer some of these questions.

Acknowledgments

This contribution is a culmination of a large, international, and multiyear research effort. This research was funded in part by the National Science Foundation's Virtual Organizations as Sociotechnical Systems (VOSS) program (Award Numbers: IIS-0838402 and IIS-0838231) in Washington, DC; the Deutsche Forschungsgemeinschaft (German National Science Foundation) in Bonn, Germany; Travian Games GmbH, Munich as well as the Jerry L. Maulden/Entergy Fund at the University of Arkansas at Little Rock. The researchers involved and contributing to these projects are Drs. Jakob J. Assmann, Munich School of Management, Ludwig Maximilians University of Munich; Marcus A. Drescher, TUM School of Management, Munich University of Technology; Nitin Agarwal, Department of Information Science, University of Arkansas at Little Rock, Little Rock, AR; Julia V. Gallenkamp, Munich School of Management, Ludwig Maximilians University of Munich; Mr. Winfried Hering, Department of Information Science, University of Arkansas at Little Rock, Little Rock, AR; M. Audrey Korsgaard, Department of Management, University of South Carolina, Columbia, SC; O. Isaac Osesina, Advanced Products Group, Aware, Inc., Bedford, MA; Arnold Picot, Institute for Information, Organization & Management, Munich School of Management, Ludwig Maximilians University of Munich; Isabell M. Welpe, TUM School of Management, Munich University of Technology; and Rolf T. Wigand, Departments of Information Science and Business Information Systems, University of Arkansas at Little Rock, Little Rock, AR and Arizona State University, Tempe, AZ. These researchers' contributions are gratefully acknowledged here. Any opinions, findings, and conclusions or recommendations expressed in this material are those of the authors and do not necessarily reflect the views of the funding agencies. The researchers gratefully acknowledge their support.

References

Abel, M. (1990). Experiences in an exploratory distributed organization. In J. Galegher, R. E. Kraut, & C. Egido (eds.), *Intellectual teamwork*. Hillsdale, NJ: Lawrence Erlbaum.

Adhikari, R. (1998, May 4). Groupware to the next level. *InformationWeek*, 106–111.

Allen, T. J. (1977). *Managing the flow of technology*. Cambridge, MA: MIT Press.

Bainbridge, W. S. (2007). The scientific research potential of virtual worlds. *Science*, 317 (5837), 472–476.

Bainbridge, W. S. (ed.). (2009). *Online worlds: Convergence of the real and the virtual*. London: Springer-Verlag.

Baker, W. E. (1992). The network organization in theory and practice. In N. Nohria & R. G. Eccles (eds.), *Networks and organizations: Structure, form, and action* (pp. 397–429). Cambridge, MA: Harvard Business School Press.

Bandow, D. (1997). Geographically distributed work groups and IT: A case study of working relationships and IS professionals. In *SIGCPR '97 Proceedings of the 1997 ACM SIGCPR Conference on Computer Personnel Research* (pp. 87–92). San Francisco: Association for Computing Machinery (ACM).

Barnatt, C. (1995). Office space, cyberspace and virtual organization. *Journal of General Management*, 20 (4), 78–91.

Beck, J. C., & Wade, M. (2004). *Got game: How the gamer generation is reshaping business forever*. Boston, MA: Harvard Business School Press.

Bélanger, F., & Watson-Manheim, M. (2006). Virtual teams and multiple media: Structuring media use to attain strategic goals. *Group Decision & Negotiation*, 15 (4), 299–321.

Bell, B. S., & Kozlowski, S. W. J. (2002). A typology of virtual teams: Implications for effective leadership. *Group & Organization Management*, 27 (1), 14.

Bell, M. (2008). Toward a definition of "Virtual Worlds." *Journal of Virtual World Research*, 1 (1), 1–5.

Benjamin, R., & Wigand, R. T. (1995). Electronic markets and virtual value chains on the Information Superhighway. *Sloan Management Review*, 2, 62–72.

Bly, S. A., Harrison, S. R., & Irwin, S. (1993). Media spaces: Bringing people together in a video, audio, and computing environment. *Communications of the ACM*, 36(1), 28–47.

Boellstorff, T. (2008). *Coming of age in* Second Life: *An anthropologist explores the virtually human*. Princeton, NJ: Princeton University Press.

Bughin, J. (2008). The rise of enterprise 2.0. *Journal of Direct, Data and Digital Marketing Practice*, 9 (3), 251–259.

Castronova, E., & Falk, M. (2008). Virtual worlds as Petri dishes for the social and behavioral sciences (December 2008). RatSWD Working Paper No. 47. Retrieved from: http://ssrn.com/abstract=1445340 (accessed November 7, 2017).

Chesbrough, H. W., & Teece, D. J. (1996). Organizing for innovation. *Harvard Business Review*, January–February, 65–73.

Churchill, E. F., & Bly, S. (1999). Virtual environments at work: Ongoing use of MUDs in the workplace. In *Proceedings of the International Joint Conference on Work Activities Coordination and Collaboration*, San Francisco, CA (pp. 99–108). New York, NY: Association for Computing Machinery (ACM), WACC '99.

Churchill, E. F., & Snowdon, D. (1998). Collaborative virtual environments: An introductory review of issues and systems. *Virtual Reality: Research, Development and Applications*, 3(1), 3–15.

Coleman, D. (1996). Electronic collaboration on the Internet and Intranets. San Francisco: Collaborative Strategies. Retrieved from: www.collaborate.com/intranet .html (accessed January 5, 2017).

Curtis, P. (1995). Mudding: Social phenomenon in text-based virtual realities. In M. Stefik (ed.), *Internet dreams: Archetypes, myths, and metaphors* (pp. 265–292). Cambridge, MA: MIT Press.

Davenport, T. H., Eccles, R. G., & Prusak, L. (1992). Information politics. *Sloan Management Review*, Fall 1992, 53–65.

Davidow, W. (1992). Virtual corporation. *Forbes*, December 7, 102–107.

Dawes, R. M. (1980). Social dilemmas. *Annual Review of Psychology*, 31, 169–193.

DeSanctis, G., & Gallupe, R. B. (1987). A foundation for the study of group decision support systems. *Management Science*, 33(5), 589–609.

DeSanctis, G., Poole, M. S., Desharnais, G., & Lewis, H. (1991). Using computing to facilitate the quality improvement process: The IRS-Minnesota project. *Interfaces*, 21(6), 23–36.

DeSanctis, G., Poole, M. S., Dickson G. W., & Jackson, B. M. (1993). Interpretive analysis of team use of group technologies. *Journal of Organizational Computing*, 3(1), 1–30.

DiMartino, V., & Wirth, L. (1990). Telework: A new way of working and living. *International Labour Review*, 129(5), 529–554.

Drescher, M. A., Korsgaard, M. A., Wigand, R. T., Welpe, I. S., & Picot, A. (2014). The dynamics of shared leadership: Building trust and enhancing performance. *Journal of Applied Psychology*, 99(5), 771–783. http://dx.doi.org/10.1037/a0036474 (accessed November 7, 2017).

Dyson, E. (1990). Why groupware is gaining ground. *Datamation*, March 1, 52–56.

Englberger, H. (2000). *Kommunikation von Innovationsbarrieren in telekooperativen Reorganisationsprozessen*. Wiesbaden: Gabler.engleberger.

Finn, K. E., Sellen, A. J., & Wilbur, S. B. (eds.). (1997). *Video mediated communication: Computer, cognition and work series*. Mahwah, NJ: Lawrence Erlbaum Associates.

Fowler, G. D., & Wackerbarth, M. E. (1980). Audio teleconferencing versus face-to-face conferencing: A synthesis of the literature. *Western Journal of Speech Communication*, 44 (Summer), 236–252.

Fukuyama, F. (1995). *Trust: The social virtues and the creation of prosperity*. New York, NY: Simon and Schuster.

Grantham, C. E. (1996). Working in a virtual place: A case study of distributed work. In *Proceedings of the ACM SIGPR/SIGMIS Special Interest Group Conference on Computer Personnel Research*, San Francisco, CA (pp. 68–84). New York: Association for Computing Machinery (ACM).

Grohowski, R., McGoff, C., Vogel, D., Martz, B., & Nunamaker, J. (1990). Implementing electronic meeting systems at IBM: Lessons learned and success factors. *MIS Quarterly*, 14(4), 369–383.

Handy, C. (1995). Trust and virtual organization: How do you manage people whom you do not see. *Harvard Business Review*, 73(3), 40–50.

Harasim, L. (1993). *Global networks: Computers and international communications*. Cambridge, MA: MIT Press.

Hart, P. (1999). Understanding colocation requirements and refining expectations about computer network use: A field study of engineering design environments. In *Proceedings of the 20th International Conference on Information Systems*, ICIS '99, Charlotte, NC (pp. 484–488). Atlanta, GA: Association for Information Systems.

Heninger, W. G., Dennis, A. R., & Hilmer, K. M. (2006). Individual cognition and dual-task interference in group support systems. *Information Systems Research*, 17(4), 415–424.

Hertel, G., Konradt, U., & Orlikowski, B. (2004). Managing distance by interdependence: Goal setting, task interdependence, and team-based rewards in virtual teams. *European Journal of Work & Organizational Psychology*, 13 (1), 1–28.

Hiltz, S. R., & Turoff, M. (1992). Virtual meetings: Computer conferencing and distributed group support. In R. P. Bostrom, R. T. Waston, & S. Kinney (eds.), *Computer augmented teamwork* (pp. 67–85). New York, NY: Van Nostrand Reinhold.

Hoffman, D. L., Novak, T. P., & Peralta, M. (1999). Building consumer trust on-line. *Communications of the ACM*, 42(4), 80–85.

Hossain, L., & Wigand, R. T. (2003). Understanding virtual collaboration through structuration. In *Proceedings of the 4th European Conference on Knowledge Management* (pp. 475–484).

Hossain, L., & Wigand, R. T. (2004). Trust for e-business management. In *Proceedings of the Fourth International Conference on Electronic Business: Shaping Business Strategy in a Networked World*, December 5–9, 2004 (pp. 893–900). Beijing, China: Tsinghua University, International Academic Publishers.

Huh, S., & Williams, D. (2009). Dude looks like a lady: Online game gender swapping. In W. S. Bainbridge (ed.), *Online worlds: Convergence of the real and the virtual* (pp. 161–174). Guildford: Springer.

Igbaria, M., Shayo, C., & Olfman, L. (1999). On becoming virtual: The driving forces and arrangements. In *Proceedings of the ACM SIGPR Special Interest Group Conference on Computer Personnel Research*, New Orleans, LA (pp. 27–41). New York: Association for Computing Machinery (ACM).

Jarvenpaa, S., & Ives, B. (1994). The global network organization of the future: Information management opportunities and challenges. *Journal of Management Information Systems*, 10(4), 25–57.

Jarvenpaa, S. L., Knoll, K., & Leidner, D. E. (1998). Is anybody out there? Antecedents of trust in global virtual teams. *Journal of Management Information Systems*, 14(4), 29–64.

Jarvenpaa, S. L., Shaw, T. R., & Staples, D. S. (2004). Toward contextualized theories of trust: The role of trust in global virtual teams. *Information Systems Research*, 15 (3), 250–264.

Jirotka, M., Gilbert, N., & Luff, P. (1992). On the social organization of organizations. *Computer Supported Cooperative Work*, 1(1), 95–118.

Jones, S., Wilikens, M., Morris, P., & Masera, M. (2000). Trust requirements in e-business. *Communications of the ACM*, 43(12), 81–87.

Joshi, A., Lazarova, M. B., & Liao, H. (2009). Getting everyone on board: The role of inspirational leadership in geographically dispersed teams. *Organization Science*, 20(1), 240–252.

Jude-York, D. (1998). Technology enhanced teamwork: Aligning individual contributions for superior team performance. *Organization Development Journal*, 16(3), 73–80.

Kanawattanachai, P., & Yoo, Y. (2007). The impact of knowledge coordination on virtual team performance over time. *MIS Quarterly*, 31(4), 783–808.

Kasper-Fuehrer, E. C., Ashkanasy, N. M., & Neal, M. (2001). Communicating trustworthiness and building trust in interorganizational virtual organizations. *Journal of Management*, 27(3), 235–254.

Kendall, L. (2002). *Hanging out in the virtual pub: Masculinities and relationships online*. Oakland, CA: University of California Press.

Kiely, T. (1993). Learning to share. *CIO*, July, 38–44.

Kirkman, B. L., & Mathieu, J. E. (2005). The dimensions and antecedents of team virtuality. *Journal of Management*, 31(5), 700–718.

Kock, N. (2000). Benefits for virtual organizations from distributed groups. *Communications of the ACM*, 43(11), 107–112.

Korsgaard, M. A., Picot, A., Wigand, R. T., Welpe, I. A., & Assmann, J. (2009). Cooperation, coordination and trust in virtual teams: Insights from virtual games (with). In William Sims Bainbridge (ed.), *Online worlds: Convergence of the real and the virtual* (pp. 251–262). London: Springer-Verlag.

Kramer, R. M., & Tyler, T. R. (eds.) (1996). *Trust in organizations: Frontiers of strategy and research*. Thousand Oaks, CA: SAGE.

Kraut, R., Egido, C., & Galegher, J. (1988). Patterns of contact and communication in scientific research collaboration. In *Proceedings of the Conference on Computer Supported Cooperative Work*, CSCW '88, Portland, OR (pp. 1–12). New York: Association for Computing Machinery.

Lucas, H. C., Jr., & Olson, M. (1994). The impact of information technology on organizational flexibility. *Journal of Organizational Computing*, 4 (2), 155–176.

Ludwig, G. S. (1999). Virtual geographic research teams: A case study. *Journal of Geography*, 98(3), 149–154.

Luhmann, N. (1986). Persöniches Vertrauen. In *Vertrauen: Ein Mechanismus der Reduktion sozialer Komplexität*, 3rd ed. (pp. 165–185). Stuttgart: Enke Verlag.

Luhmann, N. (1989). *Ecological communication*. Chicago, IL: University of Chicago Press and Cambridge, UK: Polity Press.

Luhmann, N. (2000). *The reality of the mass media*. Cambridge, UK: Polity Press and Oxford: Blackwell.

Luhmann, N. (1994). *Die Wirtschaft der Gesellschaft*. Frankfurt am Main: Suhrkamp Verlag.

Majchrzak, A., Malhotra, A., & John, R. (2005). Perceived individual collaboration know-how development through information technology-enabled contextualization: Evidence from distributed teams. *Information Systems Research*, 16, 1, 9–27.

Majchrzak, A., Rice, R. E., Malhotra, A., King, N., & Ba, S. (2000). Technology adaptation: The case of a computer-supported inter-organizational virtual team. *MIS Quarterly*, 24(4), 569–600.

Malhotra, Y., Galletta, D. F., & Kirsch, L. J. (2008). How endogenous motivations influence user intentions: Beyond the dichotomy of extrinsic and intrinsic user motivations. *Journal of Management Information Systems*, 25(1), 267–299.

Malone, T. W., & Rockart, J. F. (1993). How will information technology reshape organizations? Computers as coordination technology. In S. P. Bradley, J. A. Hausman, & R. L. Nolan (eds.), *Globalization, technology, and competition: The fusion of computer and telecommunications in the 1990s* (pp. 37–55). Boston, MA: Harvard Business School Press.

Martins, L. L., Gilson, L. L., & Maynard, M. T. (2004). Virtual teams: What do we know and where do we go from here? *Journal of Management*, 30(6), 805–835.

McLeod, P. L. (1992). An assessment of the experimental literature on electronic support of group work: Results of a meta-analysis. *Human-Computer Interaction*, 7, 257–280.

Nakamura, L. (2009). Digitizing race: Visual cultures of the internet. *Visual Studies*, 24(1), 90–91.

Nayak, N., Bhaskaran, K., & Das, R. (2001). Virtual enterprises: Building blocks for dynamic e-business. In *Proceedings of the Workshop on Information Technology for Virtual Enterprises*, Goldcoast, Queensland, Australia (pp. 80–87). Los Alamitos, CA: IEEE Computer Society.

Niederman, F., & Beise, C. M. (1999). Defining the "virtualness" of groups, teams, and meetings. In *Proceedings of the ACM SIGPR Conference on Computer Personnel Research*, New Orleans, LA (pp. 14–18). New York, NY: Association for Computing Machinery (ACM).

Ono, C., Paulson, B. C., Kanetomo, D., Cutkosky, M., Kim, K., & Petrie, C. J. (2001). Trust-based facilitator for e-partnerships. In *Proceedings of the 5th International Conference on Autonomous Agents*, Montréal, Canada (pp. 108–109). New York, NY: Association for Computing Machinery (ACM).

Overby, E. (2008). Process virtualization theory and the impact of information technology. *Organization Science*, 19(2), 277–291.

Palmer, J. W. (1996). Supporting the virtual organization through information technology in a new venture: The RETEX experience. In *Proceedings of the ACM SIGPR/SIGMIS Special Interest Group Annual Conference on Computer Personnel Research*, Denver, CO (pp. 223–233). New York, NY: Association for Computing Systems (ACM).

Papows, J. (1998). The rapid evolution of collaborative tools: A paradigm shift. *Telecommunications*, 32(1), 31–32.

Paré, G., & Dubé, L. (1999). Virtual teams: An exploratory study of key challenges and strategies. In *Proceedings of the 20th International Conference on Information Systems*, Charlotte, NC (pp. 479–483). Atlanta, GA: Association for Information Systems.

Peterson, R. A. (2001). On the use of college students in social science research: Insights from a second-order meta-analysis. *Journal of Consumer Research*, 28(3), 450–461.

Piccoli, G., & Ives, B. (2000). Virtual teams: Managerial behavior control's impact on team effectiveness. In *Proceedings of the 21st International Conference on Information Systems*, Brisbane, Australia (pp. 575–580). Atlanta, GA: Association for Information Systems.

Piccoli, G., & Ives, B. (2003). Trust and the unintended effects of behavior control in virtual teams. *MIS Quarterly*, 27(3), 365–395.

Picot, A., Assmann, J. J., Korsgaard, M. A., Welpe, I. M., Gallenkamp, J. V., & Wigand, R. T. (2009). A multi-level view of the antecedents and consequences of trust in virtual leaders. In *Proceedings of the Fifteenth Americas Conference on Information Systems*, San Francisco, CA (pp. 11–21). Atlanta, GA: Association of Information Systems.

Picot, A., Reichwald, R., & Wigand, R. (2008). *Information, organization and management*. Heidelberg: Springer-Verlag.

Raghuram, S., Gamd, R., Wiesenfeld, B., & Gupta, V. (2001). Factors contributing to virtual work adjustment. *Journal of Management*, 27(3), 383–405.

Ratnasingham, P., & Kumar, K. (2000). Trading partner trust in electronic commerce participation. In *Proceedings of the 21st International Conference on Information Systems*, Brisbane, Australia (pp. 544–552). Atlanta, GA: Association for Information Systems.

Reeves, B., Malone, T. W., & O'Driscoll, T. (2008). Leadership's online labs. *Harvard Business Review*, 86(5), 59–66.

Reips, U.-D. (2000). The Web experiment method: Advantages, disadvantages, and solutions. In M. H. Birnbaum (ed.), *Psychological experiments on the Internet* (pp. 89–117). San Diego, CA: Academic Press.

Ripperger, T. (1998). *Oekonomik des Verrauens. Analyse eines Organisationsprinzips*. Tübingen: Mohr.

Rittenbruch, M., Kahler, H., & Cremers, A. B. (1998). Supporting cooperation in a virtual organization. In *Proceedings of the International Conference on Information Systems*, Helsinki, Finland (pp. 30–38). Atlanta, GA: Association for Information Systems.

Sarker, S., & Sahay, S. (2003). Understanding virtual team development: An interpretive study. *Journal of the Association for Information Systems*, 4, 1–36.

Schmidt, J. B., Montoya-Weiss, M. M., & Massey, A. P. (2001). New product development decision-making effectiveness: Comparing individuals, face-to-face teams, and virtual teams. *Decision Sciences*, 32(4), 575–600.

Shekbar, S. (2016). *Managing the reality of virtual organizations*. Chennai, TN, India: Springer India.

Sheridan, J. H. (1996). The agile web: A model for the future? *Industry Week*, March 4, pp. 31–35.

Speier, Cheri, & Palmer, Jonathan. (1998). A definition of virtualness. *AMCIS 1998 Proceedings* (p. 191). Retrieved from: http://aisel.aisnet.org/amcis1998/191 (accessed November 7, 2017).

Sproull, L., & Kiesler, S. (1991). *Connections: New ways of working in the networked organization*. Cambridge, MA: MIT Press.

Tapscott, D. (1996). *The digital economy: Promise and peril in the age of networked intelligence*. New York, NY: McGraw-Hill.

Townsend, A. M., DeMarie, S. M., & Hendrickson, A. (1998). Virtual teams: Technology and the workplace of the future. *The Academy of Management Executive*, 12(3), 17–29.

Venkatraman, N., & Henderson, C. (1998). Real strategies for virtual organizing. *Sloan Management Review*, 40(1), 33–48.

Wakefield, R. L., Leidner, D. E., & Garrison, G. (2008). A model of conflict, leadership, and performance in virtual teams. *Information Systems Research*, 19(4), 434–455.

Warkentin, M. E., Sayeed, L., & Hightower, R. (1997). Virtual teams versus face-to-face teams: An exploratory study of a web-based conference systems. *Decision Sciences*, 28(4), 975–996.

Watson-Manheim, M. B., & Bélanger, F. (2007). Communication media repertoires: Dealing with the multiplicity of media choices. *MIS Quarterly*, 31(2), 267–293.

Webb, E. J., Campbell, D. T., Schwartz, R. D., & Sechrest, L. (1966). *Unobtrusive measures: Nonreactive research in the social sciences* (p. 237). Chicago, IL: Rand McNally.

Webster, J., & Wong, W. K. P. (2008). Comparing traditional and virtual group forms: Identity, communication and trust in naturally occurring project teams. *International Journal of Human Resource Management*, 19(1), 41–62.

Whittaker, S. (1996). Talking to strangers: An evaluation of the factors affecting electronic collaboration. In *Proceedings of the ACM Conference on Computer Supported Cooperative Work* (CSCW '96), Boston, MA (pp. 409–418). New York: Association for Computing Machinery (ACM).

Wigand, R. T. (1997) Electronic commerce: Definition, theory and context. *The Information Society*, 13, 1–16.

Wigand, R. T., & Imamura, T. (1997). Virtual organization: Enablers and boundaries of an emerging organizational form. In *Proceedings of the Americas Conference on Information Systems*, Indianapolis, IN (pp. 423–425). Atlanta, GA: Association for Information Systems.

Wigand, R. T., Picot, A., & Reichwald, R. (1997). *Information, organization and management: Expanding markets and corporate boundaries*. Chichester: John Wiley & Sons.

Williams, D., Ducheneaut, N., Xiong, L., Zhang, Y., Yee, N., & Nickell, E. (2006). From tree house to barracks: The social life of guilds in *World of Warcraft*. *Games and Culture*, 1(4), 338–361.

Williams, D., Yee, N., & Caplan, S. E. (2008). Who plays, how much, and why? Debunking the stereotypical gamer profile. *Journal of Computer-Mediated Communication*, 13(4), 993–1018.

Wise, T. P. (2016). *Trust in virtual teams*. London: Routledge.

Yee, N. (2006). The labor of fun: How video games blur the boundaries of work and play. *Games and Culture*, 1(1), 68–71.

Zhang, D., Lowry, P. B., Zhou, L., & Fu, X. (2007). The impact of individualism: Collectivism, social presence, and group diversity on group decision making under majority influence. *Journal of Management Information Systems*, 23(4), 53–80.

9

Virtual Economic Experiments

THOMAS CHESNEY, SWEE HOON CHUAH,
ROBERT HOFFMANN, WENDY HUI, AND
JEREMY LARNER

In this chapter we outline how synthetic networked environments such as multiplayer online games and virtual social worlds have recently been deployed as experimental platforms by behavioral economists. We first provide the background to behavioral economics before describing the rationale behind their use of virtual worlds for experimentation. We then develop a typology of virtual economic experiments from a survey of the main ways in which behavioral economists have used virtual worlds to conduct studies. We close with an assessment of this burgeoning area.

9.1 Background

Behavioral economics,[1] popularized in a series of bestselling books (e.g., Akerlof & Shiller, 2009; Kahneman, 2011; Thaler & Sunstein, 2008) has captured the imagination of policymakers and the wider public alike. In less glamorous terms, it is a research program designed to study economic behavior through the lens of human psychology.[2] It developed in response to what some perceived as a dead end in economic theory. In the latter half of the twentieth century, economics made great strides by predicting and explaining economic phenomena using the assumption of instrumental rationality, i.e. decision making to maximize particular objectives based on all relevant information. However, while maximization similar to *Star Trek*'s Mr. Spock rendered human agents predictable on paper, what was predicted increasingly

---

[1] Behavioral economics has little in common with classical behaviorism, which, in its strong form, ignores mental processes and only studies the observable ("behavioral") outcomes of decision making.
[2] Surveys include Angner & Loewenstein (2006); Camerer & Loewenstein (2003); Mullainathan & Thaler (2000); Weber & Camerer (2006), and Weber & Dawes (2005).

clashed with how people were found to behave in real settings as well as experimental laboratories. Behavioral economics became a banner for those economists who wanted to enrich economic theory based on how humans actually act.

In part the excitement over behavioral economics comes from the promise its novel and colorful methods seem to hold in providing new solutions to the old policy problems to which they are applied. Among these are brain scans that reveal how our minds work, questionnaires to accurately measure our happiness, and computer game–like simulations that work out the global effects of our individual decisions combined. By far the most typical and frequently used tool of behavioral economics is human participant experimentation.[3] Experiments are designed to measure the effects of systematically varying relevant decision factors on participants' behavior while controlling disturbing influences as far as possible. These latter "confounds" are controlled by being held constant or, when variable, measured and represented in the analysis (Kagel & Roth, 1995, pp. 129, 156–158, 295–296). In this way experiments are meant to establish the causal factors behind behavior beyond its mere correlates.

The experiment provides behavioral economists with a platform to instantiate economic models and to collect data on how real agents behave in them (Croson & Gächter, 2010). The factors that shape participants decisions in experiments can be classified into (1) the features of the decision situation, (2) their expectations of other participants behavior, and (3) their own inherent characteristics.[4] First, the *structural*, fixed characteristics of the experimental task that participants respond to reflect traditional economic models and include (information about) decision alternatives, task repetition and framing, the absolute and relative size of payoffs for different outcomes, as well as a number of other decision makers. A second set of *social* factors involves the influences these other participants have on a participant's behavior. These influences were recently imported into economics from social psychology and sociology and encompass fundamental social phenomena such as influence, facilitation, and intergroup effects. Third, *internal* variables reflect the nature of participants

---

[3] In principle, the concerns of behavioral economics can be pursued by a whole range of research tools (see Weber & Dawes, 2005), including agent-based simulation (Duffy, 2006; Hoffmann, 2006), neuroeconomics (Camerer, Loewenstein, & Prelec, 2005), theoretical modeling (Rabin, 1993), questionnaire and survey research (Kimball, 2015), and qualitative research approaches (Foster & Warren, 2016).

[4] Depending on purpose, there are alternative ways of grouping the factors different experiments examine. Camerer (2003b, pp. 56–59) distinguishes among methodological, structural, demographic, cultural, descriptive, and structural variables, while Ledyard (1995, p. 143) has three categories: environment, systemic, and design variables. Any categorization can only serve conceptual purposes, as it is impossible to draw definitive lines between them.

themselves such as their demographics (age, gender, academic major, ethnic origin), level of experience, attitudes, values, or even hormonal balances that moderate their decision making. These were traditionally the domain of individual difference psychology and have attracted the attention of economists only recently.

However, rather than developing into an offshoot of experimental social psychology and sociology, behavioral economics has quite deliberately and recognizably remained economic (Croson & Gächter, 2010; Laibson & List, 2015; Weber & Dawes, 2005). While economic experiments are conducted for a number of reasons (searching for new facts and regularities, evaluation of policy, as well as teaching and training; see Kagel & Roth 1995), the main one is to test and develop economic theory. Here experiments are conducted as model simulations with real agents to uncover causal factors behind behavior. Rather than establishing a patchwork of empirical facts about how people choose retrospectively, experimental economists seek to uncover the underlying choice principles that allow predicting future behavior to inform economic policy. Despite initial skepticism within economics generally, this kind of behavioral economics became feasible when it was realized that while human behavior systematically violated the assumption of instrumental rationality, it was not random but rather, in the apt term of Ariely (2008), *predictably irrational*.

Another feature differentiating behavioral economics from other empirical social sciences lies not so much in *why* or *what*[5] behavioral economics examines, but in the *how*. This differentiator lies in two features particular to the experimental method used by behavioral economists (Ariely & Norton, 2007; Croson, 2005; Hertwig & Ortmann, 2001; Weber & Dawes, 2005): in contrast to psychology, economic experiments invariably involve *incentive compatibility*, i.e., financial consequences for participants tied directly to the particular decisions they (and those they interact with) make. Performance-related decisions have been shown to address some of the response reliability issues economists worry about in questionnaire research (see Ariely & Norton, 2007; Croson, 2005; Hertwig & Ortmann, 2001). Self-reported attitudes or hypothetical decisions lack reliability because of self-generated validity (Chandon, Morwitz, & Reinartz, 2005), social desirability (Fisher, 1993), cognitive effects (Bertrand & Mullainathan, 2001), lacking construct stability (Cunningham, Preacher, & Banaji, 2001) and strength (Schwarz, 2007), as well as a modest correlation with behavior (Ajzen, 2012). The second distinguishing feature

---

[5] Behavior in realms outside the economy have been seen as fair game for economists for decades (Angner & Loewenstein, 2006; Lazear, 2000).

of experimental economics is that participants are not deceived regarding any feature of the experiment such as the task, their payoffs, or decisions of other participants. The rationale is that one's own experience or reports of others being deceived in an experiment will sever the perceived link between a participant's actions and outcomes and undermine his or her incentive to display true behavior in it (see Bonetti, 1998; Jamison, Karlan, & Schechter, 2008; Ortmann & Hertwig, 2002).[6]

9.2 Virtual Experimentation in Economics

9.2.1 Beyond the Horizon of the Lab

Despite its many early successes, behavioral economics has become somewhat hamstrung by its reliance on observing the overt decisions of student participants performing abstracted tasks in the sterile environment of the university laboratory. Doubts were raised concerning the extent to which experimental findings could be extrapolated to the real situations policymakers are interested in.[7] This problem is known as lacking *parallelism* (Smith, 1982). It has three related dimensions.

The first is doubt about the representativeness of experimental participants drawn from the student population at leading research universities (Harrison & List, 2004, p. 1016). The reason is increasing evidence that participants from different populations differ in terms of psychological characteristics as well as in the magnitude and direction of effects that various decision factors have on their behavior (Henrich, Heine, & Norenzayan, 2010, p. 78). Even basic psychological processes are subject to cultural differences (Mishra, 2001; Nisbett, 2003). Henrich et al. (2010, p. 79) conclude from their review of existing evidence that within this spectrum, traditional "WEIRD"[8] experimental participants not only lack representativeness but are also psychologically "unusual" such that caution is warranted before generalizing from their behavior.

A second issue relates to the context in which an experimental task is situated. In real scenarios a decision invariably takes place against some sort of

---

[6] In participant pools that are regularly approached both by economists and by experimenters from other disciplines following different protocols, the economic commandment of no-deception seems to rely on these participants being able to tell the difference.

[7] These growing pains of experimental economics echo the debate over the state of small-group research based on abstract laboratory experiments that raged in the 1960s (Cragan & Wright, 1980; Wheelan, 2005, p. 287).

[8] Western, educated, industrialized, rich, and democratic.

backdrop, such as continuing relationships and consequences, which experimentalists cannot and, if they can, often will not reproduce in the laboratory environment designed to achieve control (Barry, Fulmer, & Van Kleef, 2004, p. 87; Kagel & Roth, 1995). In this sense the missing context is seen as a virtue of the lab (Croson, 2005): experimentalists argue that control of contextual confounds allows the clean observation of those individual decision factors that operate in the wild of real situations on a one-at-a-time basis. But a problem arises because in real situations, the presence of particular contextual factors influences how decisions are arrived at (Loewenstein, 1999). According to theories in the *fast vs. slow thinking* tradition (Chaiken & Trope, 1999; Kahneman, 2011), it may be that the presence of confounding influences triggers specific decision processes different from those used when they are absent (Atlas & Putterman, 2011; Chuah, Hoffmann, & Larner, 2013; Sloman, 1996). If the effects of different decision factors including context are interdependent, then the experimentalist's isolation and control strategy may not work. In addition, while in one sense tasks performed in the laboratory lack the context of situated, real decisions, they may assume their own context to the extent that participants perceive an artificiality to the situation or an obligation to the experimenter that affects their behavior in ways that are often unknown (Rai & Fiske, 2010; Shweder, 2010).

A third and related issue is the social sterility of the lab. Even interdependent or group decisions are usually made individually via a computer terminal behind physical partitions that ensure anonymity and privacy, precisely so as to control such social factors that arise in face-to-face interactions that "call into play all of the social training we are endowed with" (Kagel & Roth, 1995, p. 295). In face-to-face interactions mutual presence, identification, and communication unleash different social factors (Ostrom, Gardner, & Walker, 1994) such as empathy (Batson & Moran, 1999), sympathy (Sally, 1995), social influence (Orbell, van de Kragt, & Dawes, 1988), or cues from physical features (Andreoni & Petrie, 2008). Nonverbal signals including involuntary cues can provide information about the other's intentions and emotions that affect decisions by instilling liking and attraction or disliking and repulsion (Argyle & Dean, 1965; Sprecher, 1998). The proximity of mere "bystanders" (who are not interaction or communication partners) can affect task performance positively (social facilitation) or negatively (social inhibition; e.g., Zajonc, 1965). These social factors are usually controlled to achieve clean observation of other decision factors but may need to be examined as interesting in their own right in a setting other than the standard lab. Further, as with context, control of social factors may cause the experimenter to observe behavior generated by a decision process different from that triggered had they been present.

9.2.2 Into the Virtual Wild

In response to these concerns and to achieve greater representativeness and parallelism, behavioral economists are increasingly conducting so-called *field experiments* (Carpenter, Harrison, & List, 2005; List & Reiley, 2008). These are types of experiment with non-WEIRD participants along a scale of increasing naturalism in terms of how closely their (1) tasks, (2) information, and (3) rewards as well as the (4) environment reflect real choice situations. In the resulting additive typology of field experiments proposed by Harrison and List (2004, p. 1014), an *artefactual* field experiment differs from a conventional laboratory one only in recruiting non-WEIRD participants, a *framed* field experiment additionally features a choice task participants are familiar with and for the kind of reward usually associated with it, and full-fledged *natural* field experiments also involve such participants being unwittingly observed in their natural habitats.

However, like any method, field experiments have drawbacks. To fulfil their calling, field experiments can make it impractical to control confounds effectively and/or raise the financial burden on the available research budget prohibitively (Ortmann, 2005). For example, recruiting from culturally different groups often involves international travel, potentially to remote locations (Henrich et al., 2001, 2004). As a result, according to Guala (2005) and List and Reiley (2008), the spectrum from conventional laboratory to natural field experiments represents a trade off between internal and external validity: the degree to which control helps the experimentalists uncover effects reliably is inversely correlated with the degree to which they apply elsewhere (but see Harrison & List, 2004, p. 1010; Jiménez-Buedo & Miller, 2010).

The best of both worlds would therefore involve a type of experiment with non-WEIRD subjects and other naturalistic features that afford either control or measurement of confounding factors. *Virtual* worlds have been touted as a possible new experimental platform that allows this (Fiedler & Haruvy, 2009; Fiore et al., 2008). They are graphical computer simulations of three-dimensional space in which networked users represented by avatars interact through virtual movement, avatar body language, and real audio or instant message communication.

9.3 Virtual Economic Experiments

We now survey existing economic experiments that have been conducted inside virtual worlds. The primary purpose of this survey is to discuss these experiments in methodological terms rather in terms of their findings. For the

purpose of inclusion in the survey, we define a virtual economic experiment as
an economic experiment (i.e., a controlled data collection exercise with com-
patible incentives and nondeception; see Croson & Gächter, 2010, p. 124) conducted inside a virtual world.[9] In some cases the line between virtual and other
experiments is somewhat ambiguous. To illustrate, Fiedler (2011) uses a virtual
world merely to recruit experimental participants but conducts the online experiment entirely outside that world. The participants in Chesney et al. (2016b) are
students located in a physical laboratory who control avatars inside a virtual
world to interact but record their decisions on an experimental interface on a
separate screen. To us, the defining feature should be whether the participant at
the time of data collection is immersed in the virtual world, in which case the
former study is not, and the latter is, a virtual economic experiment.

Like physical environments, virtual worlds can be used as experimental platforms in different ways associated with different merits and issues. We therefore discuss the studies in terms of different resulting types of virtual experiments. For this purpose it is tempting to adapt the typology of Harrison and
List (2004) for the virtual context to classify different virtual experiment types
based on these methodological features. However, although all types of field
experiment share the objective to add greater realism, experiments are conducted virtually for at least two separate reasons. The first is the same quest
for naturalism of field experiments. The second lies in the greater control and
measurement the computerized nature of virtual worlds is said to allow. We
therefore propose a typology leaning on Harrison and List (2004) but based on
both of these motivations behind virtual experimentation.

9.3.1 Artefactual Virtual Experiments

A major promise of virtual experiments is the convenient and economical large-
scale recruitment of participants from different cultural, socioeconomic, and
demographic groups who coinhabit virtual worlds (Reis & Gosling, 2010). This
is useful both to achieve greater representativeness and to target particular sub-
groups in terms of expertise and experience (Fiedler, 2011) as well as interests.
For example, virtual worlds can allow researchers to recruit members of clinical
populations and nefarious political interest groups who can remain anonymous
(Reips & Krantz, 2010; Reis & Gosling, 2010).

We identify a first kind of economic experiment conducted virtually to
allow for the recruitment of heterogeneous, non-WEIRD participant pools at

---

[9] Fiore et al. (2008, p. 67) use the term "virtual experiments" to denote ones performed with
immersive virtual reality and distinguish this technology from virtual worlds. See also
Harrison, Haruvy, & Rutström (2011).

Figure 9.1 The virtual laboratory of Chesney, Chuah, & Hoffmann (2009c).

economical cost and effort. Experiments of this kind recruit and observe remote users entirely within their virtual worlds. As such, these worlds need to be sufficiently popular to allow different types of participants (in terms of gender, age, occupation, and nationality) to be represented there in sufficient numbers. To remain as comparable as possible with existing results, these *artefactual virtual experiments* often reproduce standard laboratory facilities and abstract tasks. A number of studies (Atlas and Putterman, 2011; Chesney et al., 2009c, 2016a; Liibbe & Bolle, 2011) mention broadening participant representativeness as an objective.

The lack of physical presence that affords remote participation makes it difficult to establish appropriate experimental conditions and true demographics of participants. As a result, one of the very first virtual economic experiments was conducted in 2007 by Chesney, Chuah, and Hoffmann (2009c) to examine the resulting feasibility issue of virtual worlds as practical experimental platforms. To allow comparability with the conventional lab setting as far as possible, these researchers harnessed the customizability of the then-popular world *Second Life*® to create a virtual experimental laboratory in detail including participant desks and partitions programmed to make communication between them impossible (see Figure 9.1). They then used their avatars to recruit participants from among *Second Life*® users located in this world's virtual public places and teleported volunteers to the virtual laboratory. In it, the virtual participants, through their avatars, performed a range of standard interactive decision tasks including the ultimatum, dictator, minimum effort, guessing, and public good games[10] under (simulated) standard lab conditions (see Camerer, 2003a, for more details on these and similar experimental game tasks). These games were selected as established measurement tools for a range of human social motivations including fairness, altruism, cooperation, reciprocity, and coordination (see Henrich et al., 2004, pp. 55–95). In particular, copious experimental evidence from conventional lab experiments exists for these games and could serve as a benchmark for the virtual experimental results. Task behavior in the virtual lab (despite the incognito, physiologically sterile environment of the virtual world and the unverifiable identities of participants recruited entirely within it) did not differ significantly from established real-world results. One reason may be that virtual world users do not constitute, in terms of demographics, values, and motivations, an idiosyncratic niche social group (Yee, 2006) but rather represent the background population better than WEIRD undergraduate university students (Chesney et al., 2009c). The participants in this experiment hailed from North and South America, Europe, as well as Australasia.

Using virtual worlds to broaden the experimental participant pool beyond the university has proven popular. A number of subsequent experiments have also used *Second Life*® to recruit participants for experimental sessions conducted in simulated lab facilities (e.g., Atlas & Putterman, 2011). Some of these experiments have also compared experimental results from the virtual lab with comparable sessions conducted in physical settings (Fiedler, 2009; Fiedler & Haruvy, 2009; Fiedler, Haruvy, & li, 2011; Füllbrunn, Richwien, & Sadrieh, 2011; Greiner, Caravella, & Roth, 2014).

9.3.2 Controlled Virtual Experiments

As we have seen, compared to physical environments, virtual worlds allow economical recruitment of remote (non-WEIRD) participants from diverse demographic and cultural backgrounds at relatively low cost. A second affordance relates to control, the way decision factors are manipulated, and what responses are observed (Croson & Gächter, 2010, p. 124). Like experiments, virtual worlds are essentially models. Because a virtual world simulates social interactions through the computer, it allows many of their dimensions to be parameterized, varied, and measured in a way that is not possible in physical settings. The typical features of real interactions (such as participant appearance, verbal and

---

[10] In the following we use the term *game* to denote economic models of strategic situations as analyzed in the field of game theory, rather than computer games.

nonverbal communication) occur along continua and are often ambiguous to interpret and hard to measure. For example, when (and when not) is someone standing too close, dressed inappropriately, or communicating through body language? In real settings measurement is often prohibitively cumbersome, intrusive, or lacking in measurement scales that could be applied. In contrast, a virtual world limits both the number of these dimensions and the possible levels within each. For example, *Second Life* allows only a set of predefined body language signals, and standard avatar appearances come from a customizable kit. Avatar movements and instant messages can be easily recorded. Because virtual worlds are often persistent social systems, researchers can study processes that take place over longer periods of time (Bainbridge, 2007; Castronova et al., 2009), such as learning and the evolution of social norms. The virtual environment may also allow researchers to access data about participants through their user status metrics including game experience, trading activity, virtual wealth, health, and avatar race and class, which are difficult to generate outside the world but may yield powerful predictors of behavior (Duffy, 2011).

These observable parameters of virtual experiments can also be modified and customized at relatively low cost to generate experimental treatments (Duffy, 2011), such as the virtual visual cues created by Atlas and Putterman (2011). Customization allows experimenters greater control over confounds. For example, experimentalists studying the effect of communication using face-to-face settings are overwhelmed by a large number of verbal and nonverbal effects (as well as fear of post-experiment reprisal) that appear at the same time and cannot be disentangled (Roth, 1995, p. 296). Virtual "face-to-face" interactions provide an alternative because the information that is transmitted can be manipulated through communication protocols while preserving real-world anonymity (Fiedler & Haruvy, 2009; Fiedler et al., 2011). For example, Fiedler et al. (2011) employed virtual experiments to manipulate social distance in a natural context yet maintain participant anonymity. Unwanted "demand" effects of the experimenter's physical presence can likewise be mitigated (Atlas & Putterman, 2011; Reips & Krantz, 2010).

These possibilities generate a second type of virtual experiment, one that is conducted to harness the control and measurement that the electronic experimental platform affords over and above physical laboratory environments. We call studies of this kind *controlled virtual experiments*. They are often conducted with student participants who are physically present in the laboratory in order to impose greater control on who participates and under what prevailing conditions. Examples are the studies by Atlas & Putterman (2011); Chesney et al. (2016b); Fiedler (2009); Fiedler & Haruvy (2009); and Fiedler et al. (2011).

Similarly, Chesney et al. (2016b) studied the effects of social identity through the way participants modify their avatars' appearance. Chesney et al. (2016b) conducted an experiment with university student participants located in a conventional laboratory but interacting virtually through avatars they created for this purpose in *Second Life*. They performed a two-person persuasion task in which one participant (the sender) was financially incentivized to persuade another (the receiver). Interpersonal influence is a socially situated phenomenon that depends on a host of factors including the characteristics of both the sender and the receiver, the message, and the medium through which it is communicated (Cialdini, 1988; O'Keefe, 2002). As a result, observation and measurement rather than control of these factors promise progress in this area. Chesney et al. (2016b) relate the level of persuasion to the customizable appearance of sender and receiver avatars that were selected from twelve templates (see Figure 9.2, top panel). In addition, the virtual laboratory was programmed to record a host of "telemetrics" (such as data of avatar movement), chat logs, and other dimensions of the persuasion interaction. Chesney et al. (2014a) used such telemetrics data to relate avatars' appearance and their movements inside the virtual world (e.g., in terms of mean proximity to other avatars) to their social behavior.

9.3.3 Framed Virtual Experiments

In addition to sample selection and measurement, virtual worlds also offer a third benefit: the electronic nature of virtual worlds allows customization to economically create field contexts for experimental tasks. We define *framed virtual experiments* as virtual economic experiments with naturalistic character of either task or experimental incentives. Similar to the objective behind field experiments, naturalism is deemed desirable to extend the external validity of experimental results.

An example is a further series of virtual behavioral experiments (Chesney et al., 2014a, b, c, 2015) conducted as part of the Verus programme (see Chapter 1 by Chesney et al., this volume; Dieterle & Murray, 2010). These experiments involved the creation and use of a social networking world in which participants in international locations interacted and performed classic individual and group decision tasks in naturalistic frames under incentive compatibility. The vehicle was a simulated funfair (called *Sherwood*) where tasks were presented as entertainments at different booths (see Figures 9.3 and 9.4).

One of the tasks used in this experiment is the public good game (see Chesney et al., 2014b), which the authors previously used in its abstract original

Figure 9.2 Reception area (top) and virtual persuasion situation (bottom) in the experiment of Chesney et al. (2016b).

frame (Chesney et al., 2009c). Participants play in groups of four and individually allocate $10 between a "private fund" and a "group fund." The total each earns is their private allocation plus 40% of the total of everyone's combined group allocations. To generate a more naturalistic frame, this task was presented as a group duck shooting game (Figure 9.3, bottom panel). Rather than picking funds to allocate $10, the Duck Shoot requires each of the four participants to choose a mixture of red or blue bullets for his or her ten-shooter gun (the red barrel at the bottom): hitting a duck with a red bullet earns one gold coin for the participant's individual private fund; hitting a duck with a blue bullet earns two gold coins for the group fund. Participants could choose any combination of blue and red bullets and were able to practice before the game started.

Figure 9.3 The virtual funfair *Sherwood* (top) and the pop-up Duck Shoot interface (bottom). (This image is shown in full color in the Color Plates section.)

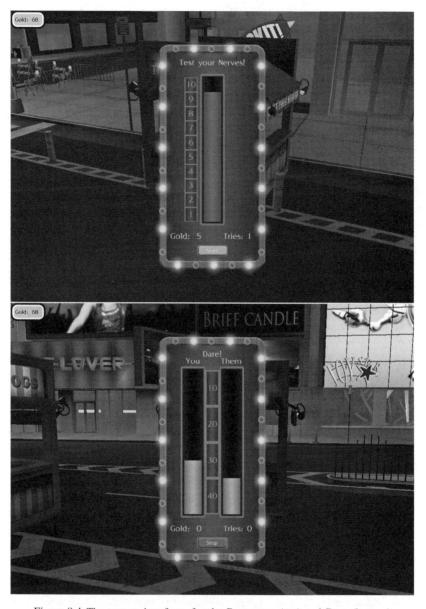

Figure 9.4 The pop-up interfaces for the Bust game (top) and Dare (bottom) inside *Sherwood*.

At the end of each round the public fund was evenly split between all members the group, and each participant was presented with a screen showing him or her the bullet colors and hit rates for all group members. The proportion of blue bullets of the ten measures a participant's level of cooperation. In the Duck Shoot, cooperation is measured in a naturalistic frame because the experimental task resembles activities that users would ordinarily encounter in virtual worlds generally or real-world settings (such as funfairs) that these worlds are meant to simulate.

The funfair also contained three other decision tasks framed as entertainment booths in similar ways. One related to individual risk preferences, i.e., to what extent people trade off the diminishing chance of winning with the increasing size of the associated prize, which is conventionally measured over pairs of abstract gambles (Eckel & Wilson, 2004; Holt & Laury, 2002). The funfair implementation was the Bust Game, in which participants were asked to stop a real-time rising gauge (see Figure 9.4, top panel) anytime before it goes bust, i.e., reaches an unknown stop point. Rewards are higher the later the participants stop but become zero upon bust. The chosen stop point measures risk-taking attitudes in an incentive-compatible but naturalistic way. A two-player version of this game, called Dare, measures *strategic* risk taking in interactive situations such as negotiation (Chuah, Hoffmann, & Larner, 2014; see Figure 9.4, bottom panel). The participant who stops the gauge first receives a lower reward. Neither receives anything if neither stops before the known bust point of 10. This game is a multistage version of the well-known chicken game called the escalation game (Chuah et al., 2013). A final classic game tasks, the dictator game, measures altruism in an incentive-compatible way by giving a participant the opportunity to give money to another participant. This game has previously been implemented in a naturalistic charity donation frame in the conventional laboratory (Eckel & Grossman, 1996). In the *Sherwood* funfair, a virtual charity booth added to the naturalism of this task.

The naturalistic behavioral measurements all these tasks generated can be related to participant characteristics as well as to virtual observations (see Section 9.3.2) of their avatar appearance choices, movements, and communications to help uncover the underlying causes of behavior. The data set captured not only the behavior of 195 participants within *Sherwood* but also in preceding in-world warm-up familiarization and customization tasks. The staging area was a simulation of Manhattan's Time Square, where avatars were given the chance to explore, socialize, as well as customize their own appearances and that of their private virtual apartments. Four broad areas of behavior were analyzed: communication, movement, avatar creation, and world customization. Communication in the form of text chat was analyzed using standard linguistic algorithms and qualitative content analysis. Movement was measured telemetrically as counts of keyboard presses to move an avatar. Avatar creation was the appearance of the avatar including hair and skin color and clothing. Lastly, world customization was the way users changed their personal space within the world (by changing colors and objects in the space).

In virtual worlds, experimental game tasks can also be used naturalistically for purposes other than data collection. For example, Abele and Stasser (2008) argue that success in coordination games within a group can enhance commonalities and accentuate shared group identity. These are games were two or more players receive a reward only if they choose the same action without communicating. The classic version is Schelling's (1960) game, in which two people must independently pick a place in New York to meet without prior arrangements. To the extent that certain alternatives (e.g., landmarks like the Empire State Building) are culturally or psychologically conspicuous or salient, participants coordinate surprisingly well in experiments (Mehta, Starmer, & Sugden, 1994). Chesney et al. (2014a) performed a version of the Schelling game in their virtual Time Square that involved groups of avatars collectively agreeing on a specific virtual location within it to meet other groups without communication between the groups. The Schelling game can be thought of as an ice breaker task that facilitated formation of group identity and dynamics that can then be studied. The server log data for these interactions allowed for an analysis of the determinants of friendship status between two users in a virtual world who are unaware of each other's real identities. Factors such as differences between two avatars' appearances, message terseness, and virtual proximity were identified as significant determinants of friendship formation between them.

9.3.4 Natural Virtual Experiments

A final affordance of virtual worlds as an experimental platform is the naturalistic environment of the world itself, to the extent that it can be used for controlled, unobtrusive, and economical observation of user behavior while maintaining the natural and familiar decision context that surrounds it (Bainbridge, 2007; Bloomfield, 2007; Castronova, 2001). Virtual worlds closely recreate natural mechanisms for meaningful social interactions such as friendship formation (Chesney et al., 2009a). Some virtual worlds are designed to function as realistic economies where users can pursue activities that have consequences in terms of in-world motivations but also real-world consequences such as convertible income generation (Mennecke et al., 2007). They can have virtual infrastructure and natural resources to induce spatial economic processes (Twieg & McCabe, 2014) and realistic environmental valuations (Fiore et al.,

2008). Worlds such as *Second Life* are generally suitable research environments for economists owing to their well-developed economies, naturally evolving markets, and active commerce (Bloomfield, 2007). This means experimental rewards can be delivered naturalistically as well as conveniently using the virtual world's currency (Chesney, Chuah, & Hoffmann, 2009b). We identify *natural virtual experiments* as ones that combine naturalistic tasks and experimental environments with virtual world users as participants, who may be unaware that they are part of an experiment.

A number of researchers conducted such experiments in massively multiplayer online games (MMOGs) that are associated with particular virtual activities and themes. Nicklisch and Salz (2008) conducted an experiment in *World of Warcraft* (WoW) with users unaware they were observed. They were hired by a principal to fish (a natural game activity) for 30 minutes and return the complete catch. The principal's social status and the wage were manipulated. Because the probability of success in fishing was directly related to an avatar's fishing experience (skill), users' efforts can be approximated by the number of fish returned. Users were more willing to work hard if they were paid more and if the principal was of a low social status. The interpretation was that agents assessed wage levels based on the principal's wealth.

Castronova et al. (2009) conducted an experiment involving student participants in *Arden*, a fantasy game these authors built. It was based on a theme of Shakespeare's Richard III and involved a medieval London quest that participants performed over the course of a month from their private computers. The forty-three participants were randomly allocated to either of two versions of the world identical in all but one dimension: the price of a quest equipment item (a health potion) was twice as high in one and served as the experimental treatment variable. The study virtually fulfills the unrealizable dream of macroeconomists to perform a fully controlled experiment with the overall economy and confirmed the law of demand: the quantity demanded was 43% lower in the high-price world.

Spann et al. (2010) used a within-subject design to compare conventional lab and virtual data. They first conducted the dictator game in WoW using an avatar to invite other users in a central in-world location to perform the game in situ. Two weeks later the researchers invited the same participants via in-world email to play the same game again using an online interface. Participation in WoW was rewarded with Gold (the virtual currency), whereas participation in the real world was rewarded with real money. Questionnaire data measured participants' altruism, preference for fairness, and feeling of presence in the virtual world and were subsequently used to explain observed behavior.

De Sousa and Munro (2012) also used in-world intercept recruitment for an in situ experiment in *RuneScape*, a Java- based role-playing MMOG. They examine the well-known endowment effect (Kahneman, Knetsch, & Thaler, 1991), where the amount for which people are willing to part with a good exceeds the amount they are willing to pay for it. The authors demonstrate and examine this effect through harnessing the naturalistic features of the virtual environment: the goods users were given (arrows, magic, and decorative artefacts) were naturalistic, and their observed behavior correlated with their in-world public records of trade and skills.

Not only macroeconomists but also institutional economists bemoan the difficulty of performing controlled experiments because of the global nature of their objects of study. Institutional economists compare governance systems (such as voting rules, property rights, etc.) that are impractical or unethical to manipulate and at any rate hard to control. Conventional lab experiments examining such issues may lack external validity. Naturally occurring virtual social systems provide an alternative. They can be used to purpose-design activities and tasks that allow the experimenter to observe how group dynamics and norms evolve while controlling for or measuring confounding factors such as the identities of or communication between participants. Twieg and McCabe (2014) created a group berry harvesting task in a customized version of *Second Life* to examine the effect of costly individual specialization on the emergence of territorial property rights. The experimental treatment variables included the layout of fields in terms of the distribution of two kinds of berry and the cost of users specializing (acquiring better picking skills) in either of them. It was found that specialization increases overall berry production and lessens territorial competition.

9.3.5 Related Types of Computer-Mediated Experiment

Virtual economic experiments are related to other computer-mediated types of experiment. One is the internet experiment or online panel. In an internet experiment (e.g., Anderhub, Müller, & Schmidt, 2001) participants are recruited over online mailing lists and websites and perform the experimental task by accessing a website at their own convenience. In recent years online participant pools have been created by professional crowd-sourcing services such as Amazon Mechanical Turk (e.g., Horton, Rand, & Zeckhauser, 2011), where anonymous people can be selected according to specific criteria and are paid modest amounts to perform tasks via the internet (Crump, McDonnell, & Gureckis, 2013). The advantage is recruitment of participants from specific and variegated demographic and cultural backgrounds for relatively small fees. Both Ander-hub et al. (2001) and Horton et al. (2011) find that the results of MTurk and online experiments generally tally with those from conventional physical labo-ratories while reducing the cost and effort involved in conducting experiments. While virtual and internet experiments afford electronic recruitment from an online pool of participants, they differ in the nature of the electronic environ-ment in which the data collection is conducted. Fiedler (2011) was able to use the virtual world *Second Life* to recruit particular types of experienced partic-ipants for (but not to perform) an experiment. Another relative of the virtual experiment is the virtual reality (VR) experiment (Fiore et al., 2008; Harrison et al., 2011). VR technology creates computer-mediated, realistic immersive sensory experiences including sight, hearing, and sometimes the other senses. On the other hand, VR, unlike virtual worlds, does not necessitate social inter-actions with other users.

9.4 Features of Virtual Experiments

Table 9.1 lists the experiments we discussed in the survey organized by their methodological features and resulting types of experiment. These features pro-vide design alternatives for virtual experimentalists that we now discuss.

The first feature refers to the particular **virtual world** used to host an exper-iment. While most experiments were conducted in the general social network-ing world *Second Life*, a number of researchers used alternative, themed virtual worlds or built their own. Existing worlds have the advantage of a preexisting and persistent society of users from across the globe. Themed worlds such as WoW have the advantage that experimental tasks may be "camouflaged" as game activities but raise the issue of robustness of results in more general set-tings. Custom-built worlds allow the experimenter greater control over access, tasks, the environment, and data collection.

Different **recruitment** methods were used in this literature. In some vir-tual experiments, researchers recruited students in traditional ways while others used online panels and websites to reach virtual world users as remote partici-pants. A third possibility is to recruit such users from inside the worlds through an intercept process using experimenter avatars. Students are often invited when demographics need to be reliably established or to provide comparison with previous experiments using student participants. In-world intercept makes the undesirable repeat participation of users difficult and can help, as in the real world, avoid selection bias. Online panels and websites can generate large sample sizes and demographic targeting but come with the issues surrounding professional participants (Horton et al., 2011).

Table 9.1 *Virtual economic experiments and their features. Question marks denote features that were described in insufficient detail in the original sources.*

Study	Virtual world	Recruitment	Participation	Tasks		Experimental interface	Experimental environment
				Controlled virtual experiments			
Chesney et al. (2016b)	Existing (*Second Life*)	Students	Physical	Persuasion task	Abstract	z-Tree interface	Laboratory
Fiedler and Haruvy (2009)	Existing (*Second Life*)	Students	Physical	Trust game with and without virtual communication	Abstract	?	Laboratory
Fiedler et al. (2011)	Existing (*Second Life*)	Students	Physical	Trust game with partner selection	Abstract	?	Laboratory
Fiedler (2009)	Existing (*Second Life*)	Students	Physical	Trust game with and without communication	Abstract	Webpage	Laboratory
				Artefactual virtual experiments			
Chesney et al. (2009c, 2016a)	Existing (*Second Life*)	Users (via intercept)	Online	Ultimatum, dictator, trust, public good, guessing and minimum effort games	Abstract	Private instant message	Laboratory
Fiedler and Haruvy (2009)	Existing (*Second Life*)	Users (via forums)	Online	Trust game with and without virtual communication	Abstract	Webpage	Laboratory
Atlas and Putterman (2011)	Existing (*Second Life*)	Users (via classified ad)	Online	Trust game with and without visual and textual cues	Abstract	Automated virtual	Laboratory
Fiedler et al. (2011)	Existing (*Second Life*)	Users (via forums)	Online	Trust game with partner selection	Abstract	?	Laboratory

Table 9.1 (cont.)

Study	Virtual world	Recruitment	Participation	Tasks		Experimental interface	Experimental environment
Greiner et al. (2014)	Existing (*Second Life*)	Users (via market research panel)	Online	Ultimatum game with and without communication	Abstract	Virtual inter-face	Laboratory
Füllbrunn et al. (2011)	Existing (*Second Life*)	Users (via in-tercept)	Online	Trust game	Abstract	Virtual inter-face	Field
Lübbe and Bolle (2011)	Existing (EVE)	Users (via fo-rums)	Online	Solidarity game	Abstract	?	?
Framed virtual experiments							
Chesney et al. (2014a, b, c, 2015)	Purpose built	Students	Physical	Escalation game, dictator game, public good game, risk task	Naturalistic	Automated virtual	Field
Twieg and McCabe (2014)	Purpose built (Second Life)	Students	Physical	Harvesting task	Naturalistic	Private instant message	Field
Natural virtual experiments							
Nicklisch and Salz (2008)	Existing (WoW)	Users (via in-tercept)	Online	Real effort task (fishing)	Naturalistic	Private instant message	Field
Castronova et al. (2009)	Purpose built	Students	Online	Trading	Naturalistic	Automated virtual	Field
Spann et al. (2010)	Existing (WoW)	Users (via in-tercept)	Online	dictator game	Abstract	Private instant message	Field
De Sousa and Munro (2012)	Existing (RuneScape)	Users (via in-tercept)	Online	Trading	Naturalistic	Private instant message	Field

Participation refers to the location of the participant during the session. In some studies participants perform the experiment wherever they happen to be, using their own computers (online). In others (physical), participants (typically students) enter the virtual spaces via computers located in physical laboratory facilities. Their demographics and experimental conditions (the situation under which a participant responds) can then be ascertained. Online participation can reduce the logistical burden on the experimenter and affords recruiting remote participant groups. On the other hand, the potentially different conditions of data collection (due to, for example, the state of the participant and his or her surrounding environment) could constitute serious experimental confounds.

The particular **tasks** used in an experiment are classified as abstract if they resemble those traditionally performed by economists in physical laboratories where framing is typically avoided to generate robustness of results beyond the context in which they were generated (Croson, 2005). Frameless tasks often include decision alternatives neutrally labeled as A or B and connotation-free descriptions of outcomes. In other virtual experiments tasks may be presented naturalistically precisely to provide context similar to the aims of field experiments discussed in Section 9.2.2.

The **experimental interface** describes the mechanism by which the decisions of participants are recorded. Simple experimental decisions, those that can be expressed as numbers (e.g., dictator game donations) or binary decisions (stop or not in the Bust and Dare games), can be transmitted between participants and experimenter via in-world private instant message. This may be cumbersome or unmanageable, especially when the participant pool is large. Other authors use extra-world web-forms or dedicated experimental interfaces such as z-Tree (Fischbacher, 2007). Although the latter method facilitates data collection, it takes the participant outside the context of the virtual world, which may disrupt an immersive experience. Virtual experimental interfaces to resemble z-Tree can also be programmed. Such systems with automated decision tasks and recording were used by Atlas and Putterman (2011) and Chesney et al. (2014b), but unless an experimenter is present in the world, participant comprehension could become an issue.

The final feature we use in our classification of virtual experiments is the nature of the **experimental environment.** Virtual laboratories are spaces designed to reproduce physical laboratory settings as much as possible in order to maximize comparability (e.g., Atlas & Putterman, 2011; Chesney et al., 2009c; Greiner et al., 2014). Virtual field settings pursue the ambitions of conventional field experiments by transporting the participant from the artificiality of the lab into the natural environment of the field.

9.5 Assessment

How well have these novel features of virtual economic experiments served researchers? The preceding sections have shown the methodological advantages of virtual economic experiments in terms of participant selection from more heterogeneous groups, measurement and observation, task framing, and naturalist environments. It should be noted that these are not unique affordances of virtual worlds. In theory, one could implement any of these in laboratory and field experiments, albeit at greater and often prohibitive costs. As in other types of production process, computer technologies, especially when networked, generally raise the efficiency and reduce the cost of different aspects of running scientific experiments, including recruitment, participant access to the experiment, data entry, and general administration (De Sousa & Munro, 2012; Reips & Krantz, 2010; Reis & Gosling, 2010). Many of these tasks can be automated, such as the data collection process used by Atlas and Putterman (2011).

These benefits do not seem to come at the cost of data collection biased toward the virtual environment in which they are collected. A number of studies have demonstrated that there are no significant *platform effects*, i.e., differences in results between virtual and conventional physical experimental settings when other experimental (social, structural, and internal) factors are the same. This goes for economic behavior in individual tasks (Chesney et al., 2009b; De Sousa & Munro, 2012), strategic games (Chesney et al., 2009b), and markets (Castronova et al., 2009). On the other hand, a number of researchers have found discrepancies between virtual and comparable physical conventional experimental results and identified potential problems with the virtual economic experimental method.

9.5.1 External Validity

One of the reasons behind virtual experimentation is the hope to recruit more representative participants for tasks in environments that resemble the real world more than the conventional lab. However, it is far from clear whether virtual experiments create conditions that are idiosyncratic in their own ways and therefore suffer from lacking external validity to the same degree. This is evidenced by researchers who found differential behavior for the tasks they study both virtually and in real environments. Füllbrunn et al. (2011) and Atlas and Putterman (2011) found virtual participants to be less trusting but more trustworthy compared to those in the conventional lab. Greiner et al. (2014) found virtual participants playing the ultimatum game to be more cooperative in *Second Life* compared to real life.

One potential explanation is that virtual interpersonal processes differ from real ones in ways that affect experimental results. Through their avatars, virtual world users may enjoy acting out and display more erratic or different behavior than their real selves. These authors suggest environmental effects could be at work. The playful and exotic nature of virtual worlds could instill greater cooperativeness compared with real settings. The perceived social distance between participants in virtual world may be smaller than between participants in the real world. These kinds of effects may be person specific: the way virtual worlds modify behavior depends on the degree a user feels immersed in the virtual world or identifies with his or her avatar (Spann et al., 2010).

An alternative explanation is a selection effect (Greiner et al., 2014). More social people may be more attracted to social networking worlds. Similarly, it is not clear to what extent virtual worlds built around fantasy themes can generate "economically normal" behavior (Castronova et al., 2009). Selection may happen on technological grounds (Reis & Gosling, 2010): only those who have access to networked computers and possess the requisite skills will be recruited into virtual experiments, while those who suffer from computer anxiety or lack of experience will not. Studies show that the more complex the technology involved in programming the online experiment, the more the samples are likely to be biased demographically and psychologically (Reips & Krantz, 2010). The same is true for members of traditional societies who are less likely to have access to online technologies (Henrich et al., 2010).

Another issue with external validity is the way in which participants respond to virtual rewards. In newer worlds there may be a relatively high valuation of money compared to the real world (Greiner et al., 2014). In maturer ones, a lower marginal utility of virtual money may arise owing to satiation and high wealth of avatars, thus failing to exert sufficient experimental incentives (Spann et al., 2010). It is therefore unclear how participants value virtual currency relative to its real-world value, thus distorting the incentive compatibility of choices (Atlas, 2008).

9.5.2 Logistics

As for external validity, the perceived logistical benefits of virtual experiments may be balanced by new logistical challenges from the physical disconnect between experimenter and participant (Reis & Gosling, 2010). In practice, it is difficult to answer participant questions about procedures or to ascertain their understanding of instructions and tasks (Horton et al., 2011). Virtual experiments may be disrupted by hardware crashes and power outages (Duffy, 2011).

While relatively cheap for some experimenters, virtual experiments entail significant costs for others. These include the high startup costs of acquiring necessary IT skills and equipment (De Sousa & Munro, 2012; Reis & Gosling, 2010). Significant economies of scale are, however, available once these investments have been made.

Other logistical issues are insurmountable for virtual experiments, such as recording of physiological responses (skin conductance, eye movement), to physically manipulate subjects (e.g., touching objects, administering substances such as oxytocin), or their environment (e.g., changing lighting).

9.5.3 Control

Experimental control of confounds, in its various forms, can again be both a benefit and a disadvantage of virtual economic experiments. On the downside of control, virtual experimenters cannot observe participants physically to assess their fitness to participate, attentiveness (do they engage on other activities at the same time?), or potential distractions in their physical environment (Chesney et al., 2009b). This can make it harder to detect cheating, collusion, and private message communication among them (Duffy, 2011; Horton et al., 2011; Reips & Krantz, 2010). Using multiple avatars, the same individual could participate repeatedly for monetary gain (Atlas & Putterman, 2011; Chesney et al., 2009b; Duffy, 2011; Füllbrunn et al., 2011; Horton et al., 2011; Reips & Krantz, 2010). Participants may feel less inhibited to disturb the experiment (Chesney et al., 2009b) or to suddenly disappear because of boredom or urgent real-world issues, or to steal their virtual rewards (De Sousa & Munro, 2012). Dishonesty is an issue also because it is hard to verify the demographic information that a participant volunteers (Atlas, 2008; Atlas & Putterman, 2011; Duffy, 2011; Horton et al., 2011), similar to online surveys. There may be incentives for giving false information when certain participants groups are targeted or excluded (e.g., minors). This raises ethical issues when experimenters cannot take steps to reliably exclude participants from vulnerable groups.

In addition, the lack of physical presence makes it difficult to control participants' beliefs about the experiment. It is hard to implement participants' common knowledge of experimental instructions, as they cannot verify whether other participants exist and/or whether they have been given the same information and instructions (Atlas & Putterman, 2011; Duffy, 2011; Horton et al., 2011). The institutional credentials of experimenters and recruiters are hard to verify for potential participants. As a result, the credibility of (and participants' trust in) the experiment may suffer if virtual participants do not believe that the experimenter will pay promised rewards, and guarantee their confidentiality and privacy (Lübbe & Bolle, 2011). Recruitment too may suffer as a result (Duffy, 2011; Horton et al., 2011).

9.5.4 Final Remarks

While virtual economic experimentation remains in its infancy one should not expect firm conclusions as to whether and how this method will mature. Many of the thorny issues discussed in the previous section are essentially empirical in nature and can be settled only to the extent that more data are collected. Such data collection should increasingly focus not on comparing virtual world results with those from standard lab (or even field) experiments when both have questionable external validity. The question is not which method is better. Instead, both of these methods could help establish greater external validity jointly by a process of triangulation. In this process of new data collection it is desirable that more standardized experimental methods and protocols for virtual environments be established.

It is also important to recognize that virtual world experiments represent neither poison not panacea for experimental research. They have specific uses that roughly follow the motivations for conducting virtual economic experiments outlined in Section 9.3. These include recruiting specific participant types likely to be represented in virtual worlds, better controlling and measuring decision factors that tend to muddy conventional lab experiments, and creating naturalistic environments at relatively low cost. Another reason for experimenting virtually may be to pilot certain designs where experimental economy is key, before committing to more costly physical experimentation. In all cases virtual economic experiments complement but do not replace other types such as lab and field experiments in physical settings.

At the same time virtual worlds are changing, with some, such as *Second Life*, becoming increasingly outmoded and newer ones emerging with new affordances for experimentalists. Alternative forms of social networking such as Facebook are increasingly competing away the user base social virtual worlds used to enjoy. For this reason they also constitute alternatives for experimentalists keen to take their methods to where their "representative agents" are most likely to be.

References

Abele, S., & Stasser, G. (2008). Coordination success and interpersonal perceptions: Matching versus mismatching. *Journal of Personality and Social Psychology*, 95(3), 576–592.

Ajzen, I. (2012). *Attitudes and persuasion* (pp. 367–393). Oxford: Oxford University Press.

Akerlof, G., & Shiller, R. (2009). *Animal spirits: How human psychology drives the economy, and why it matters for global capitalism*. Princeton, NJ: Princeton University Press.

Anderhub, V., Muller, R., & Schmidt, C. (2001). Design and evaluation of an economic experiment via the Internet. *Journal of Economic Behavior and Organization*, 46(2), 227–247.

Andreoni, J., & Petrie, R. (2008). Beauty, gender and stereotypes: Evidence from laboratory experiments. *Journal of Economic Psychology*, 29(1), 73–93.

Angner, E., & Loewenstein, G. (2006). Behavioral economics. In *Handbook of the philosophy of science*, Vol. 5. Philadelphia, PA: Elsevier.

Argyle, M., & Dean, J. (1965). Eye contact, distance and affiliation. *Sociometry*, 28(3), 289–304.

Ariely, D., & Norton, M. I. (2007). Psychology and experimental economics: A gap in abstraction. *Current Directions in Psychological Science*, 16(6), 336–339.

Ariely, Dan. (2008). *Predictably irrational*. New York, NY: HarperCollins.

Atlas, S., & Putterman, L. (2011). Trust among the avatars: A virtual world experiment, with and without textual and visual cues. *Southern Economic Association*, 78(1), 63–86.

Atlas, S.A. (2008). Inductive metanomics: Economic experiments in virtual worlds. *Journal of Virtual Worlds Research*, 1(1), 1–15.

Bainbridge, W. S. (2007). The scientific research potential of virtual worlds. *Science*, 317, 472–476.

Barry, B., Fulmer, I. S., & Van Kleef, G. A. (2004). I laughed, I cried, I settled: The role of emotions in negotiations. In M. J Gelfand, & J. M. Brett (eds.), *The handbook of negotiation and culture* (pp. 71–94). Stanford, CA: Stanford University Press.

Batson, C. D., & Moran, T. (1999). Empathy-induced altruism in a prisoner's dilemma. *European Journal of Social Psychology*, 29, 909–924.

Bertrand, M., & Mullainathan, S. (2001). Do people mean what they say? Implications for subjective survey data. *American Economic Review (Papers and Proceedings)*, 91(2), 67–72.

Bloomfield, Robert J. (2007). Worlds for study: Invitation – virtual worlds for studying real-world business (and law, and politics, and sociology, and....). *SSRN eLibrary*.

Bonetti, S. (1998). Experimental economics and deception. *Journal of Economic Psychology*, 19(3), 377–395.

Camerer, C. (2003a). *Behavioral game theory: Experiments in strategic interaction*. Princeton, NJ: Princeton University Press.

Camerer, C. F. (2003b). *Behavioral game theory*. Princeton, NJ: Princeton University Press.

Camerer, C. F., & Loewenstein, G. (2003). Behavioral economics: Past, present, future. In C. F. Camerer, G. Loewenstein, & M. Rabin (eds.), *Advances in behavioral economics* (pp. 3–51). Princeton, NJ: Princeton University Press.

Camerer, C. F., Loewenstein, G., & Prelec, D. (2005). Neuroeconomics: Why economics needs brains. *Scandinavian Journal of Economics*, 106(3), 555–579.

Carpenter, J. P., Harrison, G. W., & List, J. A. (2005). Field experiments in economics: An introduction. In J. P. Carpenter, G. W. Harrison, & J. A. List (eds.), *Field experiments in economics* (pp. 1–15). Philadelphia, PA: Elsevier.

Castronova, E. (2001). Virtual worlds: A first-hand account of market and society on the cyberian frontier. Gruter Institute Working Papers on Law, Economics, and Evolutionary Biology. Berkeley Electronic Press.

Castronova, E., Bell, M. W., Cornell, R., et al. (2009). A test of the law of demand in a virtual world: Exploring the petri dish approach to social science. *International Journal of Gaming and Computer-Mediated Simulations*, 1(2), 1–16.

Chaiken, S., & Trope, Y. (1999). *Dual-process theories in social psychology.* New York, NY: Guilford Press.

Chandon, P., Morwitz, V. G., & Reinartz, W. J. (2005). Do intentions really predict behavior? Self-generated validity effects in survey research. *Journal of Marketing*, 69(2), 1–14.

Chesney, T., Coyne, I., Logan, B., & Madden, N. (2009a). Griefing in virtual worlds: causes, casualties and coping strategies. *Information Systems Journal*, 19(6), 525–548.

Chesney, T., Chuah, S.H., & Hoffmann, R. (2009b). Virtual trust: An experimental approach. *International Centre for Behavioural Business Research Working Papers*.

Chesney, T., Chuah, S. H., & Hoffmann, R. (2009c). Virtual world experimentation: An exploratory study. *Journal of Economic Behavior and Organization*, 72(1), 618–635.

Chesney, T., Chuah, S. H., Hoffmann, R., & Larner, J. (2014a). Determinants of friendship in social networking virtual worlds. *Communications of the Association for Information Systems*, 34(72), 1379–1416.

Chesney, T., Chuah, S. H., Hoffmann, R., Hui, W., & Larner, J. (2014b). Skilled players cooperate less in multi-player games. *Journal of Gaming and Virtual Worlds*, 6(1), 21–31.

Chesney, T., Chuah, S. H., Hoffmann, R., Hui, W., & Larner, J. (2014c). A study of gamer experience and virtual world behaviour. *Interacting with Computers*, 26(1), 1–11.

Chesney, T., Chuah, S. H., Hoffmann, R., Hui, W., & Larner, J. (2015). How user personality and social value orientation influence avatar mediated friendship. *Information Technology & People*, forthcoming.

Chesney, T., Chuah, S. H., Dobele, A., & Hoffmann, R. (2016a). *Avatars: Combining the benefits of e-commerce with the benefits of brick-and-mortar retails spaces.* Unpublished manuscript.

Chesney, T., Chuah, S. H., Hoffmann, R., & Larner, J. (2016b). *Social identity and socialisation in cross-national negotiation.* Unpublished manuscript.

Chuah, S. H., Hoffmann, R., & Larner, J. (2013). Elicitation effects in a multistage bargaining experiment. *Experimental Economics*, 17, 335–345.

Chuah, S. H., Hoffmann, R., & Larner, J. (2014). Chinese values and negotiation behaviour: A bargaining experiment. *International Business Review*, 23, 1203–1211.

Cialdini. (1988). *Influence: Science and practice.* Glenview, IL: Scott, Foresman and Co.

Cragan, J. F., & Wright, D. W. (1980). Small group communication research of the 1970's: A synthesis and critique. *Central States Speech Journal*, 31(3), 197–213.

Croson, R. (2005). The method of experimental economics. *International Negotiation*, 10, 131–148.

Croson, R., & Gächter, S. (2010). The science of experimental economics. *Journal of Economic Behavior & Organization*, 73, 122–131.

Crump, M. J. C., McDonnell, J. V., & Gureckis, T. M. (2013). Evaluating Amazon's mechanical Turk as a tool for experimental behavioral research. *PLoS ONE*, 8(3), 1–18.

Cunningham, W. A., Preacher, K. J., & Banaji, M. R. (2001). Implicit attitude measures: Consistency, stability, and convergent validity. *Psychological Science*, 12(2), 163–170.

De Sousa, Y. F., & Munro, A. (2012). Truck, Barter and exchange versus the endowment effect: Virtual field experiments in an online game environment. *Journal of Economic Psychology*, 33(3), 482–493.

Dieterle, E., & Murray, J. (2010). Virtual environment real user study (VERUS): Design and methodological considerations and implications. *Journal ofApplied Learning Technology*, 1(1), 19–25.

Duffy, J. (2006). Agent-based models and human subject experiments. In L. Tesfatsion & K. L. Judd (eds.), *Handbook of computational economics*, Vol. 2. Philadelphia, PA: Elsevier.

Duffy, J. (2011). Trust in second life. *Southern Economic Journal*, 78(1), 53–62.

Eckel, C. C., & Grossman, P. J. (1996). Altruism in anonymous dictator games. *Games and Economic Behavior*, 16, 181–191.

Eckel, C. C., & Wilson, R. K. (2004). Is trust a risky decision? *Journal of Economic Behavior and Organization*, 55, 447–465.

Fiedler, M. (2009). Cooperation in virtual worlds. *Schmalenbach Business Review*, 61, 173–194.

Fiedler, M. (2011). Experience and confidence in an internet-based asset market experiment. *Southern Economic Journal*, 78(1), 30–52.

Fiedler, M., & Haruvy, E. (2009). The lab versus the virtual lab and virtual field: An experimental investigation of trust games with communication. *Journal of Economic Behavior and Organization*, 72, 716–724.

Fiedler, M., Haruvy, E., & Li, S. X. (2011). Social distance in a virtual world experiment. *Games and Economic Behavior*, 72, 400–426.

Fiore, S. M., Harrison, G. W., Hughes, C. E., & Rutström, E. E. (2008). Virtual experiments and environmental policy. *Journal of Environmental Economics and Management*, 57, 65–86.

Fischbacher, Urs. (2007). z-Tree: Zurich toolbox for ready-made economic experiments. *Experimental Economics*, 10(2), 171–178.

Fisher, R. J. J. (1993). Social desirability bias and the validity of indirect questioning. *Journal of Consumer Research*, 20(2), 303–315.

Foster, F. D., & Warren, G. J. (2016). Interviews with institutional investors: The how and why of active investing. *Journal of Behavioral Finance*, forthcoming.

Füllbrunn, K., Richwien, K., & Sadrieh, A. (2011). Trust and trustworthiness in anonymous virtual worlds. *Journal of Media Economics*, 24(1), 48–63.

Greiner, B., Caravella, M., & Roth, A. E. (2014). Is avatar-to-avatar communication as effective as face-to-face communication? An ultimatum game experiment in first and second life. *Journal of Economic Behavior and Organization*, 108, 374–382.

Guala, F. (2005). *The methodology of experimental economics*. Cambridge: Cambridge University Press.

Harrison, G. W., & List, J. A. (2004). Field experiments. *Journal of Economic Literature*, 42(4), 1009–1055.

Harrison, G. W., Haruvy, E., & Rutström, E. E. (2011). Remarks on virtual world and virtual reality experiments. *Southern Economic Journal*, 78(1), 87–94.

Henrich, J., Boyd, R., Bowles S., et al. (2001). In search of Homo economicus: Experiments in 15 small-scale societies. *AEA Papers and Proceedings*, 91(2), 73–79.

Henrich, J., Boyd, R., Bowles, S., Camerer, C., Fehr, E., & Gintis, H. (eds). 2004. *Foundations of human sociality: Economic experiments and ethnographic evidence from fifteen small-scale societies*. Oxford: Oxford University Press.

Henrich, J., Heine, S. J., & Norenzayan, A. (2010). The weirdest people in the world? *Behavioral and Brain Sciences*, 33(2–3), 61–135.

Hertwig, R., & Ortmann, A. (2001). Experimental practices in economics: A methodological challenge for psychologists? *Behavioral and Brain Sciences*, 24(03), 383–403.

Hoffmann, R. (2008). The cognitive origins of social stratification. *Computational Economics*, 28(3), 233–249.

Holt, C. A., & Laury, S. K. (2002). Risk aversion and incentive effects. *American Economic Review*, 92(5), 1644–1655.

Horton, J. J., Rand, D. G., & Zeckhauser, R. J. (2008). The online laboratory: Conducting experiments in a real labor market. *Experimental Economics*, 14(399–425).

Jamison, J., Karlan, D., & Schechter, L. (2008). To deceive or not to deceive: The effect of deception on behavior in future laboratory experiments. *Journal of Economic Behavior and Organization*, 68(3–4), 477–488.

Jiménez-Buedo, M., & Miller, L. M. (2010). Why a trade-off? The relationship between the external and internal validity of experiment. *Theoria*, 69, 301–321.

Kagel, J. H., & Roth, A. E. (1995). *The handbook of experimental economics*. Princeton, NJ: Princeton University Press.

Kahneman, D. (2011). *Thinking, fast and slow*. New York, NY: Farrar, Straus and Giroux.

Kahneman, D., Knetsch, J. L., & Thaler, R. H. (1991). Anomalies: The endowment effect, loss aversion, and status quo bias. *Journal of Economic Perspectives*, 115(1), 193–206.

Kimball, M. (2015). Cognitive economics. *The Japanese Economic Review*, 66(2), 167–181.

Laibson, D., & List, J. A. (2015). Behavioural economics in the classroom: Principles of (behavioral) economics. *American Economic Review: Papers & Proceedings*, 105(5), 385–390.

Lazear, E. P. (2000). Economic imperialism. *Quarterly Journal of Economics*, 115(1).

Ledyard, J. O. (1995). Public goods: A survey of experimental research. In J. H. Kagel & A. E. Roth (eds), *The handbook of experimental economics* (pp. 111–194). Princeton, NJ: Princeton University Press.

List, J. A., & Reiley, D. (2008). Field experiments. In S. N. Durlauf & L. E. Blume (eds.), *The new Palgrave dictionary of economics and the law*, 2nd edn. Basingstoke: Palgrave.

Loewenstein, G. (1999). Experimental economics from the vantage-point of behavioural economics. *The Economic Journal*, 109, F25–F34.

Lübbe, I., & Bolle, F. (2011). Who helps whom? Risk taking and solidarity in a virtual world experiment. European University Viadrina Department of Business Administration and Economics Discussion Paper.

Mehta, J., Starmer, C., & Sugden, R. (1994). The nature of salience: An experimental investigation of pure coordination games. *American Economic Review*, 84(3), 658–673.

Mennecke, B., Konsynski, B., Townsend, A., Bray, D., Lester, J., Roche, E., & Rowe, M. (2007). Second Life and other virtual worlds: A roadmap for Research. In: *ICIS 2007 Proceedings*. Paper 4.

Mishra, R. C. (2001). Cognition across cultures. In D. Matsumoto (ed.), *The handbook of culture and psychology* (pp. 119–136). New York, NY: Oxford University Press.

Mullainathan, S., & Thaler, R. H. (2000). Behavioral economics. *NBER Working Paper*, 7948.

Nicklisch, A., & Salz, T. (2008). Reciprocity and status in a virtual field experiment. Max Planck Institute for Research on Collective Goods.

Nisbett, R. (2003). *The geography of thought: How Asians and Westerners think differently ... and why*. London: The Free Press.

O'Keefe, D. J. (2002). *Persuasion: Theory and research*. Thousand Oaks, CA: SAGE.

Orbell, J. M., van de Kragt, A. J. C., & Dawes, R. M. (1988). Explaining discussion-induced cooperation. *Journal of Personality and Social Psychology*, 54(5), 811–819.

Ortmann, A. (2005). Field experiments in economics: Some methodological caveats. In J. P. Carpenter, G. W. Harrison, & J. A. List (eds.), *Field experiments in economics* (pp. 51–70). Philadelphia, PA: Elsevier.

Ortmann, A., & Hertwig, R. (2002). The costs of deception: Evidence from psychology. *Experimental Economics*, 5, 111–131.

Ostrom, E., Gardner, R., & Walker, J. (1994). *Rules, games and common-pool resources*. Ann Arbor, MI University of Michigan Press.

Rabin, M. (1993). Incorporating fairness into game theory and economics. *American Economic Review*, 83(5), 1281–1302.

Rai, T. S., & Fiske, A. (2010). ODD (observation- and description-deprived) psychological research. *Behavioral and Brain Sciences*, 33(2–3), 106–107.

Reips, U. D., & Krantz, J. H. (2010). Conducting true experiments on the web. In S. Gosling & J. Johnson (eds.), *Advanced methods for conducting online behavioral research* (pp. 193–216). Washington, DC: American Psychological Association.

Reis, H. T., & Gosling, S. D. (2010). Social psychological methods outside the laboratory. In S. T. Fiske, D. T. Gilbert, & G. Lindzey (eds.), *Handbook of social psychology*, 5th edn., Vol. 1 (pp. 82–114). Hoboken, NJ: John Wiley & Sons.

Roth, A. E. (1995). Bargaining Experiments. In J. H. Kagel, & A. E. Roth (eds.), *The handbook of experimental economics* (pp. 253–348). Princeton, NJ: Princeton University Press.

Sally, D. (1995). Conversation and cooperation in social dilemmas: A meta-analysis of experiments from 1958 to 1992. *Rationality and Society*, 7, 58–92.

Schelling, T. (1960). *The strategy of conflict*. Cambridge, MA: Harvard University Press.

Schwarz, N. (2007). Attitude construction: Evaluation in context. *Social Cognition*, 25(5), 638–656.

Shweder, R. A. (2010). Donald Campbell's doubt: Cultural difference or failure of communication? *Behavioral and Brain Sciences*, 33(2–3), 109–110.

Sloman, S. A. (1996). The empirical case for two systems of reasoning. *Psychological Bulletin*, 119(1), 3–22.

Smith, V. L. (1982). Microeconomic systems as an experimental science. *The American Economic Review*, 72(5), 923–955.

Spann, M., Hinz, O., Hann, I. H., & Skiera, B. (2010). Decision making in virtual worlds: An experimental test of altruism, fairness and presence. In *European Conference on Information Systems*.

Sprecher, S. (1998). Insiders' perspectives on reasons for attraction to a close other. *Social Psychology Quarterly*, 61(4), 287–300.

Thaler, R. H., & Sunstein, C. R. (2008). *Nudge: Improving decisions about health, wealth, and happiness*. New Haven, CT: Yale University Press.

Twieg, P. B., & McCabe, K. A. (2014). *The determinants of territorial property rights in a spatial commons experiment*. GMU Working Paper No. 14–40.

Weber, R., & Dawes, R. M. (2005). Behavioral economics. *The handbook of economic sociology* (pp. 90–108). New York, NY: Russell Sage Foundation.

Weber, R. A., & Camerer, C. F. (2006). "Behavioral experiments" in economics. *Experimental Economics*, 9, 187–192.

Wheelan, S. A. (2005). *The handbook of group research and practice*. Thousand Oaks, CA: SAGE.

Yee, N. (2006). The demographics, motivations and derived experiences of users of massively-multiuser online graphical environments. *Presence: Teleoperators & Virtual Environments*, 15, 309–329.

Zajonc, R. B. (1965). Social facilitation. *Science*, 149(3681), 269–274.

PART III

Understanding Culture with Games

10

A Simulated Utopia: The Social System of a Virtual Ancient Egypt

WILLIAM SIMS BAINBRIDGE*

10.1 Introduction

Unconstrained by some of the brute facts of the real world, many online multiplayer games resemble utopias, designed according to idealized principles. However, the overwhelming majority are violent, based on the Iron Law of Oligarchy within a Clash of Civilizations (Bainbridge, 2013b; Huntington, 1996; Michels, 1915). While any gameworld might serve as a cogent simulation of social forces that operate in the real world (Bainbridge, 2007), only a very few could be considered ideal representations of the kind of society people might actually want to inhabit. *A Tale in the Desert* is widely recognized as an unusual multiplayer game in that its programming prevents violence and players build a civilization based on cooperation and ethics (Sicart, 2009, p. 220). Thus it can also be conceptualized as a computer simulation of Utopia, an ideal society, that might even be a model for improving societies in the so-called "real world." Yet "utopia" means *nowhere* in Greek, was introduced in a novel published half a millennium ago (More, 1516), and seems to represent the communal human past more than the future. For a quarter century, there has been some speculation that internet-based communities make take on utopian functions (Rheingold, 1993), and this chapter explores that possibility through a case study.

10.2 Research Goals

Tale is set in ancient Egypt, where the chief of the game design team is currently called Pharaoh Pluribus, and one of the most challenging collective tasks is

---

* The views expressed in this chapter do not necessarily represent the views of the National Science Foundation or the United States.

Figure 10.1 A cluster of buildings constructed by players at a Nile crossing point.
(This image is shown in full color in the Color Plates section.)

building pyramids, as was done in Egypt more than 4,000 years ago. However, most of the work and a good deal of the social interaction is devoted to constructing more ordinary buildings, including factories, warehouses, and pens in which to keep camels and sheep. Many aspects of this virtual Egypt seem reasonably authentic, but much of the virtual technology is somewhat fanciful, even futuristic in the case of the Raeli gliderport, which is constructed from exotic materials, looks like a flying saucer, launches robot birds that paint the sky with vivid colors, and may take its name from the modern Raelian religious movement oriented toward extraterrestrials (Palmer, 2004). Thus the goal of *Tale* is not to produce a museum-style recreation of an ancient society, but to employ its tradition as the basis for a virtual utopia. Figure 10.1 offers a glimpse at the result, showing the architecture created by players at crossroads near a land bridge across the Nile.

Most of the buildings in Figure 10.1 are "compounds," where machinery can be constructed for a wide range of manufacturing tasks, owned either by individual players or by groups organized into guilds. Some of the best-loved virtual worlds allowed users to have their own homes, notably *EverQuest*, *Star Wars Galaxies*, or *Lord of the Rings Online*, but that is not the case for *Tale*, which uses architectural resources for completion of diverse manufacturing tasks that achieve gains in status and abilities for avatars, thus called *compounds* rather than *homes* or *houses*. Just below the center of the picture is a blimp, and of course the real ancient Egyptians did not have aircraft of any kind. The white blur above and to the left of it, partly obscuring the nearer of the two towers, is an artistic fountain spraying virtual water in a constantly changing complex pattern, another example of *Tale* technology the real ancients lacked.

It is interesting to note that much of the social activity in *Tale* is analogous to resource extraction and manufacturing associated with the Industrial Revolution, requiring players to cooperate because so much collective work is required to develop the infrastructure that then can be used by individuals to make specific goods. And the Industrial Revolution triggered many utopian social movements, including radical attempts to design communities of industrial workers by Robert Owen (1771–1858) and Charles Fourier (1772–1837) in Britain and France, that were then exported to the Americas (Guarneri, 1982; Kamau, 1992). Owenite and Fourierist experiments were not very successful, but given the openness of the New World, the United States became a laboratory for myriads of social experiments, and long before the end of the nineteenth century a considerable body of documentation and analysis had been written about them. Based on that period of utopian history, three main scholarly approaches were developed that shape the methodology used for this chapter.

First, there emerged a subfield of *journalism* that informed both intellectuals and the general reading public about social experiments. The best example is the book *Communistic Societies of the United States* by Charles Nordhoff (1875), who personally visited the communes he wrote about. Later decades might describe such fieldwork as *cultural anthropology*, and studies of the past mature into *social history*. The goal is rich description of each particular case, with only modest comparison across cases, thus the creation of *literature* of value for a liberal education, but perhaps not *science* in the terms of a later century.

Second, historical and observational studies of "intentional communities," as utopian experiments are sometimes called, can offer *design principles* for creating and improving them. By far the best example is *History of American Socialisms* by John Humphrey Noyes (1870), who was himself the leader of the Oneida community that features in his book, which also considers many of the competing communities in a fair-minded way (Carden, 1969). Noyes concluded that two factors would improve the survival chances of a commune – shared religious faith and prior acquaintance of the recruits with each other – as well as remarking on many specific features of the more noteworthy social experiments.

Third, quantitative studies of multiple utopias may serve as *social science* tests of general theories concerning human behavior. The clearest example, *Commitment and Community* by Rosabeth Moss Kanter (1972), was published a century after the Noyes and Nordhoff books, and showed how a set of six social factors might explain the relative success of some communes, as measured by their longevity. However, it may be that Kanter merely expanded on what Noyes had already discovered, that religion strengthens social experiments (Stephan & Stephan, 1973). This quantitative approach may be used in studying a single community, but then the unit of analysis must be individual players, avatars, or groups like guilds.

As Barthel (1984) observed in her analysis of the Amana communes, modern economies corrode the independence of any utopian movement, not the least because beneficial products and services are too numerous and diverse for any small community to produce independently. The last point in time when residents of advanced industrial societies experimented vigorously with communal experiments was the turbulent 1960s and their immediate aftermath (Gardner, 1978; Houriet, 1971; Zablocki, 1980). We may, however, have entered a new period of utopian experimentation, following a hybrid concept, in which people work at ordinary jobs and live in diverse circumstances, but come together collectively in idealized online communities. Some observers may categorize these innovations as *hybrids of reality and fantasy*, yet that same terminology could be used to describe traditional religious movements.

According to one of the more rigorously developed sociological theories of religion, humans in real life cooperate in their search for rewards, and tend to develop some degree of faith in fanciful *compensators* when real *rewards* are difficult to obtain (Stark & Bainbridge, 1987). All of the arts can also provide psychological compensation for the limits of material human existence, and their power is greatest when the audience plays active roles within them, as is distinctly the case for online role-playing games. *Tale* does not require firm *belief*, but merely *suspension of disbelief*, as I noted in a recent book about religions in virtual worlds (Bainbridge, 2013a). Anthropologist Bonnie Nardi (2010) and professor of religious studies Robert Geraci (2014) have also found a significant degree of reality in the fictional religions found in *World of Warcraft*. In two recent studies of multiple gameworlds I explored how avatars can be used as media for venerating deceased family members and social theorists, thus giving games serious social functions traditionally reserved for churches and universities (Bainbridge, 2014, 2016b; cf., Gibbs et al., 2012).

Several science fiction gameworlds possess the qualities of utopias, giving players the subjective experience of living in outer space, notably *Anarchy Online*, *EVE Online*, *Entropia Universe*, and those lamented virtual futures of the past, *Tabula Rasa* and *Star Wars Galaxies* (Bainbridge, 2011). Today, *Star Wars: The Old Republic* is deeply saturated with Jedi and Sith religion, while *Star Trek Online* offers a more secular utopian vision of human freedom in the context of rational institutions (Bainbridge, 2016a). Edward Castronova (2005, 2007) has explicitly argued that online games could improve the real world through their often admirable rules of fairness in competition. A particularly good example of the blurring line between reality and virtuality is *Communities of Play* by Celia Pearce and Artemesia (2009), which documents the historical case of *Uru* when refugees migrated from one virtual world to others, given that the coauthor is Pearce's avatar, and thus something akin to an idealized self.

10.3 A Virtual Community

Utopian experiments tend to be rather small in population, and as of November 26, 2015, *Tale* had only 933 citizens, a tiny fraction of the number of avatars in popular games. In real-world field research, I studied two modern radical religious movements organized along communal lines (Bainbridge, 1978, 2002). Although both faced a number of difficult challenges, they also exhibited some degree of endurance, although one never had a population higher than a thousand, and the peak for the other was about 10,000. Applying similar research methodologies and theories to *Tale*, I conducted virtual field research inside virtual Egypt periodically, beginning in 2009, and the data reported here mainly date from 2015. Most of the field research was conducted through my main avatar named Renhotep. One of the many unusual characteristics of *Tale* is that it is told in a series of *tellings*, each of which required Egyptians to build their civilization from scratch. The first telling began in 2003. To study a range of social conditions, I observed the middle of the fourth telling, the middle and end of the sixth telling, and here offer observations from the early weeks of the Seventh Telling, which began September 10, 2015.

Much of the action in *Tale* consists in gathering raw materials with which to build things, for example three units of mud, two units of straw, and one unit of sand to make six bricks. The mud and sand can simply be picked up from ground that happens to contain them, while straw can be made by picking grass and drying it in the sun. Many materials are hard to find, such as copper ore, and require considerable effort to extract and employ. Very soon in a telling, Egyptians band together in guilds, to help each other in many ways, but especially assembling communal equipment for constructing and storing valuable goods. This models the process of nonmilitary cooperation that built societies in the real human past.

In becoming an Egyptian, a player takes on a role, and social science offers many alternative theories of role-playing. Two contrasting classical theories illuminate the psychological dynamics of *Tale*. Undoubtedly the most important theorist in twentieth-century theatre was Constantin Stanislavski (1964), the advocate of *method acting*, in which a theater actor fully adopts the personality of the character being played. Many solo-player videogames require the player to become a prespecified *character*, acting out portions of a scripted drama, and themepark massively multiplayer online games (MMOs) do this to a noticeable degree, while giving the player some flexibility in how to play the role. The competing perspective is the *psychodrama* method developed by social scientist Jacob Moreno (1944; Moreno and Toeman, 1942), where participants in group psychotherapy act out roles in a manner especially expressive of their own personalities, thus creating *avatars*. In *Tale*, each account can have only one avatar, not a diversity of characters, and nonplayer characters do not exist.

Analogous to quests in other games, there are tasks to perform in *Tale*, but designed in such a way that the player can remain within the self-determined avatar role, and not causing that alienation sociologists call *role distance* (Goffman, 1961). These tasks are organized in seven *disciplines*, and each can be completed in either of two ways: (1) a *principle*, in which the steps required are completed most easily and one level of general experience is gained, or (2) a *test* in which one competes nonviolently for status against other players while completing the task. At the end of a telling, having such status allows one to add one's name to one of seven memorial pyramids that are constructed.

The first task in the Discipline of Architecture is to build an obelisk, the smallest one requiring 231 bricks and many other materials to pass the easy principle. To pass the competitive Test of the Obelisk, one's obelisk must be the tallest one yet built in the particular region of Egypt. As *Tale's* wiki explains, "Seeking to avoid unnecessary competition and waste, many (but by no means all) players voluntarily participate in regional obelisk queues, with each player in the queue building their obelisk in a predetermined order and height until all have passed. It is considered common courtesy to let the residents of a region sign up first for obelisk queues. Note that some people do not believe that queues should be used to determine the order in which people pass this test."[1] Renhotep did indeed notice cases in which a player jumped the queue, built a much taller obelisk than required, and thereby made the task much harder for all subsequent players.

A few kinds of architectural structure already exist when a telling begins, notably the schools where avatars learn skills and sacred altars found all across the landscape. Figure 10.2 shows a wedding ceremony being enacted at one of these altars, which allows the couple to pass a test in the Discipline of Harmony. My avatar is the one at the center with his arms raised, casting a shadow in the sacred rays of Ra the Sun God who shines from the horizon.

---

[1] www.atitd.org/wiki/tale7/Test_of_the_Obelisk (accessed November 26, 2015).

Figure 10.2 Ten citizens of Egypt enacting a marriage ritual at a sacred altar.

Supernatural ritual is common throughout the culture of *Tale*, but is the main focus of the Discipline of Worship, which emulates ancient Egyptian religion, thus enacting the theory that religion adds strength to utopias, and the wider sociological theory that religion strengthens society more generally (Durkheim, 1915; Parsons, 1964).

While it would be too much to claim that *Tale's* citizens actually believe in the ancient gods, they appreciate this sacred culture and enjoy performing the required rituals. Before beginning the first of the seven main Worship tasks, one must perform Principles of Worship, a social ritual oriented toward the ancient Egyptian deities. Two aspirants must bring various sacrificial items to the ceremony and complete the complex actions within twenty-five minutes. This requires preparation, coordination, and knowledge, so typically a third more senior person organizes everything and directs the two aspirants. In the fourth telling, Renhotep joined a special guild, Worship World, in hopes they would help him, but instead he learned through a more general guild named Helping Hands, when a level 35 woman member volunteered to conduct this ritual. She introduced him to a level 9 man who, like Renhotep, wanted to complete the principle, and together the three of them collected the required items.

At a sacred altar in Shabbat Ab, they began with the Ritual of Initiation. Under the woman's close direction, the man placed a small diamond on the left pillar of the altar, and Renhotep placed a piece of twine on its right pillar. They meditated, and the twenty-five-minute clock began counting down. For Renhotep, the crucial steps that required running a distance were dropping a beetle down a mine and learning the new skill of Ritual Item Construction at a School of Architecture for a cost of 10 linen, 200 firebricks, and 100 oil, all of which he supplied himself. The man lit a ritual torch in the deep desert and placed camel milk in a grassy field near water. The woman had scouted all these locations ahead of time, so she rushed hither and thither guiding the two aspirants. All the while they chanted:

> "Praise Horus, King of Egypt!"
> "Praise Isis, whose seed is forever fertile!"
> "Praise Osiris, who was Reborn like the Scarab!"
> "Praise Thoth, the Magician who created Science!"
> "Praise Ra, of the Blazing Eye!"
> "Praise Bastet, who teaches grace and elegance!"
> "Praise Amun, who gives us reason to celebrate!"

When the Seventh Telling began, none of the players were yet able to produce any linen or firebricks, and only a small fraction of the technological abilities could be gained simply through practice. Many skills called *tech* needed to be released by delivering large supplies of materials, which were often difficult to obtain, to the appropriate University, typically a good distance from where other activities were performed. Thus even the ancient religious rituals depended on technological progress, including some given the modern name, *research*.

10.4 Multiple Kinds of Research

There is a sense in which all *Tale* avatars were engaged in research, not Renhotep alone. Veteran players knew that the Seventh Telling would be different in some unexpected ways from earlier tellings, and even in the Sixth Telling many of them began exploring for a better location to set up camp, nearer natural resources, for example. In the Sixth telling, Renhotep had his home base in the centrally located River Plains area, on the west bank of the Nile, but he was aware that at least three other areas were rivals in terms of population and the extensive architecture that had been constructed in the extra-long Sixth Telling: Seven Lakes where he had been located in the Fourth Telling, South Egypt, and Old Egypt north on the Nile delta. For his own research purposes he decided to start in Seven Lakes this time, and like a couple hundred other players he participated in the brief *beta test* of the Seventh Telling, a test run of the updated database that allowed the developers to make a few final adjustments and thus served their special research interests. Like other veterans, he discovered that far fewer trees seemed to be standing in many of the traditionally populated areas than in earlier tellings, so he especially looked for an area with both trees and other resources, which he found rather far south in Seven Lakes, immediately at the University of Leadership where he could frequently check the constantly updated census giving the total number of Egyptian citizens as well as tabulations of their progress through the seven Disciplines that served as status rankings.

Especially during the early weeks of a telling, players invest much of their time conducting research in order to unlock capabilities, and they do so cooperatively. For example, each of the major regions of virtual Egypt has a chariot stop that permits teleporting to the chariot stop in an adjacent region. Each teleport has a cost denominated in hours earned simply by having a *Tale* avatar, for example three hours for one trip. This limits very frequent travel, but at various times a trip may be free.

At the beginning of a telling, all the chariot stops are broken and must be repaired. One learns the repair at a University of Harmony, but the ability is not available at the university in a particular region until it has been "opened," "unlocked," or "researched" by the collective investment of 12,000 bricks, 6,000 boards, 400 pieces of linen, and 800 cut stones, which as a practical matter is far beyond the ability of any one player to amass. Once River Plains residents had unlocked chariot repair, residents of other regions could undertake the long walk there to gain the skill, but by the end of September 2015 citizens of both the Seven Lakes and Old Egypt regions had invested the same daunting roster of materials to unlock chariot repair at their own universities.

This is an especially good example, clearly illustrating several things. One avatar can perform only one act of chariot repair, and only after visiting a University of Harmony that offers this skill. But one act of repair accomplishes little, and about twenty-five avatars must use up their one repair at a particular chariot stop to open the path to one of the other regions it connects to. That does not open the return route, so about fifty avatars must contribute to open any round-trip route between two chariot stops. Some tech skills can be taught by one avatar to another, but much of the exchange between players consists of virtual resources or labor. The popular image that utopias are communist obscures the fact that they are based on social exchange, with a diminished but still functional inequality between members, depending on how much each contributes.

10.5 The Guild Structure

Most popular MMOs encourage players to create enduring groups, usually called *guilds* as in *World of Warcraft*, but called *kinships* in *Lord of the Rings Online*, *fleets* in *Star Trek Online*, *legions* in *Aion*, *clans* in *Fallen Earth*, *factions* in *Perfect World International*, and *tribes* in the MMO-like television reality show, *Survivor*. As all the names except perhaps *guild* itself imply, membership has an exclusive and competitive quality. In almost every case, an avatar can belong to no more than one guild, but a player may have avatars in many different guilds. *Elder Scrolls Online* follows a different pattern, in which players, not their avatars, are guild members, and limited to five. The non-game virtual world *Second Life*, like the real world, allows people to belong to multiple *groups* simultaneously without much restriction, and this is one of the ways in which *Tale* is realistic, because Egyptians may belong to multiple guilds. Exclusive membership in one guild supports loyalty in the context of warfare, but given that *Tale* is peaceful, that limitation would serve no purpose.

Anyone may create a guild simply by building a guild hall, which can be done quite early in a telling, but requires costly research. To open guild construction for a region, players must deliver to a University of Leadership 4,000 bricks, 2,000 boards, 800 pieces of rope, and 140 pieces of canvas. This was first accomplished for the Seventh Telling in River Plains, and avatars from anywhere could travel there to learn the guild construction skill. However, for sake of convenience as well as honor, in a matter of days the people calling Midland Valley and Seven Lakes their homes had also unlocked guild construction by making identical contributions to the University of Leadership in their own region.

Once an avatar has learned guild construction, the actual job of making one requires storing up a supply of boards and bricks, then setting up a small construction site which requires one piece of canvas and four pieces of rope. The amount of boards and bricks determines how many members may join, 300 boards and 500 bricks permitting up to 10 members. Building a guild hall for 100 members from scratch would require 20,100 boards and 40,100 bricks, but guild halls can be expanded after initial construction, at greater ultimate cost in materials. Note than 100 members require more than 10 times the amount of materials as 10, thus requiring increasing investment of cooperative labor to create larger groups. All the halls appear exactly the same. Each displays the name of the guild, a public list of the members with their ranks, information about how and whether an avatar may join, and optional messages. A common practice is to ask people who want to join to *stash* boards and bricks in the hall sufficient to offset the cost of guild expansion to add them. A guild is *full* if the current number of boards and bricks will not permit addition of a new member, and *closed* if new members need special permission to join.

Guild halls cannot actually be entered, although an avatar can walk through one without encountering any barrier. Rather, they are the information hubs for members and define community property. Belonging to a guild immediately provides access to a separate text chat channel, reserved for members, and small groups of friends may create a nominal guild merely to have their own private chat channel. Materials can be stored in a guild hall for shared use, but more typically members set up boxes in work-related guild buildings and free-standing warehouses, setting permissions such as assigning the property to the guild and setting the rank in the guild an avatar must have to withdraw materials. One of the reasons for using many small boxes with a capacity of only 1,000 units, rather than a warehouse with a capacity of 25,000, is so that different permissions may be set on different containers. Another value of these small boxes is that a set of them can classify virtual goods, because there exists such a vast diversity.

This research project has collected data about guilds in many ways, but the method used at the beginning of the Seventh Telling provides the best introduction. The initial survey was done simply by searching for guild halls at locations that were popular in earlier tellings, and near the chariot stops and Nile crossings that are transportation hubs. Especially useful after that was the *friend* system in the game's user interface. The name "friend" is actually a misnomer, because unlike in other MMOs it does not imply a mutual bond between two people. In *Tale*, one may place anyone in one's private friends list, without having to have any special relationship and not requiring any action on the part of the so-called friend. Thus it is both easy and legitimate to place a name temporarily into one's friend list in order to see information about that avatar. One page of data lists all the guilds the avatar belongs to, and clicking on a name opens another page giving information about the guild, including a complete list of its members. If the list is long, and one actually needs the names rather than merely counting them, it is best to visit the guild hall, from which the member list with ranks can be downloaded via a clipboard and pasted into a spreadsheet. I did that with the two most active research guilds, in Seven Lakes and River Plains, then developed the data presented by Table 10.1 in the period September 25–27, 2015.

Seven Lakes Research (7LR) had 55 members, and River Plains Research (RPR) had 51. Three avatars, including Renhotep, belonged to both. I examined the information for guild membership of all 103 avatars, finding a total of 90 other guilds, ranging in population from 1 to 90. Of these, 18 had just 2 members, 38 had from 3 to 9, and 13 had from 10 to 19. Table 10.1 shows

Table 10.1 *Connections between Two Research Guilds and Other Large Guilds*

Name	Latitude	Longitude	Region	Members	7LR Members	RPR Members
Allied Labs of Old Egypt	6957	1012	Old Egypt	42	1	1
Midland Valley Research	4900	943	Midland Valley	36	2	3
Stuff and things	4866	929	Midland Valley	25	2	0
HHOF (Helping Hands of Friends)	4278	–50	Four Corners	22	1	3
Green Valley Falls	3395	1271	River Plains	40	4	8
Alpha	3205	1516	River Plains	20	3	5
zFree	2942	1406	River Plains	90	2	18
The HIVE	2838	1594	River Plains	40	3	13
Safari Club	2827	1587	River Plains	49	5	20
Friends of the Desert	2823	1334	River Plains	36	3	6
River Plains Research	2806	1443	River Plains	**51**	3	**51**
The Public TWERKS	2787	1424	River Plains	30	1	17
Paradise Plains Dog House	2763	2281	Hinterlands	27	0	1
The Point	1775	1299	River Plains	44	4	11
Garden of Eden	–869	1281	Seven Lakes	25	5	1
Seven Lakes Research	–937	673	Seven Lakes	**55**	**55**	3
Amigos	–973	730	Seven Lakes	74	38	4
Les Diamants du Nil	–990	1138	Seven Lakes	30	5	0
South Egypt Independent Researchers	–5572	1051	South Egypt	29	2	1

information about the 19 guilds in this network with at least 20 members. The latitude and longitude are the *Y* and *X* coordinates of the guild halls, in *Tale's* geographic system, with positive numbers being north for latitude and east for longitude.

Tale covers all of the geography of real Egypt, at a reduced scale but requiring very long walks by avatars to get anywhere, with much of the interesting territory being north–south along the banks of the Nile. So the guild hall locations vary much more in latitude, from −5572 in the far south to 6957 in the north right at the Nile Delta, than in longitude, from −50 to 2281 into the Hinterlands, which is not really a region but the designation for land outside any of the regions. Four Corners is somewhat to the west of the Nile, in an area where the Nile is rather far east of the 0 longitude. One definition of *region* is a coherent geographic area with a centrally located chariot stop, which hinterlands do not have. Four other regions are west of the Nile: Cat's Claw Ridge, Valley of the Kings, Desert of Shades, and Memphis. The remaining five are further east: Lake of Reeds, Desert of Nomads, Sinai, Cradle of the Sun, and Eastern Grounds. One explanation for why River Plains and Seven Lakes are the centers of social activity is that they are geographically central. They share the characteristic of having chariot routes to three other regions with Old Egypt, Midland Valley, and South Egypt. The others have only one or two chariot routes, while Midland Valley and Four Corners are both relatively small areas.

The last two columns of the table give the number of members of the two central research guilds who belong to each guild, including Renhotep himself, who is the only member of either who also belongs to Allied Labs of Old Egypt. The first thing to note is that fully thirty-eight members of Seven Lakes Research also belong to Amigos, which is situated only a very short distance away. In fact these guilds are partners, based on a very close cooperative relationship between their leaders. Amigos advertised itself as being very open to new players and happy to mentor them. Every weekend at the beginning of the telling, the leader of Seven Lakes Research would lead a major "dig" on land immediately beside the Amigos guild hall, where as many as eighty avatars would bring shovels and ritualistically excavate, as assistants picked up virtual stones that appeared from the ground and could be used in various manufacturing processes. Figure 10.3 shows the first dig of the Seventh Telling in Seven Lakes.

In the center is the dig hole itself, and most of the participants stand around clicking a dig command about every minute, without this generating any digging animation, although diggers must hold a shovel in their inventories, and these occasionally break, so they usually carry ten. Two Egyptians standing at the hole collect the stones that they put in inventory, for later distribution by

Figure 10.3 A group activity organized by Seven Lakes Research at the Amigos camp.

the dig leader. In the rear is the Nile River, and the small building is the first compound set up by the Amigos guild, with storage boxes inside where extra stones may be placed. The eight rectangular gardens were temporarily set up by individuals to grow flax when they were not digging. Six of the participants have text boxes over their heads, where they are communicating with the entire group in order to work on the Principles of Harmony, which requires meeting a variety of people, including avatars that had passed the principles of the other disciplines and players who had achieved great things in previous tellings. So, group meetings like a dig encourage other forms of cooperation, as well as advancing individual achievement.

At the end of each dig, each avatar would be given an equal share of the results, while half the stones were assigned to the guilds for their collective purposes. The first weekend of the telling, messages came during the dig from the evil Stranger, a supernatural rival to Pharaoh Pluribus, halting the universities and demanding a ransom of more than a thousand stones to release them. Most of Egypt was paralyzed. Communicating through common members, Seven Lakes Research and River Plains Research agreed each to pay half of the ransom, thus establishing the prominence of their two regions in Egyptian society.

10.6 Guild Diversity

At this point, it seemed that Seven Lakes Research and River Plains Research towered over all the other research guilds, yet a third actually was advancing more rapidly in its research, and a fourth was also active, both of them at the very southern end of this virtual world. The South Egypt Independent Research guild described itself thus on the wiki: "We are a friendly group of people working towards an independent South Egypt free from running for techs."[2] Remarkably, the leading research guild, Followers of Anubis, refrained from advertising itself. Table 10.2 lists the regions of Egypt, with information from October 13 about the number of techs that had been completely researched, and information about the guild most likely responsible.

Only by visiting Eastern Grounds, in the remote southeast corner of Egypt, observing passersby, and requesting help, was Renhotep able over a period of days to find the location of Followers of Anubis and learn about its social relations with the rest of Egypt. At the end of September, only three of its members belonged to any guild outside its own community, one to The Good Grub Pub, one to The HIVE, and one to both of these central Egyptian casual guilds. Followers of Anubis was a closed community that had existed for years, had built real-world relationships, and was dedicated to living by themselves within the fascinating Egyptian environment. Unlike other guilds, their members were not assigned higher or lower formal status, so this was really a commune of equals. Around a remote lake, they had built very extensive facilities, and the environment provided everything they might need to live long and happy virtual lives.

In the Sixth Telling, Renhotep had joined fully fourteen guilds, each specializing in a particular set of social functions and thus providing distinctive insights for the research. Four of them were reestablished quickly after the beginning of the Seventh Telling and are listed in Table 10.1: Helping Hands of Friends, Safari Club, The Point, and zFree. The fourteen are described in the text that follows using their own statements as much as possible, taken either from their page in the *Tale* wiki or an in-game message, with their membership numbers in parentheses, first for February 17, 2015, when Renhotep joined the last one, and then for August 5, as the telling was coming to an end. At this point in its history, *Tale* was not charging players a subscription fee, so the numbers of active avatars were lower than the formal memberships, which represented an earlier peak in activity. The Seventh Telling reintroduced subscriptions.

Helping Hands of Friends (263/265 members): This was the largest guild in Egypt. "Do Not build compounds on clay beds, or Limestone areas. This is a HHOF rule. Thank you. The Elders." "No Cussing or politics in the guild chat. This could cause reprimand HHOF. The F word and the GD words are definitely a no no. Thank you. All the Elders."

---

[2] www.atitd.org/wiki/tale7/South_Egypt_Independent_Research_(SEIR) (accessed October 13, 2015).

Table 10.2 *Early Research Permitting Industrialization in the Regions of Virtual Egypt*

| Region | Techs Completely Researched | | Guild Members | Guild Hall Location | |
	Number	Guild Probably Responsible		Longitude	Latitude
Cat's Claw Ridge	2	None	6	4378	−552
Cradle of the Sun	4	Et Tzet Ter Ra Incorporated	12	1943	6647
Desert of Nomads	5	Friends of DoN			
Desert of Shades	2	None			
Eastern Grounds	29	Followers of Anubis	20	3148	−6261
Lake of Reeds	6	Reeding Rainbow	13	4265	7616
Midland Valley	9	Midland Valley Research	40	943	4900
Old Egypt	8	Allied Labs of Old Egypt	50	1012	6957
River Plains	22	RP Research	54	1443	2806
Seven Lakes	19	7L Research	71	673	−937
Sinai	1	Sinai Central	20	3290	4766
South Egypt	11	South Egypt Independent Research	41	1051	−5574
Valley of Kings	1	None			

zFree (202/230 members): "Hiya all, welcome to zFree, a wonderful place with no drama:)" Its website in the *Tale* wiki mapped these facilities: buildings, mines, projects, camp chores, guild events, research, tests, useful info, metal treatment tanks, acoustics lab, marble and granite quarries, new player community store, and Pyramids of Heaven.

Palm Valley (193/193 members): A "closed" guild, which means that Renhotep needed permission of a leader to join. Among the facilities boasted on its wiki webpage were Raeli Ovens, Wood Treatment Recipes, Chemical Bath Recipes, Glass Class, Worship Principle (from PV altar), Pilgrimage, Salts, Aqueduct, Plantations, Ritual of Leavened Bread, Spring Boxes, and an Acoustic Lab.

Festivals (173/179 members): "The festivals altar is at 1522, 3492, in zfree camp. The main festivals will be held here, but people are welcome to sacrifice at other altars as it suits them... If the stuff you need is not in the warehouses by the altar, put your requests on this page and contact a supplier about your needs. For beers for the Osiris you are encouraged to make it yourself if you are capable, although the brewers will be happy to help you out with a recipe." In addition to the god Osiris, the goddess Hathor was prominent in the religious rituals called *festivals*.

Safari Club (140/143 members): No self-description, but the guild text chat makes it obvious that this group specializes in catching wild animals. For the Safari quest assigned at the University of the Body, very special animals must be found, and this guild's text chat distributes news about where they have been seen.

Mentors of Egypt (99/100 members): "Welcoming packet – 2 leather – 2 Nile Green – 10 jugs – 1 Pappy – 15 Pappy seeds." The wiki website says, "We are a guild dedicated to assisting and finding mentors for new trial players." With 100 members, this guild was "full," meaning that the Guild Hall would need to be expanded through investment of bricks and boards to raise the ceiling on how many could belong.

The Point (96/100 members): "The Point has 3 hades and 2 persephone furnaces: 223 1720 hades, 449 1442 hades, around 347 1681 hades, around 1275 1770 persephone, around 1350 1910 persephone." The website on the *Tale* wiki says, "The Point is focused on regional projects including research, public works and mentoring activities in RIVER PLAINS. The guild also fosters and encourages Egypt wide activities in support of every Egyptian player enjoyment of the game."

Humble Priests Devotional Groups (96/98 members): The Guild Hall offers members free construction materials, having 27,197 boards and 30,203 bricks on February 16, 2015. This guild simply provides materials for members to use in the Test of Devotion, described thus in the wiki: "Demonstrate your devotion to the gods by offering sacrifices at as many shrines as you can... To gain a point, a player must place four of the same item at an altar (on the hands and foci) then meditate which sacrifices (destroys) said items."

Pyromaniacs (69/55 members): "We are dedicated to the Test of Pyrotechnics! Our mission is 3-fold: to work together to schedule pyro shows, to work together to get more stars opened, to help Egyptians to pass the Principle of Pyrotechnics." As the wiki explains, "The Test of Pyrotechnics is one of the tests in the discipline of Art & Music. You will design colorful fireworks, which are displayed at a public Pyrotechnics Stadium and judged by your fellow Egyptians."

PV Puzzles (68/68 members): The "PV" refers to Palm Valley, and this guild is ancillary to the main Palm Valley guild, offering buildings and materials so a variety of puzzles can be constructed by players, for other players to solve, often helping both advance.

Old Egypt Public Workhouse (44/70 members): Devoted to mining stone and building a Throne of Pharaoh.

Snow Storms (59/59 members): On its website it says: "This guild was built to serve as 'chat channel' to announce snow storms, when the public [notification] boards are down... Currently the guild has been built to accept 70 members. We need more boards and bricks to expand it..." The guild hall was increased to allow as many as 100 members, but, as the telling concluded, snow storms were low in players' priorities.

Shroomers of the Darkest Night (36/40 members): Dedicated to sharing information about where rare forms of mushroom are currently growing across the huge Egyptian territory. With 40 members this guild was full, because it had not invested as many bricks and boards as had Mentors of Egypt.

Noobs Inc. (23/23 members): A small guild dedicated to helping new players.

This diversity of special-purpose guilds not only reflects the complexity of the virtual environment created by Pharaoh Pluribus and his design team, but also illustrates the fact that only simplistic stereotypes of utopia assume that all members perform the same functions and roles, when in fact utopian experiments quite frequently possess complex social structures.

10.7 Citizen Governance

Very few MMOs offer players the opportunity to participate in a formal political processes that can decide some future features of their virtual world, although within a guild players can generally organize their own political system, if the founders of the guild wish to share their original authority with the general membership. *EVE Online* is famous for having an elected advisory board of players, but among the most thoroughly developed virtual political systems is that in *A Tale in the Desert*. The complex system of guilds, and the fact that players construct enduring buildings across the landscape, also influence events in a quasi-political fashion. Here we shall use the very first voting in the Seventh Telling to understand *Tale's* referendum system, taking advantage of the facts that the players were mostly veterans, and thus had a good basis for considering changes, and analysis of the first referendum does not need to take account of prior political battles in the particular telling.

On September 24, 2015, the general System text chat announced that the winner of the first referendum election was The Agricultural Courtesy Law, with 73.227 percent of those voting being in favor. It beat out five other propositions and under the rules thus became the one that was enacted, with the proviso that Pharaoh Pluribus always retained the final authority, able to veto any proposition, adjust its details, or in some cases enact an improvement even if the citizens did not express great enthusiasm for it. Here is the main text of this petition, as it was presented to citizens:

> To better assist in the gathering of resources that all Egyptians need, the following acts of courtesy shall be made mandatory . . .
>
> - The injuring of cactuses to produce sap, when sap is gathered. Restoring the Collect Sap and Injure the Cactus menu option on the cactuses.
> - To harvest dates, saltpeter must be available in inventory to refertilize the date palm. Restoring the Gather Dates and Fertilize with Saltpeter menu option on the trees.
> - A resin wedge must be in inventory to collect resin from a tree, with the tree being renicked when the resin collected. Restoring the Gather the Resin and Nick the Tree menu option on the trees.
>
> This is a pay it forward law, ensuring that resources are available for everyone moving forward. If any part of this law is a Pluribus Veto, the other parts should still be enacted.

While each word in this proposition is familiar to any reader, the meaning is totally obscure if one lacks familiarity with the details of existence in this virtual world. That is a general point of some significance: *Laws are meaningful only within a specifiable society*. The cactus sap example is the simplest to explain. Here and there across the landscape stand plants called *royal cactus* that produce sap having religious value. In the Test of the Bedouin, an avatar obtains a supply of this sap and runs rapidly from one common altar to another, anointing each with this natural juice. Doing so at fourteen altars allows the avatar to pass a principle of the Human Body discipline, but passing this mission as a test requires being among the top anointers during a given period. Common altars are found throughout Egypt, and are used for many rituals, of which a wedding between two avatars like that shown in Figure 10.2 is especially important, as marriage combines the possessions of two Egyptians into community property of the dyad.

Prior to enactment of The Agricultural Courtesy Law, here is what happened when an avatar interacted with a royal cactus. A click on it told the avatar how many drops of sap were currently available, and offered two choices: (1) collect sap and (2) injure the cactus. Selecting the first choice gave the avatar one drop of sap each time, until the sap was exhausted. Selecting the second choice to injure the cactus would cause it to produce more sap, but none would be available for a long time. Thus in most cases, clicking the choice to injure the cactus would assist not oneself but some other person who would visit the cactus later.

This is the meaning of the phrase "pay it forward" near the end of the proposition, and the two other cases of harvesting dates and collecting resin follow the same logic. Popularized by science fiction writer Robert A. Heinlein in his 1951 juvenile novel, *Between Planets*, "pay it forward" is well explained by Wikipedia: "Pay it forward is an expression for describing the beneficiary of a good deed repaying it to others instead of to the original benefactor."[3] Heinlein intended his novels to prepare boys for a technology-rich and humanly better future, and the most obvious general analogy is that humans repay their parents' generosity by taking good care of their own children. In *Tale*, this principle is one among many that supports cooperation among all citizens, even when they do not directly interact with each other.

After The Agricultural Courtesy Law was enacted, the two options for interacting with a cactus were: (1) collect sap and injure the cactus and (2) injure the cactus. It was no longer possible to collect sap without injuring the cactus, so "pay it forward" was now programmed into the system, rather than being an individual moral choice. The reason for retaining the option of injuring the cactus without collecting sap was because many cacti were not producing sap at the time the law was enacted.

---

[3] en.wikipedia.org/wiki/Pay_it_forward (accessed September 25, 2015).

Now that we understand the social significance of the first new law enacted in the Seventh Telling, we can better understand the process by which a proposition got on the ballot for the particular referendum. The game "developers" posted the following on the *Tale* wiki:

If you wish to write up a new law and have it enforced over Egypt, here are the steps you will need to follow:

- Achieve citizen status.
- Go to the University of Leadership, click to create petition. Type your petition into the dialog box.
- Walk around and talk to people, ask them to sign your petition. They can sign by clicking on you. You can also share the petition.
- When you have enough signatures, go back to the University of Leadership, and turn in the petition.
- The developers will now classify the petition: either it is a feature request, or a petition for a law.
- If it is a feature request, the developers will put it into the feature request manager on atitd.info.
- If it is a petition for a law, it will appear at the voting booth in the game. Players will begin voting on it.
- After the voting, the petition with the most yes votes will become a law, as long as the yes votes were more than 50% of the total votes.
- After a petition becomes a law, the developers reprogram the game to enforce the law.[4]

A *feature request* would add something to *Tale* that would not be considered controversial, and thus not significantly impact the existing features, whereas a *law* in some way constrains player behavior. The game developers can decide how practical a feature request might be, and indeed whether they have the technical ability to implement it, but player input is certainly required for any new laws. At the time this referendum was conducted, petitions needed to have at least twenty-one avatar signatures to be considered, and the proposition that got the lowest support among the six, only 16 percent of those voting being in favor, simply called for this number to be increased to forty-nine. The four other unsuccessful propositions deserve some discussion.

The second-place proposition, Sheep Pox Quarantine Act, is especially interesting because it responds to a challenge the players did not yet fully understand. Virtual Egyptians commonly raise two kinds of mammals, sheep and camels, in two different kinds of pen and eating different food. Sheep eat onions

---

[4] www.atitd.org/wiki/tale7/Law (accessed September 25, 2015).

that must be grown by the avatars, and placed in the pen. If well-fed sheep in a pen are of both genders, more sheep will result up to a limit of ten. In ancient days, notably in the First Telling of *Tale*, sheep were afflicted by a highly contagious disease called *pox*. But the pox had not been seen for a decade, and few players in the Seventh Telling had any experience with dealing with it. The wiki reports some solid information about the pox, along with what appear to be frantic speculations:

> Sheep pox was a fatal illness in previous tellings requiring the slaughter of all sheep in the pen. Transmission method unknown but might be from adding sick wild sheep to the pen or other lack of good sheep farming practices like under feeding. In Tale7, sheep pox appears to work roughly how it did in Tale1. Pox can be spread by contagion, or may show up in isolated pens by random chance. Sheep in poxxed pens may not be picked up. Slaughtering sheep in a poxxed pen WILL cause an immediate contagion spread to at least the nearest sheep pens! The radius of contagion spread has not been established, but appears to be large. Starving sheep are likely to contract pox on their own, but healthy, well-fed sheep often do as well.[5]

In addition to its wiki, *Tale* has a player forum, and a new thread is started for every proposed new law, in this case one titled Law Review – Sheep Pox Quarantine Act, beginning with a statement of its terms:

PREVENTION:

1. Anyone may add food or medicine to any sheep pen at any time.

QUARANTINE:

2. Any sheep pen containing visibly diseased sheep is considered quarantined (see below).
3. Any sheep pen containing one or more sheep but zero onions is considered quarantined (see below).
4. Any pen considered quarantined is no longer considered quarantined once it either contains no sheep or contains onions without containing any visibly diseased sheep.

EPIDEMIC CONTROL:

5. Any citizen may slaughter sheep in a quarantined sheep pen by invoking the ancient law of the flock: "Baa-ram-ewe! Baa-ram-ewe! The needs of the many outweigh the needs of the few!"

---

[5] www.atitd.org/wiki/tale7/Sheep_Pen (accessed September 25, 2015).

6. Any resources gained from slaughter under section 5 of this law remain the property of the pen owner, subject to existing permissions.[6]

Two issues were raised in the forum debate: (1) Are all parts of this law necessary, given that we do not fully understand how the pox is transmitted? (2) Is it too great a violation of the rights and responsibilities of the owner of the sheep pen? The software could be revised to let a stranger kill the sheep in a pen, but not steal their wool and mutton. But then, wanton sheep-killing could become a way that evil players could circumvent the programmed restrictions preventing violence against other players. Programming good behavior into sheep slaughter used only to prevent pestilence would remove most of the gaming challenge when the designers reintroduced this plague.

The third proposition, Pharaoh's Gardiner, would have added just one more honorific to a culture that already has many, calling the player who has harvested the most vegetables Pharaoh's Gardener. The Decayed Construction Act was also rather simple, adjusting the rules for removal of unused constructions abandoned by their owners. The fifth-ranked proposition was also designed to clean up the environment, but was more interesting: "Clean Clay Act: In order to protect the delicate ecology of our clay fields, no brick rack, wood plane, flax comb, small distaff, sign, apiary, firepit, fence, or bonfire outside of a compound may be built on clay. Any such buildings already built on clay fields must be removed within a fortnight of the passage of this law or be subject to claim and removal by any Citizen of Egypt."

As in our real world, the virtual natural resources in virtual Egypt exist in many forms. Clay is found in patches of dirt near bodies of water, and gives the ground a distinctive appearance so expert clay diggers can find it fairly easily. But these areas are not common, and Egyptians generally build their homes and workplaces near water, so there is a risk of covering up the clay. Unlike grass, sand, and mud, clay cannot simply be picked up, but must be dug with a shovel while pouring water from a jug on the ground. Also, one must find a lump of clay, and refill the jug with water, by walking around the area to find a spot where either or both of these things can be done once, then continuing the same search for another spot, until much effort has been invested to get the desired quantity of clay.

In the forum and elsewhere, players argued against the removal of existing structures, because their owners had the right to build them there originally, and moving them could entail considerable inconvenience. It also seems that this proposition raised general issues about ownership of land. Some MMOs

---

[6] www.atitd.org/forum/viewtopic.php?f=2&t=1089 (accessed September 25, 2015).

Table 10.3 *Analyzing the Vote Counts in the First Referendum of the Seventh Telling*

Proposed Legislation	Percent Supporting	Number Supporting	Number Voting	Percent of 790
The Agricultural Courtesy Law	73.227	413	564	71
Sheep Pox Quarantine Act	68.029	283	416	53
Pharaoh's Gardiner	67.476	139	206	26
Decayed Construction Act	54.253	236	435	55
Clean Clay Act	38.084	163	428	54
49 Signature Law	16.209	59	364	46

allow players or guilds to own land, usually levying a periodic property tax, and competition to claim the land of players who failed to pay their tax is especially fierce in *ArcheAge*. Land as such cannot be owned in *Tale*, but mines can be because they are built using materials that are owned. One of the guilds to which Renhotep belonged invested very serious effort prospecting for copper immediately around its camp, going back and forth with a dowsing detector, intending to build a mine wherever any copper or other metal was found, effectively taking control of that exact location. Some mines are public, but typically they belong to individuals or guilds, and cannot be used by other players. Clearly, even some laws that superficially appear to be limited in scope may have implications for much wider issues of the relations between people and property.

On the evening when the results were announced, Egypt had 790 citizens, and we can wonder what fraction were voters. The reported results do not say how many Egyptians voted for or against each proposition, but the percentages are given with great precision, so it was easy to calculate within this population what integer numbers of votes could generate these percentages most precisely. For the winning proposition, 413 yes votes out of 564 cast gives 73.227 percent. The population of Egypt was constantly growing during the early weeks of the Seventh Telling, so some fraction of citizens may have been too new to consider the issues or be familiar with the voting procedures. The number 564 is 71 percent of 790, and some number a bit lower than 790 were already citizens when the voting was done, so it seems that a rather high fraction of Egyptian citizens are politically active. Table 10.3 gives the corresponding figures for all six propositions on the first ballot of the Seventh Telling.

We might hypothesize that in a referendum, the popularity of a proposition affects not only what percentage of voters will support it, but also how many citizens will express an opinion about it. Indeed, the winning proposition was judged by the greatest number of citizens, more than a hundred more than any other. However, the numbers voting are somewhat irregular across the six propositions, lowest for Pharaoh's Gardner, which was rated rather positively by those who voted. To use this virtual ancient Egypt as a testing laboratory for general theories, or a proving ground for new democratic procedures we might apply in the real world, we need to consider exactly how the referendum was done.

Citizens did not need to go through any special voter registration procedure, since paying their subscription fee and completing their training exercises on Welcoming Island renders them fully accredited citizens. Thus one of the steps that inhibits voting in the United States, voter registration, is not operative (Timpone, 1998). The voting booths can be found all over Egypt, usually at locations beside main roads and near other points of interest, such as crossing points over the Nile, chariot stops, or schools the avatar is likely to visit in the ordinary course of events. A period of time is defined for voting, such as three days, but not limited to daylight hours. To vote, the player need only click on the voting booth, select a petition from a list of their titles, read the proposition, and click to register a vote. Thus, the procedures in *A Tale in the Desert* are a model for online referendum voting in general.

10.8 The Macro Controversy

Not all controversies become political issues, as the example of macros in *Tale* illustrates. Many of the resource gathering and manufacturing actions need to be repeated hundreds or even thousands of times. Others require responses to stimuli, such as stoking a firepit when making charcoal, if the color of the flames changes and requires quick adjustment. A few of the most common tasks can be done as offline chores, but only after having completed the particular task many times manually. For example, after retrieving 1,000 pieces of slate from riverside land, or growing 2,500 cabbages, one can set a preference within the game interface such that ample quantities of the desired resource will appear in the player's inventory when logging in. But most tedious tasks cannot be avoided in this way. *Macros* are ancillary programs run simultaneously with the game program, and players differ in their use of them, as the following conversation from a regional chat illustrates, replacing the actual avatar names with descriptions:

CONFUSED: Hmm barley macro not working.
EXPERT: Some of the menu driven macros don't work.
CONFUSED: Oh it planted. Hmmm might be image thing will have to check.

EXPERT: Anything that clicks on an icon works fine. The cc [charcoal] macro works pretty good but you have to watch it carefully and close it out after each run.

SKEPTIC: Macros bah humbug I say.

EXPERT: Some things they are okay for. Saves a lot of wristing hurting clicking.

SKEPTIC: I don't use them but I can see maybe grass, or slate, menial stuff like that, that requite a lot of clicking, but not for a lot of other things.

EXPERT: I use them for hacking rake, slate, and cc.

PROGRAMMER: Use it for veggies also: D

EXPERT: Never got veggies to work. Which macro?

PROGRAMMER: Using my release? Lemme get the link. https://github.com/nigggle/VegJanitor

EXPERT: Does it work in automato?

PROGRAMMER: Yup. I made a pull request for it to be included in automato today. Not accepted yet.

EXPERT: Cool. My reflexes are damaged and veggies have gotten almost impossible.

PROGRAMMER: For now you can just manually download it. Depending on how often you have to move for pollution, you can make 1500+ an hour. Probably more like 1000 if you include running back to drop some off etc., or just bad pollution. Any problems with it just ask.

Automato is a set of macros developed by players, as explained on one of its webpages: "Automato is a LUA-based automation program which is useful for any automation task which primarily involves screen scraping and sending mouse clicks, with a special focus on automating video games. Automato was originally called *Jimbly's VeggieTales*, as it was initially developed for growing vegetables in *A Tale in the Desert*, but has grown to be used in other games as well."[7] Lua is a widely used scripting language, developed in Brazil over two decades ago, and while doing statistical research in *World of Warcraft* I made extensive use of Lua-based CensusPlus, which did not give my avatar any advantage, but tabulated the numbers and characteristics of avatars (Bainbridge, 2010).[8] The *Tale* macros do confer an advantage on players who use them, although only in reducing some of the required repetitive effort, and the lack of combat in *Tale* moderates this inequality. The *Tale* wiki explains a norm that expresses a moral principle, even if it is only seldom enforced:

Macros is the generic term for any program that does something for you in-game that means you don't need to manually do it. Whilst most games don't allow for this in online games, *A Tale in the Desert* allows them on one caveat – you don't go AFK (Away from Keyboard). What this means is that if you use a Macro, you MUST be at your computer, and must respond to any Game Master who speaks to you. You will know when this happens, as the chat box will have GM: followed by their name on it, and they will sport a banner over their avatar head that clearly

---

[7] github.com/DashingStrike/Automato (accessed October 13, 2015).

[8] www.curse.com/addons/wow/census-plus (accessed October 13, 2015).

defines them to be a Game Master... You can create your own software if you have the skills to do so, but for most people, they use software that has already been created, and then run scripts on that software to do the specific chore in the game.[9]

Online games differ in the extent to which they prohibit macros, and one of the most egregious cases was the use of a criminal add-on program to claim virtual land in *ArcheAge* a split second after the original owner lost possession of it for failure to pay taxes, faster than players who were waiting patiently around it could claim it manually.

10.9 A Criminal Act

Although direct violence between avatars is not possible in *Tale*, one avatar may cause harm to another in more subtle ways, through what gamers call *griefing*. On September 24, 2015, a few players were discussing the governmental structure of Egypt in the general chat channel called Egypt News Network, when one commented, "One concern that's cropped up now and then are so-called 'emergency laws': a proposal to immediately stop one griefer in particular, or a griefing method in general, or some other egregious situation that the vast majority of Egypt strongly feels that requires immediate attention." Pharaoh Pluribus participated in this discussion, and urged caution, because an emergency law could be abused, but did acknowledge that such a law would be possible.

At the beginning of October, the first election of the telling began, a complex process that would anoint one Egyptian as Demi-Pharaoh, with the power on rare occasions to exile another player from Egypt. One of the standard missions, Test of the Demipharaoh, required one to nominate oneself, so Renhotep did so, also letting me see the political process from inside. The nominees were divided into groups of seven, called *juries*, and given a special text chat channel in which they could privately discuss the issues facing Egypt. After three days, each jury member could go to a voting booth and nominate one of their group of seven to go on to the next phase. Renhotep was nominated by his first-phase jury to go forward, but was not nominated by his second jury to be one of the final seven candidates. Participating in two nomination phases, and observing the very public election debate, provided full experience with the political process. One of the other members of Renhotep's first-phase jury said, "My main concern at present is a griefer called Geoguy, (known as Geodude in previous

---

[9] www.atitd.org/wiki/tale7/Macro (accessed October 13, 2015).

Figure 10.4 Renhotep at his camp in Seven Lakes, early in the Seventh Telling.

tales) he has been up to his old tricks, building woodplanes over peoples compounds etc."

To illustrate the components of this form of griefing, Figure 10.4 shows Renhotep standing in front of his own home compound, which he had built using wooden boards in addition to bricks and other materials. On the left are ten brick racks, each of which can hold the materials to make six bricks as they dry in the sun. Each brick rack is made from four boards, and boards must be manufactured from logs taken from trees, by means of a wood plane. That is the prominent device on the right, which Renhotep made, and behind it is a drying rack he made for drying flax he had grown from seeds, harvested through a complex process, then placed in water so it would rot. Many pieces of equipment must be placed inside a compound like the one behind Renhotep, but wood planes can be placed outdoors because they are needed right at the beginning of an avatar's progress. Geoguy did not attack Renhotep's camp, but had he done so, he would have placed wood planes right up against the walls of Renhotep's compound building, so that it would be impossible to expand it by adding more raw materials in order to give it the capacity to hold more equipment.

By adding Geoguy as a "friend," Renhotep was able to learn that he was a level one paid subscriber who belonged to no guilds. He then sent a personal message to Geoguy, receiving a reply a couple hours later:

RENHOTEP: Rumor has it that you are disrupting Egyptian tranquility in interesting ways. Is this true?

GEOGUY: I am but a simple businessman, trying to get ahead in this dog-eat-dog worl... To be honest, my attempts thus far have generated a woefully underwhelming profit. Not a single person has taken me up on my offer of protection. Protection against coy rogues building wood planes all over their camps.

On one level, Geoguy's griefing was an unsuccessful protection racket, but on another it was a successful annoyance. He would place wood planes all around the compound of a guild or socially prominent individual player, and demand payment to remove them. For example, on October 3, he placed several immediately outside the walls of the compound belonging to the Amigos guild that was devoted to manufacture of wood and stone products. Remarkably, he was able to find the village of Followers of Anubis, despite the fact they had not occupied their remote location in earlier tellings and had hidden its coordinates from the pubic database, but its construction was already complete when he placed wood planes all around many of its buildings.

Wood planes were easy to build, did not degrade over time as some constructions do, and could not be removed by anyone other than the owner. The materials to build one consisted of six pieces of slate, two of which would be combined to make a stone blade, and slate could be obtained by walking beside a body of water, and picking one up every few steps. As noted above, after retrieving a thousand, the interface could be set so that endless supplies of slate would fill up an avatar's inventory when the player was offline. Thus, with only moderate effort, Geoguy could cover a wide area with woodplanes spaced a modest distance apart, thus preventing anyone else from building anything there. Since he chose as his targets places that were in use by dedicated players, he prevented them from expanding their facilities, as well as causing shameful eyesores.

Later, Renhotep actually met Geoguy at one of the sites where he had placed about fifty woodplanes, and interviewed him. Renhotep suggested ways Geoguy might take on a new role, earning the right to stay in *Tale* rather than be banned, but Geoguy thought this was both impossible and undesirable from his standpoint:

GEOGUY: Let's be realistic, at this point my 'reputation' is tainted beyond repair even if I wanted to try and turn things around. I would say at this point I'm on borrowed time no matter what I do... I will just stay the course and continue doing whatever I can to anger as many people as possible.
RENHOTEP: May I ask what you really gain from this?
GEOGUY: Being infamous is its own reward. I would rather be infamous than forgotten.

Later in the interview, Geoguy said he was a computer programmer and had enjoyed griefing in the non-game virtual world, *Second Life*, as well as in *Tale*.

He admitted enjoying the role of virtual "terrorist." The seven candidates of Renhotep's first-phase jury discussed the role of a demi-pharaoh in resolving disputes by providing guidance to players who seriously disagreed about something, but when this proved impossible the demi-pharaoh could ban a player from *Tale*. About Geoguy, one reported, "He did say in regional chat that he would leave 7L alone if we gave him 50 linen, but it was clear that he would just use the linen to build beehives over everyone's compounds, either here or elsewhere." Renhotep's second phase jury discussed griefing at length, including the provisions of a newly proposed anti-griefer law, and in the main campaign the final candidates also took positions on it. The law passed, clear evidence that Egyptians were quite offended by the griefer's actions. The law states:

> Part 1: Any Demi-Pharaoh may submit to any voting booth, or University of Leadership, the name of an alleged griefer. Upon such action, an immediate automatic ballot is created for the populace of Egypt to vote on, the text of which shall be as follows: "[Name] stands accused of griefing and blatantly unacceptable behavior by [Demi-PharaohName]. [Name] shall hereby be immediately and automatically banned from Egypt, and all things built by [Name], regardless of who owns them, shall be immediately salvageable by anyone, with no materials returned." On submission, a calendar event shall be created for the duration of the ballot, and a message shall appear in system announcing the start of voting, along with the name of the submitting Demi-Pharaoh, and the name of the accused griefer. Such ballot shall be available for any paid player to vote upon for a time period of 2 days. If the ballot passes with an approval rating of at least 60% of the votes submitted, Part 2 shall go into effect.
>
> Part 2: The player whose name was submitted shall be immediately banned. This ban shall not reduce the number of available bans of any Demi-Pharaoh. All items, buildings, and equipment built by such player shall become immediately salvageable by anyone, with no materials returned.

The anti-griefer law passed on October 5 with 63.590 percent of the vote, but could not be acted upon until a demi-pharaoh had been elected and given the power to ban. According to the *Tale* wiki, while demi-pharaohs may informally contribute to Egyptian community in many ways, their formal functions are limited to policing capital crimes:

> They have the ability to exile up to 7 player characters from Egypt. Any character exiled in this way will be unable to play for the remainder of the tale. This exile, or ban, applies to a character, not the actual player. A player who's had a character exiled, may create or play with a different character [which requires a different paid account].
>
> Demi-Pharaohs from previous elections retain their exile power even after a new Demi-Pharaoh is instated. In this way, they can be considered elected "for life" – or at least until the end of the current tale.

A Demi-Pharaoh who still has at least one ban left cannot be exiled by any other Demi-Pharaoh. However, if a Demi-Pharaoh has used all 7 of their bans, they are no longer immune and can be exiled by another Demi-Pharaoh just as can any other citizen.

It is possible for a Demi-Pharaoh, even in possession of 1 more [sic = or] more bans, to be exiled from Egypt if a law is passed to that effect. It is also possible for a law to be passed to strip a Demi-Pharaoh of their bans, and their position, but without actually exiling the character.

As of this writing, it is not possible for a law to be passed that would restrict or limit the power of a Demi-Pharaoh, or any aspect of the Demi-Pharaoh test itself.[10]

The high point of the election campaign was an online debate, October 12, that allowed the seven candidates to introduce themselves to the wider community. The winning candidate was a European who spoke several languages, had married a fellow player, and had served as demi-pharaoh before: "Once again I offer my services to you all and still sincerely hope I never have to intervene in a single conflict. The ban stick never left my pocket, let's try to keep it that way!" The second-place candidate had also been demi-pharaoh before, but preferred to work cooperatively behind the scenes rather than acting as Egypt's policeman. The candidate who came in third made the strongest statement about the anti-griefer law, in so doing providing us with further insights:

I have been DP twice, in T5 and T6. In T6, I wrote Anti Griefer Act, which provided a mechanism to quickly and effectively ban the obvious griefer GeoDude and his alts. That law has been pass again this tale, as a result of the resurrection of GeoGuy. In T5, before I was DP, I wrote a law (approved by majority vote) that stripped a then-DP of his DP powers because he had abused those powers in banning players which whom he had a personal conflict, solely on the basis of that conflict. I think these two events reflect the balance that a DP must maintain. In the vast majority of situations, a DP ban is inappropriate. It is an act of last resort, when the behavior of a player is categorically and undisputably damaging to Egypt as a community. Behavior that is merely unpopular, 'jerky', or generally frowned upon is not ban-worthy. However, holding to the 'defend to the death your right to say unpopular stuff' idea does not mean that we are held hostage to behavior that is solely for the purpose of destruction. Decorating someone else's camp with flax beds and woodplanes is not 'a legitimate play style' or a reasonable means of self-expression in Egypt that we need to protect. I believe strongly in the right of each player to define their own experience in a way that is most meaningful to them. There are limits to this right, though, when a player's actions directly and significantly curtail someone else's ability to shape their own experience. The reality is, however, that ban-worthy levels of destructive behavior are rare. Most

[10] www.atitd.org/wiki/tale7/Test_of_the_Demipharaoh (accessed November 25, 2015).

often disputes arise as a result of differing perspective – in this context, a DP can be a voice of mediation, to help bring differing (yet independently reasonable) perspectives to a common ground.[11]

This candidate had also married a fellow player, one sign of how seriously players experience fellowship in *Tale*. While a study of one election in one small virtual community is insufficient to test a theory, it can be instructive to consider factors at work in this particular example. Candidate 3 certainly expressed herself eloquently, and had contributed to the welfare of Egypt in past tellings. But any Demi-Pharaoh could ban Geoguy, and indeed the winner did so immediately after taking office. Candidate 3 was a member of the reclusive Followers of Anubis group, although the one member who also belonged to two conventional guilds. To what extent were players influenced by guild membership in their voting? Table 10.4 suggests it was only to a moderate degree.

Table 10.4 lists all the guilds that any candidate belonged to, in the order of decreasing membership. We see that Candidate 2, who was friendly but did not say much in the debate, may have benefitted from belonging to the largest guild, zFree, which had also been a tremendously prominent guild in the previous telling. The tiny guild "atitd.org staff" to which Candidate 2 belonged, is the small group of players who manage the wiki that is so important to citizens of Egypt. Candidate 3 did not have large-guild support, and the focus on her work in banning griefers was appreciated but reminded voters of that unpleasant topic. The winning candidate belonged to two cosmopolitan guilds of moderate size, and two small ones of the kind usually set up for small groups of close friends.

10.10 Conclusion

A Tale in the Desert may be considered a virtual laboratory experiment in utopianism, using volunteer human subjects to develop and assess social norms and institutions that could be applied in the real world. Many other online games can be understood in this way, although often not as obvious in their utopianism as *Tale*. But there is a wholly different way to conceptualize virtual utopianism. Perhaps any stable modern society fulfills most citizens' needs adequately, if not perfectly, but resists radical improvement and prevents people from setting up separate communal experiments.

Thus, in modern societies, utopian movements must be structured as overlays that use conventional society as their basis, and build unusual social forms

---

[11] www.atitd.org/wiki/tale7/Demipharaoh_Debates/2015_10 (accessed November 25, 2015).

Table 10.4 *Guild Membership of the Seven Demi-Pharaoh Candidates in October 2015*

Guilds	Members	Candidates Identified by Place in the Final Vote						
		1	2	3	4	5	6	7
zFree	115		1					
Safari Club	110							1
Amigos	99						1	
7L Research	72				1		1	
The HIVE	59			1				
Midland Valley Research	39							1
Les Diamants du Nil	37	1			1			
Garden of Eden	33	1					1	
The Good Grub Pub	28		1	1				
Vigilant Visions	24						1	
Mt Doom Vineyards and Sandwichery	20					1		
Followers of Anubis	20			1				
Discordant Accordian	18					1		
Followers of Anubis Announce	15			1				
Nothingbutt's Hand	11		1					
atitd.org staff	6		1					
7L 4 Life	5	1						
Karkady Plantation	4	1					1	
Silver Phoenix	3							1
Blue Phoenix	2							1
We Don't Bite	2				1			

on top. One sometimes sees the expression "the veneer of civilization," implying that civilization is merely a superficial appearance of social order hiding the real ugliness of human nature. Setting aside the pessimism of that metaphor, we can conceptualize virtual utopias like *Tale* as *sociocultural veneers*, perhaps powerful in their ability to enhance the experience of human life, but not fully independent from conventional socioeconomic institutions.

References

Bainbridge, William Sims. (1978). *Satan's power: A deviant psychotherapy cult.* Berkeley, CA: University of California Press.

Bainbridge, William Sims. (2002). *The endtime family: Children of God.* Albany, NY: State University of New York Press.

Bainbridge, William Sims. (2007). The scientific research potential of virtual worlds. *Science*, 317, 472–476.

Bainbridge, William Sims. (2010). *The warcraft civilization: Social science in a virtual world*. Cambridge, MA: MIT Press.

Bainbridge, William Sims. (2011). *The virtual future*. London: Springer.

Bainbridge, William Sims. (2013a). *eGods: Faith versus fantasy in computer gaming*. New York, NY: Oxford University Press.

Bainbridge, William Sims. (2013b). The Iron Law. *Journal of Virtual Worlds Research*, 6(3).

Bainbridge, William Sims. (2014). *An information technology surrogate for religion: The veneration of deceased family members in online games*. New York, NY: Palgrave Macmillan.

Bainbridge, William Sims. (2016a). *Star worlds: Freedom versus control in online gameworlds*. Ann Arbor, MI: University of Michigan Press.

Bainbridge, William Sims. (2016b). *Virtual sociocultural convergence: Human sciences of computer games*. London: Springer.

Barthel, Diane L. (1984). *Amana: From pietist sect to American community*. Lincoln, NE: University of Nebraska Press.

Carden, Maren Lockwood. (1969). *Oneida: Utopian community to modern corporation*. Baltimore, MD: Johns Hopkins University Press.

Castronova, Edward. (2005). *Synthetic worlds: The business and culture of online gaming*. Chicago, IL: University of Chicago Press.

Castronova, Edward. (2007). *Exodus to the virtual world: How online fun is changing reality*. New York, NY: Palgrave Macmillan.

Durkheim, Emile. (1915). *The elementary forms of the religious life*. New York, NY: Free Press (1965).

Gardner, Hugh. (1978). *The children of prosperity: Thirteen modern American communes*. New York, NY: St. Martin's Press.

Geraci, Robert M. (2014). *Virtually sacred*. New York, NY: Oxford University Press.

Gibbs, Martin, Mori, Jopji, Arnold, Michael, & Kohn, Tamara. (2012). Tombstones, uncanny monuments and epic quests: Memorials in World of Warcraft. *Game Studies*, 12(1).

Goffman, Erving. (1961). *Encounters: Two studies in the sociology of Interaction – Fun in games & role distance*. Indianapolis, IN: Bobbs-Merrill.

Guarneri, Carl J. (1982). Importing Fourierism to America. *Journal of the History of Ideas*, 43(4), 581–594.

Heinlein, Robert A. (1951). *Between planets*. New York, NY: Scribner.

Houriet, Robert. (1971). *Getting back together*. New York, NY: Coward, McCann and Geoghegan.

Huntington, Samuel P. (1996). *The Clash of Civilizations and the remaking of world order*. New York, NY: Simon and Schuster.

Kamau, Lucy Jayne. (1992). The anthropology of space in Harmonist and Owenite New Harmony. *Communal Societies*, 12, 68–89.

Kanter, Rosabeth Moss. (1972). *Commitment and community: Communes and utopias in sociological perspective*. Cambridge, MA: Harvard University Press.

Michels, Robert. (1915). *Political parties*. New York, NY: Hearst's International Library.

More, Thomas. (1516). *Utopia*. London: Chiswell [English translation, 1685].

Moreno, Jacob L. (1944). Psychodrama and therapeutic motion pictures. *Sociometry*, 7(2), 230–244.

Moreno, Jacob L., & Toeman, Zerka. (1942). The group approach in psychodrama. *Sociometry*, 5(2): 191–195.

Nardi, Bonnie. (2010). *My life as a Night Elf priest: An anthropological account of World of Warcraft*. Ann Arbor, MI: University of Michigan Press.

Nordhoff, Charles. (1875). *The communistic societies of the United States*. London: John Murray.

Noyes, John Humphrey. (1870). *History of American socialisms*. Philadelphia, PA: Lippincott.

Palmer, Susan J. (2004). *Aliens adored: Rael's UFO religion*. New Brunswick, NJ: Rutgers University Press.

Parsons, Talcott. (1964). Evolutionary universals in society. *American Sociological Review*, 29, 339–357.

Pearce, Celia, & Artemesia. (2009). *Communities of play: Emergent cultures in multiplayer games and virtual worlds*. Cambridge, MA: MIT Press.

Rheingold, Howard. (1993). *The virtual community*. Reading, MA: Addison-Wesley.

Sicart, Miguel. (2009). *The ethics of computer games*. Cambridge, MA: MIT Press.

Stanislavski, Constantin. (1964). *An actor prepares*. New York, NY: Routledge.

Stark, Rodney, & Bainbridge, William Sims. (1987). *A theory of religion*. New York, NY: Peter Lang.

Stephan, Karen H., & Stephan, G. Edward. (1973). Religion and the survival of Utopian communities. *Journal for the Scientific Study of Religion*, 12, 89–100.

Timpone, Richard J. (1998). Structure, behavior, and voter turnout in the United States. *The American Political Science Review*, 92(1), 145–158.

Zablocki, Benjamin. (1980). *Alienation and charisma*. New York, NY: Free Press.

11

Gaming in Multicultural Classrooms: The Potential of Collaborative Digital Games to Foster Intercultural Interaction

AMANDA ALENCAR AND
TERESA DE LA HERA CONDE-PUMPIDO

11.1 Introduction

In most European countries, schools are facing increasing numbers of students with diverse migrant backgrounds (Organisation for Economic Co-operation and Development, 2014). Recent developments in school education highlight the importance of promoting intercultural awareness and competences among teachers, as well as recommendations of a curriculum reform that can meet the challenges of teaching for diversity in Europe (EU, 2007). In line with this, education scholars Severiens, Wolff, and van Herpen (2014) argue that the main obstacles faced by teachers in culturally diverse classrooms are the development of pupils' communication skills and the promotion of positive social interactions and cultural identity among migrant students. Hence, migrant children experiencing difficulties in terms of learning achievements are very often confronted with problems of adaptation, identity formation, and interaction with native as well as with other migrant children and even with teachers (Bruin, 1985).

Evidence of this relationship has been found in the study by Suárez-Orozco and Suárez-Orozco (2000), in which pupils involved with both the native society and the new host society are usually those to achieve better studying results and attain higher levels of social and language integration at schools. Similarly, the acculturation theory of Berry et al. (2006) argues that successful adaptation of migrant children at schools is correlated with their ability to engage in interactions with both native and migrant pupils. The importance of intercultural

This work is part of the research programme "Persuasive Gaming. From Theory-based Design to Validation and Back" with project number 314-99-106 which is (partly) financed by the Netherlands Organisation for Scientific Research (NWO). This study is also in collaboration with the Research Project "Television News for Promoting Interculturalism. A Novel Step towards Immigrant Integration" funded by the European Commission in the framework of Marie Curie Actions (327228-TVNPI).

interaction in multicultural classrooms is based on the students' ability to deal across cultures, which facilitates their development and integration within the group. According to intergroup contact theory (Pettigrew, 1998), there are four main conditions that may facilitate the opportunities for intercultural interaction: equal status, support from authorities, common goals, and cooperation. Intergroup contact theory suggests that the teaching/learning methods adopted in multicultural classrooms play a major role in providing the conditions for students to engage in intercultural contact situations (Pettigrew & Tropp, 2006). For instance, an intercultural approach to education has been widely connected to improvements in social interactions of pupils in culturally diverse educational settings, as it fosters the development of competencies, attitudes, and behaviors that allow for the understanding of different cultures, and the harmonious coexistence and cooperation among students representing this diversity (Schleicher, 2012; Severiens et al., 2014). In the context of intercultural education, cooperative learning (CL) is a learning method that employs Pettigrew's contact conditions and that has been proven to encourage cross-cultural interactions of pupils coming from different migrant backgrounds (see Coelho, 1994; Johnson & Johnson, 2002; Tielman et al., 2012).

Among the many forms of implementation of the cooperative learning method, the use of digital media technologies in the classroom has gained popularity because it facilitates acceptance by encouraging cooperative learning and equal communication opportunities by the users (O'Mara & Harris, 2014; Padilla Zea et al., 2009). In this study, we particularly focus on the potential of collaborative digital games to become an effective cooperative learning tool to achieve intercultural goals and contribute to the long-term social integration process of migrant children in multicultural schools.

Although previous research has widely claimed that digital games may foster social inclusion, the majority of expectations regarding the value of this type of intervention remain largely hypothetical as research on its effective impact is still currently lacking (Bleumers et al., 2012). More extensive research in this field is necessary to enable an appropriate implementation of playful interventions aimed to support at-risk communities, such as those formed by migrant children (Haché & Cullen, 2009). Previous studies have already explored the potential of digital games to foster multicultural integration (Kayali et al., 2011; Memarzia & Star, 2011). However, the analysis of the collaborative features of research-based games used in the context of these studies – *Choices and Voices* (Playgen, 2011) and *YourTurn* (2012) – was not supported by a theoretical framework that clearly connects the benefits of collaboration with intercultural interaction. This study provides a theoretical framework based on a new implementation of the cooperative learning method (Johnson & Johnson,

1999) in the analysis of collaborative digital games as a tool for encouraging positive intercultural interactions of pupils coming from different migrant backgrounds.

This chapter has been organized in the following way. It first gives an overview of the main obstacles of culturally diverse classrooms and the importance of intercultural contact for addressing cultural differences and improving collaboration and interaction. The second part analyzes the benefits of the collaborative learning method for promoting positive intercultural interactions as well as the limitations of the approach. It is then followed by a discussion of the potential of collaborative digital games as a cooperative learning activity in a multicultural context. Finally, the chapter summarizes the main concepts and issues addressed in the sections and suggests a few directions for validating the approach.

11.2 Dealing with Differences: The Challenges of Multicultural Classrooms

Newly arrived migrant children experience a very difficult period, where they have the hard task to adapt to a new cultural environment without relying on fundamental cultural and linguistic resources related to the integration in the new host country. In this moment of high vulnerability, school can play a crucial role in providing the foundations for the future process of integration (Chomentowski, 2009; Steinbach, 2010). With the growing cultural diversity in European educational settings, acculturation processes at schools have become more complex as well as "problems" associated to cultural essentialisms in everyday classroom practices (Tupas, 2014).

More broadly, obstacles regarding migrant children's adaptation to the school environment are defined in terms of interaction with teachers as well as with other pupils in the classroom. In the former case, limitations in the language of instruction affect the ways migrant pupils relate with teachers and participate in class activities. At the same time, poor interaction between students with diverse backgrounds may be due to a lack of communication skills among them. In that respect, Chamberlin-Quinlisk (2013) highlights the importance of using meaningful systems of communication (both verbal and nonverbal) that prompt teachers and students to engage effectively in diverse educational settings.

On the other hand, challenges can also be analyzed in terms of preparation for diversity teaching (Severiens et al., 2014). The theory "stereotype threat" of

Steele (1997) describes one of the main problems regarding the lack of teacher's training that affects students' performance in multicultural classrooms. The author argues that teachers' negative expectations of certain groups of pupils influence poor performance among these groups when this stereotype becomes explicit (e.g., mentioned by instructors). Teachers should have minimal knowledge of the cultural backgrounds of their students to avoid making negative assumptions and compromising the quality of their students' performance. By way of illustration, the study by den Brok and Levy (2005) carried out in multicultural schools in the United States, Australia, and the Netherlands revealed that teacher interpersonal behavior has significant implications for immigrant minority students' outcomes than for their native peers.

Similarly, cultural background influences the ways students perceive and interpret the learning environment (Coelho, 1998). In this sense, tensions among students are in most cases related to a lack of understanding of each other's culture and these intercultural conflicts represent a big challenge for teachers in multicultural classrooms. Several studies suggest that problems of school adjustment and sociocultural integration among immigrant children are usually associated with their different cultural background (Crul & Holdaway, 2009; Lenoir et al., 2008; Tielman et al., 2012). During their school attendance, learning and interaction difficulties such as increased egocentrism and negative relationships including hostility, rejection, stereotyping, prejudice, and racism may occur as the result of the highly variety of the characteristics, language skills, and cultural background of migrant children (Johnson & Johnson, 1999).

In culturally diverse classrooms, it is also common to observe the development of undesirable attitudes (in the form of prejudices) and behaviors (in the form of discrimination). When pupils express discriminatory statements, teachers usually react by using reliable information to try to change premature judgments. However, prejudices toward minority groups is a complex problem not caused just by a lack of information and undesirable attitudes, and it is evidence that behaviors hardly ever change by the influence of alternative information (Bruin, 1985, p. 162).

It follows that alternative teaching methods capable of dealing with highly diverse classrooms are fundamental to promote positive intercultural interaction among students (Schleicher, 2012; Severiens et al., 2014). Intercultural strategies for culturally diverse pupils in learning environments should be focused on the development of interventions that support positive social interaction that help to hinder cultural differences and protect cultural diversity, but at the same time foster the integration of immigrant children at schools.

11.3 The Relevance of Intercultural Contact

In a recent European Union report (EU, 2016) on the increasing importance of promoting active educational settings that can potentially establish inclusiveness and collaborative communities, it was noted that the growing cultural diversity in European societies is not well reflected in their educational systems. This concern is echoed in the "EACEA, Eurydice" report (EU, 2004), in which special attention is given to the need for developing teaching methods that rely more and more on intercultural interactions through the promotion of teamwork, collaborative learning, and peer learning.

In this context, one of the most referred to intercultural mechanisms, highlighted by previous research, is intergroup contact theory (Pettigrew, 1998). In general, the conventional wisdom in this literature is that contact between immigrant and nonimmigrant children, especially close/friendship contact, helps in reducing prejudices, boosts mutual interests, and creates a more intercultural society with intercultural societal interests (Pettigrew & Tropp, 2006). Several authors have defended the view that knowing the "others," especially those from a different culture, leads to a fading away of prejudices, false opinions, or biased perceptions (e.g., Berry et al., 2006; Ward, 2013). Intergroup contact theory is particularly relevant for this study because it places great emphasis on the role of the educational context in providing the conditions that can potentially lead to positive cross-cultural interactions of children with diverse migrant backgrounds (Sleeter, 2013). In a study conducted by Stefanek, Strohmeier, and van de Schoot (2015) with nonimmigrant, Turkish, and former Yugoslavian immigrant youths, the authors argue about the importance of encouraging intercultural friendships in multicultural schools, as these friendships can enhance social and intercultural competencies, promote social and language integration, and create an environment free from stereotypes and discrimination.

Intergroup contact theory asserts that the friendship potential of a contact situation is determined by relevant conditions, such as intergroup cooperation and common goals between children belonging to different cultural groups (Pettigrew & Tropp, 2006). Both conditions can be fostered with the implementation of intercultural educational approaches. Such approaches are designed to integrate learning about other cultures, races, and ethnicities as part of educational instructional processes while at the same time making use of cooperative learning activities in which immigrant and nonimmigrant children have to work together to achieve a common goal (EU, 2004). In this sense, the adoption of a learning orientation has found to be useful for promoting positive intercultural interactions. For example, Migacheva and Tropp (2013) showed that individuals' primary motivation to learn new skills and capabilities as well as to enhance their knowledge is strongly correlated with their willingness to embrace intergroup contact with people from a different culture.

On the other hand, the extended model of Pettigrew's intergroup contact theory (2008) also takes into account the cultural diversity of the student body as one of the conditions to create opportunities for intercultural contact (Stefanek et al., 2015). Previous research has found that students have more chances to establish cross-cultural interactions in classes where more culturally diverse peers are present (Hallinan and Teixeira, 1987). Finally, the extended model argues that support from authorities is essential in this context. For instance, school training programs to increase the capacity of teachers to use interactive methodologies to engage pupils and at the same time to offer them a safe space for exercising their acquired intercultural competencies can function properly when these programs are implemented by the educational system.

In line with intercultural education, the cooperative learning method has gained fresh prominence among education scholars as a device for managing diversity in multicultural classrooms (Johnson & Johnson, 2002; Tielman et al., 2012). The link between IE and Cooperative Learning (CL) is evident due to their mutual interest in developing school practices that foster collaboration and integration among students in various educational contexts. The following section provides an in-depth discussion of how the cooperative learning approach utilizes the contact conditions of intergroup cooperation and common goals to support learning and cross-cultural interactions through repeated and extensive exchange among children from different cultures. The implications of scarce educational policies encouraging the use of the cooperative method in heterogeneous classrooms are also discussed both in terms of adequate training for teaching diversity and communication problems in multicultural classes.

11.4 A Cooperative Approach to Intercultural Interaction in Culturally Diverse Classrooms

As previously stated, the cooperative learning method has gained special relevance in the field of multicultural education, owing to its capacity to facilitate positive intercultural interaction. In this section, we draw on previous research on cooperative learning to argue about the potential of this method to foster the four main conditions that may facilitate the opportunities for intercultural interaction according to intergroup contact theory (Pettigrew, 1998): equal status, support from authorities, common goals, and cooperation. Furthermore, we reflect on the benefits and issues related to the use of this learning method in culturally diverse classrooms.

Cooperative learning is a learning methodology in which students share common goals that should be achieved together as a group. Cooperative learning fosters promotive interaction in comparison to individualistic and competitive learning approaches, usually prioritized as student–student inter-active patterns in educational settings, which consecutively promote no interaction and oppositional interaction (Deutsch, 1949). It follows that when individualistic efforts are fostered, no interdependence is created among goal achievements, and students do not relate their achievements to the per-formance of other students in the class. Furthermore, when competition is encouraged, students perceive their success as related to other students' fail or poor performance. In comparison, students involved in cooperative learning realize that they can only achieve their goals if other students in the class also do so (Johnson & Johnson, 2002). Thus cooperative learning is a learning methodology promoted and supervised by schools and educators, who may be considered the *authorities* in Pettigrew's (1998) terminology, and that encompasses students with *equal status* involved in an activity in which they have to *cooperate* to achieve *common goals*.

11.4.1 Benefits of Cooperative Learning in Culturally Diverse Classrooms

The social psychologists David W. Johnson and Roger Johnson have exten-sively explored the potential of the cooperative learning method in respect to different learning goals and environments (1988, 1989, 1994, 2002), including research on the benefits of this learning method in culturally diverse classrooms (1988). The authors have found that when compared to individualistic and com-petitive experiences, students involved in cooperative experiences seem to be more positive about each other regardless of differences in ethnic background (1988). Students also seem to be more effective interpersonally as a result of working together when cooperative interactive patterns are used (1988, para. 13). Furthermore, when collaborating, students seem to better develop their interaction skills, and have a more positive expectation about working with oth-ers than students from competitive or individualistic settings (1988, para. 14). By sharing common goals, students develop a sense of identity and belonging to the learning group that positively contributes to their interaction and reduces stereotypical visions about their peers (Coelho, 1998).

Johnson and Johnson (1994) also found that when cooperative interaction is fostered, it can facilitate positive outcomes related to learning in a multicultural environment, such as increased achievement and productivity, creative problem solving, growth in cognitive and moral reasoning, increased perspective-taking ability, improved relationships, and general sophistication in interacting and working with peers from a variety of cultural and ethnic backgrounds. The authors have identified five collaborative components that should be encouraged to foster the positive effects of collaborative interaction in multicultural classrooms (2002):

1. *Positive interdependence:* This happens when collaborating students are aware that their success is linked not only to their own performance, but also to the performance of their peers. This means that they acknowledge that they can benefit from their partners' performance, and that their success benefits not only themselves, but also their peers. Activities that foster positive interdependence help students to understand the personal benefits of collaborating with others and that an egocentric behavior is not always beneficial. In multicultural classrooms, students involved in cooperative experiences understand the value of people who are different from them because other participants become potential contributors to individual's success. Cultural diversity means that different ways of reasoning are brought together to contribute to achieve the common goal. In this sense, all individuals are valued regardless of their ethnic membership or their cultural background (Johnson & Johnson, 2002; Tielman et al., 2012).

2. *Individual accountability:* It takes place in situations in which all participants find a way to contribute either with their personal knowledge or personal skills. Individual accountability not only facilitates students learning to give value to their own skills, but also fosters empathy with other participants. Students participating in activities that encourage individual accountability benefit from others' personal knowledge, which helps them to acknowledge the value of cultural diversity.

3. *Face-to-face promotive interaction:* This cooperative component arises when students are involved in activities that encourage them to share their knowledge or discuss different points of view in order to achieve their goals. When sharing common goals, participants get emotionally involved in promoting the progress of their partners, which encourages them to help others by orally explaining how to solve problems or teaching their own skills. Activities that foster face-to-face promotive interaction are an opportunity to discover together how the different ways in which different cultures interpret a specific situation can complement each other and can contribute to achieve certain goals together (Johnson & Johnson, 2002).

4. *Social skills:* This is produced when in collaborative sessions students need to use their social skills in order to achieve their goals. Skills such

as leadership, conflict management, trust building, and decision making are of special value in collaborative activities. Cooperative activities that include challenges in which different types of skills are needed to achieve common goals become a tool to overcome stereotyping and prejudice in multicultural education environments (Johnson & Johnson, 1999).

5. *Group processing (self-analysis of the group):* According to Johnson and Johnson (2002) when students are encouraged to reflect together on the outcomes of a collaborative learning session to discuss whether their working relationships were effective and if they were able to achieve their goals, this can report extra positive outcomes to the activity.

Table 11.1 provides a summary of the five fundamental characteristics that improve learning and collaboration and the benefits of each collaborative component for intercultural interactions.

11.4.2 Issues of Cooperative Learning in Culturally Diverse Classrooms

The positive effects of cooperative interaction for multicultural groups of students depend on the important conditions within the educational context. Some researchers have pointed at some barriers that can limit the effectiveness of promotive interaction. On the one hand, previous research shows that cooperative learning practices when implemented by teachers usually do not meet the five conditions identified by Johnson and Johnson (2002). Fewer than half of the teachers implementing these practices are usually trained in cooperative learning methods, and only a few of them have been trained to use them in a multicultural classroom (Baker & Clark, 2010, p. 4). The lack of training of teachers might result in poor cooperative experiences that might not deliver the expected results.

Furthermore, cooperative learning requires language competence. To be able to contribute to the achievement of the common goals, students need to be able to communicate efficiently (Hijzen, 2006). However, in multicultural classrooms, students have different levels of language competence. In a study conducted by Tielman et al. (2012) in which the authors tested the effectiveness of collaborative learning activities in a secondary vocational school in the Netherlands, it was found that the vulnerability of migrant students regarding language proficiency compared to Dutch native students might prevent the formation of promotive interaction among them. Language difficulties can create difficulties related to two of the five components identified by Johnson and Johnson (1994) as relevant to achieve effective cooperation: face-to-face

Table 11.1 *Characteristics and benefits of collaborative learning practices*

Five components	Characteristics	Benefits
Positive interdependence	Collaborating students depend on each other's performance to achieve successful results.	Collaborating students can understanding how students from different cultures can help one achieve individual success.
Individual accountability	All collaborating students can offer insights and benefit from each other's personal skills.	Collaborating students can empathize with other participants and acknowledge and value their individual skills.
Face-to-face promotive interaction	Collaborating students share their knowledge and help each other by providing different perspectives on the task.	Collaborative students promote their own interpersonal skills by getting involved in each other's progress in the task.
Social skills	Collaborating students are able to use their leadership skills.	Collaborating students have the opportunity to manage intercultural conflicts and develop their communication skills and values of trust in the decision-making processes.
Group processing	Collaborating students become self-consciousness of the effectiveness of their work as a group.	Collaborating students develop their own abilities and become more committed to achieve common goals.

interaction and the use of relevant interpersonal and small-group skills. For this reason, language difficulties can become a barrier for efficient promotive interaction (Baker & Clark, 2010; Coelho, 1994; Tielman et al., 2012).

There are also dangers related to the formation of what Johnson and Johnson (1998) call "pseudo groups," defined as groups in which members that have been assigned to work together do not have interest in doing so. This can lead to students that divide up the work that has been assigned to a whole group, or groups in which one student or some of them, take the lead and do the work for all of them. In the context of multicultural classrooms, the cultural background of students also affects the proper functioning of collaborative groups. Tielman et al. (2012) stated that intercultural conflicts often emerge within groups formed by Dutch native students and students from diverse migrant background.

It follows that, although cooperative learning practices have the potential of having positive effects when used in multicultural educational settings to foster intercultural interaction of students, there are also a series of difficulties linked to this practice that need to be overcome to achieve the expected results. The following section provides a detailed description of how the use of collaborative digital games may offer the conditions to promote positive intercultural interactions as well as to overthrow some of the limitations of the collaborative approach.

11.5 Collaborative Digital Games for Intercultural Interaction

In this section we claim that collaborative digital games are able to encourage cooperative interaction and accordingly, might become a useful cooperative learning tool to foster intercultural interaction among players with diverse cultural backgrounds. Furthermore, we also claim that the interactive nature of digital games and their capacity to adjust the experience and provide feedback based on players' performances become relevant characteristics when used with this purpose, because they have the potential to help overcome the difficulties associated to cooperative learning practices, such as lack of training of teachers, language difficulties, and lack of motivation of students. These claims are based on the unique potential of digital games to engage people in collaborative activities via two basic functions: their potential to be used as tools and as social facilitators for persuasion (see Fogg, 2003). In their role as tools, digital games can be designed to influence and motivate people in specific ways by making activities easier or more efficient to do (Fogg, 2003, p. 24). Furthermore, in their role as social facilitators, digital games can be used to encourage social interaction by affording communication among players (p. 89).

Collaborative digital games are digital games in which "all the participants work together as a team, sharing the payoffs and outcomes; if the team wins or loses, everyone wins or loses" (Zagal, Rick, & Hsi, 2006). Within the game "a team is an organization in which the kind of information each person has can differ, but the interests and beliefs are the same" (Marschak in Zagal et al., 2006). A good example of collaborative digital games is the saga *Little Big*

Table 11.2 *Affordances of collaborative games in relation to cooperative learning components*

Five components	Affordances in Collaborative Games
Positive interdependence	All participants work together as a team. Players share the play-offs and outcomes. Affords team unity.
Individual accountability	Bestow different abilities upon players.
Face-to-face promotive interaction	Players have to coordinate their actions and strategies. Offer communication flexibility. Support conflict resolution and group decision making.
Social skills	Bestow different responsibilities upon players.
Group processing	Can incorporate group awareness tools.

Planet. The gameplay consists primarily, but not entirely, of platforming like jumping and avoiding obstacles to successfully navigate to the end of a level to win. The game involves a player playing in collaboration with other players to navigate through a level while collecting various "bubbles" along the way. There are also numerous collaborative parts of levels whereby certain prize bubbles can be collected only with the help of at least one player or more depending on the number of players stated in the level.

Although digital games have the potential to foster colocated and virtual non-colocated collaboration, we focus on games played synchronically by all players at the same location as the most effective way to elicit intercultural interaction in education environments. Colocated collaborative games have been shown to enhance social engagement and group cohesiveness and strengthen bonds among group players (Isbister, 2010).

To support our claim that collaborative digital games can be used as a tool to foster positive intercultural interaction, in this section we discuss in which ways they are able to elicit the five collaborative components described by Johnson and Johnson (1999), which enhances the positive outcomes related to learning in a multicultural environment. These are summarized in Table 11.2.

1. *Positive interdependence.* Collaborative games can foster positive interdependence by establishing a common goal for all players, which may help the group bond as players share in their success or failure together, including a "group life" system to achieve team accountability, establishing an evaluation process on the group rather than on each player and/or providing a player score and a group score (Padilla Zea et al., 2009). Furthermore,

digital games can include affordances "for players to have a proper sense of the team utility of certain actions" (Zagal et al., 2006, 36).

2. *Individual accountability.* Collaborative games usually "bestow different abilities upon the players" (Zagal et al., 2006, p. 37). Collaborative games can foster individual accountability by balancing players' activities in a hidden way in order to help participants with difficulties (Padilla Zea et al., 2008).

3. *Face-to-face promotive interaction.* Communication is of particular importance to a collaborative game, as players have to coordinate their actions and strategy (Zagal et al., 2006, p. 35). Sharing their knowledge, discussing different points of view and orally teaching their own skills become essential to progress in the game (Padilla Zea et al., 2008). Moreover, digital games offer communication flexibility (Zagal et al., 2006, 35) and this allows them to support conflict resolution and group decision making in ways that might be superior to face-to-face discussions (Nuñez, Aguero, & Olivares, 1998).

4. *Social skills.* Collaborative games also bestow different responsibilities on the players (Zagal et al., 2006, p. 37). Players of collaborative games must organize their tasks and make decisions that help them show, by instance, their leadership and conciliation abilities (Padilla Zea et al., 2008).

5. *Group processing* (self-analysis of the group). A group analysis of the gaming session allows examining the effectiveness of each player's contribution and how targets are being achieved. This could be a useful way to enforce an individual player's abilities and enhance the group commitment to common targets (Padilla Zea et al., 2008). A study conducted by Usart, Romero, and Almirall (2011) reported that dyads playing collaborative games incorporating knowledge group awareness tools were effective in encouraging out-of-game conversations among players. Furthermore, group discussion on individual feelings of knowledge increased feeling of another's' knowledge (2011, p. 33), which can be a useful way to overcome stereotyping and prejudice in multicultural education environments (Johnson & Johnson, 1999).

11.6 Overcoming Cooperative Learning Practices' Barriers

Up to this point we have discussed how digital games are able to elicit the five components of collaborative learning identified by Johnson and Johnson (1999). This serves to support our claim that collaborative games have the potential to foster positive intercultural interaction. This also may serve to overcome the first barrier associated to the use of cooperative learning practices:

the lack of training of teachers. Using the game as a mediating tool, teachers can promote intercultural interaction meeting the guidelines proposed by Johnson and Johnson, even when they were not specially trained on how to effectively enhance promotive interaction.

Besides this, collaborative digital games used as mediation tool to foster intercultural integration have also the potential to prevent the dangers related to the formation of "pseudo groups," defined as groups in which members who have been assigned to work together do not have interest in doing so. To this respect, digital games may incorporate small persuasive elements, called *microsuasive* elements, to motivate players to engage with an experience, complete certain tasks, gain better understanding of specific material, and/or stay on task longer (see Fogg, 2003). Microsuasive persuasive techniques implemented within collaborative digital games can therefore help to overcome the difficulties related to the lack of motivation of some participants (Baker & Clark, 2010).

Furthermore, in digital games players can be equally represented via their avatars. Players can control an avatar of any gender, age, race, and species that do not necessarily represent their physical attributes or identity (Blascovich & Bailenson, 2012), which is a way to leave outside the gaming experience players' differences that are usually related to stereotyping, prejudice, and/or racism.

The wide range of player-to-player forms of communication provide collaborative digital games with the potential to help players to overcome the difficulties associated with the lack of language competences while playing. Digital games have the potential to foster different forms of player-to-player communication that go beyond face-to-face language communication. On the top level we can differentiate between in-game communication and out-of-game communication, and both can consist of forms of communication different from language (Wiklund, 2005). On the one hand, out-of-game communication can happen while playing and/or after playing, and it may take the form of verbal communication and nonverbal communication including gestures, paralanguage, and the nonverbal part of speech. On the other hand, in-game communication includes in-character and out-character communication. In-character communication occurs while players act their own characters' personality in the game, and can consist of verbal interaction with other characters, but also nonverbal interaction with other characters at the game space. Players with low language skills can make use of in and out-of-game nonverbal communication to interact with each other.

An example of how a game can foster in-game nonverbal social interaction as a way to overcome language barriers is the game *Ghost in the Cave*

Table 11.3 *Overcoming collaborative games practices' barriers*

Barriers	Collaborative Games
Lack of teachers training	All participants work together as a team. Players share the play-offs and outcomes. Affords team unity.
Formation of "pseudo groups"	Implementation of microsuasive techniques to increase motivation. Players are equally represented in games.
Language barriers	Wide range of player-to-player forms of communication.

(KTH, 2004). In this game participants are encouraged to communicate using nonverbal emotional expressions. Players, who work as a team, control their avatars by singing or moving in front of a video camera (Rinman et al., 2004). This game explores a new form of in-game communication that illustrates how in-character nonverbal communication can be used as a form to foster social interactions among players who struggle with language barriers.

Table 11.3 summarizes ways in which barriers to collaborative games practices can be overcome.

11.7 Conclusions and Directions for Further Research

The main goal of the current study was to explore how collaborative digital games can be used to foster positive intercultural interactions by eliciting the benefits of the cooperative learning method as described by Johnson and Johnson (2002) and by helping to overcome the barriers associated with this method when applied in multicultural classrooms. The first section of the chapter provided an overview of the main challenges of culturally diverse educational settings, underpinning the importance of implementing teaching strategies that can address the problem of intercultural conflicts and foster positive interactions among pupils.

In the second section, we used the mechanisms of the intergroup contact theory to support the implementation of collaborative teaching methods in accord with the main objectives of European intercultural education (Bleszynska, 2008). Analyzing the role of the educational context through the lens of intergroup contact theory was essential to understand the importance of social interactions for enhancing intercultural competence, mitigating conflicts stirred by cultural differences, and fostering long-term processes of language and social integration among pupils in culturally diverse educational settings.

When discussing the conditions provided by collaborative learning approaches for promoting positive intercultural interactions, Johnson and Johnson's (2002) five collaborative components were presented as the main characteristics that elicit the positive effects of collaborative practices in multicultural classrooms. The limitations of the approach were argued in terms of insufficient qualified teachers, language difficulties among pupils with diverse migrant backgrounds, and the dynamics of group collaboration. These issues have already been addressed by a number of researchers who have reported that the level of teacher's preparation, the type of task and the group's cultural diversity composition will play a major role in the efficiency of cooperative learning practices (Severiens et al., 2014; Steele, 1997; Tielman et al., 2012).

The main contribution of this chapter is to propose a theoretical framework for the analysis and implementation of collaborative gaming practices for positive intercultural interaction. This theoretical framework is grounded on the cooperative learning method's benefits and barriers, and the potential of collaborative digital games to foster the former and overcome the latter. To support our claims, we discussed how collaborative digital games can promote intercultural interactions of pupils belonging to different cultures and to overcome limitations of the method. The ways in which video games support the development of collaborative behavior among players were directly related to the intercultural potential of the gaming activity. Several mechanisms of the game can be used as way to solve problems associated with the cooperative approach, and most of them have been already tested in other fields.

First, the capacity of collaborative games to promote positive interdependence was linked to common goals established for all players in the game and the inclusion of a "group life" system. Second, we have also discussed how players of collaborative games can use their unique skills to contribute to the solutions of challenges in the game, arousing individual accountability. Third, we have reflected on the relevance of player-to-player communication within collaborative games as a key feature to achieve common goals, and how this elicits face-to-face promotive interaction. Fourth, we have discussed how the different tasks that need to be accomplished within collaborative games help players to show the value or their unique social skills, such as leadership or conciliation abilities. Finally, we have highlighted in which ways collaborative games that include knowledge group awareness tools can effectively promote group processing of the gaming session.

The main value of collaborative digital games as a tool to foster intercultural interaction lies not only in their capacity to promote the benefits associated with cooperative learning practices, but also in their potential to overcome the barriers associated with these practices when implemented in multicultural settings. In this respect, we have discussed that by using collaborative games as a mediating tool, teachers can promote intercultural interaction meeting the guidelines proposed by Johnson and Johnson (2002) even when they do not have specific training on this learning method, which has been referred to as one of the main barriers associated with cooperative learning. Moreover, we have discussed how collaborative digital have also the potential to prevent the negative effects that the formation of "pseudo groups" may cause, by the use of microsuasive strategies focused on motivating players to engage with the experience and complete specific tasks within the game.

Furthermore, we have reflected on how the representation of players via their avatars within the game may serve to leave outside the experience players' differences that are usually related to stereotyping, prejudice and/or racism. Besides this, we have also discussed how the wide range of player-to-player forms of communication provided by collaborative digital games may help players to overcome the difficulties associated to the lack of language competences while playing.

The scope of this study was limited in terms of empirical research. Further work is required to study the viability of the use of video games in multicultural educational settings. In terms of directions for future research, further work should assess the impact of the approach in culturally diverse classrooms with students coming from at least five diverse cultural backgrounds. As addressed by previous research, high cultural diversity in classrooms increases the chances of intercultural contact, as it promotes more diversity in cooperation skills (Tielman et al., 2012). Also, equal-status interactions in terms of cultural background of the pupils playing the game should be implemented. The propensity of intercultural interactions is higher when both players belong to different cultures and fair equally in terms of acculturation needs. Also, it is important to carefully observe the collaborating students while playing the game. The sessions should be videotaped and notes should be taken by the researchers on their impressions of the environment and how the players behave during the game activity. Finally, the analysis of longer periods allows for investigating the evolution of interactions among pupils. At the same time, it is recommended to interview teachers involved in the task in order to have not only their perception of the collaborative process during the game activities, but also to describe their impression of their students' behavioral patterns (den Brok & Levy, 2005). Last but not least, ensuring appropriate instruction for student teachers before the gaming collaborative activities begin should be a priority for the validity and success of empirical trials.

European policies have long been emphasizing the implementation of inter-cultural policies to deal with cultural diversity in education, but little evidence on the effectiveness of the intercultural model has been proved. The increasing growth of multicultural societies in Europe as well as the decline of assimilation mechanisms associated with immigration discourses in various European countries are key factors that will impact the development of educational frameworks integrating a diverse range of ethnic groups. A key policy priority should therefore be to plan for the short-term implementation of innovative teaching/learning approaches to tackle the problems deriving from cultural diversity in educational environments. Our study concludes by claiming that the use of digital collaborative videogames has the potential to be one of these practices.

References

Asher, S. A., MacEvoy, J. P., & McDonald, K. L. (2008). Children's peer relations, social competence, and school adjustment: A social tasks and social goals perspective. In M. L. Maehr, S. Karabenick, & T. Urdan (eds.), *Advances in motivation and achievement*. Amsterdam: Elsevier.

Bailenson, J. N., Beall, A. C., Loomis, J., Blascovich, J., & Turk, M. (2004). Transformed social interaction: Decoupling representations from behavior and form in collaborative virtual environments. *Presence: Teleoperators and Virtual Environments*, 13(4), 428–441.

Baker, T., & Clark, J. (2010). Cooperative learning – A double-edged sword: A cooperative learning model for use with diverse student groups. *Intercultural Education*, 21(3), 257–68.

Banks, M. (2012). *Collocated multiplayer games and social interaction* (doctoral dissertation). London: University College London.

Baumann, G. (1999). *The multicultural riddle: Rethinking national, ethnic, and religious identities*. New York, NY: Psychology Press.

Berry, J. W., Phinney, J. S., Sam, D. L., & Vedder, P. (2006). Immigrant youth: Acculturation, identity, and adaptation. *Applied Psychology*, 55(3), 303–332.

Blascovich, J., & Bailenson, J. (2012). *Infinite reality: The hidden blueprint of our virtual lives*. New York, NY: HarperCollins.

Bleszynska, K. M. (2008). Constructing intercultural education. *Intercultural Education*, 19(6), 537–545.

Bleumers, L., All, A., Mariën, I., Schurmans, D., Van Looy, J., Jacobs, A., Willaert, K., & De Grove, F. (2012). In J. Stewart (ed.), *State of play of digital games for empowerment and inclusion: A review of literature and empirical cases*. JRC-IPTS Technical Report, Joint Research Centre; 2012. JRC77655. Retrieved from: http://ipts.jrc.ec.europa.eu/publications/pub.cfm?id=5819 (accessed July 18, 2016).

Brennen, B. S. (2013). Interviewing. In *Qualitative research methods for media studies* (pp. 26–58). New York, NY: Routledge.

Bruin, K. (1985). Prejudices, discrimination, and simulation/gaming: An analysis. *Simulation & Gaming*, 16(2), 161–173.

Chamberlin-Quinlisk, C. (2013). Media, technology, and intercultural education. *Intercultural Education*, 24(4), 297–302.

Chomentowski, M. (2009). *L'échec scolaire des enfants de migrants: L'illusion de l'égalité*. Paris: L'Harmattan.

Coelho, E. (1994). *Learning together in the multicultural classroom*. Markham, Ontario: Pippin Publishing.

Coelho, E. (1998). *Teaching and learning in multicultural schools: An integrated approach*, Vol. 13. Bristol: Multilingual Matters.

Cohen, L., Manion, L., & Morrison, K. (2000). *Research methods in education*. New York, NY: Routledge.

Côté, J. E. (1996). Sociological perspectives on identity formation: The culture–identity link and identity capital. *Journal of Adolescence*, 19(5), 417–428.

Crul, M., & Holdaway, J. (2009). Children of immigrants in schools in New York and Amsterdam: The factors shaping attainment. *The Teachers College Record*, 111(6), 1476–1507.

den Brok, P., & Levy, J. (2005). Teacher–student relationships in multicultural classes: Reviewing the past, preparing the future. *International Journal of Educational Research*, 43(1), 72–88.

Deutsch, M. (1949). A theory of cooperation and competition. *Human Relations*, 2, 129–152.

De Weyer, T., Robert, K., Hariandja, J. R. O., Alders, G., & Coninx, K. (2011). The social maze: A collaborative game to motivate MS patients for upper limb training. In M. Herrlich, R. Malaka, & M. Masuch (eds.), *ICEC 2012* (pp. 476–479). Laxenburg, Austria: International Federation for Information Processing.

Dusi, P., Messetti, G., & Falcón, I. G. (2015). Belonging: Growing up between two worlds. *Procedia-Social and Behavioral Sciences*, 171, 560–568.

EU. (2007). Report of the peer learning activity, Oslo May 2007. How can teacher education and training policies prepare teachers to teach effectively in culturally diverse classrooms? Education and Training 2010 programme, cluster Teachers and Trainers. Directorate General for Education and Culture, Lifelong Learning: Education and Training Policies, School Education and High Education.

EU. (2016). Education to foster intercultural understanding and solidarity in Europe. Retrieved from: www.eucis-lll.eu/eucis-lll/wp-content/uploads/2016/01/lllplatform_policy-paper_education-to-foster-intercultural-dialogue_jan.pdf (accessed January 20, 2016).

Eurydice. (2004) Integrating immigrant children into schools in Europe. Retrieved from: www.indire.it/lucabas/lkmw_file/eurydice///Integrating_immigrant_children_2004_EN.pdf (accessed July 4, 2015).

Fogg, B. J. (2003). *Persuasive technology: Using computers to change what we think and do*. San Francisco, CA: Morgan Kaufmann.

Gee, J. P. (2004). *Situated language and learning: A critique of traditional schooling*. London: Routledge.

González Sánchez, J. L., Cabrera, M., & Gutiérrez, F. L. (2007). Diseño de Videojuegos aplicados a la Educación Especial. In *Proceedings of eighth congreso internacional de interacción persona*, Ordenador, Zaragoza, Spain.

Gorard, S., & Taylor, C. (2004). *Combining methods in educational and social research*. London: Open University Press.

Haché, A., & Cullen, J. (2009). *ICT and youth at risk: How ICT-driven initiatives can contribute to their socio-economic inclusion and how to measure it*. Sevilla,

Spain: European Commission, Joint Research Centre (JRC), Institute for Prospective Technological Studies (IPTS).

Hallinan, Maureen T., & Teixeira, Ruy A. (1987). Opportunities and constraints: Black–white differences in the formation of interracial friendships. *Child Development*, 58(5), 1358–1371.

Hijzen, D. (2006). *Students' goal preferences, ethnocultural background and the quality of cooperative learning in secondary vocational education.* Leiden: Leiden University, Educational Sciences, Faculty of Social and Behavioural Sciences.

Hung, C.-Y. (2007). Video games in context: An ethnographic study of situated meaning-making practices of Asian immigrant adolescents. Paper presented at the *Situated Play. DiGRA 2007 International Conference*, Tokyo, Japan.

Isbister, K. (2010). Enabling social play: A framework for design and evaluation. In Evaluating user experience in games (pp. 11–22). Human-Computer Interaction Series. New York, NY: Springer Science+Business Media.

Johnson, D. W., & Johnson, R. (1989). *Cooperation and competition: Theory and research.* Edina, MN: Interaction Book Company.

Johnson, D. W., & Johnson, R. (1994). Learning together. In S. Sharan, (ed.), *Handbook of cooperative learning methods* (pp. 115–133). Westport, CT: Greenwood Press.

Johnson, D. W., & Johnson, R. (1999). Cooperative learning, values, and culturally plural classrooms. In M. Leicester, C. Modgill, & S. Modgil (eds.), *Values, the classroom, and cultural diversity* (pp. 15–28). London: Cassell PLC.

Johnson, D. W., & Johnson, R. (2002). Learning together and alone: An overview. In S. Sharan (Guest Editor), *Cooperative learning. Asia Pacific Journal of Education*, 22(1), 95–105

Johnson, R. T., & Johnson, D. W. (1988). Cooperative learning: Two heads learn better than one. *Transforming education: In context*; 18:34. Retrieved from: www.context .org/ICLIB/IC18/Johnson.htm (accessed January 20, 2016).

Kayali, F., Schwarz, V., Götzenbrucker, G., Purgathofer, P., Franz, B., & Pfeffer, J. (2011). Serious beats: Transdisciplinary research methodologies for designing and evaluating a socially integrative serious music-based online game. Paper presented to the DiGRA 2011 Conference "Think Design Play," Utrecht, the Netherlands.

KTH. (2004*). Ghost in the Cave* [collaborative game].

Lenoir, A., Lenoir, Y., Pudelko, B., & Steinback, M. (2008). Le discours québécois sur les relations entre l'école et les familles issues de l'immigration: Un état de la question. *Les Dossiers des Sciences de l:éducation*, 19, 171–190.

McFarlane, A., Sparrowhawk, A., & Heald, Y. (2002). Report on the educational use of games; 2002. Retrieved from: www.teem.org.uk/publications/teem_gamesined_ full.pdf (accessed January 20, 2016).

Media Molecule. (2015). *Little Big Planet 3* [console game].

Memarzia, M., & Star, K. (2011). Choices and voices: A serious game for preventing violent extremism. In B. Akhgar & S. Yates (eds.), *Intelligence management knowledge driven frameworks for combating terrorism and organized crime.* London: Springer

Migacheva, K., & Tropp, L. R. (2013). Learning orientation as a predictor of positive intergroup contact. *Group Processes & Intergroup Relations*, 16, 426–444.

Norman, Donald A. (1999). Affordance, conventions, and design. *Interactions* 6 (3), 38–43.

Nuñez, G., Aguero, U., & Olivares, C. (1998). Group decision-making for collaborative educational games. Paper presented at the *4th International Workshop on Groupware (CRIWG 98)*, Buzios Brasil.

Nussbaum, M., Rosas, R., Rodríguez, P., Sun, Y., & Valdivia, V. (1999). Diseño desarrollo y evaluación de video juegos portátiles educativos y autorregulados. *Ciencia al Día*, 3(2), 1.

Ohinata, A., & Van Ours, J. C. (2013). How immigrant children affect the academic achievement of native Dutch children. *The Economic Journal*, 123(570), F308–F331.

O'Mara, B., & Harris, A. (2014). Intercultural crossings in a digital age: ICT pathways with migrant and refugee-background youth. *Race Ethnicity and Education*, 19(3), 639–658.

Osterman, K. F. (2010). Teacher practice and students' sense of belonging. In *International research handbook on values education and student wellbeing* (pp. 239–260). Dordrecht: Springer.

Padilla Zea, N., González Sánchez, J. L., Gutiérrez Vela, F. L., Cabrera, M., & Paderewski, P. (2009). Design of educational multiplayer videogames: A vision from collaborative learning. *Advances in Engineering Software*, 40, 1241–1260.

Pettigrew, T. F. (1998). Intergroup contact theory. *Annual Review of Psychology*, 49(1), 65–85.

Pettigrew, T. F. (2008). Future directions for intergroup contact theory and research. *International Journal of Intercultural Relations*, 32(3), 187–199.

Pettigrew, T. F., & Tropp, L. R. (2006). A meta-analytic test of intergroup contact theory. *Journal of Personality and Social Psychology*, 90(5), 751.

Rinman, M. L., Friberg, A., Bendiksen, B., et al. (2004). *Ghost in the Cave*: An interactive collaborative game using non-verbal communication. In A. Camurri & G. Volpe (eds.), *Gesture-based communication in* human–computer interaction (pp. 549–556). New York, NY: Springer Science+Business Media.

Schleicher, A. (2012). *Preparing teachers and developing school leaders for the 21st century: Lessons from around the world*. Paris: OECD Publishing.

Sen, A. K. (1992). *Inequality examined*. Cambridge, MA: Harvard University Press.

Severiens, S., Wolff, R., & van Herpen, S. (2014). Teaching for diversity: A literature overview and an analysis of the curriculum of a teacher training college. *European Journal of Teacher Education*, 37(3), 295–311.

Silverman, D. (1993). *Interpreting qualitative data*. London: SAGE.

Sleeter, C. (2013). Teaching for social justice in multicultural classrooms. *Multicultural Education Review*, 5(2), 1–19.

Smith, H. W. (1975). *Strategies of social research: The methodological imagination*. London: Prentice Hall.

Steele, C. M. (1997). A threat in the air: How stereotypes shape intellectual identity and performance. *American Psychologist*, 52(6), 613.

Stefanek, E., Strohmeier, D., & van de Schoot, R. (2015). Individual and class room predictors of same-cultural friendship preferences in multicultural schools. *International Journal of Behavioral Development*, 39(3), 255–265.

Steinbach, M. (2010). Eux autres versus nous autres: Adolescent students' views on the integration of newcomers. *Intercultural Education*, 21(6), 535–547.

Steinkuehler, C. (2004). Learning in massively multiplayer online games. In Y. B. Kafai, W. A. Sandoval, N. Enyedy, A. S. Nixon, & F. Herreras (eds.), *Proceedings of the sixth international conference of the learning sciences* (pp. 521–528). Mahwah, NJ: Lawrence Erlbaum Associates.

Suárez-Orozco, M., & Suárez-Orozco, C. (2000). Some conceptual considerations in the interdisciplinary study of immigrant children. In H. Trueba & L. Bartolome (eds.), *Immigrant voices: In search of educational equity* (pp. 17–36). Oxford: Rowman & Littlefield.

Tielman, K., den Brok, P., Bolhuis, S., & Vallejo, B. (2012). Collaborative learning in multicultural classrooms: A case study of Dutch senior secondary vocational education. *Journal of Vocational Education & Training*, 64(1), 103–118.

Traag, T., & Van der Velden, R. K. (2008). Early school-leaving in the Netherlands. *The role of student-, family- and school factors for early school-leaving in lower secondary Education*. Maastricht: Research Centre for Education and the Labour.

Tupas, R. (2014). Intercultural education in everyday practice. *Intercultural Education*, 25(4), 243–254.

Usart, M., Romero, M., & Almirall, E. (2011). Impact of the feeling of knowledge explicitness in the learner's participation and performance in a collaborative digital game based learning activity. In M. Ma, M. Fradinho Oliveira, & J. Madeiras Pereira (eds.), *SGA 2011* (pp. 23–35). Berlin: Springer-Verlag.

Ward, C. (2013). Probing identity, integration and adaptation: Big questions, little answers. *International Journal of Intercultural Relations*, 37(4), 391–404.

Wiklund, Mats. (2005). Game mediated communication: Multiplayer games as the medium for computer based communication. In *Proceedings of DIGRA 2005 Changing Views Worlds in Play 2 Nd International Digital Games Research Association Conference June 16–20, 2005*. Retrieved from: www.digra.org/wp-content/uploads/digital-library/06278.39122.pdf (accessed January 20, 2016).

Zagal, J. P., Rick, J., & Hsi, I. (2006). Collaborative games: Lessons learned from board games. *Simulation & Gaming*, 37(1), 24–40.

PART IV

Techniques for Analyzing Game Data

12

The Power of Social Features in Online Gaming

FERNANDO KUIPERS, MARCUS MÄRTENS,
ERNST VAN DER HOEVEN, AND ALEXANDRU IOSUP

12.1 Introduction

The online gaming industry is thriving. It entertains millions of players (50% of the online population of the USA, with similar numbers reported in most developed countries), in a global market of tens of billions of dollars per year. For example, Riot's *League of Legends* alone is said to attain more than 1 billion dollars in revenues[1] yearly, but it is not the only game with revenues of this order of magnitude. Besides entertainment, the techniques developed first for online gaming are also increasingly used in enterprise training and evaluation, for example, using complex simulations that require cooperation across multiple continents and advanced visualizations (Susi, Johannesson, & Backlund, 2007); in the evacuation of large-scale disaster areas (Walker, Giddings, & Armstrong, 2011); and in education (Abulrub, Attridge, & Williams, 2011), for example, in massive open online courses. But the techniques that power new games and related applications are less introverted than ever. Online games (OGs), from the smartphone game *Bounden* (Lien, 2014) that tries to breach the social fence that prevents us from interacting with strangers, to the decade-running *World of Warcraft*, which beyond individual training incentivizes players to socialize and do activities together (World of Warcraft team, 2015), are indicating that future OGs will increasingly be social – indeed, online games will increasingly have social features, and thus be truly online *social* games (OSGs). In this chapter, we focus on how to identify, quantify, and possibly leverage such social features in OSGs.

Social game features have not simply been designed and developed; they are the complex, emergent, or only partially engineered consequences of how those in the player population interact with each other, inside and outside the

---

[1] http://goo.gl/bBKggU (gamasutra.com, September 2015).

particular game. Without social game features, the market success of recent online games would not have been obtained. For example, multiplayer online battle arena (MOBA) games (Funk, 2013) have become increasingly popular and captivate their player base by virtue of complex game mechanics and competitive nature, but also through the mechanisms they offer so that players communicate, connect, and socialize with each other while and especially beyond gaming. MOBA games, such as *League of Legends*, are typically played in independent matches, for example, a 5vs5 or 6vs6 format, in which the players of each team need to closely cooperate in their attempt to win from the other team. Collaboration is driven by communication, frequently by voice or text-based chats of predefined phrases that can be sent quickly. The competition between teams can be so sophisticated and suspenseful that professional gaming (eSport) is getting more momentum, as tens of millions of spectators gather online or offline for the purpose of watching (McCormick, 2013). Considering this wide diversity of social game features, *in this chapter we focus on understanding patterns of social interactions within the game. Which social features emerge or are designed to emerge in games? How are they emerging in practice?* This leads to numerous detailed research questions, for example: *How do teams and groups form in MOBA games?*

The presence of social game features is not in itself enough to attract the interest of the market; at the extreme, only quantifying their relationship to player retention and spending can do this. Since the number of players and revenues has grown tremendously over the past few years, with estimates often exceeding hundreds of millions of active users online (McGonigal, 2011; Newzoo team, 2016; Steam team, 2016), as a result, so has the number of online games. For a game operator, the latter means that competition is fierce and player retention is key. In other words, the players of the online game should continuously have a good *gameplay experience*; otherwise they may leave for another game operator or even trigger through their social ties departures of large groups of players to a different game operator. In the field of multimedia, this type of experience-related performance metric is called Quality of Experience (QoE) (Kuipers et al., 2010), which reflects the quality of the application/service as perceived by the user. QoE can be influenced by several aspects, such as human preconditions, social aspects, system-oriented Quality of Service (QoS) such as network delay and CPU/GPU processing power, and the quality of the content at the source. Considering, for example, MOBA games, which, by nature, demand intricate strategies to be executed in collaboration, players who contribute are valued and praised, and in some games (e.g., *Overwatch*) voted for. The opposite also happens. When team members do not follow game etiquette (either deliberately or not) or place their own interest in front of that of the team (for example, by stealing kills or resources, or focusing on personal stats instead of winning), this may result in a diminished game experience and even loss of the match. Given the intensity of the game, players who, in the eyes of their team members, misbehave may be criticized via the communication channels that were meant to coordinate the team effort, causing conflict within the team. Such conflicts bear the risk to escalate rapidly resulting in verbal assaults, shifting the focus of the players from the actual game toward harassing each other by means of profanity and harsh insults. The impact on the game experience can be dramatic, as the social features meant to foster a friendly atmosphere of collaboration are corrupted by players to create a toxic environment.This is but one example to illustrate that social features in OSGs can be beneficial for the QoE, but also that social misbehavior may cause deep player dissatisfaction, which may ultimately trigger them to leave the game, either for that single match or even forever. *We identify in this chapter ways to measure positive and negative aspects of QoE for online games with social game features.*

Understanding and learning about the nature of social interactions in games is essential to improve game design for future online social games. Rich social relationships and networks could be used to improve gaming services, such as team formation and game population retention, which are important for the user experience and the commercial value of the companies who run these games. Antisocial behavior in games may be combated combated if it can be detected and quantified and the corresponding triggers are understood. Social features might even be used to run games much more efficiently, reducing operational costs and opening the market to even more high-quality games created by indie game developers and small-and-medium sized game studios.

We identify in this chapter a common core of social interaction, sometimes explicit, other times implicit, but always strong and important for the gameplay experience. We believe this common core will lead to a unified theory of useful social game features, one in which the social experience will be at least as important as the experience derived from the gameworld itself. In this direction, *this chapter discusses ways to leverage social game features in OSGs.*

To summarize, the main contribution of this work is fivefold:

1. We motivate the importance of taking social game features into account to improve the quality of experience in online gaming. Because we consider for this chapter a general audience, we also explain the key terms and concepts used in this work, in Section 12.2.
2. We propose a socially aware model for future OSGs, in Section 12.3. The model we propose is general and focuses on three core pillars of modern

gaming operations: gameworld management, game data processing, and game content generation.

3. Also in Section 12.3, we survey methods for identifying social features in future OSGs and present examples, selected from our previous work, of using these methods in practice for today's OSGs. We also propose a new framework for identifying meaningful social relationships in online games.

4. We survey methods for using the social power in future OSGs and in Section 12.4 present examples, selected from our own work, of using these methods in practice for today's OSGs.

5. We identify and analyze several directions for future research in socially aware OSGs, in Section 12.5.

12.2 Background

The social aspects of online gaming may differ per gaming genre, so we start by enumerating the different gaming genres that exist. Unfortunately, there is no standard classification of gaming genres, and different organizations may use their own taxonomies and definitions. We have opted to classify games based on the amount of simultaneous players and to consider only games in which multiple players may interact (otherwise, the *in-game* social component is missing). We make a first coarse, high-level classification, to distinguish between (1) multiplayer online games (MOGs) and (2) massively multiplayer online games (MMOGs), and subsequently subdivide these two classes into various gaming genres.

MOGs are multiplayer games in which players play against and with each other in teams. These games admit only a limited amount of players per match (i.e., a single *game instance*). Typically, teams within such a match comprise two to sixty-four online players. However, while the amount of players in a match is modest, the number of concurrent matches may easily be thousands.

We further identify several MOG subgenres:

- *MOBA*, already described in Section 12.1: In MOBAs, each player controls in real time an in-game representation (*avatar*), and (usually two) equally sized teams of players have as objective the conquest of the opponent's main building or trophy. The game includes many tactical and strategic elements, from the team operation to the management of resources. Example games are *League of Legends*, *Dota 2*, and *Heroes of the Storm*.
- *Sports*: Sports games represent simulations of various types of popular physical sports. For example, soccer is a popular online sports game, which even offers online tournaments. This genre is of high pace, because it requires

real-time interaction and consequently low network delays. The most prominent examples are the soccer games from the FIFA series.

- *Fighting*: Fighting games are similar to sports game, but may also feature fantasy elements. They resemble a one-on-one combat by use of martial arts and combinations of moves. Example games are *Street Fighter*, *Super Smash Bros*, and *Tekken*.

- *Real-time strategy (RTS)*: An RTS game is generally played in a context of war and involves commanding troops, maintaining operational bases and managing a war economy to succeed in the battle against one or more opponents. Opposed to MOBAs, RTS games have a stronger focus on strategic elements and tactical fights with whole armies, rather than with a single avatar. Examples include *Starcraft II* and *Warcraft III*.

- *Traditional turn-based strategy (TTBS)*: TTBS games are traditional strategy games, such as chess and go, which have been played with the same rules for many (thousands of) years. In the age of the internet, they have adapted to allow for large numbers of game instances to occur simultaneously.

MMOGs offer a virtual gameworld that is populated by more than thousands of users simultaneously, allowing them to interact through (often self-created and much-tuned) characters with the in-game world or with other players.

We may distinguish several subgenres:

- *Massively multiplayer online role-playing game (MMORPG)*: This genre features a usually massively large gameworld in which player and nonplayer characters meet each other, interact, trade, and sometimes fight each other. To advance in the game, players level up their in-game character by completion of missions and quests, usually by teaming up with other players to overcome those challenges. Examples include *World of Warcraft*, *Guild Wars 2*, and *EVE Online*.

- *Massively multiplayer first-person shooter (MMFPS)*: A player in an MMFPS game owns a weapon and tries to shoot as many rivals (other players) as possible. Several playing modes may be possible, including teaming up.

- *Massively multiplayer online social game (MMOSG)*: In MMOSGs, players build their own cities or farms. Like in reality, this may involve trading with or buying goods from others. This genre is explicitly designed to interact with your friends and the community. Examples include *Farmville 2* and *Clash of Clans*.

The above classification is neither exhaustive nor unique, in the sense that some subgenres might also be played in both a MOG and MMOG setting.

To operate a MOG or MMOG requires considerable *gaming infrastructure* (*datacentres* hosting tens to hundreds of powerful *servers*). In recent years, *cloud-operated games* have emerged as a form of always-online gaming. Among the many options for cloud-operated games (Iosup, 2014), *cloud gaming* offers users the ability to stream games to their computer from a server operated by the game provider. Consequently, all the game genres mentioned above could also appear as cloud games. Since, in cloud games, all the processing and rendering is done by the service provider and streamed over the internet to the end-user, there is no need to download the complete gaming software for each game nor does one need high-end gaming hardware. Instead, a game-client suffices to, in principle, enjoy multiple games. Clearly, cloud gaming places extra stringent demands on the network QoS, since it requires sending the complete screen (server to client) and commands (client to server) in real-time and on the gaming infrastructure of the game operators.

12.3 Identifying and Quantifying Social Features in OSGs

Because social features are only partially engineered and may appear as complex emergent behavior of the local interactions between players, identifying and quantifying them is challenging. In this section, we present a model for social features that will be helpful for this challenge.

12.3.1 A General Model of OSGs

Three Main Pillars

An OSG platform typically consists of the following three pillars:

1. *Gameworld management*, which comprises game hosting, and the management of players and in-game objects in the virtual gameworld. Moreover, the OSG infrastructure and management should be scalable to serve millions of players online, match elastically the number of players, be always available, be consistent, and have low latency.

2. *Game data processing* is a selection of methods and tools to analyze game status and history. Clearly, the massive numbers of players in the gameworld collectively generate massive amounts of data: user interactions, uploaded screenshots and videos, social networking, etc. Analyzing the data can help the system designers understand player behavior and gain insight into system operation, thus allowing them to build better games for the players and to operate games more efficiently.

3. *Game content generation.* Game content, from bits such as textures to abstract puzzles and even entire game designs, is at the core of the entertainment value of games. Until the early 2000s, manual labour ensured that the quality and quantity of game content matched the demands of the playing community, but this is not scalable owing to the exponential growth in number of users and production costs. Hence, there is an increasing need for procedural generation of game content at a massive scale to provide players new incentives to keep on engaging with each other and the game.

The gameworld management pillar provides in-game data to the game data processing pillar and uses content produced by the game content generation pillar. However, not all of the requirements listed for these three pillars are being met today. Challenges remain in procedural generation of content, harnessing cloud-computing platforms for scalability, and leveraging social data and relationships to improve the gameplay experience. In this chapter, the focus is exclusively on the social aspects of online gaming.

Dimensions of Social Interaction

In addition to the three gaming pillars, we present and exemplify three dimensions of social interaction:

1. Explicit versus implicit social ties
2. Inside the gameworld versus outside
3. Long-lasting gameworld versus short-lived matches

We provide some examples to illustrate how the three social dimensions could manifest in online gaming:

- Forms of explicit association are easiest to detect and include the formation of clans and guilds. Players who have played/won/lost/conducted other activities together form an entire implicit social network with various characteristics that may be useful in improving, for example, the way players are matched to other players for a particular match.
- Explicit community work outside a single game or a set of related/unrelated games is facilitated through online meta-gaming networks (OMGNs). OMGNs are internet-based communities of online gaming players that extend in-game functionality by focusing on the relationship between game sessions, on what happens in the meantime between game sessions, and on the relationship between games. Also other means of communication, such as Short Message Service (SMS), may be used to coordinate outside of a game, for example to obtain a high chance of being teamed up with friends.

- A long lasting gameworld may lead to different relationships than brief possibly repeated encounters in short-lived instances of multiple matches.

Given that these three dimensions for social interaction in online gaming exist, the question is how to turn them to good use to improve overall performance and gameplay experience. For instance, for a social network game such as *FarmVille*, it might be more efficient to place a group of friends who interact frequently on the same server, which requires solving the question of how to use the explicit or implicit social structure of games to provision and allocate the system's resources.

In terms of QoE, a new model is needed that should consider the effect of QoS parameters as well as social aspects. While a QoE model has been developed for telephony in the past, it has already proved difficult to find one for online multimedia services, such as video-on-demand, and will be even more challenging when other elements, such as social ties, play a role.

12.3.2 Identifying Emergent Social Networks Using Interaction Graphs

In this section, we describe a graph model, presented in our previous work (Jia et al., 2015), which is able to capture social relationships in MOGs of a variety of types and strengths. In Jia et al. (2015), we have applied our model to game data and in this section we will summarize the results to show how one could leverage those networks to improve QoE.

Data

One of the three gaming pillars is game data processing, which obviously requires game data to begin with. There are a number of, for example, competitive and privacy, reasons why obtaining game data, if you are not the game operator, is challenging. Many details of the "internals" of the game infrastructure and player information are shielded from the public. Yet, some data, such as statistics, are published on websites and can be obtained by APIs or web scraping. Other means to gather data are monitoring the game-related network traffic and actually playing the game personally or by the usage of bots. To facilitate research on online gaming, the Game-Trace Archive was created to provide an open access to related data (Guo & Iosup, 2012).

For our work on identifying implicit online social gaming networks (Jia et al., 2015), we collected data corresponding to long-term activity of communities playing *DotA* (the Dota-League and the DotAlicious communities), *StarCraft II*, and *World of Tanks*, which we made available in the Game Trace

Archive (Guo Iosup, 2012). At the time these data sets were crawled, the four online communities offered each player a profile webpage that displayed information on friends and clan membership. Also individual webpages per match were published that contained the start and end times of the match, the player list, the outcome of the match (i.e., which team had won, or whether there was a draw, or if the match was aborted) and game-specific information. To reduce the effect of possible temporary webpage or network outages, each webpage was crawled at least twice and matches with zero duration were filtered out. The four types of data sets comprise

1. Friendship data from Dota-League
2. Clan membership data from DotAlicious
3. User skill levels from Dota-League and DotAlicious
4. Match data for all four communities

The four data sets together include both explicit as well as implicit social gaming information. As such, we may use tools from social network analysis, such as the use of graphs to represent user relationships even if they manifest implicitly via user interactions. Such social network studies often extract graphs based on a single, domain-specific, and usually threshold-based rule for mapping relationships to links. However, gaming involves relationships in various domains that normally do not exist in regular social networks, for example, winning together and competing with each other. Hence, to study user relationships in MOGs, all of these domains and social perspectives need to be carefully examined and compared. In Jia et al. (2015), two types of graph-based models were used to represent user relationships in MOGs: friendship and interaction graphs, discussed as follows.

Friendship Graph

The friendship graph is obtained from the friendship data of Dota-League. If two players, represented as nodes in the graph, have indicated that they are friends, a link in the graph is connecting those two nodes. Since friendship is mutual and the data did not indicate any intensity in friendship, the friendship graph is undirected and unweighted.

Interaction Graph

In the social network analysis of, for example, Facebook (Wilson et al., 2009), an interaction graph is used to represent interaction between two users. Similarly, in the context of OSGs, a link between two nodes could reflect some form of interaction between the corresponding two nodes/players. However, unlike in the Facebook study by Wilson et al. (2009), in which all interactions are assumed to be homogeneous, many different types of interactions are captured in the game data. The five types of interactions that were studied and for which interaction graphs were extracted are the following:

1. SM: Two players played in the Same Match.
2. SS: Two players played on the Same Side of a match.
3. OS: Two players played on Opposite Sides of a match.
4. MW: Two players of a Match Won together.
5. ML: Two players of a Match Lost together.

To study the social relationships in OSG interaction graphs one could consider various graph metrics, for example:

- Network size (the number of nonisolated nodes in a graph)
- Nodal degree (the number of a node's neighbors)
- Distance (the length of a shortest path between two nodes)
- Diameter (the largest distance between any two nodes)
- Clustering coefficient (the fraction of pairs of its neighbors that are linked)
- Assortativity (the average Pearson Ranking Correlation Coefficient (PRCC) of the degree between pairs of connected nodes)

Interaction graphs could be directed or undirected and weighted or unweighted. In Jia et al. (2015), the choice was made not to use link weights to capture the interaction strength, because many graph metrics are defined only for unweighted graphs. Instead, a threshold-based rule was applied, to discard interactions of low strength and to include only the interactions with sufficient strength to pass the thresholds into the graph. Two mapping thresholds were considered: the period t of effect for a user interaction and the minimum number n of interactions that need to have occurred between two users for a relationship to exist. For example, in an SM graph with t equal to one week, and n equal to ten, a link between two players exists only if the data contain at least one week in which they played at least ten games together. Indeed, the values for t and n, in this case, govern the strength of relationships reflected in the interaction graph and are important parameters. For example, both a small value of t and a large value of n would induce a graph of strong relationships.

The five aforementioned interaction graphs are undirected and unweighted. They also differ in detail, since both SS and OS constitute subclasses of SM, and both MW and ML on their turn require players to have played on the same side (SS). Consequently, for the same values of t and n, there are fewer relationships in the SM graph than in the SS and OS graphs, which in turn have fewer relationship constraints than the ML and MW graphs. Note that the list of considered interaction graphs is not exhaustive and, in principle, can handle more complex types of interaction. For example, playing against each other at least ten times during winter, while also located in the same country. Moreover, the thresholds themselves could act both as lower and upper bound. For example, we could focus on moderately interacting players (the majority of an MOG's population) by specifying, as threshold, a maximum number of interactions between two players. If two players exceed the threshold, then they are not connected by a link in the interaction graph.

Summary of Analysis Results

The analysis in Jia et al. (2015) of the four gaming communities and their various interaction graphs revealed similarities, but also differences in the social relationships and preferences among players. The differences indicate that an interaction graph analysis should be conducted not only per gaming genre, but also per game design within a particular genre. A proper analysis could serve as a reference to game designers and MOG community administrators in adjusting their designs to increase QoE. For example, players in *StarCraft II* appeared to prefer competing (by playing on the opposite side) with their rivals. Possibly, this community is more driven by trying to retaliate or redeem oneself after a previously lost match. MOG communities that are similar to *StarCraft II* could leverage such knowledge by organizing tournaments or publishing player ranks, to promote the activity level of their players, all in an attempt to increase the competitiveness of the environment.

The study in Jia et al. (2015) compared the various interaction graphs based on several graph metrics. One noteworthy metric is that of triadic closure. A closed triad is defined to be a group of three nodes that are all connected to each other. It is known, from psychology, that triadic closure is more likely to manifest with positive (a friend of my friend is likely to be a friend) rather than negative relationships (an enemy of my enemy is less likely to be an enemy). Typically, in social networks, only positive relationships are present and negative relationships could not be studied. On the contrary, in OSG networks both kinds of relationships occur, since prosocial and enmity relationships are strongly expressed. We therefore tested in Jia et al. (2015), whether positive triadic closure is indeed more pronounced than negative triadic closure. In this context, playing on the same side (SS) was assumed to indicate a positive relationship and playing on the opposite side (OS) a negative relationship (although also friends might enjoy playing against each other).

Indeed, the SS graphs for *Dota-League*, *StarCraft II*, and *World of Tanks* reflected higher triadic closure than the OS graphs. For DotAlicious, the differences between the triadic closures for both its SS and OS graphs were less pronounced. One possible reason is that the clan feature provided in

Table 12.1 *Example of an Attribute–Role–Action framework in practice*

Role	hostile	cooperative	competitive	equal	unequal	intense	superficial	socioemotional	task-oriented	informal	formal	friend list	ignore list	in party	in raid	in guild	whisper chat	party chat	raid chat	guild chat	seeing (near)	trading	giving	group leader	in combat focus target negative	in combat focus target positive	out of combat focus target	party decline	guild decline	Negatively affects "you" in world
Friend		+		+		+		+		+		+	−	+	+	+	+				+	+	+			+	+	−	−	−
Guildie		+		+		+		+		+			−	+	+	+					+	+	+			+	+	−	−	−
Social manager (guild)		+		+		+		+	+		+		−		+	+				+						+	+	−	−	−
Party member		+		+		+				+		+	−	+	+	+			+	+						+				
Management (guild)		+		+		+			+		+		−		+				+									−		−
Pugger		+		+		+	+		+	+			−	+	+			+	+									−		+
Pug leader		+		+	+	+	+	+	+		+	+	−	+	+			+	+					+				−		−
Elitist (negative)		+			+	+				+			+	−											−			−		
Guild leader						+		+	+		+	+	−	+	+	+			+	+				+				+	−	+
Rival		+	+	+		+			+			+	−	+									−		+		+	−		+
Enemy arena team			+	+		+			+				−												+					+
Temporarily same goal		+										−	−													+		−		
World pvper	+		+																											+
Scammer	+		+					+				−	+									+			+	−				+
Spectator	+						+			+	+			+	+	+	+	+	+	+	+				+	−	−	+		+

DotAlicious diminishes the significance of playing on the opposite side as a negative relationship. It remains for future work on other data sets to establish whether this conjecture is valid. In Section 12.3.5, we will closely investigate "toxicity" as a more pronounced form of negative relationship.

12.3.3 Identifying Emergent Social Networks Using the Attribute–Role–Action Framework

We describe in this section the *Attribute–Role–Action* (ARA) framework, which we see as a richer framework for identifying emergent social networks than what we have introduced in Section 12.3.2; unlike the framework from Section 12.3.2, the ARA framework still requires much work before it can be applied automatically in practice and focuses primarily on relationships within MMOGs.

The core objective of the ARA framework is that a simple set of techniques should be able to extract complex social relationships from either implicit or explicit, but fine-grained game data. Relations may be identified by not only measuring in-game interaction graphs (as in Section 12.3.2), but also by analysing indirectly related data. These data consist both of the player in-game fine-grained actions, such as conducting in-game raids or chatting in-game together, and of out-of-game actions related to forming and maintaining relationships, such as discussing over non-game channels. Data related to these *actions* can be further detailed per social *role* played during the action, from friend or enemy, to selfish behavior (being a "pugger") or being a same-party member. Roles can be defined as detailed as needed, for example, enabling the expression of degrees of social roles, from a guild leader known by all guild members, to a social manager of a guild activity, to a relatively distant party member known by few. Because roles can be infinitely many, creating a set of techniques addressing them all would be impractical without some form of clustering. We propose that a small set of *attributes* exhibited by roles could expose the dimensions used by any role, and thus be addressed by specific techniques with a wide applicability.

Table 12.1 summarizes an example of an ARA framework. Its three main columns, "Role Attributes," "Role," and "Actions," correspond to the three main dimensions of the ARA framework. The fifteen Roles are diverse, ranging from the supportive "friend" to the all-seeing, but otherwise inactive, "spectator." The "Role Attributes" describe whether the actions are performed by players with a friendly or hostile view on the acting player, or with cooperative or competitive attitudes; the attributes may indicate an equal (transitive relationship) or unequal role; may indicate that the role is superficial and thus perhaps inconsequential in the long run; may indicate a socioemotional role (such as support) or task-oriented role (such as relationship by belonging to the same guild); and whether the role is informally or formally specified. The "Actions" included in Table 12.1 are also diverse, from being included in the friend or ignore list, to indicating an action that negatively affects the player.

Symbols denote importance.

Table 12.1 already combines practical knowledge that (1) Roles such as "friend" and "guildie" (belonging to the same guild), and even "social manager" of a guild, are with respect to our dimensions very similar, and thus may be addressed by similar techniques; (2) Attributes such as "friendly" and "cooperative" are highly correlated but not identical, as sometimes cooperative players may even be hostile to each other outside a specific action; (3) many of the negative Roles, and in Table 12.1 the rows between "rival" and "scammer," have fewer Attributes and Actions terms, and thus may be easier to service; (4) Actions with strong chance of decreasing gameplay experience, such as "party decline," may be countered by techniques that increase presence of Attributes such as "friendly" and "cooperative"; the same happens for Actions with high prosocial consequences such as "giving"; (5) Actions with visceral reaction, such as "in combat focus target" may be triggered by both established rivalries and temporary roles.

To conclude, we see the ARA framework and the example in Table 12.1 as first steps toward defining a more fine-grained socially aware gaming model.

12.3.4 Quantifying QoE Using User Action Graphs and MOS Scores

Although increasing QoE is the ultimate goal, at the moment even measuring QoE for games is difficult. A common way to capture the users' perception of a service is by asking feedback from a panel of users and subsequently computing a Mean Opinion Score (MOS). Individual users from the panel are asked to rate a certain service by using a five-point scale (ITU-T P.800), where the scale runs from 1 (meaning "bad") to 5 ("excellent"). The final MOS score reflects the average of the users' assessments. Despite the frequent usage of such a panel-based method, it has obvious disadvantages: it is costly and takes a lot of time. This methodology is therefore mostly used in an attempt to derive an objective QoE model that, based for instance on QoS measurements, is calibrated to accurately reflect the subjective MOS. Several models and tools are already available to objectively quantify the QoE of video or audio (see, e.g., Kuipers et al., 2010), but not much QoE work has targeted the field of OSGs. Moreover, the few available models that do attempt to measure the QoE of online games primarily focus on the effects of the QoS parameters on the QoE (see, e.g., Antila & J. Lakkakorpi, 2003; Ries, Svoboda, & Rupp, 2008; and Wattimena et al., 2008), but ignore other important aspects, such as the influence of social ties on the QoE.

The User Action Graph

To capture the social side of playing behavior and experience, E. Dias (2014), under our supervision, investigated an MMOSG called *MagicLand*, which unfortunately is no longer available. In order to conduct that investigation, three classes of metrics were defined: (1) gameplay metrics, (2) social metrics, and (3) performance metrics, each of which will be illustrated in the text that follows.

Relevant gameplay metrics for *MagicLand* were

- *Skill level*: Very skilled players may experience a game differently in comparison to novices.
- *Time to level up*: A measure reflecting how difficult it is to advance in a game.
- *Actions*: For example, planting, harvesting, buying some assets, etc. By considering *actions per minute*, one could also study a player's involvement in a game. Inactive players may indicate a lack of enjoyment, while overly active could point to inexperienced players just clicking around. Both extremes may imply a low QoE.
- *Goals completed*: This metric to some extent depends on skill, time to level up, and actions per minute, and reflects player engagement.

Relevant social metrics for *MagicLand* were

- *Friend visits*: The number of friend visits during a game session.
- *Visit times*: The time a player spends visiting his/her friends.
- *Friend requests*: One may solicit help from friends to complete certain goals.
- *Gifting*: The act of helping friends by giving them certain items.

Relevant performance metrics for *MagicLand* included (obtaining traces on) network and server performance.

We will briefly explain how to combine these various metrics in order to reach an OSG QoE model:

1. The first stage is data collection. To validate the QoE model, we need to collect both objective data, reflected by the gameplay and social and

performance metrics, as well as subjective data, obtained via a questionnaire and reflected in an MOS score.

2. The second stage consists of correlating the objective and subjective data to determine which gaming metrics influence the QoE most and in what way.

3. In the last stage this information is used to create a model that is able to determine the overall QoE of an OSG without any subjective input.

The work in Dias (2014) on *MagicLand* was not conducted with a large enough test panel to draw significant conclusions and to develop a QoE model for *MagicLand*. It did, however, lead to the following observation: *Playing with friends leads to a higher QoE and faster level-up times, but this mostly holds for experienced players and not as much for the novices.*

In the following section, we will illustrate that social (mis)behavior can also have a negative effect on the QoE.

12.3.5 Identifying In-Game Toxicity Using Natural Language Processing

In this section, we will summarize our main findings from Märtens et al. (2015), which used natural language processing (NLP) to detect profanity, or so-called toxicity, in the chat-logs of a game. Toxicity is a clear example of a negative form of social behavior and could seriously affect a player's gameplay experience.

Data

The chat data used in Märtens et al. (2015) was crawled from the DotAlicious platform, one of the DotA communities studied in Section 12.3.2. The data set comprised both the all-chat as well as the ally-chat logs. All-chat communication is accessible to all players of the match, while the ally-chat (which accounted for nearly 90% of all chat communication) is only visible by allied players (players in the same team).

Unfortunately, the DotAlicious site is no longer available, and we cannot release the data publicly in order to protect the privacy of the players, especially when dealing with such a sensitive topic as personal insults. Some of the data may be available on request.

Extracting Meaning from Data Using Natural Language Processing

The data obtained from DotAlicious contained all chat logs for 10,305 matches of DotA. The logs were tokenized into single words by white-space splitting, maintaining the information of the corresponding sender. Contrary to standard practice in the field of NLP, our tokenizer kept symbols such as exclamation marks attached to words and regarded different capitalizations as different tokens. This was done as different capitalization and symbols such as smileys are frequently used to emphasize statements and carry thus valuable information about the sentiment of the corresponding sender. Since the chats took place while playing fast-paced matches, the spelling of the words leaves much to be desired for and also contains many abbreviations and game-specific commands. In general, the language used rarely follows any grammatical structures, but is rather elliptic and extremely abbreviated, often consisting of technical slang terms not found in standard dictionaries. This is another reason why standard procedures (e.g., part-of-speech tagging and spelling correction) are largely inapplicable. Although different languages appeared, English was the dominant language in the corpus.

After the tokenization process, we attached labels to each word, marking it, for example, as profanity, technical term, smiley, stop word, or expression of laughter. To assign a label to a word, three different classes of rules were considered:

1. Pattern: The word includes or starts with certain symbols.
2. List: The word appears a predefined list (dictionary).
3. Letterset: The set of letters of the word equals the set of letters of a word from a predefined list.

The letterset rules have been particularly useful to alleviate the impact of bad spelling. For example, a commonly used insult is the word "noob," which is somehow derived from "newbie" and used to typify a player as such. Many different ways of stating "noob" were found in the corpus, for example, "NOOOOOOOOb," "nooobbbbb," and "noonb," pointing to deliberate and unintentional misspellings of the word. Considering lettersets allows classifying all those words to a same class, as long as no other meaningful recombination of the letters appears in the corpus. The text corpus analyzed in Märtens et al. (2015) consisted of 7,042,112 words, of which 286,654 were distinct.

What Is Toxicity and How to Detect It?

Toxicity has not been established as a well-defined term in literature yet, but is frequently used to refer to all forms of displeasing antisocial behavior of players. Part of this behavior is language used for verbal assault and harassment of other players. For our purposes, we interpret it as the act of sending a chat message with the aim to insult another player within the same team.

While the extraction of profane words and insults (via list and letterset rules) might give an idea about the atmosphere of the particular match, the detection of profanity is not sufficient. A highly competitive game as DotA may trigger strong emotions that result into swearing, which is an expression of an immediate dissatisfaction, but not necessarily meant to hurt a teammate. In fact, people might sympathize with a swearing person, in case he was the victim of an unfortunate event. Thus, we found that in order to detect toxicity, considering the context is crucial.

One way of taking the context into account is the use of n-grams. An n-gram is a contiguous sequence of n words that appear in a temporal context. That context could comprise all words sent by a single player no more than 1 second before and/or after a word labelled as profane. As such, in Märtens et al. (2015), for all players who participated in at least 10 matches, the 100 most frequently used n-grams for $n = 1, 2, 3, 4$ that contained at least one profane word were retrieved and analyzed manually to determine which of them were toxic. The rule for toxicity was that the corresponding n-gram could be understood as an insult directed toward another person ("you noob") and not some self-referential humor: "I am so noob."

Results Analysis

Of the 10,305 matches analyzed in Märtens et al. (2015), 6,528 contained at least one toxic remark. As our selection of toxicity was conservative and very strict to avoid false positives, the total amount of toxic remarks was modest and generally no more than five toxic remarks were made per match. The maximum amount of toxic remarks registered for a single match was twenty-two.

To investigate potential causes or triggers for toxicity, toxicity was further evaluated against

- The win rate for each player, i.e., the amount of matches won divided by the amount of matches played in total
- The expected game-outcome
- In-game events like kills of player characters

The results in Märtens et al. (2015) indicated that, surprisingly, there seems to be no strong linear correlation between the win rate and the level of toxicity. Profanity and toxicity seem to be used regardless of success in the game. To gain deeper insights, analyzing the distribution of toxicity over all matches is not insightful, but the distribution and usage of toxicity within the matches paints a different and more intuitive picture. Considering the progress of the game, the team that will lose is observed to use more toxic remarks on average in the later stages of the match in comparison to the opposing winning team. A possible explanation is that the level of toxicity increases with the frustration experienced in the face of a more and more inevitable defeat.

As indicated, frustration may spark toxic behavior and certain game events may be at the root of that frustration. One obvious game event players try to avoid is that of their avatar (temporarily) being killed. To test whether such kill events were indeed triggers of toxicity, the data were analyzed to examine whether each of the 16,950 detected toxic remarks were preceded by a kill event taking place not more than 10 seconds before the actual remark. For comparison, an equivalent amount of 16,950 random chat lines were used as a null model to analyze whether there have been any kill events in the same time window. As expected, toxic remarks turned out to be indeed more frequently preceded by kill events than random remarks, roughly by a factor of 2.

The methodology described in the preceding text can be adapted to other MOBAs and possibly even games of different genres, as long as protected textual chat communication within teams is a social feature. As language (and corresponding insults) used by players may be strongly game dependent, one would need to redefine the list and pattern rules for word labeling according to the specific terms used in the game under consideration.

12.4 Using Social Features in Future Online Social Games

There are many possible applications of social features, as defined in this chapter, for OSGs. We discuss several such applications.

12.4.1 Match Recommendation in Online Social Games Based on Interaction Graphs

Match recommendation in a MOG community can be seen as an attempt to predict player pairs that are likely to form gaming relationships in the future. Match recommendation often includes two types of predictions: (1) predicting new relationships between players who previously had no relationships at all, and (2) predicting renewed relationships between players who have interacted in the past.

In multiplayer games, your "click" with fellow players may have a big influence on your QoE. Consequently, good matchmaking algorithms should help to improve user experience, and hence, the commercial value of MOGs. For example, in Dota-League, players could only join a waiting queue, and, only when there were enough players, teams were formed considering the skill levels of the players in the game. Although such an approach enforces balanced matches, it does not take into account the social relationships of players. As a possible consequence, many of the games in *Dota-League* were aborted at the very beginning of the match. Instead, the findings of McGonigal (2011) and our own research have pointed out that matches played by players with strong social ties are enjoyed to a higher extent than those played together with players to which one has weak or no social ties. We therefore believe that matchmaking in OSGs stands to gain by including predictions on which player pairs are likely to "click" and form social gaming relationships in the future. A socially aware match recommendation algorithm was devised in Jia et al. (2015) as follows: For all players who are online and have not been assigned to a match, we compute their connected components based on the interaction graphs extracted with a large value for threshold n. Those components are ranked in decreasing order of their size, and then all players from the same component are assigned to the same match as long as it does not exceed the permissible match size. Otherwise the component is split, ensuring that the number of players per part equals the match size, and the same methodology is applied. Such an algorithm could be made more advanced, by also including other features such as location and the toxicity profile of players, but in Jia et al. (2015) we have shown that even such a simple algorithm can already increase the QoE.

12.4.2 Social Climate Engineering for Online Social Games

The toxicity detection method we have developed in our previous work (Märtens et al., 2015) is based on contextual information to distinguish simple swearing from deliberate insults. Although already effective, it could also serve as a building block for a monitoring system that can be used together with player reports to identify toxic players. Clearly, giving such players incentives to prevent further toxicity from happening is important, but there are also other emotional states expressed by the players that are worth monitoring and that have been part of our work as well. For example, encouraging and motivating behavior should be helpful to improve team spirit and cope with difficult situations. Kindness and forgiveness may motivate fellow players to not give up and continue giving their best effort.

By using standard supervised learning methods on TF-IDF features (term frequency–inverse document frequency) over the used words by the players toward their allies, predictions about the game outcome were already possible to 0.7 accuracy after two-thirds of a match were over. Although cause and effect need to be more carefully examined, this could mean that the language used by the players is critical for success.

Refining the prediction methods toward QoE measures rather than match outcome could provide a "barometer" of the emotional state of the corresponding players. Understanding what factors make a match enjoyable will provide feedback for game designers to balance the competitiveness of the game in favour of an improved experience.

In fact, our analysis supports the hypothesis that toxicity is mainly fuelled by the inherent competitiveness (i.e., killing each other) of the MOBA game under consideration, while being seemingly uncorrelated to the actual outcome of a match. Consequently, if players can be successful despite being toxic, they need a different incentive to cease insulting and to behave more pleasantly. Possibly, the matchmaking systems that ensemble the teams could be altered to take toxicity into account to avoid creating a social powder keg. Although preventing toxicity entirely seems to be a utopia, controlling it to some degree would ensure a much more positive game experience.

Possible in-game mechanisms to combat toxicity could also consist of awareness campaigns that target at toxic players with the goal to rehabilitate them. While winning in a difficult competitive match might still be the main reason for players to engage with the game, cosmetic aspects exist, that is, items that decorate and dress in-game avatars that are highly desirable by a large subpopulation of players. In fact, cosmetic items are a considerate source of income for the game developing company. This proves that there can be artificial incentives created that influence player behavior despite the prospect of game success.

Future games might use these or similar incentives to steer the social behavior between players into a more positive direction, without taking the edge from the competitiveness. Understanding under which circumstances toxic and friendly behavior arises will be the first step (trigger-condition) of such a future system.

12.4.3 Scaling Games with Socially Aware Techniques

Scaling the gameworld to operate well for large amounts of units and/or players is not trivial. All entities in the gameworld might be able to interact with one another. Processing all the actions (interactions) that entities want to execute requires an increasing amount of processing power as the number of entities and actions increases. This load needs to be partitioned to achieve scalability. If all entities can interact with all other entities at any time, and if they need to know the state of all other entities, then the servers handling those entities would quickly be overwhelmed by the amount of information generated by an increasing entity count. Two related techniques are commonly used to achieve scalability in practice: *interest management* (Morse, 1996) tries to disregard information that is less relevant or even entirely irrelevant, and *load partitioning* (Drain, 2008) tries to divide the information management problems across the participating processing nodes and player machines. The use of both of these techniques is currently oblivious to social features. We encourage focusing on socially aware techniques for scaling games, along the following directions.

First, many interest management techniques already exist (Liu & Theodoropoulos, 2014; Morse, 1996; Shen, 2015), but it would be interesting to extend their filtering of in-game information with filtering of nonfriends, inclusion of information for arbitrarily distant acquaintances, and other social features. Such criteria could be prime candidates to filter for information that is arbitrarily relevant to the player, in that the social features could be linked to the likeliness of interaction or even their potential impact on gameplay experience.

Second, load partitioning leads to similar opportunities as interest management, but with different techniques (Drain, 2008; Nae, Iosup, & Prodan, 2011). The current approaches in practice, in both commercial games such as Runescape and community gaming platforms such as OpenRA, assume that either contiguous areas (*zone-based partitioning*) or largely fixed sets of in-game objects (*object-based partitioning*) are leading to most of the interaction, and should thus be handled by one server each. This idea could be extended by including social features in the partitioning process, for example, by clustering by social features when deciding the set of in-game objects to be assigned to a server.

12.5 Conclusion and Directions for Future Research

The convergence of technological and social networks, if understood and managed, creates opportunities for better system design, and also for better user experience. Implicit social relationships between users, such as direct communication, direct exchange of data, and acting together can be seen as strong social relationships (ties) between users. However, social behavior could also be social misbehavior (toxicity), leading to reduced gameplay experience. To put the power of social features in OSGs to good use, much research still needs to be conducted:

- There is a need for a QoE model to objectively capture the user's gameplay experience. This includes tools to capture the social aspect in gaming and to translate those into an experience score.
- There are challenges in properly defining and measuring toxicity. Once that is possible across game genres, one should investigate what are its

short-term effects, for instance on the QoE, but also what are its long-term effects, for example, is it "contagious"? Moreover, given that toxicity is unwanted behavior, how could a game operator best deal with it?

- While, in this chapter, we mostly considered the social behavior and relationships in online gaming, there is still much research to be done on how to leverage such information. For instance, social ties may bring about certain "social" workload patterns, which might be used by a data centre scheduler to improve overall network and system performance.

Acknowledgments

The key findings as summarized in this chapter could not have been presented here without the instrumental work of our many collaborators, whom we thank: Ruud van de Bovenkamp, Emanuel Dias, Dick Epema, Adele Lu Jia, and Siqi Shen.

References

Abulrub, A.-H. G., Attridge, A., & Williams, M. A. (2011). Virtual reality in engineering education: The future of creative learning. *iJET*, 6(4), 4–11.

Antila, J., & Lakkakorpi, J. (2003). On the effect of reduced quality of service in multiplayer on-line games. *International Journal of Intelligent Games & Simulation*, 2(2), 89–95.

Dias, E. (2014). *A model to evaluate QoE of online social gaming*. MSc thesis, Delft University of Technology.

Drain, B. (2008). EVE evolved: EVE Online's server model. Retrieved from: http://massively.joystiq.com/2008/09/28/eve-evolved-eve-onlines-server-model/ (accessed October 11, 2017).

Funk, J. (2013). MOBA, DOTA, ARTS: A brief introduction to gaming's biggest, most impenetrable genre. Retrieved from: www.polygon.com/2013/9/2/4672920/moba-dota-arts-a-brief-introduction-to-gamings-biggest-most (accessed October 11, 2017).

Guo, Y., & Iosup, A. (2012). The Game Trace archive. In 11th International Workshop on Network and Systems Support for Games (NetGames) 2012: 1–6, Venice, Italy.

Iosup, A., Shen, S., Guo, Y., Hugtenburg, S., Donkervliet, J., & Prodan, R. (2014). Massivizing online games using cloud computing: A vision. In Multimedia and Expo Workshops (ICMEW), 1–4.

Jia, A. Lu, Shen, S., van de Bovenkamp, R., Iosup, A., Kuipers, F. A., & Epema, D. H. J. (2015, October). Socializing by gaming: Revealing social relationships in multiplayer online games. *ACM Transactions on Knowledge Discovery from Data*, 10(2), 11:1–11:29

Kuipers, F., Kooij, R., De Vleeschauwer, D., & Brunnstrom, K. (2010). Techniques for measuring quality of experience. In *Proceedings of the 8th International Conference on Wired/Wireless Internet Communications (WWIC'10)*, Luleå, Sweden.

Lien, T. (2014, August 11). What if video games could help us flirt? Retrieved from: www.polygon.com/2014/8/11/5990319/game-oven-bounden-flirt (accessed October 11, 2017).

Liu, E. S., & Theodoropoulos, G. K. (2014). Space-time matching algorithms for interest management in distributed virtual environments. *ACM Transactions on Modeling and Computer Simulation*, 24(3), 1–23.

Märtens, M., Shen, S., Iosup, A., & Kuipers, F. A. (2015). Toxicity detection in multiplayer online games. In *Proceedings of 14th International Workshop on Network and Systems Support for Games (NetGames)*, Zagreb, Croatia.

McCormick, R. (2013). 'League of Legends' eSports finals watched by 32 million people. Retrieved from:www.theverge.com/2013/11/19/5123724/league-of-legends-world-championship-32-million-viewers (accessed October 11, 2017).

McGonigal. J. (2011). *Reality is broken: Why games make us better and how they can change the world*. London: Jonathan Cape.

Morse, K. L. (1996). Interest management in large-scale distributed simulations. Technical Report. Information and Computer Science, University of California, Irvine.

Nae, V., Iosup, A., & Prodan, R. (2011). Dynamic resource provisioning in massively multiplayer online games. *IEEE Transactions on Parallel and Distributed Systems*, 22(3), 380–395.

Newzoo team. (2016). Global eSports market report. Reports an audience of over 130 million esports. Retrieved from: https://newzoo.com/insights/countries/global/ (accessed October 11, 2017).

Ries, M., Svoboda, P., & Rupp, M. (2008, June). Empirical study of subjective quality for massive multiplayer games. In *Proceedings of the 15th International Conference on Systems, Signals and Image Processing*, Bartislava, Slovakia.

Shen, S., Hu, S-Y., Iosup, A., & Epema, D. H. J. (2015). Area of simulation: Mechanism and architecture for multi-avatar virtual environments. *TOMCCAP*, 12(1), 8.

Steam team (2016, February 28). Steam and game stats. Continuously updated numbers indicate millions of online players, from a base of over 100 million players. Retrieved from: http://store.steampowered.com/stats/ (accessed October 11, 2017).

Susi, T., Johannesson, M., & Backlund, P. (2007). Serious games – An overview. Technical Report HS-IKI-TR-07-001. School of Humanities and Informatics University of Skövde, Sweden.

Walker, W. E., Giddings, J., & Armstrong, S. (2011). Training and learning for crisis management using a virtual simulation/gaming environment. *Cognition, Technology & Work*, 13(3), 163–173.

Wattimena, A. F., Kooij, R. E., van Vugt, J. M., & Ahmed, O. K. (2006). Predicting the perceived quality of a first person shooter: The quake iv g-model. In *Proceedings of NetGames*, New York, NY.

Wilson, C., Boe, B., Sala, A., Puttaswamy, K. P. N., & Zhao, B. Y. (2009). User interactions in social networks and their implications," In *Proceedings of the 4th ACM European conference on computer systems* (EuroSys), Nuremberg, Germany.

World of Warcraft team. (2015, August). Expansion features for The Legion Awaits. Mentions "in-game communities," "social groups," and attention to "form the perfect group to play your way." Retrieved from: http://eu.battle.net/wow/en/legion/#features (accessed October 11, 2017).

13

Profiling in Games: Understanding Behavior from Telemetry

RAFET SIFA, ANDERS DRACHEN, AND
CHRISTIAN BAUCKHAGE

13.1 Introduction

The game industry is facing a surge of data, which results from increasingly available highly detailed information about the behavior of software and software users. The data can come from a variety of channels, behavioral telemetry, user testing, surveys, attribution models, forums etc., be high dimensional, time dependent, and potentially very large (Drachen et al., 2013b; Feng, Brandt, & Saha, 2007; Hadiji et al., 2014; Sifa, Bauckhage, & Drachen, 2014a). The old adage of big data having volume, velocity, variety and volatility holds very true for behavioral telemetry from games (Drachen et al., 2013b; Feng et al., 2007; Runge et al., 2014; Sifa et al., 2013; Weber et al., 2011).

Profiling users has emerged across multiple data science application areas as a way of managing complex user data and discovering underlying patterns in the behavior of the player base. Profiling of users allows for a condensation and modeling of a complex behavioral space. Profiles allow us to consider players in a nonabstract and quantifiable way, building an understanding about who the players are and how they play the game or games being investigated.

Player profiling has been performed for a variety of different reasons and based on similarly varied methodologies, from work focused on customer profiling, psychological modeling, cohort analysis, and more. In this chapter, the focus is on behavior profiling based on telemetry data. That is, models of player behavior are generated based exclusively on telemetry data obtained from logs of player behavior, either during gameplay or in relation to it. Telemetry-driven profiling is one of the central challenges in game analytics, and focuses on condensing varied, high-volume, and often volatile data into descriptions that highlight the patterns in player behavior (Bohannon, 2010; Drachen et al., 2013b; Luton, 2013).

The idea of using customer data to inform marketing and product design has an extensive history in information science, where user profiling was developed to deal specifically with the problem of data overload. This is a prevalent issue in any user/customer-focused industry today, and certainly so in games. In games, we easily extract dozens to hundreds of features from direct user-game interactions and supplement these with data from marketing, attribution, play-testing, social networks, and more. To make things even more challenging, data are usually collected from large numbers of players, from potentially long-term interaction periods and are typically temporally volatile (Bauckhage, Drachen, & Sifa, 2015).

Despite these challenges, behavioral profiling plays an important role in game analytics. However, the general application of analytical principles to large-scale behavioral data in games is still relatively recent and has a fragmented history. Behavioral profiling in games originates in game design and game artificial intelligence (AI) (Bohannon et al., 2010; Drachen et al., 2013b; Mellon, 2009; Zoeller, 2011), and work in these areas has been carried out for more than two decades. However, with the recent introduction of large-scale behavioral tracking in online environments and games in particular, accompanied by the emergence of non-retail–based business models, new data sources have led to a proliferation of work focusing on pattern finding and definition in the behavior of players. For example, focusing on play styles, strategies, prediction, profiling, etc. (Bartle, 1996; Drachen & Schubert, 2013; Hadiji et al., 2014; Miller & Crowcroft, 2010; Nozhnin, 2012, 2013; Sifa et al., 2013). The purposes of telemetry-driven profiling can be many, from design evaluation, progression analysis, AI/bot behavior generation and monetization to user experience evaluation. Jointly, profiling helps build an understanding of the users. However, behavioral profiling in digital games is not a straightforward task due to the common high dimensionality in the data and the lack of clear guidelines for which types of behavioral features to incorporate into profiles. There is also a human element in the decisionmaking process that has a direct impact on the relative strength and applicability of behavioral profiles (Drachen et al., 2013b). These problems are especially present in games where players have wide degrees of freedom in how they want to approach and play the games, e.g., massively multiplayer online games (MMOGs), open-world games (OWGs) (also referred to as "sandbox" games because of their design), and some action-adventure games. Persistent online games featuring large virtual environments and broad player affordance can be particularly challenging due to the high-dimensional nature of the behavioral features that can be needed for behavioral profiling (Drachen et al., 2012; Sifa et al., 2016). Examples include games such as *The Elder Scrolls: Skyrim, World of Warcraft, Minecraft*, and *EVE Online*.

13.1.1 Overview of This Chapter

In this chapter the background of player profiling will be outlined and a review of the state-of-the-art presented. Furthermore, we present a number of case studies showcasing different profiling techniques and approaches, providing the first overview of the topic and a reference for future work in the domain. Section 13.2 provides a brief introduction to player profiling and introduces core concepts. Sections 13.3 and 13.4 review and analyze the state-of-the-art in behavior profiling in games across academia and industry. Sections 13.5 to 13.8 provide examples and in-depth discussions of different techniques for telemetry-driven profiling. Finally, Section 13.9 gathers these various threads and summarizes the current status of profiling within the domain of game analytics and highlights future research directions.

13.2 Player Profiling: An Introduction

Behavioral profiling in games provides the ability to consider the users in a nonabstract and quantifiable way. Profiling techniques essentially condense the behavioral space so that any patterns can be located or hypotheses tested (The techniques available for behavioral profiling in games rest on a variety of factors, as shown in Figure 13.1). Following that, profiles need to be refined into a format that permits action to be taken on them by the stakeholder on the receiving end. For example, for a level designer, profiles could be descriptions of how players overcome a specific challenge in a game, with clear indications as to where things go right and wrong.

In games, there are typically two overall goals of player profiling:

- **Correlation**: To correlate profiles with specific behaviors such as game completion potential, user experience, monetization, churn, retention, cross-game transportation, cross-promotion, social influence, and so on
- **Inference**: To investigate how and why specific behaviors occur as a function of user traits and/or behaviors.

We can also consider how profiles are developed, usually either in a bottom-up or top-down manner. The former is explorative, focused on locating patterns we did not know existed. This approach is useful as soon as data are available, but is usually feature intensive. Top-down profiling focuses on testing hypotheses, e.g., how valid already established profiles are given a new player cohort. This approach is typically employed late in production and during the live period of a game, notably for consistency-testing and updating previously defined profiles.

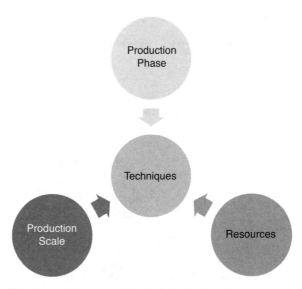

Figure 13.1 The techniques available for behavioral profiling in games rest on a variety of factors, notably: (1) the active production phase of a game, which determines what kinds of data are available; (2) the production scale, which determines the variety of data available, from a few key features to hundreds or more; and (3) the overall level of resources dedicated to analytics in the company and the active production. (This image is shown in full color in the Color Plates section.)

Profiles can be generated either to target individual or groups of players. Individual profiles seek to discover characteristics of specific people, and is based on data from only that person. Group profiling, which is the most common due to the typical large number of players involved in analysis (see, e.g., Drachen et al., 2013b; Normoyle & Jensen, 2015; and Sifa et al. 2015a), tries to categorize individuals as a kind of individual – i.e., a type or group. Group profiling is less precise than individual profiling but often required in practice to manage high-dimensionality data sets. Every group profile will have a *fit* that is the quality of the profile in terms of what it is applied to. Fit is an important component when considering how to distribute players into profiles or taking action on players who fall into specific profiles (Drachen et al., 2009; Mahlmann et al., 2010; Sifa et al., 2013). If a profile is 100% distributive it means that all properties apply fully to everyone in a group, e.g. *all bachelors are unmarried*. In practice, analytically generated group profiles are nondistributive to a greater or lesser degree. This is a key concern when considering how to act on profiles in an industrial or academic context. In general, the more detailed we try to make profiles, the fewer players they apply to and there is a definite element of cost–benefit balancing in play here.

Finally, player profiles can also be classified according to the information they are built from. Two core types are protean and player profiles (Drachen, 2014). The latter is based on actual behavioral, attitudinal, or other data, while the former is based on theoretical models and design intent (Canossa & Drachen, 2009a,b; Solomon, 2014; Taylor & Todd, 1995). Data-driven profiles can be developed from the earliest user testing and they are ideally updated throughout production and during post-launch. Protean profiles are commonly used in game design and can be defined from day 1. Importantly, they must be kept updated as a function of design changes in order to remain useful. They must also be integrated across the team to ensure coherence in their use (Drachen, 2014).

The process of building profiles rests on well-established guidelines for knowledge discovery in IT, irrespective of the specific algorithms or models used for pattern recognition (ranging from simple but effective tools such as cohort analysis to machine learning) (Drachen et al., 2013b):

1. **Discovery:** A knowledge discovery process is performed to provide sets of correlated data for profiling, i.e., information about which patterns and correlations we see in the data. For example, kill/death ratio appears to be important to progression in an FPS.
2. **Selection:** We decide which patterns to use and which behaviors to employ in further work with developing profiles. For example, if we are interested in churn, we use patterns showing correlations between behavior and players leaving/staying in the game. Via experimental work we can also investigate causal relationships. Various types of machine learning algorithms can be employed to search the variance space, with clustering being a popular example.
3. **Interpretation:** In this step, we define the profiles. This can be done in a variety of ways, but a sharp eye on the application is important. This is an often overlooked or underprioritized phase leading to problems in the fourth step.
4. **Application:** This vital step involves taking actions based on the information contained in the profiles. This step is possibly the most difficult to execute in practice as it often involves communication between stakeholder groups that may speak completely different languages.

The process is ideally cyclic, because players change behavior, the composition of the population changes over time, as does game design in persistent or semipersistent games. Hence, profiles should be continually updated as new data become available. It is also worth noting that profiling at all levels is not an objective process. The process relies on choices, such as the algorithm or model used, data preprocessing, feature selection, interpretation, etc. Because of these choices, there is a potential for bias and error in all of the foregoing steps.

13.3 Related Work: Player Profiling in the Lab and in the Wild

Behavioral profiling in games based on telemetry data is a relatively recent endeavor, distributed across a variety of subdomains and purposes within the overall confines of game research and game development, notably game analytics and game user research (Bohannon, 2010; El-Nasr, Drachen, A., & Canossa, A., 2013; Fields & Cotton, 2011; Lim, 2012). However, within game AI, agent modeling and adaptive games, the use of profiling for modeling autonomous entities has a history stretching over two decades, although the use of player-derived telemetry data in AI modeling is more recent (Kim et al., 2008; Sifa & Bauckhage, 2013; Thurau, Bauckhage, & Sagerer, 2004; Yannakakis, 2012).

Profiling players has a long history stretching back to, for example, the work of Bartle (1996), Nacke, Bateman, & Mandryk (2014), and Bateman and Boon (2006); the original and newest work of Yee (2014) and Yee and Ducheneaut (2015), and others who used design principles and motivational and psychological theory, combined with observation and surveys, to build the first frameworks categorizing player behavior. Trying to infer player motivation, personality, or similar based on in-game behavior forms an emergent key topic in game analytics, which connects psychology, social science, and analytics but is not the topic of the current work. Focusing on the use of behavioral or attitudinal data to profile players specifically, the current developments are generally driven by the recent availability of large-scale behavioral data from games, thanks to the adoption of tracking technologies and the business necessity of being able to take advantage of such data in order to remain competitive (Bauckhage et al., 2015; Fields & Cotton, 2011; Kersting et al., 2010; Lim and Harrell, 2015). Today, telemetry-driven behavioral profiling in industry and academia can take a variety of forms, from simple cohort analyses or segmentation of players, to machine learning-driven methods. It may also address a variety of goals, including design evaluation, monetization, optimization, debugging and exploration (Bauckhage et al., 2015; Drachen et al., 2012, 2013b; Mellon, 2009; Normoyle & Jensen, 2015; Nozhnin, 2013; Sifa et al., 2013; Yannakakis and Togelius, 2015).

13.4 Telemetry-Driven Profiling

Early work on telemetry-driven profiling originated in the industry, notably from Microsoft Studios Research, which championed the adoption of telemetry in game user research (Canossa, Drachen, & Sorensen, 2011; Kim et al., 2008; Thompson, 2007). In the past few years, every major publisher in the world has added analytics competencies, not only for free to play (F2P) mobile games, but across all game projects (Mellon, 2009; Zoeller, 2011; El-Nasr et al., 2013). The rise of F2P games has notably added to the industry's focus on behavior analysis. These are games with no up-front cost to the customer and with revenue depending on In-App Purchases (IAPs) (and sometimes associated branded products). Revenue thus depends on the ability of the developer to convince some portion of the customer base to purchase virtual items for real money. In order to be successful as a business model, these games require continued analysis of player behavior and are challenged by changes in player behavior and the shifting composition of the player base (Drachen et al., 2014a; Fields & Cotton, 2011; Luton, 2013; Mellon, 2009; Sifa et al., 2013).

Academic-industry partnerships, too, are increasingly common in game analytics (Drachen et al., 2009; Hadiji et al., 2014; Runge, 2014; Runge et al., 2014; Weber et al., 2011) although there remains a general lack of knowledge and data transfer due to confidentiality requirements versus academic publishing needs. The recency of game telemetry as a research topic also means that most available work is case based, e.g., application of a specific algorithm to behavioral data from a specific game. However, industry work in F2P mobile games are seeing the beginnings of shared underpinnings on the types of metrics that can be used for different types of analysis, e.g., segmentation, funnel analysis, and churn prediction (Drachen et al., 2013b; Fields & Cotton, 2011; Hadiji et al., 2014; Luton, 2013; Nozhnin, 2012, 2013; Runge et al., 2014; Sifa et al., 2015b).

Current work on behavioral and behavioral-attitudinal profiling in games can be categorized according to the method used, whether it is mainly descriptive or rests on unsupervised or supervised machine learning. Machine learning techniques can, for example, be classified according to their model complexity, their required input data, etc. However, the approach adopted here categorizes current work based on the intended application (use), because this better matches the real-use context of behavioral profiling in games. Additionally, the available literature is readily organized in this manner due to the applied focus of the work in the domain. In short, as illustrated in Figure 13.2, the five categories for profiling are snapshot, dynamic, predictive, psychological, and spatiotemporal profiling. It is important to note that specific machine learning approaches such as clustering, affinity mining, or prediction can be applied in one or more of these.

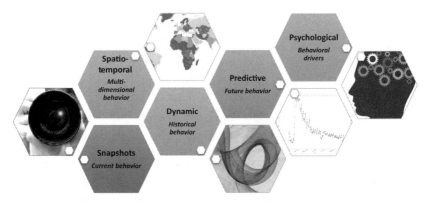

Figure 13.2 Current work on behavioral profiling in games can be divided into five categories depending on the overall purpose of the analysis: snapshot, dynamic, predictive, psychological, and spatiotemporal profiling. Each category targets specific aspects, dimensions, or properties of player behavior in games.

13.4.1 Snapshot Profiling

Snapshot profiling focuses developing an understanding of the patterns of behavior as they occur at the operational level. The majority of the work on telemetry-based behavior profiling in games has been based on snapshot data. The earliest work directly focusing on profiling is possibly by Drachen et al. (2009), who used data from *Tomb Raider: Underworld* to generate profiles of 1365 players based on Emergent Self-Organizing Networks. Four clusters of were located, encompassing more than 90% of the sampled players. The profiles were expressed in game design language to enable game designers to take action on them. Around the same time, Thurau, Kersting, and Bauckhage (2009) applied nonnegative matrix factorization to find clusters of player guilds in *World of Warcraft*. This characterizes much of the research on behavioral profiling in games, i.e., that while direct player profiling is not the end goal, the results ultimately provide profiles of one kind or another that informs design, monetization, server load balancing, or other aspect of games. This work was followed up by Drachen et al. (2012), who built snapshot profiles of players from the MMOG *Tera Online* and *Battlefield 2*, using a variety of clustering methods. Drachen et al. (2013a) investigated four different clustering techniques in terms of how useful they were for generating interpretable behavioral profiles in games, using data from *World of Warcraft*. Drachen, Sifa, and Thurau (2014b) adopted dimensionality reduction techniques to investigate patterns in character names in *World of Warcraft*. Bauckhage and Sifa (2015) presented k-maxoids, a k-means variant, and described its usefulness for clustering behavioral telemetry. The authors presented a case study of vehicle usage data from *Battlefield 3*, identifying seven clusters of behavior showcasing the preferences of players for specific vehicles in this game. Finally, Bauckhage et al. (2015) summarized the state of the art of using clustering to analyze behavioral telemetry in games. The authors outline multiple future perspectives on behavioral profiling in games, including the application of spatiotemporal analytics.

Pattern searching of player behavior was also performed by Thawonmas and Iizuka (2008), who used used frequency analysis to find behavior patterns in the MMOG *Cabal Online*, focusing specifically on bot-detection via identifying aberrant behavior. Bot-detection is a recurring topic in game analytics for MMOGs where in-game resources represent considerable value both internally and in terms of real-world value. Focusing on the real-time strategy game *StarCraft*, Weber and Mateas (2009) employed a series of classification algorithms for recognizing player strategy, employing regression in order to predict the production of units or buildings. Müller et al. (2015) classified player behavior in *MineCraft* using principal component analysis (PCA). The focus is on the distribution of time players put into four main categories of behavior, namely building, mining, fighting and exploring. Lim and Harrell (2015) used the archetype analysis approach of, e.g., Drachen et al. (2012) to investigate social phenomena in *Ultima IV* and to model identity representations in *The Elder Scrolls IV: Oblivion*. Holmgard et al. (2015) used Monte Carlo Tree Search controlled procedural personas to simulate players in the puzzle game *MiniDungeons 2*. Normoyle and Jensen (2015) used Bayesian semiparametric clustering to investigate choice–outcome relationships in *Battlefield 3*. Normoyle and Jensen (2015) used Bayesian clustering for grouping players. Finally, Suznjevic, Stupar, and Matijasevic (2011) modeled player behavior in the MMOG *World of Warcraft* as a function of five different types of behaviors, exploring temporal trends. The overall aim was to contribute to the problem of predicting network traffic in MMOGs accurately.

In esports analytics (as defined by Drachen et al., 2014c), a small number of publications have focused on clustering or profiling player behavior. Gao et al. (2013) targeted the identification of the heroes that players are controlling and the role they take. They defined a basic model with three roles a player can fulfill. Eggert et al. (2015) built on the work of Gao et al. (2013) and applied supervised machine learning to classify the behavior of *DOTA* players in terms of their hero roles or play styles. The authors used attribute evaluation techniques to develop a series of hero roles that were then evaluated again DOTA match data. Southey et al. (2005) developed a general-purpose analysis tool (SAGA-ML) to analyze metrics data from the game *FIFA '99*. The aim was to identify faults in the game design that permits maneuvers that can be used to repeatedly score goals.

13.4.2 Dynamic and Predictive Profiling

Player behavior changes as a function of time (Drachen et al., 2014a; El-Nasr et al., 2013; Fields & Cotton, 2011; Mellon, 2009; Sifa et al., 2013, 2014b; Zoeller, 2011). Furthermore, persistent games that see the same players interacting with a game over potentially long temporal periods experience a constant change in the population of players (Drachen et al., 2014a; Fields & Cotton, 2011; Mellon, 2009; Sifa et al., 2014b). This is notably the case for F2P games, which have persistence as a key design factor in order to support the underlying business model (Drachen et al., 2014a; El-Nasr et al., 2013; Fields & Cotton, 2011; Hadiji et al., 2014; Luton, 2013; Mellon, 2009; Nozhnin, 2012, 2013; Runge et al., 2014; Sifa et al., 2014b). Games themselves can also change over time, e.g., via patches, updates, or expansions. These three factors jointly mean that profiles generated based on snapshot data have a limited period during which they are valid as representations of the player base. In the industry it is therefore increasingly common to see player profiles being iteratively generated as a function of predefined time intervals, e.g., 24 hours. While the underlying unsupervised machine learning methods are similar for snapshot and dynamic profiling, the latter are constantly regenerated and additionally permit historical viewpoints on changes in the behavior of the players (or systems), and also act as a starting point for predictive analytics (Drachen et al., 2013b; Hadiji et al., 2014; Nozhnin, 2012, 2013; Runge et al., 2014).

Some of the earliest temporal analyses of player behavior originated in network analysis. For instance, Feng et al. (2007) investigated long-term patterns in playtime and session intervals in MMORPGs. Similarly, Sifa et al. (2014b) described large-scale cross-games patterns in playtime and retention patterns for more than 3,000 titles. Sifa et al. (2013) and Drachen et al. (2014a) used temporal bins in conjunction with iterative profiling to investigate the evolution of player profiles as a function of game progression and MMOG game lifetime, respectively. Thawonmas et al. (2011) studied revisitations to the game or specific area of the gameworld in an MMOG. Nozhnin (2012, 2013) provided insights into the practical development of churn prediction models in game development, working with the MMOG *Aion*. Hadiji et al. (2014), Runge et al. (2014), and Sifa et al. (2015b) focused on churn prediction in F2P games, categorizing players according to whether or not they were predicted to churn and at what point. Sifa et al. (2015b) also outlined methods for predicting which players would make IAPs. Yang, Harrison, and Roberts (2014) presented an approach for discovering and defining patterns in combat tactics among winning teams in the MOBA *DOTA*, based on graph representation. The authors attributed features to the graphs using frequent subgraph mining that allowed them to describe how different combat tactics contributed to team success in specific situation. Also in the area of e-sport analytics, Ong, Deolalikar, and Penge (2015) applied clustering to learn optimal team compositions for the the MOBA *League of Legends*. The goal was to develop descriptive play style groupings for informing a win/loss prediction model.

While predictive profiling can be as detailed and multidimensional as required, the currently most common techniques outside Game AI can generally be classified as delivering *shallow* profiles, i.e., profiles that are generated based on a small number of features and with a resulting binary classification such as *churner* and *nonchurner* (Hadiji et al., 2014; Nozhnin, 2012; Runge et al., 2014). This is in contrast to *deep* profiling, which categories or classifies players according to many features or dimensions. There is no agreed-on boundary between these definitions, and their use depends on the context of analysis. Adapting content to players, whether for the purpose of retention, monetization, experience, or learning, is generally aided by a more detailed categorization of the players that provides information about their specific behavior, and ideally the kinds of challenges they encounter in progressing in the game, making in-game social connections, accomplishing goals, etc. (Hadiji et al., 2014; Runge et al., 2014; Sifa et al., 2015b).

Prediction has a less pronounced role beyond the F2P game context, but is also finding use to predict player navigation in 3D environments, predict how far specific players will get into a game, predict what kind of problems specific players will encounter, and so on. The vast majority of the current knowledge about these application areas rests within the industry and is generally available only through industry talks and presentations. Game AI should again be mentioned as a domain where predictive behavioral models have been a focus of work for, e.g., guiding bot behavior (Bauckhage & Thurau, 2004; Sifa & Bauckhage, 2013; Tastan, Chang, & Sukthankar, 2012).

The problems associated with imbalanced data sets are of direct importance in predictive profiling in F2P games (Sifa et al., 2015b). Imbalance issues usually appear when analyzing rare events such as purchase within an interval or fraudulent activities. Training pure supervised machine learning models, e.g., to detect rare events, without accounting for this issue yields poor generalizations (Sifa et al., 2015b). It is important to note that this is not a unique problem for games (Chawla et al., 2002; Kubat, Holte, & Matwin, 1997), but F2P games form a situation that is different from subscription-based or retail-based business models (and outside of games entirely, e.g., retail). First, F2P games follow a freemium model, which means that the life cycle of these games is different than non-freemium situations. Second, F2P games do not change as a function of a purchase. As noted by Sifa et al. (2015b), installing an F2P game is not a commitment at the same level as buying a product in advance and this is one of the main reasons for the imbalance issue. For more information on how to deal with imbalance issues in behavioral telemetry, see, for instance, the work from Sifa et al. (2015b).

Another important problem in predictive profiling is the determination of the right model input features. There is relatively little publicly available knowledge on this issue, but Drachen et al. (2013b); Feng et al. (2007); Hadiji et al. (2014); Nozhnin (2012, 2013); Runge et al. (2014); and Sifa et al. (2014b, 2015b) discuss this problem in more detail.

13.4.3 Spatiotemporal Profiling

All games contain spatial and temporal elements, whether digital or nondigital. Especially in 3D digital games, the spatial dimension is often important to the perceived experience of the game. Furthermore, spatial navigation and positioning are key gameplay elements in games such as first-person shooters and many multiplayer games (Bauckhage et al., 2014; Drachen and Schubert, 2013; Sifa et al., 2016). A number of approaches for, e.g., trajectory analysis and classification have been adapted for use in game AI and game analytics to detect churners, study player tactics or to train nonplayer characters (NPCs) (Bauckhage et al., 2014; Sifa & Bauckhage, 2013; Sifa et al., 2016; Thurau et al., 2004). Behavioral analysis can be carried out without considering the temporal and spatial dimensions of play (these are referred to as static analysis); however, it is often necessary to include one or more of these in order to build the required insights. Snapshot profiling can be done without historical or spatial data, whereas dynamic profiling invariably ends up providing temporal patterns. Similarly, predictive modeling requires temporal information. Neither profiling approach requires spatial information, however. Spatial behavioral data are usually included only when needed given the purpose of the analysis. Additionally, spatiotemporal game analytics can be cumbersome and require that interpretation is performed in relation to the actual virtual environment. Ignoring this step in the analysis cycle leads to the risk of misinterpretation of the root causes of the observed behaviors (Drachen & Schubert, 2013).

While a full overview of the literature is beyond the scope of this chapter, simply because of the sheer variety of applications of spatiotemporal behavioral data in game AI and game analytics, a few key publications need to be mentioned. First, Drachen & Schubert (2013) provide a relatively recent overview of spatial and spatiotemporal game analytics. The use of spatiotemporal telemetry for visualizing player behavior originates about a decade back, e.g., with the work of Hoobler, Humphreys, & Agrawala (2004) on the multi-player first-person shooter *Return to Castle Wolfenstein.* Drachen and Canossa (2009) applied Geographic Information Systems to characterize player behavior in games, focusing on *Tomb Raider: Underworld.* The work was expanded to include, e.g., overlay analysis by Drachen & Canossa (2011). Miller and Crowcroft (2010) investigated group movement in the Arathi Basin battleground of *World of Warcraft,* grouping trajectories of players based on waypoint modeling. Bauckhage et al. (2014) adopted DEDICOM to not only cluster players of *Quake III Arena* based on their in-game behavior, but also develop directional waypoint graphs for behavior-based partitioning of game environments. Within es-ports, Drachen et al. (2014c) investigated skill-based differences in the behavior of *DOTA* players. Rioult et al. (2014) used topological measures in the same game to investigate player positioning and the influence of this on predicting match outcomes. Campbell, Tremblay, & Verbrugge (2015) presented work on path clustering of player trails. Finally, Sifa et al. (2016) introduced the use of tensor models for learning spatiotemporal features to predict retention in games.

13.4.4 Psychological Profiling

Telemetry data are only one source of information about players, and a relatively recently introduced one at that. While the focus here is on telemetry-driven approaches, it should be mentioned that behavioral profiling has an extended history based on information derived from user-testing, surveys, marketing data, etc., and has there given rise to the concept of Psychographic customer modeling (Raghu et al., 2001). With the work of Bartle (1996) and others, the idea of tying in observations from gameplay to profiling, or use gameplay behavior as the sole basis for profiling, was introduced. Initially such models were based on observation only. In the early 2000s, authors such as Bateman and Boon (2006), Nacke et al. (2014), Ryan, Rigby, & Przybylski (2006), Yee (2014), and Yee and Ducheneaut (2015) began using online surveys to build profiles based on the motivations/needs or personalities of players; however, these were not initially tied to in-game telemetry but to the perceptions of the players themselves about their in-game behavior and motivations driving these. In recent years, the idea of using telemetry data to draw inferences about player psychology has emerged, with, however, only early work having been done so far.

For example, van Lankveld et al. (2011) used a custom module from *Neverwinter Nights* generated using the AURORA engine to investigate correlations between player behavior and the Five Factor Model of personality, measured using the NEO-PI-R questionnaire. The experimental work indicated that it was possible correlating at least some aspects of the five personality traits in the model and in-game behavior. In follow-up work, Spronck, Balemans, and van Lankveld (2012) investigated whether the same relationships were present in *Fallout 3*, measuring personality traits using the NEO-FFI survey this time. The results generally supported the previous work, although sample sizes this time also were understandably small given the laboratory-based nature of the work. Canossa, Martinez, and Togelius (2013) triangulated behavioral telemetry from *MineCraft* with the Reiss Motivation Profiler serving as a hermeneutic grid. Canossa et al. (2013) investigated correlations between in-game behavior in *Kane & Lynch: Dog Days* and player frustration in a mixed-methods study.

Psychological profiling based on behavioral telemetry remains in its infancy. It is unknown what the state of the art of these methods is within the industry due to confidentiality requirements. It is possibly a near-future major new topic in game analytics, as there is an obvious interest in tying in-game behavior with player psychology, as this provides the basis for marketing that targets the specific interests of the players, as well as for adaptive games that modify themselves to the inferred motivations and personalities of the players (Yannakakis, 2012; Yannakakis & Togelius, 2015). Finally, this perspective is important in learning games where the motivation to engage with teaching material is crucial.

13.5 Snapshot Profiling in Games

Typically, data used for snapshot profiling consists of aggregate metrics about the players and/or their behavior. Generally, historical data are not used but rather information about the state of the players at the present. Typical examples include dimensionality reduction of high-variety data sets about player characters in MMOGs or other online multiplayer games, in order to obtain an understanding about the composition of the current player base (Bauckhage & Sifa, 2015; Drachen et al., 2012; Gao et al., 2013; Feng et al., 2007).

Although there are various methods that can be used for this task, the usually preferred methods for snapshot profiling in the game industry are based on manual segmentation using predefined features (Bauckhage et al., 2015). These methods usually do not capture interesting patterns that are related to relationships with data sets. However, statistical machine learning tools not only help in finding interesting patterns but also provide possibilities to identify important features.

For the task of profiling in this section, we will start with snapshot profiling, which is commonly the first level of profiling performed for multidimensional behavioral data sets. For the sake of generality, we will continue this section with an overview over the theoretical foundations of one of the most commonly used algorithms for snapshot profiling and a profiling case study from Sifa et al. (2015a) which covers a large-scale playtime based analysis of millions of players.

13.5.1 k-Means Clustering

The simplicity of its derivation and implementation has made the k-means algorithm arguably one of the most popular (clustering) procedure in data science (Wu et al., 2008). Specifically in game analytics, it is often used to find central behavioral clusters (Bauckhage & Sifa, 2015; Bauckhage et al., 2015; Drachen et al., 2012).

The main objective of k-means algorithm is to group a given set of data points into a predefined number of clusters. Formally, given $k \in \mathbb{N}$ and a set of data points $X = \{\mathbf{x}_i \in \mathbb{R}^m | i = 1, \ldots, n\}$, the k-means algorithm finds appropriate centroids $Z = \{\mathbf{z}_i \in \mathbb{R}^m | i = 1, \ldots, k\}$ by minimizing

$$\min_{\mathbf{z}_i} RSS = \sum_{i=1}^{k} \sum_{\mathbf{x}_j \in C_i} ||\mathbf{x}_j - \mathbf{z}_i||^2. \tag{13.1}$$

The algorithm randomly initializes the centroids and determines the clusters as

$$C_i = \{\mathbf{x}_j \in X | ||\mathbf{x}_j - \mathbf{z}_i||^2 \leq ||\mathbf{x}_j - \mathbf{z}_l||^2 \quad \forall l \neq i\}. \tag{13.2}$$

After that each new cluster will be updated as being the center of the assigned points by

$$\mathbf{z}_i = \frac{1}{|C_i|} \sum_{\mathbf{x}_j \in C_i} \mathbf{x}_j. \tag{13.3}$$

Repeating the steps in (13.2) and (13.3) until convergence will yield suitable centroids. With respect to our discussion further in the text that follows, we also remark that the problem of k-means clustering is equivalent to a constrained matrix factorization problem (Bauckhage, 2015).

13.5.2 Case Study: Cross Game Player Profiling

Now we turn our attention to a snapshot profiling study by Sifa et al. (2015a) that aimed at revealing how players distribute their time playing particular games. The results we discuss here are but the first part of the player-based analysis in that work. Having analyzed the time 6 million players (of a multigame

Table 13.1 *Snapshot profiling results from Sifa et al. (2015a) that show player-wise gameplay distributions of 6 million players.*

Profile Identifiers	Ratio	Characteristics
Customizers	3.1	Valve's flagship customization game TF-2 and Garry's Mod
DOTA 2	9.7	Typical *DOTA-only* players
FPS	5.2	Played only famous FPS games: CS: Source, CoD and TF-2
Left 4 Dead 2	0.8	FPS players with a heavy emphasis on Left 4 Dead 1 and 2
CS: Source	8.6	Playing mostly CS: Source
Counter-Strike Original	10.6	Player of the original CS game
Civilization V	1.0	Sid Meier's Civilization V players
Active Steam Players	38.8	Played variety of games across different genres nearly equal amount of time
Balanced DOTA 2	5.4	DOTA2 players that are more inclined to play other games
TF-2	15.6	Mostly played TF-2
Counter-Strike Alternative	1.2	CS Condition Zero and original CS players

Each identified profile shows a tendency toward a particular type of game genre or a flagship game.

social networking platform called *Steam*) spent on more than 3,007 games using *k*-means clustering, the authors found eleven different behavioral profiles and reported more than half of the players are *specialized* in one particular game.

Table 13.1 shows the summarized results where the profiles are described in terms of their representation ratio and characteristics. The results indicate inclinations of game preferences with respect to particular titles or set of titles (such as *Team Fortress 2* (TF-2) players or *Counter Strike* (CS) series) or to particular game genres such as first person shooter (FPS) game players in general.

These types of insights help the analysts reveal interesting player behaviors and give a first impression about the data set at hand.

13.6 Dynamic Profiling with Extremes

Considering the cases of dynamic player profiling, it is vital to know the coverage of the existing data to provide meaningful and actionable insights

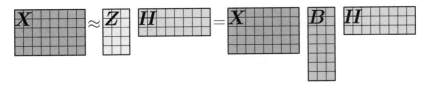

Figure 13.3 A pictorial representation of archetypal analysis. The data matrix $\mathbf{X} \in \mathbb{R}^{m \times n}$ is factorized into $\mathbf{Z} \in \mathbb{R}^{m \times k}$ which is the matrix of archetypes and a belongingness matrix $\mathbf{H} \in \mathbb{R}^{k \times n}$ which is column stochastic. When representing the archetypes as a convex combination of actual data points a further column stochastic matrix $\mathbf{B} \in \mathbb{R}^{n \times k}$ is also introduced.

to designers and the developers for decision making (Bauckhage & Sifa, 2015). In this context, archetypal analysis plays an important role owing to its unique structure. It not only reveals extreme behavioral basis vectors that are easy to interpret, but also allows for soft clustering through the stochastic belongingness coefficients. In the following we give an introduction to archetypal analysis that includes its matrix factorization formalization as well as approaches to find the archetypes. Following that we present a case study covering level-wise profiling of players of an action-adventure game.

13.6.1 Archetypal Analysis

Introduced by Cutler and Breiman (1994), archetypal analysis is a soft clustering method based on representing data entities with respect to archetypes that are defined to be extremal data points (Figure 13.3). Formally, given a data matrix $\mathbf{X} = [\mathbf{x}_1, \mathbf{x}_2, \ldots, \mathbf{x}_n] \in \mathbb{R}^{m \times n}$ and an integer k s.t. $k \ll n$, archetypal analysis performs the following factorization:

$$\mathbf{X} \approx \mathbf{ZH} \approx \mathbf{XBH}, \tag{13.4}$$

where $\mathbf{Z} = [\mathbf{z}_1, \mathbf{z}_2, \ldots, \mathbf{z}_k] \in \mathbb{R}^{m \times k}$ contains the k archetypes, $\mathbf{H} = [\mathbf{h}_1, \mathbf{h}_2, \ldots, \mathbf{h}_n] \in \mathbb{R}^{k \times n}$ contains the stochastic belongingness coefficient vectors for each data point to the archetypes, and $\mathbf{B} = [\mathbf{b}_1, \mathbf{b}_2, \ldots, \mathbf{b}_k] \in \mathbb{R}^{n \times k}$ contains the stochastic coefficient vectors to represent the archetypes as convex mixtures of actual data points. After calculating the archetypes and coefficient matrices, a data point $\mathbf{x}_i$ can be represented as

$$\mathbf{x}_i \approx \mathbf{Zh}_i = \sum_{j=1}^{k} \mathbf{z}_j h_{ji} = \sum_{j=1}^{k} \sum_{p=1}^{n} \mathbf{x}_p b_{pj} h_{ji}. \tag{13.5}$$

As a matrix norm minimization problem, the task of finding appropriate archetypes can be formally cast as minimizing the residual sum of squares

$$\min_{H,B} RSS = ||\mathbf{X} - \mathbf{XBH}||^2 \tag{13.6}$$

with the following constraints

$$b_{ij} \geq 0 \wedge \sum_{i=1}^{n} b_{ij} = 1 \wedge h_{ji} \geq 0 \wedge \sum_{j=1}^{k} h_{ji} = 1. \tag{13.7}$$

Numerous approaches have been proposed for finding $\mathbf{H}$ and $\mathbf{B}$ minimizing (13.6) (Bauckhage & Thurau, 2009; Kersting et al., 2010; Morup & Hansen, 2012; Sifa et al., 2014b; Thurau, Kersting, & Bauckhage, 2010). The first algorithm proposed by Cutler & Breiman (1994) aimed to solve convex least squares problems to find archetypes and its coefficients. To handle large data sets, the method has been modified using active set approaches (Bauckhage & Thurau, 2009). A distance geometry based approach, called simplex volume maximization (SIVM), has been introduced by Thurau et al. (2010) showing the relation between increasing the volume of the data simplex and reduction of error in (13.6). By constraining the archetypes to be actual data points, i.e., constraining $\mathbf{B}$ to be a sparse and nonoverlapping binary matrix, SIVM first finds the datapoints that maximize the Cayley–Menger determinant as being the archetypes and finds the appropriate belongingness coefficients $\mathbf{H}$ by solving (13.6) with fixed $\mathbf{B}$. Furthermore, a formalization of finding archetypes and coefficients as gradient descent optimization has been shown by Morup and Hansen (2012) that also allows for capturing nonlinearity through kernelization (Bauckhage & Thurau, 2009; Morup & Hansen, 2012; Sifa et al., 2014b).

13.6.2 Case Study: Level-wise Player Profiling in an Action-Adventure Game

To provide a practical impression of how archetypal analysis performs, we present a case study (Sifa et al., 2013) that is based on an analysis of 62,000 players of the AAA-level jump and run game *Tomb Raider Underworld* (TRU). TRU offers a third-person level oriented adventure- and platformer-type gameplay where the player controls a fictional character and protagonist Lara Croft. Including the storyline and a skippable prologue, the game offers its players nearly 200 puzzles to solve. The main concentration of the case study is to observe behavioral profiles and their evolution throughout the level progression using archetypal analysis to help designers and developers understand how the players progress levels and interact with the game. At this stage, game and task-specific feature selection plays an important role to be able to build actionable profiles. Namely, considering the highly granular data sets (such as the one analyzed in this case study) and the level of analysis needed, aggregating numerous features capturing important aspects of the gameplay helps the designers have an overall idea about how the players are interacting in complex games such as TRU. For that reason, Sifa et al. (2013) extracted gameplay, playtime, and interaction based features that are listed as follows.

- **Playing time**: The aggregated time of the player spent playing the game, which is also analyzed population-wise by Bauckhage et al. (2012).
- **Player death**: Represents the total number of deaths of a player, which can have variety of causes and depend on activity distribution of the player.
- **Help-on-demand**: Frequency of requests through the help on demand (HOD) system that provides hints and answers to solve puzzles.
- **Causes of death**: The frequencies of main causes of deaths in the games that are categorized under four groups: deaths caused by melee enemies, ranged weapons, environmental factors (e.g., fire or traps), and falling.
- **Adrenaline used**: Represents the number of adrenaline-type attacks used that allow the player to lock on to the enemies and and hit them.
- **Rewards**: Numbers of ancient artifacts, shards, and relics collected by the player.
- **Setting changes**: Represents the number and type of personalization based game features that the player has performed. The player adjustments can be performed under carriable ammo, hit points of NPCs and the players themselves and the recovery time for jumping.

Having identified features and gathered them in a data matrix X, Sifa et al. (2013) used SIVM to extract level-wise behavioral profiles. It is important to note that the basis vectors that are used to describe the profiles correspond to actual players with extreme behavior, which gives the ability to the designer not only to interpret the results but also to understand how extreme the players might be (Bauckhage & Sifa, 2015; Sifa et al., 2013). The profiles resulting from running SIVM with six archetypes and their characterization for each of the levels of TRU are listed as follows.

- **Level 1**: Having the highest playtime among the profiles, the most populated profile contains more than 76% of the players who have low death rates that are caused mainly by falling damage. This profile also indicates finding many rewards (which we label as the SLOW archetype). Ten percent of the players are characterized by low completion time, minimal use of the HOD system, but many death events, notably from falling and environmental causes, and also very high reward scores. Among the remaining four archetypes, making use of the savings adjustment system is common.

- **Level 2**: For the second level in TRU, the players are more divided across the six archetypes, showing a higher overall diversity in play styles. Forty-five percent of the players are characterized by low completion rates but heavy use of the HOD system (labeled as HODUSE profile), indicating some trouble with the puzzles in the game for this cluster – notably because remaining archetypes do not use the HOD system. These players complete the level quickly and die very little. Twenty-six percent of the players exhibit slow completion times and high reward rates, with limited deaths. This profile was also evident in level 1 (SLOW archetype), but is much less frequent in level 2 indicating greater diversification of play styles. Twenty-one percent of the players exhibit the same quick completion rate as the first cluster described, but do not use the HOD system and – maybe as a consequence – die a lot (the most of any of the clusters), mainly from falling. Perhaps this indicates a group of players who have trouble with the jumping mechanic in TRU.
- **Level 3**: The third level sees players falling into one large cluster (75%) characterized by having the longest completion time, high rewards, and low death counts (SLOW archetype). This cluster was also prevalent in level 1 and formed a smaller component in level 2. Eleven percent fall into a profile exhibiting faster completion times, but also heavy use of the HOD system and more deaths than the main cluster. This pattern is reminiscent to the largest cluster in level 2. Two smaller clusters are characterized by (4%) high use of the adrenaline feature, quick completion and high reward scores, but also fairly high death scores, mainly from falling; 6% fall into a cluster characterized by high death scores, with their deaths being mainly from ranged enemies.
- **Level 4**: Similar to level 2, players form form three main clusters. The mostly populated cluster here is the SLOW archetype covering 46% of the players. Twenty-four percent of the players fall into the profile with a large number of deaths by mostly ranged weapons and fast level completion whereas the 11.6% of the players frequently use the HOD system, obtained high scores through rewards and have high number of deaths caused by the environment and falling. Nine percent of the players are described as having fast completion times and high frequency of deaths through melee and ranged enemies which characterizes the players as good navigators that are challenged by movable enemies (Sifa et al., 2013).
- **Level 5**: In this level the overall picture painted by the six archetypes changes. At this point there are only about 12,000 players out of the original 62,000 who have reached this far into the game. One cluster dominates (89%), characterized by heavy use of the HOD system (HODUSE profile), but otherwise rapid completion and low deaths indicating highly skilled play but either

not caring about or having trouble with the puzzles in the level. The second biggest cluster, just shy of 7% of the players, are characterized by not using the HOD system heavily, but contrarily dying a lot, and mainly from falling.

- **Level 6**: Sees a return to a more diversified profile in the archetypes. Fifty-five percent are characterized by very quick completion rates, limited use of the adrenalin feature but using the savings grab adjustment heavily. This is in tune with the levels design which features many difficult jumps. Remaining clusters do not use the savings grab adjustment. Twenty-one percent of the players similarly complete the level fast, die mainly from environmental causes, and use the HOD system heavily and are reminiscent of the HODUSE profile identified in previous levels, although there are some variations across the levels (as would be expected given the variations in the design of these, notably the increasing difficulty). Finally, 11% fit the SLOW profile, which also appears to occur in all the levels.
- **Level 7**: Fifty-five percent fit the overall characteristics of the SLOW profile (slow completion time, low deaths, high reward scores). Twenty-four percent are characterized by rapid completion times and overall low scores, including few rewards found, but a return to using the savings changes in the game which are otherwise concentrated on the first two levels of the game. Eleven percent are characterized by having high death scores, from diverse causes, but rapid completion, zero use of the HOD system, and high reward scores. This profile to some degree fits the five smallest of the clusters in level 7, with some individual variations, e.g., heavy use of the adrenalin feature or use of the savings changes. But they are all generally characterized by highly skilled play, which is to be expected perhaps given that there are now only one sixth of the players left at this point in the game.

It is important to note that the aforementioned results are one out of the three analyses performed for profiling TRU players. A more detailed discussion regarding playtime and level-based profiling through archetypal analysis can be found in Sifa et al. (2013). Nevertheless, in this section, we have seen how archetypal analysis can reduce the dimensionality by yielding representative players for the profiling players in complex and high-dimensional data sets.

13.7 Predictive Profiling in Freemium Games

Predictive profiling changes the focus from the foregoing unsupervised approaches to supervised techniques. Predicting player behavior is one of the central and most common challenges in game analytics, notably owing to the mobile F2P section of the game industry, which depends on predictive modeling to be able to monitor, control, and forecast their revenue flow. In F2P games, which operate under the freemium business model, only a small fraction of the people starting the game turn into long-term players, social network enablers, and/or buyers of in-game content. Given this imbalance, the ability to predict who these players are is therefore important as it enables an optimization of Customer Relationship Management (CRM), and tailoring game content to the specific profiles of these users (Hadiji et al., 2014; Runge et al., 2014; Sifa et al., 2015b; Xie et al., 2015).

13.7.1 Decision Trees and Random Forests

An important aspect of all game analytics work is that the results need to be described in such a way that the relevant stakeholder (game designer, system designer, marketer, community specialist, manager, producer, or artist) can act on them. Predictive models should therefore ideally have relative transparency in addition to being accurate. For this reason, decision trees are broadly used for predicting player behavior (Drachen et al., 2013b; Sifa et al., 2015b; Weber & Mateas, 2009).

An example of the use of decision trees for prediction was presented by Mahlmann et al. (2010), who employed 11 behavioral features as well as player progress in *Tomb Raider: Underworld*, to investigate patterns in said progress. The authors describe for example how time spent on a specific level early in the game combined with finding few hidden rewards led to a tree branch that ultimately predicted players would leave the game relatively early. Conversely, completing the early level relatively quickly meant players were predicted to be retained until the later levels in the game. Decision tree–based models like these can be employed on a wide variety of behavioral variables to determine which are the most important to predict a specific behavior.

Decision trees, irrespective of the specific variant, apply a graphical approach to compare alternative explanations and assign values to these alternatives, describing problems in terms of sequential decisions. This perspective fits the perspective of the player progressing through a game well. Given the range of models available, decision trees are also relatively powerful analytically, and robust within a range of data types and levels of measurement (Rokach & Maimon, 2008).

Formally, decision trees are greedy split-based learning methods that are realized in divide and conquer manner (Breiman, 2001; Quinlan, 1996). Given an input and output space that are denoted by H and D respectively, decision trees learn the mapping $f : H \rightarrow D$. For profiling players, we usually define H

to be the space formed by the accumulated behavioral features and D to be the target variable such as the binary indicator for churning or numeric value for number of purchases (Hadiji et al., 2014; Runge et al., 2014; Sifa et al., 2015b). Considering the structure of the decision tree models, they usually contain two atomic entities: *conditional nodes* that steer the search direction with respect to the condition they entail and *leaf nodes* that contain the conclusion, i.e., the classification results. The models are learned by splitting the training data based on particular attributes into chunks that minimize a given error. While this error is task specific, it is usually defined as the heterogeneity (or impurity) for binary classification. For classification tasks, heterogeneity measures yield how uncertain, or mixed, a particular split is and can be quantified using the *Gini Impurity Index*. For binary classification, given a node q as a collection of some data entities, its Gini Impurity Index is gives as

$$\text{gini}(q) = 1 - P(q = True)^2 - P(q = False)^2, \qquad (13.8)$$

where $P(q = True)$ and $P(q = False)$ indicate the probability of entities in q belonging to *True* or *False* classes respectively. The splitting works recursively until all data entities are perfectly separated with respect to the classes or a predefined tree depth is reached. The stopping conditions can also be restricted by setting a threshold on the minimum number of elements in the leaves. It is important to note that the stopping condition might directly affect the overall generalization of the learned function. Perfectly grown trees might learn the mapping in the training data with almost zero error; however, they might not necessarily perform well on unseen entities. In machine learning and statistics, this is called *overfitting*. For decision trees, this can be prevented, for instance, by pruning the trees. For more information on avoiding overfitting in the context of decision tree learning using tree-pruning, we refer the reader to Mitchell (1997).

Another method to reduce the chances of overfitting has been proposed by Breiman (2001) and uses an ensemble of decision trees called a *Random Forest*. The main idea behind Random Forests is to incorporate randomness with sampling and tree construction to obtain numerous trees that reduce the variance toward finding the actual underlying function that is learned. Using the foregoing terminology, the trees are constructed as follows: (1) we generate $l \in \mathbb{N}$ data samples by selecting data entities *with replacement* (a.k.a. bootstrap samples); (2) for each data sample we train decision trees using the particular sample *with randomly selected $c \in \mathbb{N}$ features*; (3) for each new entity to classify we feed the input to all of the learned trees and combine the output, for instance, by majority voting of the class labels or averaging the resulting probabilities.

13.7.2 Case Study: Prediction Profiling through Purchase Decision and Churn Identification in F2P Mobile Games

Predictive profiling plays a major role in the product development of any F2P game for resource planning. For example, estimating player retention behavior might help find critical players that are about to quit (Runge et al., 2014). We now present a combined case study for predictive profiling in mobile F2P gaming environments that is based on the churn analysis by Hadiji et al. (2014) and purchase decision analysis of Sifa et al. (2015b), where both consider a decision tree–based approach. The main aim here is to predict future player activities given player's metadata and their historical activities. Even though profiling was not the main objective of both studies, using decision tree models provides a supervised profiling framework that can also handle nominal attributes such as country or flags indicating particular activities. That is, analyzing the selected features that increase the information gain from the learned tree or set of trees provides us useful insights about the important features to consider that lead to the people to leave the game or purchase in-game items (Hadiji et al., 2014; Sifa et al., 2015b). In both works, the authors considered features that are general and largely game independent such as *the number of sessions played* or *the current absence time until the decision date* for applicability to other games. Additionally, to capture the temporal trends in changes of some important behavioral features such as playtime, Hadiji et al. (2014) used parameters of a playtime model as features whereas Sifa et al. (2015b) used the correlation and deviation in time. We group the full list of features used for this case study under the type of analysis in the following.

- **Churn prediction**: Number of sessions, number of purchases, average playtime per session, average spending per session, premium user flag, number of days, retention value, predefined spending category, average time between sessions, parameters of the playtime model, current absence time.
- **Purchase decision prediction**: Country, device, move count, active opponents, logins and game rounds, skill level, reached goals, world number, number of interactions with other users, number of purchases, amount spent, playtime, last inter-session time, last inter-login time, inter-login time distribution, inter-session time distribution, correlation on time, mean and deviation on time, country segments.

Starting with churn prediction analysis, Hadiji et al. (2014) performed two types of data generation procedures to train their models. The first type of the data generation model analyzed only the churned players up to a cutoff date by assigning their complete profile as churning and generated randomly sampled nonchurning (synthetic) examples to train a player churn classifier. On the other hand the second data generation type introduced the notion of *soft churn window* to simulate real-world applications, where players were considered churning or not churning based on their appearance in a predefined time window. For more insights about the data generation process with a pictorial illustration we refer the reader to Hadiji et al. (2014). In the following, we analyze the results from the latter data generation type as it aligns with the purchase decision prediction study as well. Having built decision tree–based binary classification models for players of five different F2P mobile games the authors found that average time between sessions plays the most important role in players' upcoming departure. Namely as also indicated by Feng et al. (2007) for multiplayer game players, the decision tree model trained to predict churn has also found that an increase in the time between sessions results in players quitting the game. Other important features found to be affecting the departure of the players were number of sessions, current absence time, number of days, and the predefined spending category of the players.

Moving on with purchase prediction decision analysis, Sifa et al. (2015b) considered a decision tree learning–based prediction approach in which given the history of player activities, they predict whether an upcoming purchase will be made, and if so, its quantity. They modeled the former as a binary classification problem and the latter as a regression problem. In this section we explain the former as it built on the churn analysis from above. For this task the authors consider three supervised learning models which included decision trees, random forests and support vector machines for three observation windows of length 1, 3, and 7 days. Additionally, it is important to note that the game analyzed in this study was of freemium type and the objective defining the information gain here was whether the player will have made a purchase or not. These caused a highly imbalanced class distribution where the majority of the players were nonpaying users, which made the prediction of paying users really difficult. To overcome this problem, the authors created synthetic players as convex combinations of randomly selected premium players to obtain the best result with random forests. Similar to the foregoing decision tree model for churn analysis, random forests also provide a way of determining important features for the defined objective (Breiman, 2001; Sifa et al., 2015b). Considering the best model trained to predict the player purchases for the seven-day window, Sifa et al. (2015b) reported that Number of Purchases and Amount Spent are the most important indicator features for further purchases. That is, players that have already spent money in games will be most likely also spend money in the future. Additionally, the authors also report the importance of the social interactions with other players and some game-related features such as count of the moves and the worlds.

13.8 Spatiotemporal Profiling with DEDICOM

For many contemporary games in the market, spatiotemporal activities play an important role in user engagement. This especially becomes important for open world games that allow the user to freely navigate through the maps (Bauckhage et al., 2014; Campbell et al., 2015). Spatial layouts of such gameworlds are constantly growing and become more and more comparable to the real world in terms of scale. For instance, *Just Cause 2* comes with a game map of one thousand square kilometers and *The Elder Scrolls II: Daggerfall* offers an area of more than 160,000 square kilometers to its players. Considering the three-dimensional nature of such game environments, intelligent analysis techniques are required to provide designers important feedback with respect to behavior of the players. This feedback process is particularly vital for massively multiplayer online open world games that are gradually improved and extended based on the behavior of the players.

Regarding the spatial analysis of player behavior, current methods heavily rely on two- or three-dimensional heatmaps (see the examples in Figure 13.5) that color-code visited locations with respect to frequency of appearance. The main issues of heatmaps is the lack of coverage of directional and temporal information that form the basis of movement. In order to tackle these challenges and capture the movement information, Bauckhage et al. (2014) used asymmetric matrix factorization techniques called Decomposition Into Directed Components (DEDICOM) and Decomposition Into Simple Components (DESICOM). Both these methods allow for reducing the dimensionality of higher order directional data sets while preserving temporal information. The results of the models can be used to mine hidden patterns in player trajectories and allow for comparative player analysis. In the following, we introduce DEDICOM and DESICOM partitioning models and present a case study for how such methods can be used to analyze game trajectory data.

13.8.1 DEDICOM Model

As a counterpart to the well known methods of Principal Component Analysis (PCA) and Multidimensional Scaling (MDS), DEDICOM as introduced by Harshman (1978) allows for analyzing pairwise similarities that may be asymmetric. Given a matrix $\mathbf{S} \in \mathbb{R}^{n \times n}$ that represents the asymmetric relations

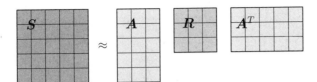

Figure 13.4 A pictorial representation of *Two-Way DEDICOM* partitioning. Asymmetrical relationships given in $\mathbf{S} \in \mathbb{R}^{n \times n}$ are decomposed into a combination of a latent factor matrix $\mathbf{A} \in \mathbb{R}^{n \times k}$ and an asymmetric mode transition matrix $\mathbf{R} \in \mathbb{R}^{k \times k}$.

among n objects, i.e., $\mathbf{S} \neq \mathbf{S}^T$, DEDICOM performs the following partition:

$$\mathbf{S} \approx \mathbf{ARA}^T \qquad (13.9)$$

where $\mathbf{A} \in \mathbb{R}^{n \times k}$ and $\mathbf{R} \in \mathbb{R}^{k \times k}$. The columns of $\mathbf{A}$ represent the k latent factors behind the relationships encoded in $\mathbf{S}$ and matrix $\mathbf{R}$ encodes the relations among these latent components. DEDICOM approximates the individual relationships between two data entities i and j as

$$s_{ij} \approx \mathbf{a_{:i}}^T \mathbf{R} \mathbf{a_{:j}} = \sum_{b=1}^{k} \left(a_{ib} \mathbf{r_{:b}} \right)^T \mathbf{a_{:j}} = \sum_{b=1}^{k} \sum_{c=1}^{k} a_{ib} r_{bc} a_{jc} \qquad (13.10)$$

where $\mathbf{a_{:i}}$ and $\mathbf{a_{:j}}$ represent the ith and jth row of $\mathbf{A}$ respectively and $\mathbf{r_{:b}}$ represents the bth row of $\mathbf{R}$. Figure 13.4 provides a pictorial representation of two-way DEDICOM partitioning.

Solving DEDICOM can be cast as a problem of minimizing a matrix norm

$$\min_{\mathbf{A}, \mathbf{R}} ||\mathbf{S} - \mathbf{ARA}^T||^2 \qquad (13.11)$$

which is convex in $\mathbf{R}$ but not in $\mathbf{A}$. This leads us to consider alternating least squares minimization procedures to find the optimal factors $\mathbf{R}$ and $\mathbf{A}$ minimizing (13.11) (Bader, Harshman, & Kolda, 2007; Bauckhage et al., 2014; Sifa, Ojeda, & Bauckhage, 2015c). Updating $\mathbf{A}$ in a scalable fashion has been tackled by approximating the normal equations by holding $\mathbf{A}^T$ fixed (Bader et al., 2007; Bauckhage et al., 2014) or by projected gradient descent (Sifa et al., 2015c). Subsequent to that, fixing $\mathbf{A}$, updating $\mathbf{R}$ becomes a matrix regression problem with a close form solution (Bader et al., 2007; Bauckhage et al., 2014; Sifa et al., 2015c). The resulting low rank factors can be used to reveal the hidden directional patterns and summarize the overall behavior in a compressed representation.

13.8.2 Interpretability through Constraints

It is important to note that the presence of three factors in the approximation of each factor in (13.10) might restrict the interpretation of the resulting factor matrices $\mathbf{A}$ and $\mathbf{R}$ to consider only the nonnegative values (Kiers, 1997; Sifa et al., 2015c). This is especially important for hard or soft clustering interpretation of the factorization requiring additional constraints on $\mathbf{A}$ and $\mathbf{R}$, which might increase the fitting error in (13.11) for the cost of interpretability (Bauckhage et al., 2014; Kiers, 1997; Sifa et al., 2015c). In the following we explain special DEDICOM based models: *Semi-Nonnegative DEDICOM* constraining $\mathbf{R}$ to be nonnegative and DESICOM constraining $\mathbf{A}$ to be nonnegative and sparse.

Introduced by Sifa et al. (2015c), semi nonnegative DEDICOM constrains the affinity matrix $\mathbf{R}$ to be nonnegative. This becomes important when we consider only positive valued asymmetric similarity values such as counts or probabilities. Additionally, having nonnegative $\mathbf{R}$ allows us to interpret both positive and negative loadings that are encoded in $\mathbf{A}$. Formally, since setting the negative entities in $\mathbf{R}$ for its update does not always guarantee the global minimum of (13.10) for fixed $\mathbf{A}$ with nonnegativity constraint, Sifa et al. (2015c) showed how the optimization procedure for $\mathbf{R}$ can be formalized as a nonnegative least squares problem. The resulting algorithm has been shown to find hidden migration patterns among players.

Decomposition Into Simple Components (DESICOM), which is a sparsity based DEDICOM model, was introduced by Kiers (1997) to obtain interpretable (i.e., *simple*) factors. The model constrains $\mathbf{A}$ to be row sparse, that is, each row contains only one nonnegative value while others are zero-valued. The algorithm suggested by Kiers (1997) works in alternating least squares fashion by updating each row of $\mathbf{A}$ at a time and $\mathbf{R}$ by matrix regression by keeping $\mathbf{A}$ fix. Although the run time of this algorithm is longer than that of the algorithms suggested for traditional DEDICOM models, DESICOM offers aspects of interpretability of the models (Bauckhage et al., 2014; Kiers, 1997).

The algorithm presented by Kiers (1997) minimizes the objective function in (13.11) by simultaneously updating $\mathbf{A}$ and $\mathbf{R}$ and keeping the other factor matrix fixed. Compared to the algorithms to find DEDICOM factors (e.g., the ones in Bader et al., 2007; Bauckhage et al., 2014; Sifa et al., 2015c), here the update of A is done row-wise and simultaneously. Namely, by keeping the other rows fixed, each row $\mathbf{a}_{:i}$ can be updated by minimizing a function that is derived from (13.11) to depend only on $\mathbf{a}_{:i}$. Since we require to have only one nonnegative entry in every $\mathbf{a}_{:i}$ and reduce the total error in (13.11), the algorithm finds the dimension $l \in [1 \ldots k]$ that yields the smallest error value and sets the value of a_{il} to the minimizer and all other values (i.e., $m \in [1 \dots k] | m \neq l$) of $\mathbf{a}_{\cdot i}$ to zero. The advantages of DESICOM regarding interpretability are threefold. First, the cluster assignment is done by assigning each entity to the cluster indexed by the single nonnegative value. Second, considering the factorization of nonnegative similarity matrices, the resulting loadings will or can be turned into positive values (Kiers, 1997). Third, having nonnegative loadings we can consider a scaling to interpret the loadings as probabilities indicating the *representativeness* values that show how much an entity contributes to the clusters. Further mathematical details (including the optimization process) and implementation details of DESICOM are discussed by Bauckhage et al. (2014) and Kiers (1997). In the next section, we present a use case of DESICOM for comparative spatiotemporal player profiling.

13.8.3 Case Study: Spatiotemporal Profiling of Player Traces in FPS Games

In this section, we show how DEDICOM–based models can be used for profiling players based on how they have moved around the game map. The case study presented is part of the comparative analysis of player trajectories in famous first-person shooter games by Bauckhage et al. (2014). The authors compared the behavior of DEDICOM and DESICOM to well known clustering methods in terms of trajectory-based profiling. The main aim of this study is to provide insights to the designers about different kinds of behavior-based partitionings of maps. As a first step the authors consider encoding the spatiotemporal interactions on the game map through *waypoint-map* generation in which the spatial data is divided into Voronoi cells. After that a *waypoint transition matrix* is generated such that it captures the movements between the waypoints by assigning every positional point of a player to its closest waypoint and counting the transitions between the waypoints afterwards. Namely, an arbitrary entry of the waypoint transition matrix s_{ij} encodes the interaction between waypoint i and waypoint j. It is important to note the asymmetry of such a matrix, as players might be able to move from one particular sector of the game map to another, while the opposite is not physically possible. Teleportation in *Quake III* or falling down of the pit on *Unreal Tournament*'s DM-1on1-Serpentine may serve as examples of such a type of the spatiotemporal asymmetry in the movements of the players. After the extraction of the waypoints and their transition matrices, Bauckhage et al. (2014) compared the behavior of k-means, spectral clustering, DEDICOM, and DESICOM for partitioning of the players traces of maps of *Quake III* and *Unreal Tournament*. While k-means performed poorly in capturing reasonable structures owing to the variance minimization nature of the algorithm, spectral clustering captured the spatial partitioning of the player behavior without the temporal information. On the other hand, DEDICOM and DESICOM captured not only the spatial partitioning, which can be read off from the columns of **A**, but also temporal directions among the partitioning, which can be directly read off from the values of **R**. As a use case for a comparative player trajectory analysis using DEDICOM family, we now present the insights where we analyze the results of DESICOM for two players (the complete analysis with three players can be found in Bauckhage et al., 2014). Having extracted 250 common waypoints from the analyzed *Quake III* players played on the well-known map *q3dm17*, Bauckhage et al. (2014) ran DESICOM with the same number of components over each of the player traces and analyzed the spatiotemporal profiles. We show the profiles of two of the players in Figure 13.5. Based on the nonnegative and sparse loadings in **A** the authors could identify the belongingness of the sector to its particular cluster and through **R**.

Figure 13.5a shows a *camper* player behavior that interacted mostly in a certain area of the map without moving around. DESICOM highlights this type of behavior by providing a high amount of affinity from the yellow sector to the green sector (but not vice versa). It is also important to note that, comparing the rows of the affinity matrix of this player, the high self-affinities are indicating that this player has not moved around but within the found sectors. Unlike the first player, Figure 13.5b shows a *mover* type player that explored the map more intensively. Through the yellow, red, and blue sectors, DESICOM, identified the players most frequently visited areas. Moreover, compared to other players, the higher affinity values between the sectors lead to the conclusion that the player has not specifically moved around the found sectors, showing no particular pattern. Through intelligent trajectory analysis such as DEDICOM and DESICOM, the highly complex player interactions can be compressed into more interpretable sectors and affinities between sectors. Methods like these are of obvious interest to game designers and analysts who seek more insights about the players' physical interactions in virtual worlds.

13.9 Discussion and Future Work

With the broad availability of detailed behavioral telemetry data in the game industry, and the increasing focus on freemium business models, there is a keen interest in techniques that permit evaluating player behavior in digital games. Behavioral profiling is one approach toward managing the common high-complexity, high volume, veracious and volatile telemetry data that

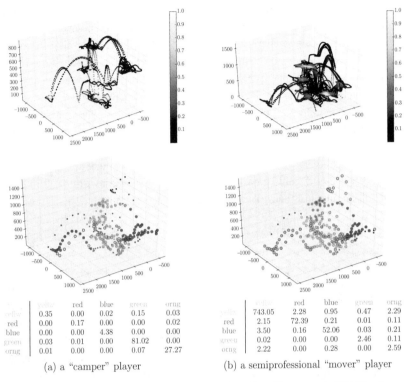

	yellw	red	blue	green	orng
yellw	0.35	0.00	0.02	0.15	0.03
red	0.00	0.17	0.00	0.00	0.02
blue	0.00	0.00	4.38	0.00	0.00
green	0.03	0.01	0.00	81.02	0.00
orng	0.01	0.00	0.00	0.07	27.27

	yellw	red	blue	green	orng
yellw	743.05	2.28	0.95	0.47	2.29
red	2.15	72.39	0.21	0.01	0.11
blue	3.50	0.16	52.06	0.03	0.21
green	0.02	0.00	0.00	2.46	0.11
orng	2.22	0.00	0.28	0.00	2.59

(a) a "camper" player   (b) a semiprofessional "mover" player

Figure 13.5 Comparative analysis (derived from Bauckhage et al. (2014)) of movements of two different players on the *Quake III* map *q3dm17*. From top to bottom, each part of the figure respectively illustrates a heatmap indicating the frequently visited areas on the map, waypoints (in black) and DESICOM clusters (shown in color), and, finally, automatically determined affinities between the identified clusters. (This image is shown in full color in the Color Plates section.)

characterize game development. Profiling provides for a condensation and modeling of potentially complex behavioral spaces, and permits the consideration of users in a quantifiable fashion, toward building an understanding about how people have played, how they are playing, and how they will play a game.

The specific techniques used for profiling exercises vary from simple aggregate statistics to machine learning. Each approach has its strengths and weaknesses and provides different venues of insights into the underlying consumer behavior. Profiling is carried out for a variety of purposes, including informing game design, driving monetization decisions, studying human behavior, driving adaptive systems, and so forth. Shared in all of these purposes is the fact that they attempt to provide data-driven insights to the relevant stakeholders, irrespective of whether they are from industry or academia. Game analytics is a domain that, at the time of this writing and presumably in the near future, is in a state of rapid development owing in part to the relatively recent introduction of big data scale telemetry data, and in part owing to the fast pace of innovation in games, as exemplified by the drive in recent years toward virtual reality and augmented reality games. For these reasons, it is difficult to use the state-of-the-art to generate predictions of the future evolution of the field. However, there are specific gaps in the current knowledge which require future work, and that can pave the way not only for insights useful to the game industry, but also to the study of human behavior in online environments. These could be characterized as flagship areas in game analytics, and behavioral profiling has a role to play in all of them. These include but are not limited to the following.

1. **Cross-games profiling:** Given the high costs associated with acquiring players to a game – the User Acquisition Cost (UAC), there is a general interest in discovering techniques for migrating players between games in a company's portfolio. Doing so requires the ability to predict when someone will stop playing a particular game, and consumer profiles that can drive personalized advertising in order to try to convince a player to try out another game in the portfolio, rather than moving a competitor's game, i.e., profiles that inform what types of advertising strategies to leverage to drive players of a particular type to migrate (Runge et al., 2014; Sifa et al., 2015c).

2. **Deep profiling in retention and monetization:** In most cases today the goal of predictive analytics is to drive a binary classification of players, e.g., into buyers and nonbuyers, churners and non-churners. However, there appears to be an increasing interest in a broader classification that includes more detail, i.e., a more nuanced basis to make decisions on. Furthermore, given the variety in the motivations for playing games, the variety of experiences games can provide and the varied personalities of consumers, deep profiling provides a toolbox for integrating varied player behaviors and experiments on potential correlations with player psychology.

3. **Modeling human behavior in online environments:** Unlike virtually any other online application, games can provide high-frequency and longitudinal telemetry data about human behavior in online environments. Some games are played by players over several years. These data provide a unique opportunity to study human behavior, not just in terms of direct observation, as exemplified by Sifa et al. (2014b), who observed regular patterns in playtime across more than 3000 game titles, or Feng et al. (2007), as well as Pittman and GauthierDickey (2010), who investigated long-term behavioral patterns in an MMOG; but also from an experimental angle, i.e., trying to manipulate

online environments to study how people react. There is a decades-long tradition for this kind of work in games research, e.g., in behavioral economics (see, e.g., Knowles, Castronova, & Ross, 2015).

4. **Adaptive games:** Adaptive games have been a topic of investigation in game AI for more than a decade (Laviers et al., 2009; Yannakakis, 2012; Yannakakis & Hallam, 2009; Yannakakis & Togelius, 2015). With the introduction of detailed telemetry streams, real-time adaptation has become possible and has already been integrated in some commercial games, e.g., the *Left 4 Dead* series. Adaptation thus has a certain history in major commercial retail-based titles, but has also recently become a topic of interest in F2P games, across casual, mid-core, and hardcore genres. The interest relates to the potential for improving retention, user experience, and monetization in games via real-time adaptation to individual or groups of players. Dynamic and predictive profiling here comes into play by providing the information required by adaptive systems.

5. **Cradle-to-Grave profiling:** As discussed at the beginning of this chapter, profiling can be driven by a variety of qualitative and quantitative data, across every phase of a product life cycle. A practical challenge in this regard is ensuring the continuity of profiles across game productions and the integration of different data sources. Drachen (2014) introduced the concept of cradle-to-grave profiling to describe this challenge, emphasizing that to accommodate the variations in data sources and technique availability throughout a product's life cycle, player profiles would need to be iteratively updated in order to remain useful across changes in design, business goals, player behavior, and the composition of the underlying user community.

In this chapter an overview and analysis of the state-of-the-art in player-focused, telemetry-based behavioral profiling has been presented, highlighting five main categories in contemporary work: snapshot, dynamic, predictive, spatiotemporal, and psychological profiles. Each have their strengths and weaknesses and are applied to solve arrays of problems that inform decision-making processes. Focusing on telemetry-driven profiling, examples have been given for each of the four first categories. Within each category a broad range of statistical and machine-learning–based methods can be utilized by professionals and researchers to evaluate player behavior. As the current work in behavioral profiling in games indicates, there is a substantial room for future work across industry and academia and every phase and aspect of the profiling process, e.g., algorithms, feature engineering, application, and actionability of results, method evaluation and not the least communication of profiling results to stakeholders.

References

Bader, B. W., Harshinan, R. A., & Kolda, T. G. (2007). Temporal analysis of semantic graphs using ASALSAN. In *Proceedings of IEEE ICDM*.

Bartle, R. (1996). Hearts, clubs, diamonds, spades: Players who suit MUDs. *Journal of MUD Research*, 1(1).

Bateman, C. M., & Boon, R. (2006). *21st century game design*. Newton Center, MA: Charles River Media.

Bauckhage, C. (2015). k-Means clustering is matrix factorization. arXiv preprint arXiv:1512.07548.

Bauckhage, C., & Sifa, R. (2015). k-Maxoids clustering. In *Proceedings of KDML-LWA*.

Bauckhage, C., & Thurau, C. (2004). Towards a fair 'n square aimbot using mixtures of experts to learn context aware weapon handling. In *Proceedings of GAME-ON*.

Bauckhage, C., & Thurau, C. (2009). Making archetypal analysis practical. In *Pattern Recognition*. Lecture Notes in Computer Science, Vol. 5748. New York: Springer Science+Business Media.

Bauckhage, C., Kersting, K., Sifa, R., Thurau, C, Drachen, A., & Canossa, A. (2012). How players lose interest in playing a game: An empirical study based on distributions of total playing times. In *Proceedings of IEEE CIG*.

Bauckhage, C., Sifa, R., Drachen, A., Thurau, C, & Hadiji, F. (2014). Beyond heatmaps: Spatio-temporal clustering using behavior-based partitioning of game levels. In *Proceedings of IEEE CIG*.

Bauckhage, C., Drachen, A., & Sifa, R. (2015). Clustering game behavior data. *IEEE Transactions on Computational Intelligence and AI in Games*, 7(3), 266–278.

Bohannon, J. (2010). Game-miners grapple with massive data. *Science*, 330(6000), 30–31.

Breiman, L. (2001). Random forests. *Machine Learning*, 45(1), 5–32.

Campbell, J., Tremblay, J., & Verbrugge, C. (2015). Clustering player paths. In *Proceedings of FDG*.

Canossa, A., & Drachen, A. (2009a). Patterns of play: Play-personas in user-centered game development. In *Proceedings of DIGRA*.

Canossa, A., & Drachen, A. (2009b). Play-personas: Behaviors and belief systems in user-centered game design. In *Proceedings of ACM INTERACT*.

Canossa, A., Drachen, A., & Sorensen, J. (2011). Arrrgghh!!!: Blending quantitative and qualitative methods to detect player frustration. In *Proceedings of FDG*.

Canossa, A., Martinez, J. B., & Togelius, J. (2013). Give me a reason to dig Minecraft and psychology of motivation. In *Proceedings of IEEE CIG*.

Chawla, N., Bowyer, K., Hall, L. O, & Kegelmeyer, W. (2002). SMOTE: Synthetic minority over-sampling technique. *Journal of Artificial Intelligence Research*, 16(1), 321–357.

Cutler, A., & Breiman, L. (1994). Archetypal analysis. *Technometrics*, 36(4), 338–347.

Drachen, A. (2014). *Behavioral profiling in game user research*. Presentation at the 4th International Game Developers Association Game User Research Summit.

Drachen, A., & Canossa, A. (2009). Analyzing spatial user behavior in computer games using Geographic Information Systems. In *Proceedings of MindTrek*.

Drachen, A., & Canossa, A. (2011). Evaluating motion: Spatial user behaviour in virtual environments. *International Journal of Arts and Technology*, 4(2), 294–314.

Drachen, A., & Schubert, M. (2013). Spatial game analytics. In M. S. El-Nasr, A. Drachen, & A. Canossa (eds.), *Game analytics: Maximizing the value of player data* (pp. 365–402). New York: Springer Science+Business Media.

Drachen, A., Yannakakis, G. N., Canossa, A., & Togelius, J. (2009). Player modeling using self-organization in tomb raider: Underworld. In *Proceedings of IEEE CIG*.

Drachen, A., Sifa, R., Bauckhage, C., & Thurau, C. (2012). Guns, swords and data: Clustering of player behavior in computer games in the wild. In *Proceedings of IEEE CIG*.

Drachen, A., Thurau, C., Sifa, R., & Bauckhage, C. (2013a). A comparison of methods for player clustering via behavioral telemetry. In *Proceedings of FDG*.

Drachen, A., Thurau, C., Togelius, J., Yannakakis, G., & Bauckhage, C. (2013b). Game data mining. In M. S. El-Nasr, A. Drachen, & A. Canossa (eds.), *Game analytics: Maximizing the value of player data*. New York: Springer Science+Business Media.

Drachen, A., Baskin, S., Riley, J., & Klabjan, D. (2014a). Going out of business: Auction house behavior in the massively multi-player online game glitch. *Entertainment Computing*, 5(4), 219–232.

Drachen, A., Sifa, R., & Thurau, C. (2014b). The name in the game: Patterns in character names and gamer tags. *Entertainment Computing*, 5(1), 21–32.

Drachen, A., Yancey, M., Maquire, J., Chu, D., Wang, Y. I., Mahlman, T., Schubert, M., & Klabjan, D. (2014c). Skill-based differences in spatio-temporal team behaviour in defence of The Ancients 2 (DotA 2). In *Proceedings of the IEEE Consumer Electronics Society Games, Entertainment, Media Conference*.

Eggert, C., Herrlich, M., Smeddinck, J., & Malaka, R. (2015). Classification of player roles in the team-based multi-player game Dota 2. In *Proceedings of Entertainment Computing*.

El-Nasr, M. S., Drachen, A., & Canossa, A. (2013). *Game analytics: Maximizing the value of player data*. New York: Springer Science+Business Media.

Feng, J., Brandt, D., & Saha, D. (2007). A long-term study of a popular MMORPG. In *Proceedings ACM SIGCOMM WNSSG*.

Fields, T., & Cotton, B. (2011). *Social game design: Monetization methods and mechanics*. San Mateo, CA: Morgan Kaufmann.

Gao, L., Judd, J., Wong, D., & Lowder, J. (2013). Classifying dota 2 hero characters based on play style and performance. Retrieved from: http://spotidoc.com/doc/163929/classifying-dota-2-heroes-based-on-play-style-and-perform

Hadiji, F., Sifa, R., Drachen, A., Thurau, C., Kersting, K., & Bauckhage, C. (2014). Predicting player churn in the wild. In *Proceedings of IEEE CIG*.

Harshman, R. A. (1978). Models for analysis of asymmetrical relationships among N objects or stimuli. In *Proceedings of the Joint Meeting of the Psychometric Society and the Society for Mathematical Psychology*.

Holmgard, C., Liapis, A., Togelius, J., & Yannakakis, G. N. (2015). Monte-Carlo tree search for persona based player modeling. In *Proceedings of AIIDE Player Modeling Workshop*.

Hoobler, N., Humphreys, G., & Agrawala, M. (2004). Visualizing competitive behaviors in multi-user virtual environments. In *Proceedings of VIS*.

Kersting, K., Wahabzada, M., Thurau, C., & Bauckhage, C. (2010). Hierarchical convex NMF for clustering massive data. In *Proceedings of ACML*.

Kiers, H. A. L. (1997). DESICOM: Decomposition of asymmetric relationships data into simple components. *Behaviormetrika*, 24(2), 203–217.

Kim, J. H., Gunn, D. V., Schuh, E., Phillips, B. C., Pagulayan, R. J., & Wixon, D. (2008). Tracking real-time user experience (true): A comprehensive instrumentation solution for complex systems. In *Proceedings of ACM CHI*.

Knowles, I., Castronova, E., & Ross, T. (2015). Virtual economies: Origins and issues. *The international encyclopedia of digital communication and society*.

Kubat, M., Holte, R., & Matwin, S. (1997). Learning when negative examples abound. In *Proceedings of ECML*.

Laviers, K., Sukthankar, G., Molineaux, M., & Aha, D. (2009). Improving offensive performance through opponent modeling. In *Proceedings of AAAI AIIDE*.

Lim, C., & Harrell, D. F. (2015). Revealing social identity phenomena in videogames with archetypal analysis. In *Proceedings of AISB*.

Lim, N. (2012). Freemium games are not normal. Retrieved from: www.gamasutra.com/blogs/NickLim/.

Luton, W. (2013). *Free-to-play: Making money from games you give away*. New Riders.

Mahlmann, T., Drachen, A., Togelius, J., Canossa, A., & Yannakakis, G. N. (2010). Predicting player behavior in Tomb Raider: Underworld. In *Proceedings of IEEE GIG*.

Mellon, L. (2009). *Applying metrics driven development to MMO costs and risks*, http://maggotranch.com/.

Miller, J.L., & Crowcroft, J. (2010). Group movement in World of Warcraft battle-grounds. *International Journal of Advanced Media and Communication*, 4(4), 387–404.

Mitchell, T. M. (1997). *Machine learning*. New York, NY: McGraw-Hill.

Morup, M., & Hansen, L. K. (2012). Archetypal analysis for machine learning and data mining. *Neurocomputing*, 80(March), 54–63.

Müller, S., Kapadia, M., Prey, S., et al. (2015). Statistical analysis of player behavior in minecraft. In *Proceedings of FDG*.

Nacke, L. E., Bateman, C, & Mandryk, R. L. (2014). BrainHex: A neurobio-logical gamer typology survey. *Entertainment Computing*, 5(1), 55–62.

Normoyle, A., & Jensen, S. T. (2015). Bayesian clustering of player styles for multi-player games. In *Proceedings of AAAI AIIDE*.

Nozhnin, D. (2012). Predicting churn: Data-mining your game. *Gamasutra*.

Nozhnin, D. (2013). Predicting churn: When do veterans quit? *Gamasutra*.

Ong, H. Y., Deolalikar, S., & Penge, M. V. (2015). Player behavior and optimal team composition in online multiplayer games. Retrieved from: http://arxiv.org/abs/1503.02230.

Pittman, D., & GauthierDickey, C. (2010). Characterizing virtual populations in mas-sively multiplayer online role-playing games. In *Proceedings of MMM*.

Quinlan, J. R. (1996). Improved use of continuous attributes in C4.5. *Journal of Artificial Intelligence Research*, 4(1), 77–90.

Raghu, T. S., Kannan, H. R., Rao, A., & Winston, B. (2001). Dynamic profiling of con-sumers for customized offerings over the Internet: A model and analysis. *Decision Support Systems*, 32(2), 117–134.

Rioult, R., Metivier, J.-P., Helleu, B., et al. (2014). Mining tracks of competitive video games. In *Proceedings of AASRI Conference on Sports Engineering and Computer Science*.

Rokach, L., & Maimon, O. (2008). *Data mining with decision trees: Theory and applications*. Singapore: World Scientific.

Runge, J. (2014). *Predictive analytics set to become more valuable in light of rising CPIs*. http://www.gamasutra.com/blogs/.

Runge, J., Gao, P., Garcin, F., & Faltings, B. (2014). Churn prediction for high-value players in casual social games. In *Proceedings of IEEE CIG*.

Ryan, R. M., Rigby, C. S., & Przybylski, A. (2006). The motivational pull of video games: A Self-Determination Theory approach. *Motivation Emotion*, 30(4), 344–360.

Sifa, R., & Bauckhage, C. (2013). Archetypical motion: Supervised game behavior learning with archetypal analysis. In *Proceedings of IEEE CIG*.

Sifa, R., Drachen, A., Bauckhage, C., Thurau, C., & Canossa, A. (2013). Behavior evolution in Tomb Raider underworld. In *Proceedings of IEEE CIG*.

Sifa, R., Bauckhage, C., & Drachen, A. (2014a). Archetypal game recommender systems. In *Proceedings of KDML-LWA*.

Sifa, R., Bauckhage, C., & Drachen, A. (2014b). The playtime principle: Large-scale cross-games interest modeling. In *Proceedings of IEEE CIG*.

Sifa, R., Drachen, A., & Bauckhage, C. (2015a). Large-scale cross-game player behavior analysis on steam. In *Proceedings of AAAI AIIDE*.

Sifa, R., Hadiji, F., Runge, J., Drachen, A., Kersting, K., & Bauckhage, C. (2015b). Predicting purchase decisions in mobile free-to-play games. In *Proceedings of AAAI AIIDE*.

Sifa, R., Ojeda, C., & Bauckhage, C. (2015c). User churn migration analysis with DEDICOM. In *Proceedings of ACM RccSys*.

Sifa, R., Srikanth, S., Drachen, A., Ojeda, C., & Bauckhage, C. (2016). Predicting retention in sandbox games with tensor factorization-based representation learning. In *Proceedings of IEEE CIG*.

Solomon, M. R. (2014). *Consumer behavior: Buying, having, and being*. Upper Saddle River, NJ: Prentice Hall.

Southey, F., Xiao, G., Holte, R. C., Trommelen, M., & Buchanan, J. (2005). Semi-automated gameplay analysis by machine learning. In *Proceedings of AAAI AIIDE*.

Spronck, P., Balemans, I., & van Lankveld, G. (2012). Player profiling with Fallout 3. In *Proceedings of AAAI AIIDE*.

Suznjevic, M., Stupar, I., & Matijasevic, M. (2011). MMORPG player behavior model based on player action categories. In *Proceedings of NetGames*.

Tastan, B., Chang, Y., & Sukthankar, G. (2012). Learning to intercept opponents in first person shooter games. In *Proceedings of IEEE CIG*.

Taylor, S., & Todd, P. (1995). Decomposition and crossover effects in the theory of planned behavior: A study of consumer adoption intentions. *International Journal of Research in Marketing*, 12(2), 137–155.

Thawonmas, R., & Iizuka, K. (2008). Visualization of online game players based on their action behaviors. *International Journal of Computer Games Technology*, 2008(Jan.), 906931.

Thawonmas, R., Yoshida, K., Lou, J.-K., & Chen, K.-T. (2011). Analysis of revisitations in online games. *Entertainment Computing*, 2(4), 215–221.

Thompson, C. (2007, September). Halo 3: How Microsoft labs invented a new science of play. Wired Magazine.

Thurau, C., Bauckhage, C., & Sagerer, G. (2004). Synthesizing movements for computer game characters. In *Joint Pattern Recognition Symposium*.

Thurau, C., Kersting, K., & Bauckhage, C. (2009). Convex non-negative matrix factorization in the wild. In *Proceedings of IEEE International Conference on Data Mining*.

Thurau, C., Kersting, K., & Bauckhage, C. (2010). Yes we can: Simplex volume maximization for descriptive web-scale matrix factorization. In *Proceedings of ACM CIKM*.

van Lankveld, G., Spronck, P., Van Den Herik, J., & Arntz, A. (2011). Games as personality profiling tools. In *Proceedings of IEEE CIG*.

Weber, B., & Mateas, M. (2009). A data mining approach to strategy prediction. In *Proceedings of IEEE CIG*.

Weber, B. G., John, M., Mateas, M., & Jhala, A. (2011). Modeling player retention in Madden NFL 11. In *Proceedings of IAAI*.

Wu, X., Kumar, V., Quinlan, J. R., et al. (2008). Top 10 algorithms in data mining. *Knowledge and Information Systems*, 14(1), 1–37.

Xie, H., Devlin, S., Kudenko, D., & Cowling, P. (2015). Predicting player disengagement and first purchase with event-frequency based data representation. In *Proceedings of IEEE CIG*.

Yang, P. Harrison, B., & Roberts, D. L. (2014). Identifying patterns in combat that are predictive of success in moba games. In *Proceedings of FDG*.

Yannakakis, G. (2012). Game AI revisited. In *Proceedings of ACM Computing Frontiers Conference*.

Yannakakis, G. N., & Hallam, J. (2009). Real-time game adaptation for optimizing player satisfaction. *IEEE Transactions on Computational Intelligence and AI in Games*, 1(2), 121–133.

Yannakakis, G. N., & Togelius, J. (2015). A panorama of artificial and computational intelligence in games. *IEEE Transactions on Computational Intelligence and AI in Games*, 7(4), 317–335.

Yee, N. (2014). *The proteus paradox: How online games and virtual worlds change us – and how they don't.* New Haven, CT: Yale University Press.

Yee, N., & Ducheneaut, N. (2015). The gamer motivation model in handy reference chart and slides. Retrieved from: http://quanticfoundry.com/2015/12/15/handy-reference/.

Zoeller, G. (2011). Game development telemetry. In *Game Developers Conference*.

14

Using Massively Multiplayer Online Game Data to Analyze the Dynamics of Social Interactions

ALIREZA HAJIBAGHERI, GITA SUKTHANKAR,
KIRAN LAKKARAJU, HAMIDREZA ALVARI,
ROLF T. WIGAND, AND NITIN AGARWAL

14.1 Introduction

The natural flux of people's changing social ties and interests generates a dynamic social network. This network can be observed by capturing daily or weekly snapshots of user activities in massively multiplayer online games (MMOGs), allowing these environments to serve as "laboratories" for studying large-scale human behaviors. It is informative to visualize these data as a set of graphs for each time period, where vertices correspond to users and edges represent interactions. Multiple types of dyadic associations can be represented by encoding the data as a multiplex network, where the links at each layer represent a different type of interaction between the same set of nodes. Often these network layers coevolve, owing to interdependencies between the social processes represented by different layers. The main goal of our research is to study large-scale human behaviors in coevolving multiplex networks (Figure 14.1). Owing to the lack of good standardized data sets, there has been relatively little research on dynamic multiplex networks, as compared to static single layer ones. Our research has been conducted using a dynamic multiplex network data set collected from the *Travian* massively multiplayer online game.

Most online social media platforms are optimized to support a limited range of social interactions, focusing primarily on communication and information sharing. In contrast, relations in MMOGs are often formed during the course of gameplay and evolve as the game progresses. Even though these relationships are conducted in a virtual world, they are cognitively comparable to real-world friendships or co-worker relationships (Yee, 2006). The amount and richness of social intercourse makes it possible to observe a broader gamut of human experiences within MMOGs such as *World of Warcraft* (Thurau &

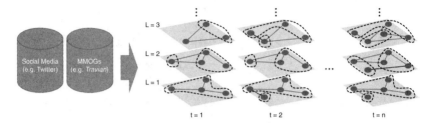

Figure 14.1 A dynamic multiplex network with changing community structure. Each person is associated with a node in a network. The network structure is *dynamic* and changes over time as new users join and social connections are formed. Adding *multiple layers* to the network allows a variety of interactions to be represented within the same network. Users self-organize into *communities* based on shared interests that also change over time.

Bauckhage, 2010), Sony *EverQuest II* (Keegan et al., 2010; Roy et al., 2013), and *Travian* (Korsgaard et al., 2010; Wigand et al., 2012) than can be done with other data sources. They have been particularly valuable for studying groups, teams, and organizations, since banding together yields economic and combat advantages in most games. Geographically separated players must work together to achieve shared goals using a similar combination of email, chat, and videoconferencing as remote employees; hence game guilds can be viewed as analogous to virtual workplace organizations (Korsgaard et al., 2010; Wigand, Chapter 8, this volume). By observing the changing social interactions within the *Travian* MMOG, we have been able to model the evolution of the social network and its constituent communities while comparing the model predictions against ground truth information collected from player logs. Moreover, it is possible to study the concurrence of different types of social interactions within multiplex networks. This chapter presents an overview of our research on link prediction and community detection within the *Travian* MMOG.

14.2 *Travian* MMOG

Travian is a popular browser-based real-time strategy game with more than 5 million players. Games can be played in more than 40 different languages on more than 300 game servers worldwide. Playing with up to 20,000 users on one server with scarce resources, actors soon find themselves in a social dilemma (Dawes, 1980), which is typical for organizations, project teams, and economies where parties need to both coordinate and compete with one another. Participants start the game as chieftains of their own villages and can choose to be a member of one of three tribes (Gaul, Roman, or Teuton). Each of these three tribes has its own advantages and disadvantages. For instance, Teutons produce the cheapest military units and are the best raiders, whereas Gauls are the best at living in peace and have fast units and merchants. Players seek to improve their production capacity and construct military units in order to expand their territory through a combination of colonization and conquest. Each game cycle lasts a fixed period (a few months), during which time the players vie to create the first civilization to complete construction on one of the Wonders of the World. In the race to dominate, actors form alliances of up to 60 members under a leader or a leadership team. Alliances are equipped with a shared forum, a chat room, and an in-game messaging system. As in the real world, teamwork and negotiation skills play a crucial role in game success.

Conflicts in *Travian* can be divided into two categories: attacks and raids. The goal of an attack is to destroy its target, whereas raids are meant to gather bounty and are much less vicious. The armies will do battle until at least one side is reduced in strength by 50 percent, and therefore the loss on both sides is usually smaller. A trade is an exchange of different resources (gold, wood, clay, wheat) necessary to upgrade a village's buildings. In *Travian*, villages may trade their resources with other villages if both villages have a marketplace. *Travian* has an in-game messaging system (IGM) for player communication. IGMs can also include broadcast messages, i.e., messages sent to all players by the game moderators. Note these messages were not included in our experiments, as their volume could introduce bias in the results. For our analysis, we used data collected from a server in Germany specifically designed for research purposes. The data set contains a variety of tables including logs and reports from different actions of users. To study the dynamics of social processes within the game, we structured the multiplex network into raid, trade, and communication layers.

14.3 Network Analysis

Network structure analysis has become an increasingly important aspect of understanding user behavior on social media platforms. This methodology places relations and links among entities, or people, at the center of investigation. In the last decade, much research has been performed on characterizing the dynamics of complex systems and extracting nontrivial properties using massive network data from social, biological, and technological sources. Example applications include predicting future links among the actors of a network (Bringmann et al., 2010; Liben-Nowell & Kleinberg, 2007), detecting and studying the structure of communities (Alvari et al., 2016), and mining common user behavior patterns (Benevenuto et al., 2009; Cook et al., 2010).

Many studies on online social networks, the WWW, and biological networks have focused on the macroscopic properties of static networks (Albert & Barabási, 2002; Broder et al., 2000; Faloutsos et al., 1999; Strogatz, 2001). However, social networks are not static. They are dynamic structures that evolve over time either by the addition of new vertices or by new connecting edges. Thus, modeling network dynamics is important and the focus of a number of research efforts (Backstrom et al., 2006; Barabási & Albert, 1999; Leskovec et al., 2008). Also in the real world, networks are often multiplex, containing multiple types of relationships; in some cases, aggregating different interaction types loses information about the structure and function of the original system (Buldyrev et al., 2010; Kurant & Thiran, 2006). For instance, the same set of individuals in a social system can be connected through friendship, collaboration, communication, and colocation relationships; in MMOGs, players have a variety of interactions such as trading, messaging, and attacking. In these systems, each type of relationship may have a different semantic meaning, relevance, importance, and cost, so that treating all the links as being equivalent discards key information. Multiplex networks serve as a better description of these systems; each node appears in a set of different layers, and each layer describes all the edges of a given type.

Recently, a considerable amount of effort has been devoted to the characterization and modeling of multiplex networks, with the aim of creating a consistent mathematical framework to study, understand, and reproduce the structure of these systems. For instance, it is feasible to model multiplex networks using a statistical mechanics approach (Bianconi, 2013). Another alternative is to simply extend classical network metrics to handle multiple layers (De Domenico et al., 2013a; Sole-Ribalta et al., 2013) and to model the growth of systems of this kind (Nicosia et al., 2013). An active research area is characterizing the dynamics and the emergent properties of multilayer systems, especially with respect to contagious properties (Saumell-Mendiola, Serrano, & Boguná, 2012), information propagation (Buono et al., 2014; Min & Goh, 2013), cooperation (Gómez-Gardenes et al., 2012), diffusion processes (Gomez et al., 2013), and random walks (De Domenico et al., 2013b). The subsequent sections of the chapter chronicle a set of studies that we completed using multiplex networks extracted from the *Travian* MMOG, and the algorithms that we developed for modeling the evolution of communities and the dynamics of link formation.

14.4 Analyzing the Effects of Aggression on Network Structure

MMOGs have been a fertile testing ground for many types of human studies, enabling scientists to overcome key difficulties in studying social dynamics by providing an experimental platform for collecting high-resolution data over longer time period (Korsgaard et al., 2010; Roy, Borbora, & Srivastava, 2013; Thurau & Bauckhage, 2010; Wigand et al., 2012). One research question of interest is how conflict shapes the underlying social network; in MMOGs, conflict and cooperation are inextricably linked since many attacks are launched by coalitions of players to gain resources, control territory, or subjugate enemies. It is easier to study aggression in virtual worlds because it is both more common and simpler to quantify.

In real life there are myriad potential motivations for choosing to fight. Humphreys and Weinstein (2008) categorized key determinants of participation in conflicts as being long-term grievances (i.e., economic or political disenfranchisement), selective incentives (money or safety), and community cohesion. Community cohesion predicts that people are more likely to join the conflict if they are members of a tightly knit community and their friends have already joined. This factor is the most relevant to fighting within MMOGs. Not only are there conflicts between guilds and alliances, but also pick-up groups may spontaneously form to tackle larger challenges such as boss fights (Bennerstedt, Ivarsson, & Linderoth, 2012).

In *Travian*, attacking (raiding) is one of the easiest pathways for gaining the necessary resources for growing one's civilization, and players need to rush to grow their civilizations within a short period of time. Here we study (1) how the structure of the attack layer differs from the communication and trade layers and (2) how communication, trade, and geographic connections affect the likelihood of two players engaging in hostilities. For this study, we used data from one *Travian* game cycle played on a high speed server in an expedited game (a period of 144 days). Our analysis was conducted on a 30-day period in the middle of the game cycle. This period has fewer transient bursts of activity and a more stable network than the early period (which has many fewer committed players who drop out) and the late period where the focus is on the Wonder of the World construction.

Table 14.1 shows the statistics for attack, trade, and message networks during the time period selected for this analysis. In these networks, each node represents an individual player, and directed edges represent attacks, trades, and messages between players. The attack graph in *Travian* has a higher

Table 14.1 Travian *attack, message, and trade network statistics*

Parameter/Network	Attack	Message	Trade
No. of vertices	4,418	3,092	2,649
Frequency	633,105	451,669	271,039
Diameter	17	9	10
Avg. path lengths	5.312	3.471	2.849
Avg. degree	7.998	14.591	32.828
Avg. clustering coefficient	0.065	0.319	0.154

diameter, lower average degree, and lower clustering coefficient than either the message or trade graphs.

The degree distributions of attack, messages, and trades conform to a power law distribution (Figure 14.2). Clauset, Shalizi, and Newman (2009) proposed a robust estimating technique to estimate the parameters of a power law; to verify the distributions, we used this method, which employs a maximum likelihood estimator. This model calculates the goodness-of-fit between the data and the power law. If the resulting value is greater than 0.1, the power law is a plausible hypothesis for the data otherwise it is rejected.

Assortativity is a preference for a network's nodes to attach to others that are similar in some way. Though the specific measure of similarity may vary, network theorists often examine assortativity in terms of a node's degree. Correlations between nodes of similar degree are found in the mixing patterns of many observable networks. For instance, in social networks, highly connected nodes tend to be connected with other high-degree nodes. This tendency is referred to as assortative mixing, or assortativity. On the other hand, technological and biological networks typically show disassortative mixing, or dissortativity, as high-degree nodes tend to attach to low degree nodes (Newman, 2002).

For *Travian*, as shown in Figure 14.3, while the message network displays disassortative mixing, attack and trade networks tend to show a nonassortative mixing. This suggests that players who send more messages are in contact with others who rarely send messages; communication in *Travian* often flows from alliance leaders outward to the other alliance members, reflective of a spoke–hub communication structure. In contrast, the degree of the members appears to be an unimportant consideration in dictating connectivity in the attack and trade networks. Nonassortative networks may arise either because the networks possess a balanced number of assortative and disassortative links or because a greater number of links in one direction is counterbalanced by a greater weight in the other (Piraveenan et al., 2012).

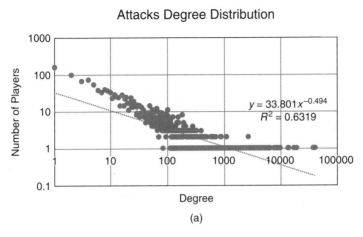

(a)

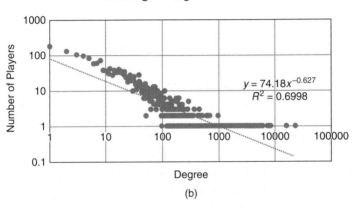

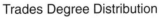

(b)

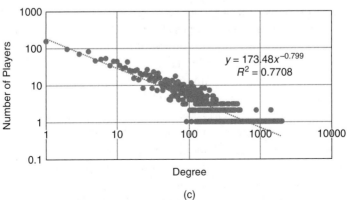

(c)

Figure 14.2 Degree distribution (log-log scale) for (a) attack, (b) message, and (c) trade networks.

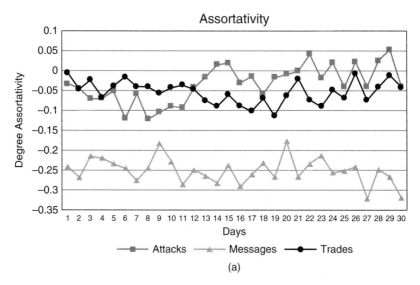

Figure 14.3 *Travian* node degree assortativity.

Attacks in *Travian* are generally inversely proportional to other types of activity. In *Travian*, in 41 percent of cases, players do not attack other players with whom they have been in contact at least once (Figure 14.4). A large number of players do not attack players with whom they have traded resources. As shown in Figure 14.5, 28 percent of the attacks in *Travian* occurred between two players without any trade history. Trading with other players indicates that they have desirable resources, making them worth attacking, and after only one trade, the players are unlikely to have established the sense of trust that may deter an attack. We believe that in some cases players who have never traded together or exchanged messages are geographically separated; hence they are less likely to attack each other because they are unaware of each other's existence. To test this hypothesis, we analyzed the probability of attack based on the distance between player territories in *Travian* (Figure 14.6). To estimate distance, we calculated the territory centroids by averaging the latitudes and longitudes of the villages. Then, standard Euclidean distance was used to measure the distance between each pair of players in the attack network. Our analysis shows that attacks between immediate neighbors are frequent. Attacks with close (but not immediate) neighbors are common, followed by a decay in attack activity with distance. Attacks are generally rare between alliance and guild members, indicating a strong level of trust in those relationships. In *Travian*, 4 percent of the attack edges are between two players within the same alliance.

PDF Attacks vs. Messages

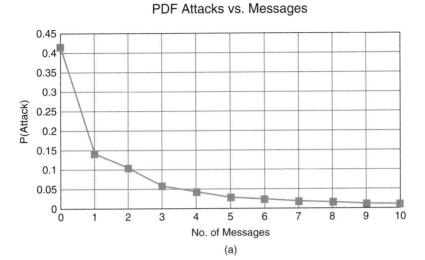

(a)

Figure 14.4 Probability of attacks occurring between a pair of users vs. the number of messages they have exchanged (P(Attack and Message=x)).

PDF Attacks vs. Trades

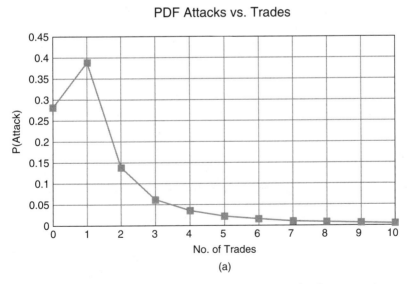

(a)

Figure 14.5 Probability of attacks occurring between a pair of users vs. the number of trades they have made (P(Attack and Message=x)).

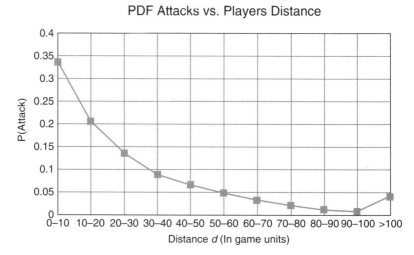

Figure 14.6 Probability of attacks based on players' distance from each other.

Similar to real life, social structures play a significant role in the likelihood of interplayer conflict. In summary, our analysis reveals the following:

1. The attack network has a higher diameter, lower average degree, and lower clustering coefficient than either the message or the trade networks.
2. All networks have similar power law degree distributions, but different degree assortativity. The *Travian* attack network shows nonassortative mixing.
3. The general trend is that attacks are inversely proportional to message frequency, trade frequency, and distance, with some specific exceptions. Players rarely attack fellow alliance or guild members.

14.5 Modeling the Evolution of Alliance Structures

In addition to facilitating our understanding of aggression, *Travian* is also an interesting testbed for studying cooperation, since forming a strong alliance is an important stepping stone toward achieving the final objective of creating the Wonder of the World. Here we analyze how alliances change and evolve during the course of the *Travian* game cycle. Although lacking in formal alliances, most real-world social networks are inherently dynamic and are composed of communities that are constantly changing in membership. As a result, recent years have witnessed increased attention toward the challenging problem of

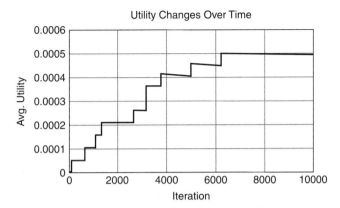

Figure 14.7 Change in average utility summed over all nodes vs. iteration for the *Travian*-Trades data set (one snapshot with 964 nodes). The algorithm converges after 6,680 iterations which requires 2.8 seconds to complete.

detecting evolving communities. As the network changes, user communities evolve and can grow, shrink, or disappear. Intuitively we expect more edges inside the community compared to its outside; i.e., intraconnections tend to be more common than interconnections. Community detection can help us understand the hidden social structure of the user populations, but the dynamic aspect of networks can pose problems for standard algorithms.

Formally, given snapshots $\mathbf{T} = \{T^t | \forall t, t = 1, \ldots, M\}$ of a dynamic network and their corresponding underlying graphs $\mathbf{G}^t = (V^t, E^t)$, with $n^t = |V^t|$ vertices and $m^t = |E^t|$ edges, where $t = 1, \ldots, M$, we aim to detect community structure $\mathbf{C} = \{C^t | \forall t, t = 1, \ldots, M\}$ of the network. The process of community detection is treated as an iterative game performed in a dynamic multiagent environment in which each node of the underlying graph is a selfish agent who decides to maximize its total utility u_i. For every snapshot of the network, a set of agents, one representing each node in the graph, is created to play the community formation game. The community structure is initialized either with a set of singleton communities or with communities passed from previous snapshots. During gameplay, an agent is randomly selected (without replacement) from the pool; it selects an action (join, leave, switch, or no op) by calculating the action that yields the highest utility. After the agent plays, the community structure is updated. The game is played until the number of agents changing communities between permutations falls below the threshold, or the maximum iteration is reached. Figure 14.7 shows an example of the convergence in utility versus iteration. The algorithm maintains a candidate set of multiple community assignments per agent until the last iteration and

Table 14.2 *Data set summary*

Data	Messages	Trades
Min no. of nodes	1,373	964
Max no. of nodes	2,100	1,336
Min no. of edges	8,511	8,080
Max no. of edges	19,242	10,221
No. of snapshots	30	30

then selects the assignment with the highest utility function as the final disjoint partition. Our method, D-GT (**D**ynamic **G**ame **T**heoretic community detection, originally introduced in Alvari et al., 2016), outperforms several other state of the art methods for detecting changing alliances within the *Travian* game. We also created a version of the algorithm, **D-GTG** (D-GT with passing Ground Truth) to handle cases in which the alliance structure is partially known. For instance, MMOG guilds and alliances often have a leadership council that is openly publicized or easily inferred based on the content of chat messages. D-GTG leverages this information by using a select seed group of ground truth communities with predefined size to initialize the algorithm.

14.5.1 Evaluation

For this evaluation, we used two layers of *Travian* multiplex network: Messages and Trades. *Travian* has an in-game messaging system (IGM) for player communication that was used to create our Messages network. Each player can submit a request to trade a specific resource. If another player finds this request interesting, he or she can accept it and the trade will occur; this data was used to build the Trade network. About 70% of messages are exchanged between users in the same alliance (community), making it more predictive of community structure than the Trades network since only 30% of edges in this network represent trades occurred between players within the same alliance. The structural changes in both *Travian* data sets are shown in Figures 14.8 and 14.9; statistics are provided in Table 14.2. Modeling the evolution of alliances is harder during periods of significant structural change, when large numbers of edges are being added and deleted.

We compare D-GT with the following community detection baselines:

- **LabelRankT** (Xie, Chen, & Szymanski, 2013). LabelRankT functions according to the generalized LabelRank, in which each node requires only local information during label propagation processing. Several parameters

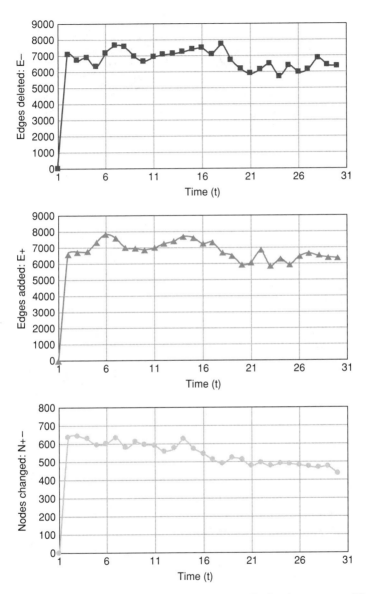

Figure 14.8 The structural changes in the *Travian* Trades data set over 30 snapshots

must be set before running the algorithm on the data; we used the best performing values reported in the original paper.

- **iLCD** (Cazabet, Amblard, & Hanachi, 2010). iLCD is another well known community detection approach for dynamic social networks which works by

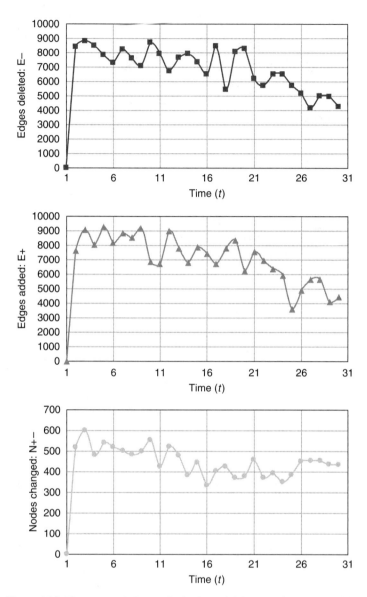

Figure 14.9 The structural changes in the *Travian* Messages data set over thirty snapshots.

first adding edges and then merging the similar ones. It takes the dynamics of the network into account.

- **OSLOM** (Lancichinetti et al., 2011). The Order Statistics Local Optimization Method (OSLOM) is a versatile community detection algorithm that can handle most types of graph properties including edge directions and weights, overlapping communities, hierarchies, and community dynamics. It is based on the local optimization of a fitness function expressing the statistical significance of clusters with respect to random fluctuations.

- **InfoMap** (Rosvall & Bergstrom, 2008). InfoMap is a static community detection method that calculates the probability flow of random walks and decomposes the network into modules by compressing a description of the flows. Since this is a static algorithm, we run it separately on each snapshot.
- **Louvain** (Blondel et al., 2008). The Louvain method is a static community detection approach designed to optimize modularity using heuristics. Small communities are found by optimizing modularity locally for all nodes. Then each community is grouped into a single node, and the first step is repeated. We run this algorithm separately on every network snapshot.

Algorithms were evaluated together on a system with 12G of RAM and an Intel CPU 2.53 GHz, and all reported results were averaged over ten repetitions. The best way to measure the performance of a community detection algorithm is to determine how similar the partition delivered by the algorithm is to the desired partition, assuming ground truth information about the community membership exists. Out of several existing measures (Fortunato, 2010), we selected the standard version of normalized mutual information (NMI) (Danon et al., 2005), which is computed as follows:

$$\mathbf{I}_{norm}(\mathbf{X}, \mathbf{Y}) = \frac{2I(X, Y)}{H(X) + H(Y)}, \tag{14.1}$$

where $I(X, Y)$ is mutual information between two random variables X and Y (i.e. two community partitions) (MacKay, 2003):

$$\mathbf{I}(\mathbf{X}, \mathbf{X}) = \sum_{x} \sum_{y} P(x, y) \log \frac{P(x, y)}{P(x)P(y)}. \tag{14.2}$$

Here $P(x)$ indicates the probability that $X = x$ and joint probability $P(x, y)$ equals to $P(X = x, Y = y)$. $H(X)$ and $H(Y)$ are the entropies of X and Y, respectively. NMI lies in the range [0,1], equaling 1 when two partitions X and Y are exactly identical and 0 when they are totally independent.

Figure 14.10 shows the average performance of D-GT versus OSLOM, LabelRankT, iLCD, InfoMap, and Louvain. Unlike many social media data sets, the *Travian* data set contains ground truth alliance membership information that can be used to calculate the NMI. D-GT outperforms all other methods ($p < .01$) on this metric. Figure 14.11 shows D-GT's performance at predicting the number of alliances, as measured by summed absolute difference between predicted and actual community numbers (lower is better). Note that it is

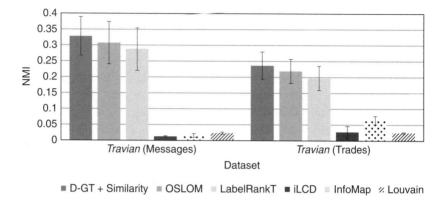

Figure 14.10 Normalized mutual information (NMI) evaluation metric on the two *Travian* data sets with ground truth community membership information; results are averaged over all snapshots.

possible to do acceptably well on the NMI metric while still incorrectly estimating the actual number of communities in the data set. OSLOM also scores well on both metrics (NMI and number of communities). Additionally, it is useful to examine how the number of predicted communities varies between consecutive snapshots. In most cases, the number of communities should remain relatively stable, since the structure of real-world communities rarely changes completely in a short period of time. This is definitely true in *Travian*, where the number of

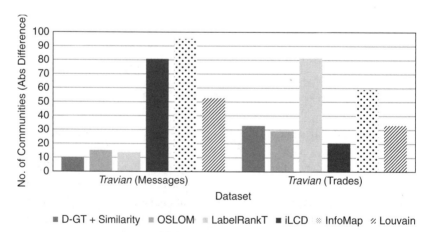

Figure 14.11 Absolute difference between the predicted number of communities and the actual number for the two *Travian* data sets. D-GT and OSLOM achieve the best performance overall at correctly predicting the number of alliances.

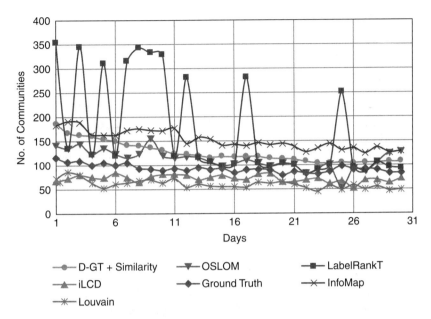

Figure 14.12 Number of predicted communities versus time for the *Travian* (Trades) data set. LabelRankT's predicted number of communities varies drastically between time steps, whereas all other algorithms make more consistent predictions.

alliances changes relatively slowly. Figure 14.12 shows the number of predicted communities versus time on the *Travian* (Trades) data set; all of the methods make more consistent predictions over time than LabelRankT.

In some scenarios, it is plausible that the community membership of a small number of agents is known in advance, and the community detection procedure should leverage this information. To handle this problem, we developed a variant (D-GTG: D-GT with passing Ground Truth). Figure 14.13 shows the performance improvements from increasing the size of the seed groups from 0–20% of the total number of agents for the *Travian* (Messages) data set, and Figure 14.14 shows the performance increase for *Travian* (Trades). Note that extracting community membership information from the network structure of *Travian* (Trades) is a difficult problem because only 30% of the edges in *Travian* (Trades) occur between players within the same alliance (community). Also the data set has a high number of isolated nodes; about 50% of the nodes do not belong to any alliance.

In summary, our results demonstrate that D-GT can accurately track the evolution of alliance structure. For this task, it outperforms other dynamic

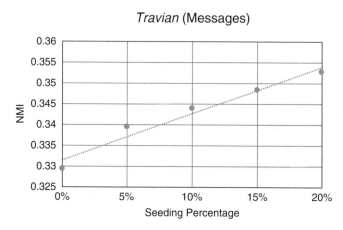

Figure 14.13 D-GTG NMI vs. seed group size on *Travian* (Messages).

community detection methods including LabelRankT, iLCD, and OSLOM. In cases where the community membership of a small number of players (e.g., the guild leadership) is known D-GTG can leverage this information to improve the NMI score.

14.6 Rate Prediction Model for Link Formation

Many social networks are constantly in flux, with new edges and vertices being added or deleted daily. Fully modeling the dynamics that drive the

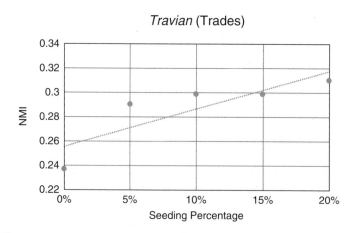

Figure 14.14 D-GTG NMI vs. seed group size on *Travian* (Trades).

evolution of a social network is a complex problem, owing to the large number of individual and dyadic factors associated with link formation. Here we focus on predicting one crucial variable – the *rate* of network change. Not only do different networks change at different rates, but individuals within a network can have disparate tempos of social interaction. This section describes how modeling this aspect of network dynamics can ameliorate performance on link prediction tasks. We introduce a new supervised link prediction framework, RPM (Rate Prediction Model). In addition to network similarity measures, RPM uses the predicted rate of link modifications, modeled using time series data.

14.6.1 Problem Formulation

The problem of link prediction in dynamic networks is defined as: Let graph G be the social network of interest denoted as (V, E), where V is the set of nodes and $E \in V \times V$ is the set of (directed or undirected) interactions. Let G_t be the subgraph of G containing the nodes and edges recorded at time t. In turn, let G_{t+1} be the subgraph of G observed at time $t + 1$. Using network structure up to time t, our goal is then to predict future structure of the network at time $t + 1$.

14.6.2 Background

Link prediction approaches commonly rely on measuring topological similarity between unconnected nodes (Al Hasan & Zaki, 2011; Getoor & Diehl, 2005; Wang, Satuluri, & Parthasarathy, 2007). It is a task well suited for supervised binary classification because it is easy to create a labeled data set of node pairs; however, the data sets tend to be extremely unbalanced with a preponderance of negative examples where links were not formed. Topological metrics are used to score node pairs at time t in order to predict whether a link will occur at a later time t' ($t' > t$). However, even though these metrics are good indicators of future network connections, they are less accurate at predicting *when* the changes will occur (the exact value of t'). To overcome this limitation, we explicitly learn link formation rates for all nodes in the network; first, a time series is constructed for each node pair from historic data and then a forecasting model is applied to predict future values. The output of the forecasting model is used to augment topological similarity metrics within a supervised link prediction framework. Prior work has demonstrated the general utility of modeling time for link prediction (e.g., Berlingerio et al., 2009; Huang & Lin, 2009; Potgieter et al., 2009); our results show that our

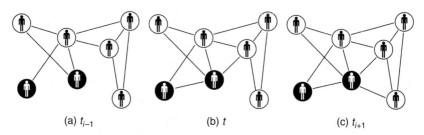

(a) t_{i-1} (b) t (c) t_{i+1}

Figure 14.15 Evolution of a network over time. Black nodes have higher *rates* of link formation. This behavior can be captured by taking temporal information into account; RPM identifies these nodes through the use of time series.

specific method of rate modeling outperforms the use of other types of time series. Networks formed from different types of social processes (e.g., trades vs. communication) may vary in their dynamics, but our experiments show that RPM outperforms other standard approaches on multiple types of data sets.

14.6.3 Time Series

To construct the time series, the network G observed at time t must be split into several time-sliced snapshots, that is, states of the network at different times in the past. Afterwards, a window of prediction is defined, representing how further in the future we want to make the prediction. Then, consecutive snapshots are grouped in small sets called frames. Frames contain as many snapshots as the length of the window of prediction. These frames compose what is called Framed Time-Sliced Network Structure (S) (Soares & Prudêncio, 2012). Let G_t be the graph representation of a network at time t. Let $[G_1, G_2, \ldots, G_T]$ be the frame formed by the union of the graphs from time 1 to T. Let n be the number of periods (frames) in the series. And let w be the window of prediction. Formally, S can be defined as

$$S = \{[G_1, \ldots, G_w], [G_{w+1}, \ldots, G_{2w}], \ldots [G_{(n--1)w+1}, \ldots, G_{nw}]\}$$

For instance, suppose that we observed a network from day 1 to day 9, and our aim is to predict links that will appear at day 10. In this example, the forecast horizon (window of prediction) is one day. Our aim here is to model how the networks evolve every day in order to predict what will happen in the forecast horizon. Figure 14.15 shows an example of the evolution of network over time.

14.6.4 Network Similarity Metrics

Here, we use a standard set of topological metrics to assign scores to potential links:

1. Common Neighbors (CN) (Newman, 2001) is defined as the number of nodes with direct relationships with both members of the node pair:

$$CN(x, y) = |\Gamma(x) \cap \Gamma(y)| \qquad (14.3)$$

   where $\Gamma(x)$ is the set of neighbors of node x.
2. Preferential Attachment (PA) (Barabási et al., 2009; Liben-Nowell & Kleinberg, 2003) assumes that the probability that a new link is created is proportional to the node degree $\Gamma(x)$. Hence, nodes that currently have a high number of relationships tend to create more links in the future:

$$PA(x, y) = |\Gamma(x)| \times |\Gamma(y)| \qquad (14.4)$$

3. Jaccard's Coefficient (JC) (Tan, Steinbach, & Kumar, 2005) assumes higher values for pairs of nodes that share a higher proportion of common neighbors relative to total number of neighbors they have

$$JC(x, y) = \frac{|\Gamma(x) \cap \Gamma(y)|}{|\Gamma(x) \cup \Gamma(y)|} \qquad (14.5)$$

4. Adamic-Adar (AA) (Adamic & Adar, 2003), similar to JC, assigns a higher importance to the common neighbors that have fewer total neighbors. Hence, it measures exclusivity between a common neighbor and the evaluated pair of nodes:

$$AA(x, y) = \sum_{z \in |\Gamma(x) \cap \Gamma(y)|} \frac{1}{\log(|\Gamma(z)|)} \qquad (14.6)$$

These metrics serve as (1) unsupervised baseline methods for evaluating the performance of RPM and (2) are also included as features used by the supervised classifiers.

14.6.5 Method

RPM treats the link prediction problem as a supervised classification task, where each data point corresponds to a pair of vertices in the social network graph. This is a typical binary classification task that could be addressed with a variety of classifiers; we use the Spark support vector machine (SVM) implementation. All experiments were conducted using the default parameters of the Spark MLlib package: the SVM is defined with a polynomial kernel and a cost parameter of 1. Algorithms were implemented in Python and executed on a machine with Intel(R) Core i7 CPU and 24GB of RAM.

To produce a labeled data set for supervised learning, we require timestamps for each node and edge to track the evolution of the social network over time. We then consider the state of the network for two different time periods t and t' (with $t < t'$). The network information from time t is used to predict new links that will be formed at time t'. One of the most important challenges with the supervised link prediction approach is handling extreme class skewness. The number of possible links is quadratic in the number of vertices in a social network; however, the number of actual edges is only a tiny fraction of this number, resulting in large class skewness.

The most commonly used technique for coping with this problem is to balance the training data set by using a small subset of the negative examples. Rather than sampling the network, we both train and test with the original data distribution and reweight the misclassification penalties. Let $G(V, A)$ be the social network of interest. Let G_t be the subgraph of G containing the nodes and edges recorded at time t. In turn, let $G_{t'}$ be the subgraph of G observed at time t'. To generate training examples, we considered all pairs of nodes in G_t. Even though this training paradigm is more computationally demanding it avoids the concern that the choice of sampling strategy is distorting the classifier performance (Lichtenwalter, Lussier, & Chawla, 2010).

Selecting the best feature set is often the most critical part of any machine learning implementation. In this dissertation, we supplement the standard set of features extracted from the graph topology (described in the previous section), with features predicted by a set of time series. Let $F_t (t = 1, \dots, T)$ be a time series with T observations with A_t defined as the observation at time t and F_{t+1} the time series forecast at time $t + 1$. First, we analyze the performance of the following time series forecasting models for generating features:

1. **Simple Mean:** The simple mean is the average of all available data:

$$F_{t+1} = \frac{A_t + A_{t-1} + \cdots + A_{t-T}}{T}$$

2. **Moving Average:** This method makes a prediction by taking the mean of the n most recent observed values. The moving average forecast at time t can be defined as:

$$F_{t+1} = \frac{A_t + A_{t-1} + \cdots + A_{t-n}}{n}$$

3. **Weighted Moving Average:** This method is similar to moving average but allows one period to be emphasized over others. The sum of weights must

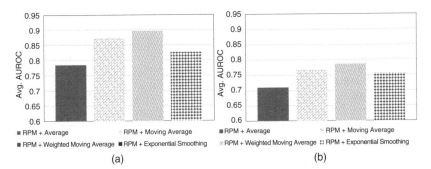

Figure 14.16 Performance of RPM using different forecasting models on (a) *Travian* Messages and (b) *Travian* Trades. Weighted Moving Average is the best performer and is used in RPM.

add to 100% or 1.00:

$$F_{t+1} = \sum C_t A_t$$

4. **Exponential Smoothing:** This model is one of the most frequently used time series methods because of its ease of use and minimal data requirements. It only needs three pieces of data to start: last period's forecast (F_t), last period's actual value (A_t), and a value of smoothing coefficient, α, between 0 and 1.0. If no last period forecast is available, we can simply average the last few periods:

$$F_{t+1} = \alpha A_t + (1 - \alpha)F_t$$

We identify which time series prediction model produces the best rate estimate, according to the AUROC performance of its RPM variant. Parameters of weighted moving average and exponential smoothing were tuned to maximize performance on the training data set. Figure 14.16 shows that the best performing model was Weighted Moving Average with $n = 3$ and parameters C_1, C_2, and C_3 set to 0.2, 0.3, and 0.5 respectively.

14.6.6 Results

Table 14.3 gives the network statistics for each of the data sets used in the evaluation. Our evaluation measures receiver operating characteristic (ROC) curves for the different approaches. These curves show achievable true positive (TP) rates with respect to all false-positive (FP) rates by varying the decision threshold on probability estimations or scores. For all of our experiments, we report area under the ROC curve (AU-ROC), the scalar measure of the performance

Table 14.3 *Data set summary*

Data	*Travian* (Messages)	*Travian* (Trades)
No. of nodes	2,809	2,466
Link (Class 1)	44,956	87,418
No link (Class 0)	7,845,525	5,993,738
No. of snapshots	30	30

over all thresholds. Since link prediction is highly imbalanced, straightforward accuracy measures are well known to be misleading; for example, in a sparse network, the trivial classifier that labels all samples as missing links can have a 99.99% accuracy.

In all experiments, the algorithms were evaluated with stratified 10-fold cross-validation. For more reliable results, the cross-validation procedure was executed 10 times for each algorithm and data set. We benchmark our algorithm against **Supervised-MA** (Soares & Prudêncio, 2012). Supervised-MA is a state-of-the-art link prediction method that is similar to our method, in that it is supervised and uses moving average time series forecasting. In contrast to RPM, Supervised-MA creates time series for the unsupervised metrics rather than the link formation rate itself. **Supervised** is a baseline supervised classifier that uses the same unsupervised metrics as features without the time series prediction model. As a point of reference, we also show the unsupervised performance of the individual topological metrics: (1) **Common Neighbors**, (2) **Preferential Attachment**, (3) **Jaccard Coefficient**, and (4) **Adamic-Adar**. Table 14.4 presents results for all methods on *Travian* (communication and trade layers). Results for our proposed method are shown using bold numbers in the table; in all cases, RPM outperforms the other approaches. Two-tailed, paired t-tests across multiple network snapshots reveal that the

Table 14.4 *AUROC performance*

Algorithms / Networks	*Travian* (Messages)	*Travian* (Trades)
RPM	**0.8970**	**0.7859**
Supervised-MA	0.8002	0.6143
Supervised	0.7568	0.7603
Common Neighbors	0.4968	0.5002
Jaccard Coefficient	0.6482	0.4703
Preferential Attachment	0.5896	0.5441
Adamic/Adar	0.5233	0.4962

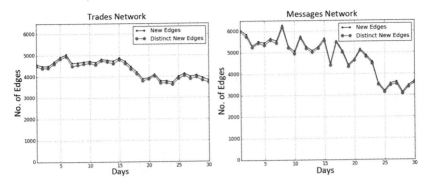

Figure 14.17 Dynamics of the *Travian* network (trades: left and messages: right). The line with square markers shows the new edges added, and the line with circle markers shows edges that did not exist in the previous snapshot.

RPM is significantly better ($p < .01$) on all four data sets when compared to Supervised-MA. Figure 14.17 shows the dynamics of the *Travian* network.

We discover that explicitly including the rate feature (estimated by a time series) is decisively better than the usage of time series to forecast topological metrics. The rate forecast is useful for predicting the source node of future links; hence RPM can focus its search on a smaller set of node pairs. We believe a combination of topological metrics is useful for predicting the destination node, but that relying exclusively on the topological metrics, or their forecasts, is less discriminative.

The performance of RPM relies on three innovations: (1) explicit modeling of link formation rates at a node level, (2) the usage of multiple time series to leverage information from earlier snapshots, and (3) training and testing with the full data distribution courtesy of the Spark fast cluster computing system. Rate is an important concept in many generative network models, but its usage has been largely ignored within discriminative classification frameworks. For instance, the stochastic actor-oriented model of network dynamics contains a network rate component that is governed by both the time period and the actors (Snijders, van de Bunt, & Steglich, 2010). RPM does not attempt to create a general model of how the rate is affected by the properties of the actor (node), but instead predicts the link formation rate of each node with a time series. By accurately identifying the most active individuals in the social network, RPM achieves statistically significant improvements over related link prediction methods. Our experiments were performed on networks created by a variety of social processes, including communication and trading; they show that the rate of link generation varies with the type of network.

14.7 Link Prediction in Coevolving Multiplex Networks

As social media platforms offer customers more interaction options, such as *friending, following*, and *recommending*, analyzing the rich tapestry of interdependent user interactions becomes increasingly complicated. Although standard social network analysis techniques (Scott, 2012) offer useful insights about these communities, there is relatively little theory from the social sciences on how to integrate information from multiple types of online interactions. Rather than organizing these data into social networks separately chronicling the history of different forms of user interaction, dynamic multiplex networks (Kivela et al., 2014) offer a richer formalism for modeling the social fabric of online societies. This section introduces a comprehensive framework, MLP (Multiplex Link Prediction), in which link existence likelihoods for the target layer are learned from the other network layers. These likelihoods are used to reweight the output of a single layer link prediction method that uses rank aggregation to combine a set of topological metrics.

A multiplex network is a multilayer network that shares the same set of vertices across all layers. This network can be modeled as a graph $G = <V, E >$ where V is the set of vertices and E is the set of edges present in the graph. The dynamic graph $G = \{G_0, G_1, \ldots, G_t\}$ represents the state of the network at different times. The network is then defined as: $G_t = <V, E_t^1, \ldots, E_t^M>$ with $E_t^\alpha \subseteq V \times V, \forall \alpha \in \{1, \ldots, M\}$, where each set E_t^α corresponds to the edge set of a distinct layer at time t. Thus a dynamic multiplex network is well suited for representing diverse user activities over a period of time. Here, we address the problem of predicting future user interactions from the history of past connections. Assuming the data are represented as a graph, our goal is then to predict the structure of graph G_t with α as the target layer, using information from previous snapshots as well as other layers of the network.

MLP is a hybrid architecture that utilizes multiple components to address different aspects of the link prediction task. We seek to extract information from all layers of the network for the purpose of link prediction within a specific layer known as the target layer. To do so, we create a weighted version of the original target layer where interactions and connections that exist in other layers receive higher weights. After reweighting the layer, we employ the collection of node similarity metrics on the weighted network. To express the temporal dynamics of the network, we use a decay model on the time series of similarity metrics to predict future values. Finally, the Borda rank aggregation method is employed to combine the ranked lists of node pairs into a single list that predicts links for the next snapshot of the target network layer. Each component of the model is explained in more detail in the following sections.

14.7.1 Multiplex Likelihood Assignment and Edge Weighting

This component leverages information about cross-layer link co-occurrences. During the coevolution process, links may be engendered due to activity in other network layers. Some layers may evolve largely independently of the rest of the network, whereas links in other layers may be highly predictive of links in the target layer. In our proposed method, a weight is assigned to each layer based on its influence on the target layer. Weights are calculated using a likelihood function:

$$w_i = Likelihood(\text{Link in } L^{Target} | \text{Link in } L^i) \qquad (14.7)$$

where L^i and w_i represent the ith layer and the weight calculated for it respectively. $LTarget$ indicates the target layer for which we want to predict future links. The $Likelihood$ function computes the similarity between the target layer and the ith layer; to do this, we use the current ratio of overlapping edges. Next, we calculate weights for every node pair by checking the link correspondence between two layers using the likelihood of a link being present in the target layer given the existence of the link in the other layer at any other previous snapshot. This orders other layers in terms of their relative importance for a specific target layer. The process assigns higher weights to node pairs that occur in more than one layer (multiplex edges). The rate of link formation is incorporated into the model as the first term of the edge weight. Algorithm 14.1 shows the process of assigning likelihoods to layers and reweighting the adjacency matrix.

Algorithm 14.1 Likelihood Assignment and Edge Weighting

1: Input: Edge sets $(E1, \ldots, E^M)$ for M layers where E^α is the edge set of target layer
2: Output: E_w^α weighted adjacency matrix for layer α (target layer)
   //Calculate weights for the layers
3: **for** $i \in \{1, 2, \ldots, M\} - \{\alpha\}$ **do**
4:   $w_i = Likelihood (Link \text{ in } L^\alpha | Link \text{ in } L^i)$
5: **end for**
   //Weighting target layer
6: **for** edge $e \in E^\alpha$ **do**
7: $w_e = rate + \sum_{i=1 \& i \neq \alpha}^{M} w_i \times linkExist(e)$
8: **end for**

The term $rate$ is defined as the average value of the source node's out-degree over previous timesteps. Function $linkExist$ is used to obtain information about a link's existence in other layers during previous snapshots. It checks each layer for the presence of an edge and returns 1 if an edge is present in that layer.

14.7.2 Node Similarity Metrics

This section provides a brief description of the topological and path-based metrics for encoding node similarity that are used within our MLP framework to create ranked score lists for each node pair. These techniques are often used in isolation as unsupervised methods for link prediction. Note that $\Gamma(x)$ stands for the set of neighbors of vertex x while $w(x, y)$ represents the weight assigned to the interaction between node x and y. We use the same metrics used by RPM: (1) common neighbors (CN), (2) Jaccard's coefficient (JC), (3) preferential attachment (PA), and (4) Adamic-Adar coefficient (AA). Additionally, MLP uses the following metrics:

- **Resource Allocation (RA)**

  RA was first proposed in Zhou, Lü, and Zhang (2009) and is based on physical processes of resource allocation:

  $$RA(x, y) = \sum_{z \in \Gamma(x) \cap \Gamma(y)} \frac{w(x, z) + w(y, z)}{\sum_{c \in \Gamma(z)} w(z, c)} \tag{14.8}$$

- **Page Rank (PR)**

  The PageRank algorithm (Brin & Page, 2012) measures the significance of a node based on the significance of its neighbors. We use the weighted PageRank algorithm proposed in Ding (2011):

  $$PR_w(x) = \alpha \sum_{k \in \Gamma(x)} \frac{PR_w(x)}{L(k)} + (1 - \alpha) \frac{w(x)}{\sum_{y=1}^{N} w(y)} \tag{14.9}$$

  where $L(x)$ is the sum of outgoing link weights from node x, and $\sum_{y=1}^{N} w(y)$ is the total weight across the whole network.

- **Inverse Path Distance (IPD)**

  The Path Distance measure for unweighted networks simply counts the number of nodes along the shortest path between x and y in the graph. Note that $PD(x, y) = 1$ if two nodes x and y share at least one common neighbor. In this article, the Inverse Path Distance is used to measure the proximity between two nodes, where:

  $$IPD(x, y) = \frac{1}{PD(x, y)} \tag{14.10}$$

IPD is based on the intuition that nearby nodes are likely to be connected. In a weighted network, IPD is defined by the inverse of the shortest weighted distance between two nodes.

- **Product of Clustering Coefficient (PCF)**

  The Clustering Coefficient of a vertex v is defined as:

  $$PCF(v) = \frac{3 \times \text{no. of triangles adjacent to } v}{\text{no. of possible triples adjacent to } v} \qquad (14.11)$$

  To compute a score for link prediction between the vertex x and y, one can multiply the clustering coefficient score of x and y.

14.7.3 Temporal Link Structure

Given the network history for T time periods, we need to capture the temporal dependencies of the coevolution process. To do so, our framework uses a weighted exponentially decaying model (Acar, Dunlavy, & Kolda, 2009). Let $\{Sim_t(i, j), t = t_0 + 1, \ldots, t_0 + T\}$ be a time series of similarity score matrices generated by a node similarity metric on a sliding window of T successive temporal slices. An aggregated weighted similarity matrix is constructed as follows:

$$Sim_{(t_0+1)\sim(t_0+T)}(i, j) = \sum_{t=t_0+1}^{t_0+T} \theta^{t_0+T-t} Sim_t(i, j) \qquad (14.12)$$

where the parameter $\theta \in [0, 1]$ is the smoothing weight for previous time periods. Different values of θ modify the importance assigned to the most or least recent snapshots before current time $t + 1$. This procedure generates a composite temporal score matrix for every node similarity metric. $Sim_{(t_0+1)\sim(t_0+T)}$ (shortened to Sim) is used by the algorithm as a summary of network activity, encapsulating the temporal evolution of the similarity matrix.

14.7.4 Rank Aggregation

Before describing the final step of our approach, let us briefly discuss existing methods for *ranked list aggregation/rank aggregation*. List merging or list aggregation refers to the process of combining a number of lists with the same or different numbers of elements in order to get one final list including all the elements. In rank aggregation, the order or rank of elements in input lists is also taken into consideration. The input lists can be categorized as *full, partial, or disjoint lists*. Full lists contain exactly the same elements but with a different ordering, partial lists may have some of the elements in common but not all, and disjoint lists have completely different elements. In this case, we are only dealing with full lists since each similarity metric produces a complete list for the same set of pairs, differing only in ordering.

In rank aggregation, distance metrics are used to find the disagreement between two lists/rankings. In general, any method of rank aggregation is desired to produce an aggregate ranking with minimal total disagreement among the input lists. Two well-known distance measures are:

- **Spearman Footrule Distance:** This computes the distance between two ranked lists by computing the sum of differences in rankings of each element. Formally, it is given by

$$F(L_1, L_2) = \sum_{i \in n} |L_1(i) - L_2(i)| \qquad (14.13)$$

- **Kendall Tau Distance:** This counts the number of pairs of elements that have opposite rankings in the two input lists, i.e., it calculates the pairwise disagreements.

$$K(L_1, L_2) = |(i, j) \text{ s.t. } L_1(i) \le L_2(j) \& L_1(i) \ge L_2(j)| \qquad (14.14)$$

where L_1 and L_2 are the input lists and $L_1(i)$ and $L_2(i)$ represent the ranks of element i in the two lists correspondingly.

Rank aggregation methods can be categorized into two types: order-based and score-based. Order-based methods use the rank information (Liu et al., 2007) while score-based aggregation methods use score information from individual rankers. Several rank aggregation methods are described in (Sculley, 2007), including Borda's, Markov chain, and median rank methods. Borda's method is a *rank-then-combine* method originally proposed to obtain a consensus from a voting system. Since it is based on the absolute positioning of the rank elements and not their relative rankings, it can be considered a truly positional method. For every element in the lists, a Borda score is calculated and elements are ranked according to this score in the aggregated list. For a set of complete ranked lists $L = [L_1, L_2, L_3, \ldots, L_k]$, the Borda score for an element i and a list L_k is given by:

$$B_{L_k}(i) = \{count(j) | L_k(j) < L_k(i) \& j \in L_k\} \qquad (14.15)$$

The total Borda score for an element is given as

$$B(i) = \sum_{t=1}^{k} B_{L_t(i)} \qquad (14.16)$$

Borda's method is computationally cheap, which is a highly desirable property for link prediction in large networks.

Algorithm 14.2 shows our proposed framework, which incorporates edge weighting, the temporal decay model, and rank aggregation to produce an accurate prediction of future links in a dynamic multiplex network. The Borda function produces the final output of the MLP framework. Results of the proposed algorithm are compared with other state-of-the-art techniques in the next section.

Algorithm 14.2 Multiplex Link Prediction Framework (MLP)

1: Input: Weighted target layer edge sets for T previous snapshots
2: Output: Temporal aggregated score matrix S for the target layer
3: **for** each node similarity metric u **do**
4:     **for** $t \in \{1, \ldots, T\}$ **do**
5:         Calculate score matrix Sim_{t0+t}^{u}
6:     **end for**
7:     Calculate temporal similarity matrix Sim^{u}
8: **end for**
9: Final score matrix $S = Borda(Sim^{1}, \ldots, Sim^{u})$

14.7.5 Experimental Study

To investigate the impact of each component of our proposed method, not only do we compare our results with two other approaches for fusing cross-layer information, but we also analyze the performance of ablated versions of our method. The complete method, MLP (Hybrid), is compared with MLP (Decay Model + Rank Aggregation) and MLP (Weighted + Rank Aggregation). All of the algorithms were implemented in Python and executed on a machine with the Intel(R) Core i7 CPU and 24GB of RAM for the purpose of fair comparison. Our implementation uses Apache Spark to speed the link prediction process.

14.7.6 Analysis of Cross-layer Interaction

Figure 14.18 shows log scale box–whisker plots that depict the frequency of interactions between users who are connected across multiple layers. We compare the frequency of interactions in cases where the node pair is connected on all layers versus the frequency of being connected in a single layer. As expected, in cases where users are connected on all layers, the number of

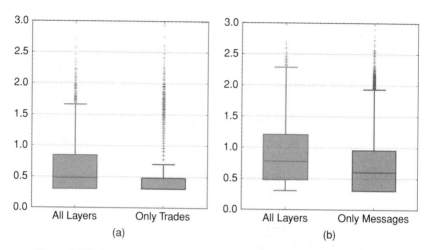

Figure 14.18 Log scale box–whisker plots for user interactions in different layers of the network: (a) *Travian* (Trades) and (b) *Travian* (Messages).

interactions is higher. The heatmap of the number of overlapping edges between different network layers (Figure 14.19) suggests that a noticeable number of edges are shared between all layers. This clearly indicates the potential value of cross-layer information for the link prediction task on these data sets (Table 14.5). Our proposed likelihood weighting method effectively captures the information revealed by our analysis.

14.7.7 Performance of Multilayer Link Prediction

For our experiments, we adopted a moving-window approach to evaluate the performance of our temporal multiplex link prediction algorithm. Given a

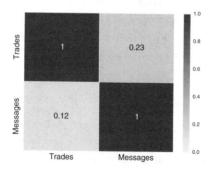

Figure 14.19 Heatmap representing the edge overlap between pairs of layers for the *Travian* data set.

Table 14.5 *Data set summary; Number of edges,*
nodes, and snapshots for each network layer

Data set		Travian
No. of nodes		2,809
No. of snapshots		30
Layers/no. of edges	Trades	87,418
	Messages	44,956

specified window size T, for each time period $t(t > T)$, graphs of T previous periods $(G_{t-T}, \ldots, G_{t-1})$ (where each graph consists of M layers) are used to predict links that occur at the target layer α in the current period (G_t^α). To assess our proposed framework and study the impact of its components, we compare against the following baselines:

- **MLP (Hybrid)**: incorporates all elements discussed in the framework section. It utilizes the likelihood assignment and edge weighting procedure to extract cross-layer information. Node similarity scores are modified using the temporal decay model and combined with Borda rank aggregation.
- **MLP (Likelihood + Rank Aggregation)**: This method uses only the aggregated scores calculated from the graphs weighted with cross-layer information. It does not consider the temporal aspects of network coevolution.
- **MLP (Decay Model + Rank Aggregation)**: This method does not use the cross-layer weighting scheme and relies on temporal information alone to predict future links. The final aggregated score matrix is calculated based on forecast values at time t for each node similarity metric using the decay model.
- **Likelihood:** Weights generated by the cross-layer likelihood assignment procedure are treated as scores for every node pair. We then sort the pairs based on their score and calculate the AUROC.
- **Rank Aggregation:** This method is a simple aggregated version of all unsupervised scoring methods using Borda's rank aggregation method applied to node similarity metrics from the target layer.
- **Unsupervised Methods:** The performance of our proposed framework is compared with eight well-known unsupervised link prediction methods described in the proposed method under node similarity metrics. All unsupervised methods are applied to the binary static graph from time 0 to $t - 1$ in order to predict links at time t. Only the structure of the target layer is used.

- **Average Aggregation:** In order to extend the rank aggregation model to include information from other layers of the network, we use the idea proposed in Pujari and Kanawati (2015). Node similarity metrics are aggregated across all layers. So for attribute X (Common Neighbors, Adamic/Adar, etc.) over M layers the following is defined:

$$X(u, v) = \frac{\sum_{\alpha=1}^{M} X(u, v)^{\alpha}}{M} \qquad (14.17)$$

where $X(u, v)$ is the average score for nodes u and v across all layers and $X(u, v)^{\alpha}$ is the score at layer α. Borda's rank aggregation is then applied to the extended attributes to calculate the final scoring matrix.

- **Entropy Aggregation:** Entropy aggregation is another extended rank aggregation model proposed in Pujari and Kanawati (2015), where $X(u, v)$ is defined as follows:

$$X(u, v) = -\sum_{\alpha=1}^{M} \frac{X(u, v)^{\alpha}}{X_{total}} \log \left(\frac{X(u, v)^{\alpha}}{X_{total}} \right) \qquad (14.18)$$

where $X_{total} = \sum_{\alpha=1}^{M} X(u, v)^{\alpha}$. The entropy-based attributes are more suitable for capturing the distribution of the attribute value over all dimensions. A higher value indicates a uniform distribution of attribute values across the multiplex layers.

- **Multiplex Unsupervised Methods:** Finally, using the definition of core neighborhood proposed in Hristova et al. (2015), we extend four unsupervised methods (Common Neighbors, Preferential Attachment, Jaccard Coefficient, and Adamic/Adar) to their multiplex versions.

Table 14.6 shows the results of different algorithms on the *Travian* data set. Bold numbers indicate the best results on each target layer considered; MLP (Hybrid) is the best performing algorithm.

14.7.8 Discussion

In this section, we discuss the most interesting findings:

Does rank aggregation improve the performance of the unsupervised metrics? As shown in Table 14.6, although the aggregated scores matrix produced by Borda's method achieves better results than unsupervised methods in one case (*Travian* message) and comparable results on *Travian* trade, it is not able to significantly outperform all unsupervised methods in any of the networks. As discussed before, we are using the simple Borda method for the rank aggregation which does not consider the effect of each ranker on the

Table 14.6 *AUROC performances for a target layer averaged over all snapshots with a sliding time window of T = 3*

Algorithms / Networks	Trade	Message
MLP (Hybrid)	**0.821 ± 0.001**	**0.803 ± 0.002**
MLP (LH/RA)	0.802 ± 0.001	0.790 ± 0.0021
MLP (DM/RA)	0.722 ± 0.002	0.731 ± 0.002
Likelihood	0.770 ± 0.033	0.760 ± 0.041
Rank Aggregation	0.694 ± 0.001	0.712 ± 0.001
Common Neighbors	0.656 ± 0.002	0.667 ± 0.002
Jaccard Coefficient	0.628 ± 0.002	0.680 ± 0.003
Preferential Attachment	0.709 ± 0.002	0.637 ± 0.001
Adamic/Adar	0.635 ± 0.003	0.700 ± 0.003
Resource Allocation	0.625 ± 0.005	0.690 ± 0.003
Page Rank	0.595 ± 0.0016	0.687 ± 0.002
Inverse Path Distance	0.572 ± 0.003	0.650 ± 0.003
Clustering Coefficient	0.580 ± 0.002	0.633 ± 0.003
Average Aggregation	0.744 ± 0.030	0.752 ± 0.020
Entropy Aggregation	0.731 ± 0.004	0.763 ± 0.020
Multiplex CN	0.729 ± 0.0040	0.643 ± 0.013
Multiplex JC	0.666 ± 0.031	0.619 ± 0.012
Multiplex PA	0.722 ± 0.010	0.646 ± 0.012
Multiplex AA	0.671 ± 0.010	0.690 ± 0.031

Variants of our proposed framework are shown at the top of the table, followed by standard unsupervised methods. The algorithms shown in the bottom half of the table are techniques for multiplex networks proposed by other research groups. The best performer is marked in bold.

final performance. While adding weights to the rankers or using more complex rank aggregation models such as Kemeny might achieve better results, it has been shown that those approaches have high computational complexity, which makes them less suitable for large real-world networks (Pujari & Kanawati, 2012; Tabourier et al., 2014). Despite the fact that the rank aggregation alone does not significantly improve the overall performance of the link prediction task, it enables us to effectively fuse different kinds of information (edge and node features, nodes similarity, etc.).

On the other hand, the Average and Entropy Aggregation methods, which are designed to consider attribute values from other layers, are able to outperform regular Rank Aggregation and MLP (Decay Model + Rank Aggregation). However, both methods use the static structure of all snapshots from time 0 to

$t - 1$, while MLP (Decay Model + Rank Aggregation) incorporates only the past T snapshots, which makes it more suitable for large networks.

Does the likelihood assignment procedure outperform the unsupervised scores? To study the ability of our likelihood weighting method to model the link formation process, we generate results for two methods: using likelihood explicitly as a scoring method as well as using the values to generate a weighted version of the networks. First, the *Likelihood* method is used in isolation to demonstrate the prediction power of its weights as a new scoring approach. Table 14.6 shows significant improvements on unsupervised scores as well as the aggregated version of them. As expected, the more overlap between the target layer and predictor layers, the more performance improvement *Likelihood* achieves. As an example, Likelihood achieves ~ 7% of improvement on *Travian* (Trade) compared with ~ 5% of improvement on *Travian* (Message). Not only is there a lower rate of overlapping edges between those layers, but also the number of interactions is higher than in the two other layers.

On the other hand, the method introduced in Algorithm 14.1 generates a weighted version of input graphs which is used to generate a weighted version of unsupervised methods to produce the final scoring matrix. This paired with the rank aggregation method generates significantly better average AUROC performance compared with other proposed methods. Also, when temporal information from previous snapshots of the network is included, MLP (Hybrid) outperforms other variants of MLP as well as well-known unsupervised methods. This indicates the power of overlapping links in improving the performance of link prediction in coevolving multiplex networks.

Does including temporal information improve AUROC performance? The importance of incorporating temporal information into link prediction has been discussed in our previous work (Hajibagheri, Sukthankar, & Lakkaraju, 2016). However, here we are interested in analyzing the impact of this information on improving the performance of MLP. For that purpose, first, the decay model is employed in MLP (Decay Model + Rank Aggregation) to determine whether it improves the results generated by the aggregated score matrix. The final aggregated score matrix is calculated based on forecast values at time t for each unsupervised method using the decay model. As expected, this version of MLP is able to achieve up to ~3% of AUROC improvement using only information from the last three snapshots of the *Travian* network. On the other hand, we observed the same pattern when the decay model was added to MLP (Hybrid) along with likelihood and rank aggregation. Using the scores generated by our hybrid approach outperformed all other proposed and existing methods. The results presented here have been obtained using $T = 3$ for the *Travian* data set. While for *Travian* layers, increasing the value of T

tends to improve the prediction performance slightly until $T = 3$, higher values of T may decrease the performance. Similarly, the value of θ is set to 0.4.

In summary, MLP (Decay Model + Rank Aggregation) is able to achieve results comparable to other baseline methods except Average and Entropy Aggregation since they benefit from the entire graph structure. Although rank aggregation by itself is not able to significantly improve the performance of unsupervised methods, paired with decay models and taking temporal aspects of the network, it can achieve better performance. On the other hand, the multiplex versions of the neighborhood-based unsupervised methods are able to improve average AUROC performance, however the results are inconsistent and they achieve lower performance in many cases. Finally, both MLP (Hybrid) and MLP (Likelihood + Rank Aggregation) achieve higher performance compared with all other methods, illustrating the importance of the cross-layer information created by the network coevolution process. A paired two-sample t-test is used to indicate the significance of the results produced by each method where the p-value is smaller than .0001. It is worth mentioning that, even though MLP (Hybrid) is able to outperform all other methods, its performance is not significantly better than MLP (Likelihood + Rank Aggregation) in the case of *Travian* (Message).

In summary, MLP (Multiplex Link Prediction) employs a holistic approach to accurately predict links in dynamic multiplex networks using a collection of topological metrics, the temporal patterns of link formation, and overlapping edges created by network coevolution. Our analysis on real-world networks created by a variety of social processes suggests that MLP effectively models multiplex network coevolution.

14.8 Conclusion

The *Travian* massively multiplayer online game has served as a valuable testbed, enabling us to evaluate our social modeling algorithms in a complex and rich environment. Owing to the dearth of publicly available data, many of the published prediction models have been tested only on coauthorship networks, such as DBLP and arXiv. However, our results show that networks formed through different social processes (e.g., aggression vs. communication) exhibit different characteristics, necessitating experimentation on many types of data sets. Although most of the research described in this chapter has been conducted on the communication and trade layers of the *Travian* multiplex network, our current work focuses on the problem of leveraging information from the attack layer to improve our models of alliance evolution and link formation. The attack network layer is particularly challenging since it contains fewer interactions, and the standard topological metrics are not good predictors of its future structure. Also we plan to include additional network layers to represent alliance membership and geographic proximity; these relationships are semantically slightly different from the other layers because they are based on long-term relationships, rather than a series of transactions. Using a combination of our three techniques, D-GT, RPM, and MLP, we are able to successfully model the changes in community structure, rate of link formation, and the coevolution of different network layers. In the future we plan to introduce a single unified model, capable of exploiting dependencies between the dynamics of different processes.

Acknowledgments

This contribution is a culmination of a large, international and multi-year research effort. It is funded in part by the US National Science Foundation (IIS-0838402, IIS-0838231, IIS-1110868, and ACI-1429160), US Office of Naval Research (N000141010091, N000141410489, N0001415P1187, N000141612016, and N000141612412), US Air Force Research Lab, US Army Research Office (W911NF-16-1-0189), US Defense Advanced Research Projects Agency (W31P4Q-17-C-0059), the Deutsche Forschungs-gemeinschaft (German National Science Foundation) in Bonn, Germany, research grants, Travian Games GmbH, Munich and the Jerry L. Maulden/En-tergy Fund at the University of Arkansas at Little Rock to Nitin Agarwal and Rolf Wigand. Any opinions, findings, and conclusions or recommendations expressed in this material are those of the authors and do not necessarily reflect the views of the funding organizations. The researchers gratefully acknowledge the support.

References

Acar, Evrim, Dunlavy, Daniel M, & Kolda, Tamara G. (2009). Link prediction on evolving data using matrix and tensor factorizations. In *Workshops at IEEE International Conference on Data Mining* (pp. 262–269).

Adamic, Lada A, & Adar, Eytan. (2003). Friends and neighbors on the web. *Social Networks*, 25(3), 211–230.

Al Hasan, Mohammad, & Zaki, Mohammed J. (2011). A survey of link prediction in social networks. In *Social network data analytics* (pp. 243–275). New York: Science+Business Media.

Albert, Réka, & Barabási, Albert-László. (2002). Statistical mechanics of complex networks. *Reviews of Modern Physics*, 74(1), 47.

Alvari, Hamidreza, Hajibagheri, Alireza, Sukthankar, Gita, & Lakkaraju, Kiran. (2016). Identifying community structures in dynamic networks. *Social Network Analysis and Mining*, 6(1), 77.

Backstrom, Lars, Huttenlocher, Dan, Kleinberg, Jon, & Lan, Xiangyang. (2006). Group formation in large social networks: Membership, growth, and evolution. In *Proceedings of the ACM SIGKDD International Conference on Knowledge Discovery and Data Mining* (pp. 44–54).

Barabási, Albert-László, & Albert, Réka. (1999). Emergence of scaling in random networks. *Science*, 286(5439), 509–512.

Barabási, Albert-László, et al. (2009). Scale-free networks: A decade and beyond. *Science*, 325(5939), 412.

Benevenuto, Fabricio, Rodrigues, Tiago, Cha, Meeyoung, & Almeida, Virgílio. (2009). Characterizing user behavior in online social networks. In *Proceedings of the ACM SIGCOMM Conference on Internet Measurement* (pp. 49–62).

Bennerstedt, U., Ivarsson, J., & Linderoth, J. (2012). How gamers manage aggression: Situating skills in collaborative computer games. *Computer-Supported Collaborative Learning*, 7, 43–61.

Berlingerio, Michele, Bonchi, Francesco, Bringmann, Björn, & Gionis, Aristides. (2009). Mining graph evolution rules. In *Machine learning and knowledge discovery in databases* (pp. 115–130). New York, NY: Springer Science+Business Media.

Bianconi, Ginestra. (2013). Statistical mechanics of multiplex networks: Entropy and overlap. *Physical Review E*, 87(6), 062806.

Blondel, Vincent D, Guillaume, Jean-Loup, Lambiotte, Renaud, & Lefebvre, Etienne. (2008). Fast unfolding of communities in large networks. *Journal of Statistical Mechanics: Theory and Experiment*, 2008(10), P10008.

Brin, Sergey, & Page, Lawrence. (2012). Reprint of: The anatomy of a large-scale hypertextual web search engine. *Computer Networks*, 56(18), 3825–3833.

Bringmann, Björn, Berlingerio, Michele, Bonchi, Francesco, & Gionis, Arisitdes. (2010). Learning and predicting the evolution of social networks. *IEEE Intelligent Systems*, 25(4), 26–35.

Broder, Andrei, Kumar, Ravi, Maghoul, Farzin, et al. (2000). Graph structure in the web. *Computer Networks*, 33(1), 309–320.

Buldyrev, Sergey V, Parshani, Roni, Paul, Gerald, Stanley, H Eugene, & Havlin, Shlomo. (2010). Catastrophic cascade of failures in interdependent networks. *Nature*, 464(7291), 1025–1028.

Buono, Camila, Alvarez-Zuzek, Lucila G, Macri, Pablo A, & Braunstein, Lidia A. (2014). Epidemics in partially overlapped multiplex networks. *PloS ONE*, 9(3), e92200.

Cazabet, Rémy, Amblard, Frédéric, & Hanachi, Chihab. (2010). Detection of overlapping communities in dynamical social networks. In *IEEE International Conference on Social Computing* (pp. 309–314).

Clauset, Aaron, Shalizi, Cosma Rohilla, & Newman, Mark EJ. (2009). Power-law distributions in empirical data. *SIAM Review*, 51(4), 661–703.

Cook, Diane J, Crandall, Aaron, Singla, Geetika, & Thomas, Brian. (2010). Detection of social interaction in smart spaces. *Cybernetics and Systems: An International Journal*, 41(2), 90–104.

Danon, Leon, Diaz-Guilera, Albert, Duch, Jordi, & Arenas, Alex. (2005). Comparing community structure identification. *Journal of Statistical Mechanics: Theory and Experiment*, 2005(09), P09008.

Dawes, Robyn M. (1980). Social dilemmas. *Annual Review of Psychology*, 31(1), 169–193.

De Domenico, Manlio, Solé-Ribalta, Albert, Cozzo, Emanuele, et al. (2013a). Mathematical formulation of multilayer networks. *Physical Review X*, 3(4), 041022.

De Domenico, Manlio, Sole, Albert, Gomez, Sergio, & Arenas, Alex. (2013b). Random walks on multiplex networks. arXiv preprint arXiv:1306.0519.

Ding, Ying. (2011). Applying weighted PageRank to author citation networks. *Journal of the American Society for Information Science and Technology*, 62(2), 236–245.

Faloutsos, Michalis, Faloutsos, Petros, & Faloutsos, Christos. (1999). On power-law relationships of the internet topology. In *ACM SIGCOMM Computer Communication Review*, Vol. 29 (pp. 251–262).

Fortunato, Santo. (2010). Community detection in graphs. *Physics Reports*, 486(3), 75–174.

Getoor, Lise, & Diehl, Christopher P. (2005). Link mining: A survey. *ACM SIGKDD Explorations Newsletter*, 7(2), 3–12.

Gomez, Sergio, Diaz-Guilera, Albert, Gomez-Gardenes, Jesus, Perez-Vicente, Conrad J, Moreno, Yamir, & Arenas, Alex. (2013). Diffusion dynamics on multiplex networks. *Physical Review Letters*, 110(2), 028701.

Gómez-Gardenes, Jesús, Reinares, Irene, Arenas, Alex, & Floría, Luis Mario. (2012). Evolution of cooperation in multiplex networks. *Scientific Reports*, 2.

Hajibagheri, Alireza, Sukthankar, Gita, & Lakkaraju, Kiran. (2016). Leveraging network dynamics for improved link prediction. In *Proceedings of the International Conference on Social Computing, Behavioral-Cultural Modeling, and Prediction*.

Hristova, Desislava, Noulas, Anastasios, Brown, Chloë, Musolesi, Mirco, & Mascolo, Cecilia. (2015). A multilayer approach to multiplexity and link prediction in online geo-social networks. arXiv preprint arXiv:1508.07876.

Huang, Zan, & Lin, Dennis K. J. (2009). The time-series link prediction problem with applications in communication surveillance. *INFORMS Journal on Computing*, 21(2), 286–303.

Humphreys, M., & Weinstein, J. (2008). Who fights? The determinants of participation in civil war. *American Journal of Political Science*, 52(2), 436–455.

Keegan, B., Ahmed, M., Williams, D., Srivastava, J., & Contractor, N. (2010). Dark Gold: Statistical properties of clandestine networks in massively multiplayer online games. In *IEEE International Conference on Social Computing* (pp. 201–208).

Kivela, Mikko, Arenas, Alex, Barthelemy, Marc, Gleeson, James, Moreno, Yamir, & Porter, Mason. (2014). Multilayer networks. *Journal of Complex Networks*, 2, 203–271.

Korsgaard, M., Picot, A., Wigand, Rolf, Welpe, I., & Assmann, J. (2010). Cooperation, coordination, and trust in virtual teams: Insights from virtual games. In *Online worlds: Convergence of the real and the virtual* (pp. 253–264). New York, NY: Springer Science+Business Media.

Kurant, Maciej, & Thiran, Patrick. (2006). Layered complex networks. *Physical Review Letters*, 96(13), 138701.

Lancichinetti, Andrea, Radicchi, Filippo, Ramasco, José J, et al. (2011). Finding statistically significant communities in networks. *PloS One*, 6(4), e18961.

Leskovec, Jure, Backstrom, Lars, Kumar, Ravi, & Tomkins, Andrew. (2008). Microscopic evolution of social networks. In *Proceedings ofthe ACM SIGKDD International Conference on Knowledge Discovery and Data Mining* (pp. 462–470).

Liben-Nowell, David, & Kleinberg, Jon. (2003). The Link Prediction Problem for Social Networks. In *Proceedings of the International Conference on Information and Knowledge Management* (pp. 556–559).

Liben-Nowell, David, & Kleinberg, Jon. (2007). The link-prediction problem for social networks. *Journal of the American Society for Information Science and Technology*, 58(7), 1019–1031.

Lichtenwalter, Ryan N., Lussier, Jake T., & Chawla, Nitesh V. (2010). New perspectives and methods in link prediction. In *Proceedings of the ACM SIGKDD International Conference on Knowledge Discovery and Data Mining* (pp. 243–252).

Liu, Yu-Ting, Liu, Tie-Yan, Qin, Tao, Ma, Zhi-Ming, & Li, Hang. (2007). Supervised rank aggregation. In *Proceedings of the International Conference on World Wide Web* (pp. 481–490).

MacKay, David JC. (2003). *Information theory, inference and learning algorithms*. Cambridge: Cambridge University Press.

Min, Byungjoon, & Goh, K-I. (2013). Layer-crossing overhead and information spreading in multiplex social networks. arXiv preprint arXiv:1307.2967.

Newman, M. E. J. (2001). Clustering and preferential attachment in growing networks. *Physical Review E*, 64, 025102.

Newman, M. E. J. (2002). Assortative mixing in networks. *Physical Review Letters*, 89(20), 208701.

Nicosia, Vincenzo, Bianconi, Ginestra, Latora, Vito, & Barthelemy, Marc. (2013). Growing multiplex networks. *Physical Review Letters*, 111(5), 058701.

Piraveenan, Mahendra, Chung, Kon Shing Kenneth, & Uddin, Shahadat. (2012). Assortativity of links in directed networks. In *Foundations of Computer Science Conference*. Retrieved from: www.academia.edu/1892630/Assortativity_of_links_in_directed_networks.

Potgieter, Anet, April, Kurt A, Cooke, Richard JE, & Osunmakinde, Isaac O. (2009). Temporality in link prediction: Understanding social complexity. *Emergence: Complexity & Organization (E: CO)*, 11(1), 69–83.

Pujari, Manisha, & Kanawati, Rushed. (2012). Supervised rank aggregation approach for link prediction in complex networks. *Proceedings of the International World Wide Web Conference* (pp. 1189–1196).

Pujari, Manisha, & Kanawati, Rushed. (2015). Link prediction in multiplex networks. *Networks and Heterogeneous Media*, 10(1), 17–35.

Rosvall, Martin, & Bergstrom, Carl T. (2008). Maps of random walks on complex networks reveal community structure. *Proceedings of the National Academy of Sciences of the USA*, 105(4), 1118–1123.

Roy, A., Borbora, Z., & Srivastava, J. (2013). Socialization and Trust Formation: A Mutual Reinforcement? An Exploratory Analysis in an Online Virtual Setting. *IEEE/ACM International Conference on Advances in Social Networks Analysis and Mining* (pp. 653–660).

Saumell-Mendiola, Anna, Serrano, M Ángeles, & Boguná, Marián. (2012). Epidemic spreading on interconnected networks. *Physical Review E*, 86(2), 026106.

Scott, John. (2012). *Social Network Analysis*. SAGE.

Sculley, D. (2007). Rank Aggregation for Similar Items. In *SIAM International Conference on Data Mining* (pp. 587–592).

Snijders, T., van de Bunt, G., & Steglich, C. E. G. (2010). Introduction to actor-based models for network dynamics. *Social Networks*, 32, 44–60.

Soares, Paulo Ricardo da Silva, & Prudêncio, Ricardo Bastos Cavalcante. (2012). Time series based link prediction. In *International Joint Conference on Neural Networks* (pp. 1–7). IEEE.

Sole-Ribalta, Albert, De Domenico, Manlio, Kouvaris, Nikos E, Diaz-Guilera, Albert, Gomez, Sergio, & Arenas, Alex. (2013). Spectral properties of the Laplacian of multiplex networks. *Physical Review E*, 88(3), 032807.

Strogatz, Steven H. (2001). Exploring complex networks. *Nature*, 410(6825), 268–276.

Tabourier, Lionel, Bernardes, Daniel Faria, Libert, Anne-Sophie, & Lambiotte, Renaud. (2014). RankMerging: A supervised learning-to-rank framework to predict links in large social network. arXiv preprint arXiv:1407.2515.

Tan, Pang-Ning, Steinbach, Michael, & Kumar, Vipin. (2005). *Introduction to data mining*, 1st edn. Boston, MA: Addison-Wesley Longman.

Thurau, C., & Bauckhage, C. (2010). Analyzing the evolution of social groups in World of Warcraft. In *IEEE International Conference on Computational Intelligence in Games* (pp. 170–177).

Wang, Chao, Satuluri, Venu, & Parthasarathy, Srinivasan. (2007). Local probabilistic models for link prediction. In *Seventh IEEE International Conference on Data Mining* (pp. 322–331).

Wigand, R., Agrawal, N., Osesina, O., Hering, W., Korsgaard, M., Picot, A., & Drescher, M. (2012). Social network indices as performance predictors in a virtual organization. In *International Conference on Computational Analysis of Social Networks* (pp. 144–149). Retrieved from: http://ieeexplore.ieee.org/xpl/mostRecentIssue.jsp?punumber=6396507.

Xie, Jierui, Chen, Mingming, & Szymanski, Boleslaw K. (2013). LabelrankT: Incremental community detection in dynamic networks via label propagation. arXiv preprint arXiv:1305.2006.

Yee, N. (2006). The labor of fun: How video games blur the boundaries of work and play. *Games and Culture*, 1(1), 68–71.

Zhou, Tao, Lü, Linyuan, & Zhang, Yi-Cheng. (2009). Predicting missing links via local information. *The European Physical Journal B*, 71(4), 623–630.